TARNISHED GOLD THREAD
Memoir of Life, Mission, and the Call to Love

Barbara Dowdy

SparkPoint
PRESS

Dedication

I dedicate this book to my family, hoping my children, grandchildren, and future generations will understand my life and times better. I also dedicate this book to my many friends who have been so wonderful to me throughout my life.

I intend for this book to serve as a remembrance of God's faithfulness and love for His children.

Author's Note

I wrote this book over many years, and it has been a work of emotional strain. I have written my memoir in the way I remember things or as they were told to me. My intent is to be as honest as possible. (If someone else were writing this same story from their perspective, it would be different, I'm sure.)

During the course of writing this book, I changed computers three times, and my main manuscript and disk were stolen or misplaced in a move. All of this contributed to its difficulty.

I've taken much of the material from letters I wrote to my children while living in Africa. (Bless Ken and Peggy's hearts for saving all my letters.) I also drew some of the material for this book from my own journals.

This book is written in my voice, telling my story to capture the historical chronology of my life and events for future generations of my family.

Everything that happened to me — good, bad, and in between — molded me into who I have become with the help of God. I hope you will read and enjoy and love the people I have loved so well.

—B.D.

"And we know that in all things God works for the good of those who love him who have been called according to his purpose."

–Romans 8:28

Table of Contents

PROLOGUE: **My Roots & Ancestry**

1 **My Birth & Family of Origin**
2 **Growing Up in The Great Depression**
3 **Through the Eyes of Early Childhood**
4 **Lessons in Religion, Money, & Sex**
5 **School Days & Social Strata**
6 **Teen Times & First Call to Ministry**
7 **Courtship & Engagement**
8 **Melding Families & Personalities**
9 **Wedding Daze**
10 **Honeymoon & Early Marriage**
11 **Church, Children, & Family**
12 **Starting Our Business**
13 **Family Life in Ryan Place**
14 **Ryan Place: The Dark Years**

15 The Call Finally Answered
16 New Building for Copy & Litho
17 Orienting for Mission
18 Into Africa
19 Building Our Malawi Home
20 Settling into Lilongwe Life
21 Family Visit: Christmas in Malawi
22 Navigating Sensitive Issues
23 Connections & Common Ground
24 Nerve Jangling Shortages
25 Convention & Relationships
26 Capital City Baptist Church
27 At Home in Lilongwe
28 Ministry & Culture
29 Malawi Lens of Tradition
30 Stateside for Peggy's Wedding
31 Work & Strife
32 Eslet Chacwanira
33 Yet Another Robbery
34 First Johannesburg Trip
35 Group Dynamics
36 Bridging Realities
37 Betrayal & Moral Struggles
38 Delicacies & Reprieves
39 First Furlough
40 Chongoni Retreat
41 Trouble at Copy & Litho
42 Kilimanjaro
43 Unexpected Adventures
44 Feet First
45 Matters of Life & Death in Malawi
46 Home from Africa
47 Called Again to Serve
48 World of War: Somalia
49 Mogadishu Mission Work
50 Fun in Kenya
51 Back to Farm & Fort Worth
52 End Notes

My Roots & Ancestry

Note to readers: Much of the Ancestry information for this side of my family was written by Lura Elliott McConnell for my nephew, Roger Allen Ashinhurst, in 1973. Roger is the son of my sister, Doris, and her husband, John Lindy Ashinhurst. Lura passed away in Sherman, Texas, at the age of 94.

My Great Grandfather was William Nicholson, born in 1814. He was a Merchant in North Carolina. William Nicholson was a wealthy landowner with many acres and owned many slaves. He married Martha, who was from Mississippi. They lived in a Colonial Mansion and had seven children; William A. b. 1837, Mary D. b. 1842, Sarah E. b. 1844, Joseph or Josephus Love b. 1846, Virginia D b. 1849, Martha G. b. 1851, and Francis N. b. 1853.

The girls were given slave girls as playmates. One of the girls remembered that her slave girl's name was Roxie. They loved each other like sisters, and there was a strong bond between them, and they would protect each other as long as they lived.

The children had a Negro Mammy who did everything for the girls. The Mammy bathed, combed hair, laced up shoes, and dressed them. The Nicholson girls were pampered and spoiled and always the belle of the ball.

When the Civil War broke out, the colonial families would host parties for the soldiers on bivouac. On one such occasion, a young soldier named Joseph Love Nicholson came through town. Later he was known as Joe.

One evening at one of these parties, held at a Hotel in Meridian, Mississippi, Joe met Frankie Ross, a lovely girl whose family owned a large plantation and many slaves. Indulged all her life, Frankie grew up in one of the Colonial Mansions in Meridian, Mississippi. Roxie was her maid friend.

When Frankie first saw Joe Nicholson, the unknown soldier, her eyes lit up and her heart began to flutter. From the first time she saw him, she had eyes for no one else.

Frankie's parents, however, put their thumbs down on that romance. For all they knew, Joe was a rag-tag soldier and a nobody — he was not on their social scale.

Frankie just thought that Joe was the sweetest thing she had ever seen, and it did not matter to her what her parents thought.

"That boy is a nobody," they said, "a fly-by-night soldier. Don't you ever see him again."

But young love isn't so quickly squelched. Frankie insisted that she would marry Joseph Love Nicholson. Her father said that if she did, she would be struck from the family Bible, no longer be his child, and not inherit anything.

And so it was.

After they were married, Frankie discovered that the Nicholsons owned many slaves and had a vast plantation, mostly cotton and sugar cane. In their kitchen, separate from the main house, Negro cooks prepared their food, and younger Negro girls served the meals in the vast dining hall. Everyone dressed for dinner.

There were numerous cabins where the Negro slaves lived. There were two big smokehouses where the slaves cured and smoked the meat with hickory chips. Frankie said it took days to hang and smoke all the meat. It took a lot of meat to feed the slaves and the Nicholson family, but in all likelihood, the slaves saw precious little meat.

The slaves also made hominy by the barrel. They soaked the corn in lye water, then ran it through ashes until the husk came off. Then they boiled it, poured it into jars, and stored it in the springhouse, a large room built over a natural spring so the water would run through the house and keep the canned goods and the milk cool.

———•••———

Time went on, and the war was over. The emancipation proclamation freed the slaves on January 1, 1863. For the next couple of years, however, the freed slaves stayed on the plantation and continued to work.

When the former slaves eventually learned that they did not have to work and the Plantation owner could not make them stay, many of them left. The Nicholsons had to do something.

They sold their land to the former slaves for confederate cash, which was no good, and moved to Texas. They bought a farm at Ethel near Whitesboro. Joseph Love's father fell in a creek, got pneumonia, died, and was buried in the Ethel Cemetery.

The family then moved to Farmington, Texas, near Van Alstyne. Although their lavish lifestyle was over, the farm they purchased had good rich soil, and the farmers there were prosperous.

There were three churches: Methodist, Baptist, and Christian. There was a cotton gin, three stores, a blacksmith shop, a school, and several two-story houses. Joe and Frankie had five children, and Frankie passed away, leaving Joe with children to raise.

Octavia Burgess Norman Ferguson was born in West Virginia on May 14, 1864. For some reason, her family had moved near Farmington. She was single and had one son named Oather Ferguson. Octavia and Joe married and had four more children: Una Dorine, Anna Lou, Josie Love, and Ralph Wesley.

Ralph Wesley grew up to become my father, born on May 11, 1901. Ralph always said the children were mean to him as a little boy. His real sisters had neighbors about their ages, and he was a tag-along with them. Ralph's half-brothers and half-sisters were older, and they picked on him, too. He always looked taller than he actually was because he was so thin. Because his family had a problem with walking straight and tall, he always made a point of it. Regardless of the load upon him, my father prided himself on his good posture.

————•••————

Grandpa Joe told the children tall tales on bad weather days. The winters were cold, and the houses were not heated well. The family would gather in one room with a fireplace, and Joe would say, "All right, all you chaps come ovah heah by the fiah place, and we will talk of the past." He spoke with an accent and pronounced the words door as "doah" and sister as "Sistah."

In one story, the Feds and Confederates had a big battle. The battle was in the swamps, and the Feds put the Rebs to fight. It was a hot battle, and many got killed. The rest ran away in every direction. Joe said he got lost and wandered around for several days, hitching rides with farmers when he could and wandering around in between.

One day he came upon a little house with settlers. A woman was in the yard with a child in the shade of a tree. He yelled out at the woman, and she became terrified. She started running, but he said he would not hurt her. He was just hungry.

He asked the woman to make him a peach pie big enough for five men. She cooked him the pie, and he ate the whole thing. He later told the chaps that they did not know what a good pie tasted like.

————•••————

Grandpa Joe also had a terrible temper. He would pick up a hickory stick and hit the neighbor kids just the same as his own. He would say, "scat!" and the kids scatted. Grandpa was an elder in the Ferguson Chapel Church, and he said the blessing before each meal, except when he was mad. Then he would skip the blessing. Everybody knew they better keep quiet and be on their best behavior, or they would get "it."

Grandpa and Grandma had a long table with a bench on either side. With so many children, they needed a lot of spaces. When Grandpa skipped the blessing, the kids would kick each other under the table. Later they would say, "I guess he is mad at God." When he was mad, the kids would say Grandpa was on a "high horse."

Grandpa stacked his hay by hand. He put a pole in the center, then spread the hay and tramped it down until he reached the top point, and it looked like a colossal tepee. Grandpa then laid down the law to the chaps. He would have several haystacks but always put a great big one by the hay loft.

The big stack beside the loft was always the first put in the mangers. When winter came, Grandpa sure was cranky about those haystacks. (He called them "hay cocks"). He would round the kids up and say that the first one he caught climbing on those hay cocks would get it.

The kids would wait until he got settled in the house reading his paper, and they would slip out behind the barn and begin to slide down the hay cocks. They would be having a great time and soon began to yip and holler like a bunch of Comanche. The kids also did not understand that their heads could be seen from the house when they climbed to the top of the haystack.

Pretty soon, here came Grandpa with his "hickory." They would scatter in all directions, but Grandpa was able to catch two or three, and they would get a beating.

———•••———

There was a steep hill on the south side of the house and a creek below it. There were three or four mulberry trees on the hilltop, and the kids would climb those trees and fill up on those sweet black mulberries.

One day, Lura, a cousin of Ralph and Josie, was going someplace, and their Grandma Nicholson had the girls all dressed up. Lura wore a new plaid dress her mother had made for her.

Grandpa had always warned the kids to stay out of the creek behind the house, but he never explained why they were not supposed to get into the creek. On this day, they decided to go across the creek. When they got there, they started walking down the creek. Lura, who was in the lead, suddenly began to sink into the sand. She quickly grabbed her dress, yanked it off, and threw it to Josie. She said her mother would kill her if she messed it up.

Lura continued to sink into the sand. By this time, Ralph and Josie had gotten out of the water. Ralph grabbed a stick and handed it to Lura, pulling her out of the quicksand. They were all scared half to death, never told their parents what they had done, and never got in that creek again.

———•••———

Grandpa and Grandma's house was two stories in front, and the kitchen was one story. There were two bedrooms upstairs. Uncle Smith, Frank, and Aunt Lissa stayed in the two bedrooms. The kids slept in the hall at the top of the stairs.

The wall only went halfway up, so you could see the space over the kitchen from the hall. When Grandma got mad at the kids, she would tell them that she would throw them into the "Dark Hole," the dark area over the kitchen that was always dark — and cold in the winter and hot in the summer. Grandma told the boys old raw meat and "Bloody Bones" lived up there and would get them and eat them up, and it scared them half to death.

Grandma was a patient woman. Nobody remembers her ever spanking any of the kids. Grandpa never forgot how he had once lived. He told them they lived in a storeroom over a porch before he moved.

Grandpa bought apples by the barrel, wrapped each in tissue paper, and stored them in the barrel. He would also buy brown sugar by the barrel and syrup, good old sorghum. Not the kind sold now, but unrefined. When it got damp, the sugar would harden into lumps. Grandpa also stored dried fruit and red peppers, strung on strings and hung on the rafters.

These stored items were a reserve supply, and the kids knew it. But gee, how good that sugar tasted, and the apple was so sweet and mellow. Stolen sweets are always best — until you get caught — then payday comes, sure as shooting, and it was the old hickory again. The "hickory" was really a peach limb, but Grandpa called it a "hickory."

Grandma died, but the memory of those alluring treats still burned bright and clear. Lura's mother said that after our first Grandma died and before he married the second Grandma, Grandpa got to running around with some pretty tough guys, and they would get dog drunk. He got

14

pretty rough, and the younger kids were scared of him.

Once when my dad was dating Mother, Grandpa came home one night pretty well lit up. Uncle Frank got close to mother and said, "Sis, I wish Bud were here, don't you?" (The kids all called mother "Sis", and my dad's nickname was "Bud.")

Grandpa took a notion to move to East Texas, so they moved to Hopkins County and bought a farm. They came back to visit us one summer in a covered wagon. He brought stalks of ribbon cane and several gallon buckets of Ribbon Cane Syrup.

———————

Josie walked in her sleep. Once when she and her siblings were sleeping on the porch on pallets, she got up and roamed over into a neighbor's pasture where there were "jillions" of thistles — they called them sticker weeds.

Anyway, Lura awoke and heard Josie yelling, "Oh, Sis!"

I couldn't find her, so I awoke my dad and Grandpa. They got a lantern, followed the sounds of her voice, and brought her back. Her feet were full of stickers.

———————

After the family came back from East Texas, they lived on the Paul Bean Place. There were two houses on it. Grandpa lived in one, and Uncle Frank, who had married Aunt Lizzie in East Texas, lived in the other.

During this time, my uncles and aunts got married. (I won't try to tell who married who because it becomes too confusing to me, so I know it would bog you readers down, too).

Grandpa moved from the Carruth Farm to the old Buck Tolbert home place. It had a great big barn with a large dome on top where owls roosted up there. Josie, Ralph, Leslie, and some other kids — a boy named Rayward, Beulah Lavender, and the girl the Brooks raised — climbed up into the barn loft.

These kids took turns grabbing a rope and swinging across the loft. It seemed very dangerous, and some of the kids would not try it. That rope never broke, and nobody ever fell. The Good Lord must have taken care of them because they were always doing something risky.

———••———

Josie, Anna Lou, Ralph, and Una had a white mare and an old white mule. They rode them to school in Howe, Texas. One night Lura was spending the night with Josie. Ralph went home with Leslie, Anna Lou and Una rode the mare, and Josie and Lura rode the mule.

If you let the mule put her head down, she would buck like a rodeo pony. Josie was in the saddle, and she rode up by the school porch so Lura could get on.

Her book satchel slipped just as Lura was climbing on, and as Josie grabbed at the satchel, she let the reins loosen. That old mule started bucking plumb across the schoolyard and then across the road.

The Methodist Church faced the school, and there was a deep ditch between the road and the churchyard. Josie and Lura yelled and screamed. The children on the playground began to cry and scatter.

Well sir, that old mule's front feet went down in that ditch. The saddle broke, and Josie flew right over the mule's head. Over went Lura, right on top of Josie. Once that old mule got rid of them, she brayed as loud as she could, kicked up her hind legs, and started running toward home.

Lura and Josie picked themselves up, collected their books, lunch pails, and coats, and started on that long walk home, about four miles. It was after dark when they drug in, and the mule got home before they did.

———••———

Kids didn't smoke in those days — it was unheard of. However, they did plenty of other unheard-of things. When you put seven kids together, they can think up a lot of things that they think would be fun. They were adventurous and would try anything.

Grandpa had a hired hand, and he smoked. Josie and the others gathered up all the snipes, put them in a matchbox, and saved them. There were cigarettes, cigars, and cheroots. The snipes got intense, waiting to gather enough to smoke.

16

It was wintertime and sleeting and snowing and cold as a tomb. The kids brought their collection of snipes upstairs and passed out the smokes. Lura happened to get a cheroot, and suddenly she keeled over. Scared those kids half to death.

They had an old velvet sofa in their room. They raised a North window, put Lura on the couch, and pushed it close to the window. She finally revived in the sleet and snow, finishing their smoking forever.

———— •••————

Ruby Celeste Ray Nicholson was the daughter of William Thomas ("Tater") and Hattie Pate Ray. She was born on September 26, 1902. Ruby was the fourth born, following Jewel, Opal, and J.C. After Ruby came George Washington, known as Dub, William Thomas, known as Bill, then Estelle, Oline, and the one that died as a newborn baby. She was always referred to as Little Liddie.

Ruby did not get much formal education. She could read and write a little, and she attended school through the sixth or seventh grade. Ruby Ray was a beautiful young girl, and she thought she was pretty, too, making her a little cocky and feisty. She was the apple of her father's eye when she was growing up, and he had been a farmer all his life.

Tater indulged Ruby with material things he probably could not afford, like high-top lace-up shoes. She always dressed better than the other Ray girls. When Ruby was about 12, she began to eye the boys. And with much glee, they responded just as enthusiastically.

When she was about 15, a young man named Paul asked Ruby to go to the box supper with him. Ruby dressed in her lace-up shoes, a new petticoat, and the bright red taffeta bloomers her mother had made her.

Oh, how Ruby loved those bloomers! Although her petticoat rubbing against taffeta bloomers made a rustling sound when she walked, Ruby was concerned that nobody could see her beautiful new gathered bloomers that fit tightly around her legs just below the knees. A ruffle at the edge of the bloomers made them come almost to the calf of her legs.

Ruby hoped Paul would notice her new bloomers and petty coat.

Paul pulled up with his nice buggy and horse, tied the horse to the hitching post, and went to the door. He escorted Ruby to the buggy, and after helping her up into her seat, he proudly perched himself beside her.

Casually, Ruby reached down and slid her dress up just a little, just enough so that her bloomers showed just a little.

Paul did not comment.

So, she reached down and slid her dress up a little higher.

Paul could tell this time that she had raised her dress intentionally. Nice girls did not show their bloomers, so he was unsure what he should say. Finally, he said, "you sure have pretty bloomers."

"Thank You," Ruby said. She grinned sheepishly and then, acting embarrassed, pushed the hem of her skirt down.

Ruby's flirtation got her into a lot of trouble. Tatter demanded high moral standards from all his girls. Occasionally, Tatter had to have a heart-to-heart with Ruby, which sometimes also included a spanking.

While just a teenage girl, Ruby and three or four girlfriends decided to play hooky from school, caught an interurban train in Howe, and went to Sherman. Even though Sherman was only five miles from Howe, it was quite a journey for little country girls to venture out independently.

After shopping for a while, they returned to the interurban station to go home. Ruby sat on one of the benches, and the other girls went to the restroom. A handsome man in his 20s came over to sit beside Ruby. She recognized him as someone she had seen in Howe and was flattered that he seemed to know her.

The man began talking to her and asked if she would like to go to the movies with him. She knew she should not go because she did not know anything about him, but she could not resist saying yes.

"Wait here a few minutes," he said, "and I will make sure my wife is going to be working for the next couple of hours."

Ruby was scared almost to death — she did not know the man was married! She did not know what she was going to do.

Fortunately, before the man returned, the interurban came, and she jumped on it as quickly as she could and headed home. It did not take her long to recover from the mess she had gotten herself into, but she never forgot the incident.

The Nicholsons were neighbors of the Rays, and Euna Nicholson and Ruby were good friends. Euna had a brother named Ralph, and Ruby and

Ralph had grown up together.

One Sunday, as the Rays and the Nicholsons attended church, Ruby had eyed Ralph, so she was thrilled when he asked to take her home in his buggy. They got into the buggy and headed home, and the family took another buggy and headed home.

Ralph decided to take the long road home, and Ruby had no objections. By the time they got home, the family had already finished lunch.

Tatter took Ruby behind the barn and beat her so hard that she never forgot that beating. She told me about that beating only two months before her death, and she said that she thought her father was going to beat her to death.

———◆◆◆———

Ralph and Ruby were married in Tioga, Texas, in about 1922. The only possession they had was a little car that Ralph had purchased. They lived in Howe for a few years and then moved to the Old Backus Place in Van Alstyne, Texas.

Ruby was tiny, five foot two, with stunning blue eyes. Her hair was fine and a deep, shiny brown with just enough curl to give her a sweet flock of waves and curls caressing her face.

Ruby could be as sweet as an angel — and a real spitfire when things did not suit her. If her children did not mind, she could spank the tar out of their little "hineys." She would cut a little switch from a tree or use the razor strap. Or, more often than not, she would just tear into them with her hand, leaving her small, red handprints that would soon disappear.

She would tell the kids, "I'm going to beat you to the death," but she never hurt one of them. I think that was her way of compensating for her small stature. She accepted the responsibility of caring for her family and was always willing to "work like a dog," she often said.

Life was not easy on the farm, but most of their neighbors and friends were struggling to make a living also. They were a proud family and would not mention any difficulties of putting food on the table. They tried to pretend that they were not as poor as they were. They were doing better than some folks.

They had an inferiority complex from being poor that they never quite overcame for as long as they lived. They did as well as they could, and they always made up for their lack of material possessions with plenty of love. (If my brother, Duane, was writing this, he might say that our family was well off, because we had an old truck, and most people did not have a vehicle at all. My perception was one way and my brother's was completely different.)

Ruby was a loving and affectionate woman while Ralph was not as gregarious. Down deep the kids knew their father loved them, but what Ralph lacked in his ability to express in love, Ruby made up the difference.

1 My Birth & Family of Origin

"She is the prettiest baby I have ever seen," Ralph said as the doctor laid the baby in Ruby's arms.

This was not a wanted pregnancy. In fact, as Ruby tearfully told the doctor when he confirmed the news, they really couldn't afford another mouth to feed. When the doctor refused to even consider terminating the pregnancy (and they felt so ashamed for even asking, but they had heard that was a thing that could be done), Ruby and Ralph had their fourth baby on the way.

Nine months later, early in the morning of June 6, 1934, Ruby awakened with a severe cramp in her abdomen. There was not an ounce of fat on her body, but she had been retaining water, so her face, legs, and feet were puffy, and the skin was stretched tight across her protruding belly. (Ralph teased her and said she looked like she had swallowed a watermelon.) Between the shortage of food, overworking in the fields, and the unbelievable heat, Ruby did not feel much like laughing or joking about anything.

As another pain gripped her, and she burst out in a sweat. She knew the time had come for her to deliver her fourth child. Remembering that the doctor had been somewhat concerned about the delivery since she was anemic and in a weakened condition, Ruby told Ralph that he better get the doctor.

It was just beginning to get daylight when Ralph got into his old Model T truck and headed down the road to the nearest phone. Dr. Strother, who had his practice in Sherman, was summoned.

Some of the family who lived nearby came in and stayed with Ruby while she struggled and agonized; she moaned and groaned. The doctor was about ten miles away; at that time, most country folks still had their babies at home. (Ruby had given birth to all her other children at home.)

By the time Doctor Strother arrived, Ruby was in hard labor. The sun was up, and there was not a breath of air anywhere. The children (and Ralph) were sent outside.

Ralph went outside and sat under a shade tree in front of the house. He chewed on a twig he had fashioned into a toothbrush as he waited. The waiting was difficult — he always wanted to fix everything for Ruby, but there was nothing he could do this time. Finally, the doctor came out and announced that it was a girl.

That little baby girl was me.

———◆◆◆———

Van Alstyne, Texas, was not much of a town, but it was a place where good people lived, and of course, there were a few not-so-good ones, too. Every day around daybreak, the menfolk met on the street in front of the dry goods store to start the day.

They would chew their tobacco, dip their snuff, and spit into the street as the farmers in their horse-drawn wagons went by. They lifted their hand with each of these encounters and spoke to one another in a friendly sort of way.

Occasionally a lady in her bonnet would walk by, and the men would tip their hats. The dust from the street would fog around, but nobody seemed to mind too much. It gave the men something to talk about.

About three miles east of town, past the cemetery, at the bend in the road sat the little two-bedroom house where I was born. Before I arrived, it was the home of Ralph and Ruby Nicholson and their three children: Billy Duane, the oldest, was born May 25, 1923; James Bobby was born September 23, 1925; and then Ola Doris was born October 6, 1927.

Duane was eleven years old when I was born, tall and skinny as a rail, with freckles and a cowlick. Bobby was a quiet child with fair, smooth skin. He was a beautiful child but a little "slow." (People would say, "isn't he pretty?") Bobby never gave anybody any trouble, but he did have a temper, and occasionally he would get mad. Doris was the third child. She had straight dark brown hair, as did all the Nicholson kids — and freckles. (Her uncles would tease her and tell her that someone had thrown a hand full of bran in her face.) Doris always wanted to please, and she was a hard worker.

As an adult, Ralph was so thin his "Big Mac" overalls always hung limply across his shoulders. The pressure of trying to carve out a living from the soil showed on his face. The workload was almost unbearable, but he still prided himself on his excellent posture. Life on the farm was far different from the old Colonial Mansion times, generations before him he had heard about in his family.

In those days, everybody in the family worked in the fields — they'd hoe the corn, pick the cotton, and do whatever else needed to be done — and kids made for cheap labor. In fact, most people had large families, so the children could help support the family.

The cost of raising kids back then was not that great. If the boys had two pairs of overalls and a pair of shoes, they were well off. Most of the kids went barefoot in the summer anyway. But the winters were frigid.

———•••———

For several days after my birth, my mother was so weak that it was hard for her to muster up even a little smile. She was too weak to get up and help the family because she had lost so much blood (she didn't have any to spare, to begin with). Ruby's mother, my grandmother, Hattie Pate Ray, came to stay for a few days to help out because Ralph was not much good when it came to cooking and caring for the baby.

Slowly, Ruby began to recover. When it became apparent that this baby needed a name to put on the birth certificate, my parents chose Barbara Ann. I always felt that I was a little extra special to Mother and Daddy, but I didn't understand why until many, many years later when Mother shared with me that I had started out as their "unwanted child," who became the special gift God had sent to them.

In the years to follow, Mother, Daddy, my two brothers, one sister, and I worked hard to live and survive in that two-bedroom house. Daddy was a sharecropper, meaning that the land belonged to someone else, and Daddy did the work and shared the crop with the landowner.

We had some relatives who lived in Oklahoma, and when they got "starved out," Daddy got in his Model T Truck and went to Oklahoma. He loaded up the seven and their belongings and brought them back to Texas.

The older boys stayed with us, and Daddy hired them to work on the farm. Mother would feed them, and she charged them by the meal. At mealtimes, these boys would eat all they could, then walk around the table to try to pack their food down so they could eat some more. They wanted to be sure they were getting their money's worth.

Sometimes the boys would come in from the fields and lean against the tree, and Bobby or Duane would take them some bread and a syrup pail. They would dig into that like they were starving to death. (The fact is they probably were about to starve.)

Daddy probably saved the entire family by bringing them back to Texas. We did not have much, but Daddy was willing to share with the family. Several times through the years, different family members would come and stay with us when they hit on hard times.

2 Growing Up in The Great Depression

To share my life as I perceive it is also essential for me to share a little about what was going on in America. I turned 5 in June of 1939, ten years after Tuesday, October 29, 1929 that American History remembers as "Black Tuesday."

The stock market had risen to new highs during the past year, and then it would drop, but analysts were still bullish on the market. Small investors began to want in on the quick money and began to invest. This infusion of capital helped to stabilize the market and caused it to climb even more. The market kept inflating until that famous day when the balloon burst, and the walls came tumbling down.

———•••———

Today we understand that the stock market crash did not start the depression. Still, it certainly contributed to the mindset of the people of that day since fear was one of the main ingredients.

Automobile sales dropped from 4.5 million to 1.1 million, and this caused a downward spiral that affected not only the thousands of men who lost their jobs in the auto industry but also the steel mills and all the peripheral industries.

Thousands of people were laid off. Because there was a shortage of money to buy goods, companies wound up with goods that could not be sold, and even more people were laid off.

With no jobs, people could not pay their loans, houses were repossessed, and 1300 banks closed their doors in 1930. By two years later, 3700 more banks had closed their doors. Because of these bank closures, people could not get their money out of the bank; therefore, they had no money to buy the goods produced by the industrial revolution.

President Herbert Hoover tried to convince the people that economic recovery was just around the corner. Still, fear and discouragement aggravated and fueled the depression. The government got involved in lending money to businesses to stimulate the economy, but this did not restore order to the now-devastated society.

Then the government got involved in purchasing the overproduction of agriculture because people lacked funds to buy produce. Hoover even encouraged constituents to increase gifts to charitable institutions, and the charities would help needy people.

State and local relief agencies established ways to help the needy. In 1929, the Federal Farm Bureau spent millions of government dollars buying surplus wheat and cotton.

All of this strife directly affected our family, even if we never collected any of these government giveaways. Things that started in Washington took a few years to take effect in Texas.

When farmers were paid not to plant cotton or wheat, some landowners could collect more from the government to not plant than they would earn if they did plant.

As sharecroppers, we were affected, as were millions of other sharecroppers who lost their homes and their ability to feed their families. All the money went to the landowner, and the poor, uneducated sharecroppers were turned out without "a pot to pee in," so the saying goes.

The downward economic spiral continued, so 40% of the workforce was unemployed by 1932. At that time, virtually no women worked outside the home, so this 40% constituted the one breadwinner of the families. (Some places like Pennsylvania experienced unemployment of 66%.)

My family was fortunate not to be immediately hit by the sharecropper's plight, so they continued to farm. Then in 1930, a drought hit Texas, and most of the South, destroying hope for crops. Before there had been plenty of food but insufficient funds to purchase it; now, food was also in short supply.

By 1931, Europe was beginning to feel the depression also, and they suspended all their World War I debt payments. Now the once-rich U. S. government was starting to run out of money. Between unpaid debts, the inability to collect taxes from the unemployed, and the robust giveaway programs, the government was on the brink of collapse.

Long bread lines were prevalent in big cities throughout the States. By 1932, thousands were facing starvation, and "shanty towns" sprung up in every major city in America. Even Washington, D.C., was having problems with people throwing up housing made of cardboard boxes and tin. Two thousand soldiers and their families settled just outside the capital in ramshackle communities called "Hoovervilles."

Men began to tie a bundle of personal items into a little cloth and tie this bundle onto a stick they would throw across their shoulders and hit the road. These men were called tramps. (Even though this could be a derogatory term, most people at that time understood the helplessness and despair that consumed the lives of these men.)

Often these men would knock on our back door and ask for something to eat, and mother always tried to share something with them. As little as we had, I guess we had more than the tramps. Mother and Daddy prided themselves in never turning anyone away empty-handed, even though I am sure they went to bed with their stomachs growling from time to time.

Yet there were many rich people in the land, too, and Congress looked at many plans to redistribute the wealth without going to outright communism. Some considered the Russian-type government very favorably as a possible solution to our plight.

———•••———

By 1932 it was clear to many that President Hoover could not pull the people together and get the country on track. The people had lost confidence in the country and Hoover, so Franklin Delano Roosevelt was elected President based on his "New Deal" campaign that promised "a chicken in every pot." As Roosevelt began his presidency, "The Great Depression" reached its lowest point of suffering.

The banking industry disintegrated, and again people were the losers. But in Roosevelt's inaugural address, he stated that "the only thing we have to fear is fear itself...." His charismatic, persuasive air transcended the fear and spurred action. Franklin D. Roosevelt's first 100 days in office are still well remembered in the history books.

Early in his presidency, Roosevelt established The Federal Depository Insurance Corporation (FDIC) with money backed by gold and put government-funded work programs and Welfare programs into effect.

My family certainly could have qualified for welfare, but Daddy would have nothing to do with it; he had too much pride to become any part of that. He said that the government was killing pigs and destroying the meat while families were starving.

He wasn't wrong. What he was referring to, I now understand, was because the government still believed farmers were producing too many commodities and causing prices to be too low, it was paying farmers not to grow cotton and many other commodities, so once again, many sharecroppers lost their homes and ability to make a living because the landowners could earn more money by plowing the crops under or not planting than if they produced. Since the landowners collected all the money, the poor sharecroppers were literally left out in the cold. (I really didn't intend this to be a lesson in American History, but I wanted you to know the reason for the mindset of the people, and their children, who lived through the Great Depression.)

———◦•◦———

Living through these troubled times, people developed an insecurity that guided them throughout their lifetime. This mindset almost always included the need to save for a "rainy day." Save for the future. Don't buy anything unless you really need it. Sometimes this was carried to the extreme, and at times children were not even taken to the doctor when they were sick because it cost money.

So, by the time 1934 came along, and I was born, my parents and most of the people we knew were as poor as "Job's Turkey." The country was far from recovered. Bread lines still existed, tramps still hitch-hiked rides on trains, and beggars and panhandlers still roamed the streets.

3 Through the Eyes of Early Childhood

By the time I was one year old, my family had managed to save $80.00 from the sale of crops. The insurance companies had lent money before the depression, and people could not repay these loans, so the insurance companies wound up with an abundance of real estate. To liquidate some of their holdings, they let some of the farm property go for a reasonable price and then agreed to carry the note.

Mother and Daddy found two 40-acre plots of land that backed up to each other, making one 80-acre plot. The soil was not particularly fertile, but it had an old two-story frame house on the land. Daddy felt that if he could make a living sharecropping, he should be able to grub out an existence for the family on these 80 acres. They had hoped and dreamed of owning a little land one day.

So, with their $80.00 in hand, they went to the insurance company and bought the land for $800.00. They agreed to put the $80.00 down and pay $80.00 every six months until the loan was repaid. With their old Model T Ford, one old milk cow, four "young uns," and an old dog, they packed their limited belongings onto the truck and headed for Southmayd, Texas. Their dream lay ten miles West of Sherman and five miles North of Southmayd.

That last five miles over the years became a mud hurdle that would "make a preacher cuss," and a little girl (me) hate the country. Daddy would gun that truck, and Mother and all us kids would push that truck out of the mud holes. Sometimes we would slip down in the murky mire, and sometimes the wheels would just sling mud all over us. I should have been thankful that we had a truck that would travel part of the way, but as a child, I never seemed to find the bright side of life when mud was involved.

———•••———

The farmhouse stood like a gaping gray monster, naked of trees or grass. There were no telltale signs that anyone had ever painted the house, and the gray shiplap boards scarcely covered the gaping holes in the walls. It stood upon a hill with only a few trees in the distance to break the cold North wind. (If you have ever wondered where the wind starts, it's five miles North of Southmayd.) That had to be one of the coldest houses in North Texas.

Downstairs were two bedrooms, a kitchen, and a small back porch. Between the two bedrooms was a small hall that the stairway connected. There were two bedrooms upstairs. The heater was in Mother and Daddy's bedroom, which connected to the kitchen and also served as the living room.

The inside walls had once enjoyed canvas and wallpaper, but now the torn paper revealed the old boards beneath. I don't remember seeing daylight straight through the outside, but the wind came through the walls and around the old windows and doors. It was impossible to keep warm in the winter, but it did let a nice cool breeze blow through in the summer.

———•••———

Daddy bought an old mule and began to plow up what land was level enough to plant a crop. The land was so hard the plow would not go into the ground, and Daddy would walk behind the plow while the old mule pulled as hard as possible. All the family got out there and helped work the land, sowing cotton seeds and eagerly awaiting the rains.

The rains came, but the land was not fertile enough to produce much of a crop. The cotton came up and grew to a stunted height. Mother sewed kneepads on our pants or made kneepads that would tie around our knees. Mother and Daddy bought white cotton gloves for everyone except me that year. I was too young to get in on this great family togetherness.

Children were exempt from cotton picking until they were about four. Then they were expected to pick cotton or pull bolls and put it into their mother's sack. Mother bought canvas ducking (a heavy, plain-woven cotton fabric) and carefully measured each kid for their cotton sack. It had to be just so long, the strap around the neck had to be the correct length, and the opening had to be just so that you could grab the cotton and quickly stuff it into the sack.

As Daddy perused the fruits of his labor, he could not help but be disappointed. The crop was a dismal failure, yielding little more than the seed money as profit. So, the family hired out to the neighbors and picked cotton for them.

As years went by, I distinctly remember Mother pulling her sack down between two rows of cotton. The sun blistered down and sweat and dirt consumed Mother's frail little body. She would head down the rows picking cotton or pulling bolls as fast as she could. She would get out to the field shortly after daylight.

Before she got to the field, however, she had to prepare breakfast for the family, wash the dishes and prepare a sack lunch made of biscuits and syrup (or, if we were lucky, there might be sausage or egg instead of syrup.) She then wrapped a jar of iced tea or water in a wet cloth and placed it under a tree to keep it cool. Not until then was she ready to head for the cotton fields.

As Mother's cotton sack would begin to get full, she would stop and pull up the top of her sack and shake the cotton down. She would continue to pull up and shake that sack down until it was packed tight, and the end of the sack would lie on the ground, all rounded.

Mother would stand and pick cotton until her back got too tired, and then she would get down on her knees and pull. Every time the cotton would fill her sack to the top, she would stop and shake it down until the cotton was packed all the way to the top of the sack.

Then whenever the sack was packed full, she would turn toward the sack, bend over it, and with a big heave, she would lift the sack, throw it over her shoulder, and walk towards the wagon where they weighed and emptied the cotton.

She would lift the sack's end onto the scales, pull the other end up so that it was entirely off the ground, and wrap the other end of the sack into enough of a knot to stay on the scales. Then she would move the little weight toward the end of the scales. Fifty or sixty pounds she had drug along behind her and then carried to the wagon.

Now came the hardest part — lifting the sack into the wagon. With Mother barely five feet tall and less than one hundred pounds, this was an obstacle even she could not maneuver alone. Sometimes one of us kids would help her. Hopefully, others bringing their cotton in to weigh and empty could help so that everybody could help everybody else. Once the cotton was in the wagon, the sack was tugged on and shaken until the last boll tumbled from the sack.

Then the cotton pickers trampled around the wagon to mash down the cotton. (The cotton owner wanted to see nice, clean cotton without any green leaves.) Then they would climb out of the wagon, get a drink of water, return to the rows where they left off, and start filling their sack all over again.

Most years, Duane, Bobby, and Doris were kept out of school for two months, so they could pick cotton. They pulled plenty of bolls. We called this time "picking cotton," whether we just picked the cotton out of the boll or pulled cotton bolls as well as the cotton.

Doris was always a really hard worker. She would put on her knee pads and bonnet every morning and head for the fields, and she would throw that bonnet back when she got hot so that she could get a breath of air. Mother would holler at her as soon as she saw Doris not wearing her bonnet.

"Get that bonnet on, Doris!"

And Doris would pull that bonnet back on without ever missing a lick. But it was only a few minutes until she would have that bonnet pushed back off her head again.

Bobby seemed to just go along and do his very best, whatever it was. Duane, however, did not like any part of farm life. He definitely did not like to pull bolls, but after a reasonable amount of grumbling, he would put in a pretty good day's work.

I was not wholly exempt from pulling bolls, but I must admit I never had it as hard as my brothers and sister. I did wear out many a pair of little white gloves, and I had those cotton burrs stick my hands until my hands bled, and at night I would have to get a needle and pick out little pieces of burrs that had broken off in my hands. I can remember that pain of sore knees and sore hands.

Mother sewed herself, Doris, and I bonnets. She saved oatmeal boxes and cut them into strips so that they would slide nicely into the little slits she always put into the brims. These cardboard strips were called slats, maybe because they resembled bed slats. Our bonnets had to be just right, even though they were work bonnets.

Mother only wore pants during cotton picking time, no matter how cold it got in the winter. She would back up to that pot-bellied wood stove to warm her legs.

Ladies did not wear long pants, no matter how cold their legs got — it simply was not ladylike. Our bonnets were to protect our skin from the sun, not because it would cause skin cancer but because ladies' skin was supposed to be white as snow. We would not want people to know that we had to work out in the hot sun to have food to fill our bellies.

If there ever was a woman who loved her family, my mother qualified. She was no different than many other women in that day, but she gave her all and then some. After she got home from the fields at dusk, dead tired, she had to prepare supper. Our meals were not exotic —they usually consisted of pinto beans, fried potatoes, and cornbread.

Somehow, with all the family working until they almost killed themselves, Daddy was able to make those $80.00 farm payments. I might have been small, but I remember my parents discussing where the money would come from that month. Finally, when I was five and a half years old, Daddy made that last payment, and the farm was our very own. What pride and delight my parents must have felt.

We had even managed to trade the old Model T truck for a used car, a 1936 black Ford Sedan. Daddy also managed to acquire a few old cows that would either raise calves, or we could milk.

Sometimes Bobby would get his little red wagon and have me get into it. He would pull me down the country road and then turn around and head back to our house. All would be fine, except when he pulled into our driveway too fast, the wagon would turn over, and out I would tumble and start to cry. I can still remember the grit and taste of dirt in my mouth, crunchy between my teeth. I would run into the house to Mother, and she would always make everything better.

Then in a few days, Bobby would ask me to ride in his wagon, and in I would climb, and the same thing would happen. I even got to where I would ask him to slow down at the drive, but he was pulling as hard as he could go. His intention was not to hurt me; he was just focused on pulling his wagon.

Bobby did not have any cars to play with, so when Mother emptied a Watkins vanilla bottle, she would give it to him to use as one of his cars. He would take it out into the yard, make car sounds, and push that bottle around on the ground. Bobby was a good-size boy, but he would get on his knees, and round and round he would go. He must have worn holes in his pants because Mother often had to sew patches on the knees of his pants.

Neighbor kids would come over, and we would play "Annie Over." Some kids would get on one side of the house, and others would get on the other.

One side would take a ball, and whoever had the ball would say, "Annie!"

Then the other side would yell "Over!" and the ball would be thrown over the house.

The kids would watch for the ball, and whoever caught the ball would again yell, "Annie!"

The other side would again say, "Over!" and the ball would be thrown again.

And so went the game, sometimes for what seemed like hours.

Sometimes we would play "Follow the Leader." Whoever was in front would do something, and everybody who followed had to do the same thing. Sometimes they would jump off the barn or something equally dangerous, and we'd all do it, too.

One day I was following them (I was always the tag along because my brothers and sister and their friends were several years older than me.), and we climbed up on the barn. It looked a long way down to me, and I was the last one to jump. They had been laughing about someone who had put their legs straight out and jumped, and I thought that would be funny. I jumped and put my legs out and landed on my buttocks. I think my brains were scrambled that day. (Maybe I would have been a different person otherwise. Who knows?)

We had an old, dead grape vine down in the pasture, and it had been a long time since it had produced fruit. The kids would break off a little twig, light it, and smoke it. They gave me one of their twigs, and I drew in real big and burnt my tongue. That was the last time I tried to smoke.

I loved to play "hopscotch," "pick up sticks," and "jacks." All our games were very simple.

———•••———

Uncle Bill would sometimes come to visit us, and he delighted in telling a story about when Daddy's milk cow died. He would say that she was the best milk cow in the county. After she died, they cut her utter off and hung it on a fence post, and she continued to give five gallons of milk a day for three days. Then he would just laugh and laugh. I never knew why that was funny.

People like to brag about how many gallons of milk their cows would give daily. Or they would compare how fast their cars would run. Or they would brag about the good mileage their car would get. I would hear my Daddy brag about how good mileage his Ford would get, and I never saw him fill the car — he bought one dollar's worth of gas at a time.

———•••———

Just as we began to see the light at the end of the tunnel, tragedy hit. Mother got "milk leg." (At least that is what Doctor Strother called it. Now I think it could have been a blood clot.) Mother began to have a high fever and was in excruciating pain. She lay prone all the time with her foot propped up, and the Doctor thought she might die.

Daddy tried to take care of the family, but his household skills had not improved since I was born (you had to give him "A" for effort). One morning he got up, went into the kitchen, and made biscuits. He mixed them up, rolled them out, cut them, and put them in the pan, just as Mother did every morning. He was proud of this accomplishment.

Next, he picked up the pan, headed for the stove, and plop — down went the pan into the middle of the floor. Biscuits flew everywhere. After a few choice words (my "cussing vocabulary" increased that day), he bent over, put the biscuits back into the pan, and cooked them. They were pretty good, besides being a little crunchier than Mother's.

36

After lying in bed for a month, Mother recovered from her milk leg. She never completely recovered all her strength.

4 Lessons in Religion, Money, & Sex

Religion, money, and sex are the three things that have basically ruled my life, and usually in that order. Still, from time to time, anyone could take precedence.

Being raised on a farm exposes children to sex in a very natural way. The old rooster chases the hen, jumps on her back, pecks the back of her head, goes through a few vibrations, and jumps off. Both go their own way. Then we raised cows, and the old bull would follow the cow and smell her back end. If the odor was to his liking, he would jump up on her hindquarters, and without any difficulty, one could see the bull's penis inserted into the cow.

Of course, we never discussed these things. If a small child asked a question about it, the immediate hushing conveyed that this was not a topic for polite conversation. So, I grew up knowing that there are some things that you don't discuss with your parents, and sexual matters are one of them.

———•••———

When I was four or five years old, I got my first lesson in contraceptives. Mary Larkin, Mother's neighbor and best friend, was visiting my mother, and they were sewing. The living room, sewing room, and my parents' bedroom were all in one. I crawled under the bed and found this white rubbery thing. I stuck my hand in my Big Mac coveralls.

These were boys' coveralls, so they had a fly in the front, and there was an opening in the pocket. (I guess this was so it would be handier for little boys.) I stuck my finger out of the fly and put the prophylactic or ("rubber" is all I knew until I was grown) on my finger and said, "Look, Mommy."

Well, Mother threw a "hush! hush!" fit, and I was not sure just what line I had crossed, but whatever it was, I knew that you don't do such things in public. I have no recollection of where the idea came from, but evidently, I had heard something or seen something that was a no-no in our culture.

The next exposure I had to a contraceptive was when I started school.

I caught the school bus daily and rode about 30 minutes to an hour to school each way, depending on which route the bus was assigned.

Maudie Lou Woods was in the same grade as me, and I think it must have been the year we were in the second grade. When I got on the bus, Maudie Lou pulled out a rubber and began blowing it up like a giant white balloon.

Some of the older kids began to snicker. Mrs. Shankles, the algebra and Spanish teacher, was sitting up front, and when she heard the giggles, she turned around to see what was going on. Since the bus was not her responsibility, she just turned around and ignored the situation.

The bus driver looked through the rear-view mirror and also ignored the situation. The kids stared at Maudie Lou, but it did not seem to faze her. Much to her delight, she just kept blowing up her balloon.

Finally, I bent over and told her to stop blowing that thing up. (I didn't know its name.) At first, she ignored me, and I guess she did not understand what I meant since I was not very good at explaining this was a no-no item. Finally, she got the drift and put it away, and some teacher took it away from her when she got to school.

Even before I started school, my parents had fusses and verbal fights. (Maybe I should say that both of them cussed each other, and Daddy would hold Mother's hands to keep her from hitting him.) On a Saturday afternoon, Daddy would say, "Barbe-ann (that's what Daddy called me), "go get my dress socks out of my shoes and wash them." Daddy and Mother each had one pair of work shoes and one pair of dress shoes.

I would get Daddy's socks and put them in the wash pan in the kitchen. I would take the dipper, dip water out of the pail, and wash the socks. I would hang them on the line to dry. Daddy only had one pair of good socks.

When nighttime came, Daddy would put on his dress socks and shoes, get dressed in his best kicky pants and shirt, jump in the car, and head off. He and Floyd Larkin, Mary's husband, would go out "honkytonking."

Sometimes during these drinking bouts, Daddy found him another woman, and Mother found out and did she ever get her dander up! Daddy and his friends would drink beer until they were completely drunk and then head back home.

Sometimes, Daddy would come home late at night, and Mother was furious. That is when the fights would start. Daddy wanted to sing and laugh, but Mother saw nothing funny about the situation.

She had gone out in the cold and chopped wood for the stove to keep us warm. At times I would go out and get sticks of wood, pile two or three on my arms, and hobble back into the house. Doris, Duane, and Bobby all helped at times, too. I hated the cold wind; sometimes, it was dark before Mother realized we had no chopped firewood.

———◆◆◆———

Mother had gotten very frail after she had the "milk leg." She was now down to about 80 pounds. She felt trapped. She had four children, no education, and no way to provide for her family. I think she would have left Daddy if it had not been for us kids. She always contended that she loved Daddy and set out to figure out how to make him stay home and take care of the family. There was hardly any food to eat, and Daddy would take what little money there was and spend it on beer and women.

Mother continued to cook, wash the dishes, work in the fields, plant a garden, can food, wash the clothes, iron, help milk the cows, chop the wood when necessary, and do anything else we needed.

When mother began to get sick and have fainting spells, I will give my Daddy credit; he showed genuine concern for her. Maybe he really loved Mother — or perhaps he did not want to be stuck with four kids.

To be fair to Daddy, I will note that he did some work also. If my brothers or sister were writing this, they would give a different slant on my father. They thought my father hung the moon.

———•••———

We went to see Grandma Ray, my maternal grandmother, one Saturday. She had moved from Van Alstyne to Sherman. We always went to town on Saturdays to buy groceries or other essentials. Grandma lived with Estelle, Mother's sister. Grandpa Ray had died before I was born, leaving Grandma destitute.

Estelle worked at Leeds Ladies Apparel as a saleslady. Oline Ray Tye, Mother's sister, was visiting Estelle. Mother and her sisters would whisper about how Mother could catch Daddy with this other woman. Estelle agreed to keep the kids that Saturday night, and they decided Mother would accompany Daddy to the honkytonk. Mother hated beer because of her exposure to the effects of beer when she was growing up.

On Saturday, while we were at Grandma's house, Estelle, Oline, and Mother insisted that Mother go with Daddy that night. He never had a chance to refuse.

When Mother and Daddy got to the beer joint, they went in and began to drink. Mother danced with Daddy, but she kept her eyes peeled for a dark-headed woman that acted as if she knew Daddy.

When Mother had fought with Daddy in the past, she always accused him of having a red-headed woman, but someone had told her that Daddy had been seen out with a black-headed woman.

Later in the evening, Daddy asked Mother if he could dance with this dark-headed woman, quickly pointing out to Mother that the woman did not have red hair. While Daddy danced with this woman, Mother went out to the car and began to kick the dashboard, scream, holler, and throw a wall-eyed fit.

Someone saw her and went in and told Daddy what was going on out in the car, so Daddy rushed out to the car to see. He got there just before Mother completely demolished the car. Mother was so mad she couldn't see straight, and she couldn't talk. Daddy accused her of being crazy, and that just made Mother angrier. Daddy cursed Mother for embarrassing him.

They fought and cursed for several days. It was a terrible scene, and mother cried in total despair. When it was all over, she had fought for her man and won. To the best of my knowledge, Daddy stopped at least some of his carousing after that.

During the day, Daddy would take us to town on Saturday and park the car down at the Jockey Ground at the West end of Sherman. He would go off drinking until the wee hours of the night. Mother and us kids would just sit in the car and wait for him to return. Mother did not know how to drive and was too humiliated to go to her mother's house, so we would just sit there. We spoke few words while we sat in the car.

We would not have eaten supper, and there was no money to buy food. People would drive by, and there we sat late at night.

Everybody in town knew that Daddy was chasing around. I was so embarrassed. These experiences placed in me a hatred for my Daddy that I had great difficulty ever overcoming.

The night I was left with Estelle so that Mother could go out with Daddy, I got my first exposure to sex personally. I must have been about six years old, and my Uncle Dub was visiting Estelle and Grandma Ray.

Uncle Dub had always paid me a lot of attention. He would talk to me, hold me in his lap, kiss me, and make me feel special.

With all the turmoil that was going on in our household, there was little love and affection wasted on any of us kids.

When it came bedtime, Uncle Dub said I could sleep with him. After we went to bed, he hugged, kissed, and snuggled up to me. I felt safe and secure.

Then he began to tell me dirty jokes. Usually, I did not understand them, but he would explain them to me and then laugh and laugh.

Soon he began to rub me in places that made me feel less than secure. Even though I didn't have words for this, I knew he was sexually molesting me.

Since these matters were a no-no for discussion, I knew better than to mention them to my mother. Anyway, Uncle Dub led me to believe that this was part of my sex education; he told me this was our little secret.

Every time Uncle Dub came to spend the night with us, or I spent the night with Grandma, I endured "our little secret."

I hated him with a passion. Just being in the same room with him made me sick to my stomach. He told me that one day I would thank him.

I begged him not to touch me. I begged Mother to let me sleep with someone else, and she thought I was just being difficult.

Finally, one night Uncle Dub came to visit, and he informed Mother that I could sleep with him on the couch. By then, I was between nine and eleven years of age.

When we went to bed, I told him in no uncertain terms that he'd better not touch me, or I would tell Daddy. I had never threatened him before.

I suppose that by the tone of my voice, he knew I meant what I said. He never touched me again.

The next morning at the breakfast table Uncle Dub announced to everyone that Barbara was growing up.

Growing up and wising up, and being educated in the school of hard knocks I thought as I glared at him.

———••———

Another thing that inadvertently affected my sex education was a baby calf. We had this calf, and Daddy said he would give it to me if I took care of it. It was red with a pretty white face. I would feed that calf, rub the hair on its back, and scratch behind its ears. I felt so alone and was delighted to pour my love into this calf.

The first thing I would do in the evening when I got off the school bus was run up the hill to the house, throw my books on the bed, and go to the barn to see my calf.

As usual, I ran out to the barn one afternoon, and my calf was gone. I ran to the house as fast as I could and asked Mother, "Where is my calf?"

I could tell that she hated to tell me. "Your Daddy has taken him to the auction in Durant," she said. "He is going to sell your calf."

When Daddy came home, I asked him about my calf. I had never had much to say to my father, and I had never confronted him about anything. He was usually a very quiet man; he just chewed on his pipe and said little to anyone.

He admitted that he had sold the calf. I knew that there was nothing that I could do about it. I was young but understood that once cattle are sold, they are gone forever. There was nothing else to do but accept that my calf was gone.

The next thing to do was ask for the money the calf had brought at the auction.

Daddy had no intention of giving me the money, and he was surprised that I was spirited enough to ask him for the money. Had it been one of my brothers or my sister, I don't think they would have dared ask for the money. Over the next two or three days, I continued to express my feelings that he had taken my calf and that the money should be mine.

Between these incidents, a fundamental distrust of men began to grow in the back of my mind. Little did I realize the impact this would play on my life.

5 School Days & Social Strata

When I was six years old, I was all excited about being old enough to go to school. Going to school meant getting new dresses, a pair of shoes, and maybe even some ribbons for my hair. Mother pulled bolls out while I went to school. She made me five new dresses. It did not matter to me that some were made from flour sacks, some from cow-feed sacks, and maybe one was made from five-cent-a-yard fabric from Kress's. I could not have been more pleased if the dresses had been Paris originals.

Duane and Bobby must have quit school the year I started. Doris and I walked the quarter mile down the hill to catch the bus. At first this was fine. Then it was dark, and I had to climb out of bed, eat breakfast, and walk down the hill.

At times it was cold and rainy. I hated the mud road we had to walk down, because my shoes got wet and muddy, and I had to wear them all day.

It seemed that only the poorest kids must live on muddy roads. I developed an inferiority complex if I did not already have one. Everybody was poor so we were all poor together, but not everybody had those muddy, wet shoes.

Mrs. Lois McAlister was my first-grade teacher, and I really liked her. Eddie Vessel and I were the best readers in the class, so "Miss Lois," as we called the teacher, would let us read and then we could go to the back of the room and play in the sand box.

Sometimes she had crookneck gourds she wanted me to put my hands down into and pull out the seeds. She used these gourds in her art class. Mother would help me with my reading at night and that is the only way that I was able to read, because it was not long until I was just an average reader.

Miss Lois was in charge of an elaborate Christmas Program at school each year. The entire school participated. Southmayd School was a very small school from the first through twelfth grades.

When I started school there were around twenty students in my class and when I graduated from high school there were twenty-two and many were the same ones that I started school with.

When Christmastime came, each class was assigned certain songs to sing. There were angels in white robes with big wings covered with tinsel that glittered. There were bright robes for the King and the wisemen, and the Shepherds had their costumes with staffs in hand.

Many students were given poems to memorize, and I always got one of the longest poems to learn of anyone. I always worked and worked to memorize those poems.

There would be a Mary and Joseph, and of course, a doll that lay in a manger to represent Baby Jesus. This annual event was a very special time. Everyone got out of their classes to practice for the play. Since Miss Lois's husband was the school principal, there was no complaint. (This was before there was any problem with Christianity in the schools.)

After months of work, that special night would come when we would share that program with people from Southmayd and all over Grayson County, Texas. People would come to see the Christmas Play, and I felt like a super star.

We had assemblies once a week. Mr. McAlister would get up and read I Corinthians 13 or other Bible verses. We openly prayed to God in Jesus name. The school was the next thing to going to church, and there was as much Christian influence as if it had been a religious school.

Mrs. Biggers was my second-grade teacher. She was very kind and good. She was tall and thin and had a pleasant smile. Her hair was short, brown, and wavy. She had a sharp clear voice. While in her class the photographer came and took pictures of the classes and each student.

Usually, we could not afford to buy any of the pictures. Still, occasionally we would buy a group picture or the packet of my individual pictures. That year we purchased my packet, and Daddy carried one of my pictures in his billfold for as long as he lived. Mrs. Biggers had combed my hair and pulled a whisper of hair around my face; that gave me a sweet, soft appearance. Mother had dressed me in my best school dress. The dress was blue and white stripped cotton with small pink and white flowers. I felt really good about myself.

One year, the photographer photographed me and Nellie Don Reece. Nellie Don was not the prettiest girl in the class, but she was one of the cutest and best loved. I had skinned knees, which was typical of me, and I seemed to be skinnier and clumsier than any other girls. I did not like sports when we were in elementary school (grade school is what we called it then). But the teachers would make me go outside and play anyway.

Sometimes we would line up for teams and two people would choose who would be on their team. I was always one of the last ones picked, and I still remember hoping I would not be the last one chosen.

As I grew older, I must have gotten my coordination to work a little better and began to be one of the first chosen. Still, I never considered myself a very good athlete. I had sense enough to see some of my classmates' abilities and realized that some were great athletes.

Joyce Hames was a large girl with older brothers who was good at any sport. She played guard on the girls' basketball team and usually was the pitcher with baseball. Nellie Don Reese could run backward faster than any of the other girls. Rose Mary Blazek was swift and good. Mildred Hazelwood was more like me, tall and lanky. She had a knack for writing.

Lou Allie Andrews was my best girlfriend. She was a star forward on the basketball team. She was tall, excellent posture, thin face but filled out, muscular legs. She drove the tractor while her father pulled corn and threw it into the trailer. She helped with the milking and helped with the chickens. We spent a lot of time together. I would spend the night with her, or she would spend the night with me. She was more mature than me in many ways. She and Nellie Don were the ones who helped to pull me out of my shell. All the girls in my class became very close. Our class of 20 or 22 students became very close over our twelve years together.

-----•••-----

I had always made a straight "A" report card until I started into the third grade. Miss May Bumpus was my teacher, and she was the prettiest teacher. She had been married, but I think her husband had died or maybe they were divorced. Miss May had a beautiful daughter who was about the age of Duane. Miss May's mother lived with her, and people said all her mother would eat was bread and milk.

Miss May looked very nice in her clothes, but I am sure it was not easy for her to care for her family. When I looked at her, she was my idol and stood for everything I admired. She was pretty, sophisticated, self-sufficient, intelligent, and educated.

That's the year that the cows died. One of the wealthier men in the neighborhood came over to our house and wanted to sell Daddy some cows, I think there were twenty-three. He offered to sell the cows to Daddy at a really good price. Daddy did not have enough money to buy that many cows, but the more the man talked the deal became irresistible. So, Daddy went to the M & P Bank on Travis Street in Sherman. The Banker lent Daddy the money to buy the cows on Daddy's signature; maybe he put the cows up as collateral.

The man hauled the cows over to our house immediately. Everything seemed so rushed, and Daddy was excited about his purchase.

That first night five of the cows died. It seems that they all had hoof and mouth disease or something, and over the next few days ALL the cows died.

Daddy was so mad about being so gullible and ignorant. Daddy had only gone to the sixth grade and did not have a lot of book learning, but he had always prided himself on having common sense. This experience

48

devastated his ego. I don't know that he ever said anything to the man from whom he purchased the cows, but he learned that the man knew the cows were sick when he sold them.

So now here we were — no money, no cows, and a big loan. Fortunately, Mother and Daddy had just made the final payment on the farm, and we were just beginning to get on our feet financially for the first time in Mother and Daddy's marriage.

So, there was only one thing to do. Mother and Daddy held us kids out of school and the entire family hired out to the neighbors and picked cotton from sunup to sundown. When the cotton was all picked in our area we loaded up in our black, 1936 Ford and headed for Lubbock to pick cotton out there.

We found a small cabin and set up housekeeping with two or three pots and pans, clothes, and quilts. Mother and Daddy decided that I would stay with my Uncle J. C. and Aunt Ruby in Lubbock and go to school with their twin daughters, Connie and Mollie.

So, I went to school with my cousins, but the school would not admit me because I was not vaccinated. They put me in the hall, and I sat there all day long and watched the other children go up and down the hall. Every once in a while, Connie or Mollie would come by and say something to me. I don't know what they thought. I was embarrassed. I felt like some kind of a country bumpkin.

At the end of the day Connie and Mollie came by and told me that their music teacher said I could go to their music class with them. She said I must sit in the back of the class, but I could sing along.

They sang, "When Those Caissons Go Rolling Along" and other World War I songs. I had never heard them before, and I don't think I realized a war had gone on. Anyway, by the end of the class I was beginning to learn the songs and singing as big as anyone.

At the end of the day, we went back to their home. The next day I stayed home alone. Uncle J. C. and Aunt Ruby had to go to work. I felt so frightened to be alone in a strange town. I stayed by myself every day until the weekend. Somehow, they delivered a message to my parents that I could not attend that school, and Mother and Daddy came into town and got me and took me back out to the cotton fields. There was no money for vaccinations.

I put on my cotton sack and had one row of bolls to pull. Mother, Doris, Duane, and Bobby would pull two rows each, and Daddy would pull two or three. The cotton fields were white with cotton, and the bolls would be bulging and hanging down with cotton pouring out of them.

Instead of pulling each boll, you would strip the stalk. You would place your hands around the bottom of the stalk, cup your hands, and pull your hands up the stalk and with a swift swish you would stuff the cotton into your cotton sack.

My hands were so small that I had difficulty maneuvering this procedure, but I tried my best. Doris said she worked like a "trojan" and would complain about my laziness. I don't think I was lazy, but I must admit that I probably was not very enthusiastic. For whatever reason, I was not a very big asset to paying off the debt. Duane would complain; he hated picking cotton, milking cows, or anything related to farming. We seemed to have this in common.

Finally, after eating pork and beans from a tin can, sleeping on the floor, and surviving on the most meager existence possible, we returned home. I guess we had earned and saved enough money to pay off the debt. Mother had stood by her man without criticizing him for making such a mistake.

My family worked together and pulled together. They survived together and saved their dignity. Daddy paid off the bank and never had difficulty borrowing money after that. The cost was high, but our honor was intact.

We might have been short on money and material possessions, but our lessons in honesty and integrity were well worth the cost. So, when I started back to school at Southmayd, although my first report card did not have all "A's," I probably learned one of the most valuable lessons in my life that year. I worked hard in school for the remainder of the school year and was able to catch up.

Other children had been out picking cotton also, Mildred and Charles Freeman and Rose Mary and Frankie Blazek. The Freeman kids did not have a mother and were probably much worse off than us. Mildred had to do the cooking, dish washing, clothes washing, and all the housework. Mildred was one of the smartest kids in our class, and Rose Mary Blazek became one of my very best friends.

6 Teen Times & First Call to Ministry

School was both fun and miserable. The kids would line up by class in front of the old, white, two-story grade school building. When the bell rang, we would march to our classes. Sometimes we would take the erasers outside and beat the chalk dust out of them, banging them against the sidewalk.

At lunch time we would line up to go to lunch. Everybody would jockey for position. Certain ones wanted to sit by certain people. I never was out going enough to try to push in to sit by someone special and nobody was fighting to get to sit by me. Going to lunch was a painful time for me because I thought nobody wanted to sit by me. I don't think that is how it was, but because of my shyness and lack of self-confidence, this is how I felt.

As the years went by, I got better at baseball and was not half bad at basketball. My grades were good, so I felt I must not be too dumb. We moved over to the High School Building where the students from the sixth or seventh grade through twelfth attended. It was on the same campus, and we all ate in the same lunchroom.

One day at lunch time, as the girls were walking from the High School to the lunchroom in the grade school building, Nellie Don Reese called to me, as I was following behind all the other girls, not close enough to be a part of the group, but not far enough behind to be alone.

"Come on Barbara," she said, "up here with us!"

There is no way to express what that did for my ego. It does not sound like much, but this was the first clue I ever had that somebody wanted my company.

Nobody had ever treated me badly or made fun of me. Nobody had been rude or ugly to me in any way, but still I just did not feel wanted.

From that day forward I would take my position with all the other girls, and I began to blossom. I began to exert myself and see myself in a completely different light. After a while, I began to see myself as a leader.

I was one of the best academically in my class. I was still shy with the boys, and even though they seemed to like me just fine, there seemed to be a difference in how they treated me.

This difference could have been partly because of how they saw me and my relationship with God. They probably saw me as some kind of religious fanatic. I got along with the boys just fine and acquired a great deal of respect from them.

The year before ninth grade there was a drought all summer long.

The tank dried up and we had to pump water for the cows. By this time, we were milking cows for a living, and I was more involved with cows than I ever was with cotton. I would go out into the back yard and call "soo-uk, soo-uk," and the cows on the back forty acres could hear me and start toward the barn.

When the drought came there was no water for the cows to drink. I pumped up and down on the pump attached to the water well. As my arms pushed down on the pump handle and pulled up on the pump handle, little did I notice that my breast began to change shapes.

Then as I moved my arms my nipples were so sore that I could hardly stand for my dress to rub across my breasts.

By the time I started back to school my body had changed from a little girl to that of a full-breasted woman. To further exaggerate the situation, sweaters were in fashion with full circular skirts or tight sweaters with pencil slim skirts. We would tie a scarf around our necks and pull the knot to one side of our necks and let the two ends tousle in the wind. Oxfords with colored anklets were in style. These tight sweaters emphasized my newly developed breasts.

Algebra was my best subject and Mrs. Shankles taught that class. One day she sent me and a boy to the black board to work a problem simultaneously. I was always happy to be sent to the blackboard because I felt certain she would not give me any problem I could not work with. I was wearing one of those pencil-slim skirts that was light colored.

She gave us the problem and I began to work the problem so I could beat the boy. When I finished working the problem, Lou Allie approached the black board and asked me to go with her.

I could not imagine what she wanted with me. I looked at the teacher and then at Lou Allie without saying anything. Lou Allie marched me out into the hall and into the rest room as quickly as possible.

When we got to the rest room, I discovered a large spot on my skirt. I was menstruating, and I don't remember much else besides the shock and horror of that big spot of blood on the back of my pastel skirt.

Lou Allie helped me get my skirt off and I got the spot washed off, but it left a large wet spot on my bottom. By the time we got the problem taken care of, the Algebra class was over, and it was lunch time.

Nobody ever teased me or said anything to me. Getting your period was just one of those things you did not discuss, one of those no-no subjects. For that I was grateful. Most of the girls got their period that year or they had already gotten their period. This big landmark seemed to thrust us all from being little girls to becoming women.

———•••———

Miss Lois taught us about personal hygiene. We were taught everything from how much toilet paper to use to wipe our behinds to how to dispose of our sanitary pads. She told us to shower every day after basketball practice, what to eat, and how to eat. We also learned how to do the Virginia Drill and Square Dance. We had plays of all sorts and I continued to get a big part in the plays.

By the time graduation day came, I was a better-rounded person.

Basketball was everything in our community, and everything seemed to revolve around the basketball team. When I was in the tenth grade, I broke my arm playing basketball. Then in the eleventh grade I worked as hard as possible to make the team but could never quite make the first string. (I was not that good, so I understood.)

We practiced basketball before school in the morning, at every break, at lunch time, and then for a couple hours in the afternoon. During the free practice time, I felt like I was on the first string, because the other five girls from my class who were on the first string always wanted me to be the sixth.

But I was left on the bench when the coach picked the team. At least my peers wanted me to be a part of them, which was more important than the coach. I would always sit on the bench next to the coach because that is where the coach wanted me. I got substituted regularly and got to play a lot, but I never got to start.

———•••———

When I started the twelfth grade, I told myself that this was my last shot at making the first team. We had a championship team, the best team in North Texas for our size school. We would play Sherman, a big city school by our standards, and we either won or gave them a real run for their money.

My name was not on the list when the coach picked the starting lineup. I went to a few games and continued to practice, but to no avail. Then I did something I don't think any girl in that school had ever done.

I told the coach that I quit. I did not need the credit to graduate, and I told the coach I would prefer to use that time to study instead of play basketball. The coach tried to talk me into staying, but Miss Lois understood.

Miss Lois had coached the girls' team, but when it came time to pick the lineup Mr. McAlister, Miss Lois's husband, picked the team. He sat on the bench and acted as if he was the girls coach when in reality, he had done nothing.

So, from that day on instead of going to the gym in the afternoon, I went to the study hall and read and studied. I wanted to go to college but knew there was no way I could go. I didn't even talk to any of the teachers about my desire, or they probably could have shared information that might have allowed me to go.

When graduation came, there was great excitement about what the girls would wear. We talked about our hats and gloves and dresses or suits. Mother had made me a pink linen suit. Irish linen was expensive, but Mother had purchased the material I wanted for this special occasion.

Daddy had worked on the railroad for a while, then he had worked at Perrin Field as a fireman, and now he was working in Fort Worth at Convair (later to become General Dynamics), so our money situation had improved greatly.

We rented caps and gowns, and then the discussion arose on whether to wear the caps and gowns to the baccalaureate service at church or wear our new dresses. I wanted to wear my suit and began talking to the other girls and found out that each one had a new dress.

I especially talked to the girls I thought might be unable to get a new graduation dress. Occasionally, I would hear the boys mention something about a new suit. So, the class voted on whether to wear caps and gowns.

But before we voted Miss Lois got up before the class and told all the reasons why we should wear the caps and gowns. Some of her reasoning, I thought, was out of line. It was like she was putting on a campaign to sway the class in a certain direction without giving equal time to the opposing side.

When the class voted, I cast the only descending vote — so we wore caps and gowns to the baccalaureate service. That was fine with me, but Miss Lois called me in for a little talk, and I thought she had acted inappropriately.

She began talking to me about my descending vote as if I did not have the right to vote my conscience, and that by voting in the way I had voted, I had committed some wrong. To me, I felt that in a democratic society that is what democracy is all about. She talked and talked, and I kept quiet. After a while, I got mad and began to cry. I cried and cried, and she talked and talked. I was crying so hard that I could never state my point of view.

After leaving that room that day, I vowed to never cry again. I would hold back the tears so I would be able to argue my point of view. I told myself that if I cried, I had lost the battle, and it did not matter what I thought if I was not strong enough not to cry. I kept that promise to myself, but somehow some of my softness disappeared.

7 Courtship & Engagement

On June 3, 1955, I met Jerry Dowdy. I was working at Burroughs Corporation, at the Regional Accounting Office, on Mockingbird Lane, Dallas, Texas. There was a young lady named Ima Jean Angel, and she said there was a young man who worked at the Lone Star Gas Company in Dallas with her husband, George, whom she would like me to meet. She suggested we go out on a double date together so I could meet this young man.

One of the other girls in the office had asked me to have a blind date with her husband's brother, a Dallas policeman. I had gone out with him, and it was the worst dating experience I'd ever had, so when Ima Jean asked me to have a blind date with this guy at the gas Company, I was not sure I wanted to go. I liked Ima Jean, though, and thought everything would probably be satisfactory if she and her husband went along.

I was dating a couple of other guys at the time but was not seriously interested. I was twenty-one and had dated so many guys since graduating from high school that I was tired of the dating scene.

All girls were expected to get married, have children, and become "housewives." Still, times were changing, and now men expected their wives to work at least until they got pregnant.

I liked my work but did not particularly like one of the married men at the office who kept saying little things to me that did not mean much of anything, but at the same time, it made me feel uncomfortable. Sometimes I had to go into the office where his desk was, and I was reluctant to go over there. Walking down the hall, I could feel the men peering through the glass and staring at me as I walked. Maybe I should have been flattered, but it made me uncomfortable.

———•••———

At one time, I had done some nude photo modeling for a friend of Francis Bell. (One of those crazy choices you make as a teenager and later regret.) Looking back, I can't, in my wildest imagination, figure out why I agreed to such a thing. I have never been modest and visiting art museums and seeing paintings of naked women seemed culturally appropriate. When this man asked me to model for him, I agreed to pose for him two or three times. He was always dignified and never did anything inappropriate.

Anyway, he insisted that I take some of the pictures. I really had no desire for them, but he said that when I was old and fat I would appreciate them. So, I took the pictures and showed them to my roommates, and I took some of the less provocative ones and showed them to some of the girls at the office and even to my parents. My mother did not say much, but my daddy was appalled. Daddy never said much, but he had a way of letting you know what he thought.

I put the pictures in my lingerie drawer in the apartment. One day I was looking in the drawer and noticed that the pictures were gone. I really hated for them to wind up in the hands of dirty old men or people who would not see them as a work of art or something of beauty God had created. The human body was a beautiful creation, which may be why I posed in the first place.

Sally Scoggins had moved into the apartment with Frances, Doris, and me. I attended school with Sally Scoggins and Tommy Pence. They were dating then, and Tommy had gotten a job at Burroughs in the warehouse.

I always wondered if Sally had shown the pictures to Tommy without my permission — and if he had stolen them, taken them to the office, and showed them to some of the men at Burroughs. This may be my imagination.

I share this background to express some of the feelings I was experiencing when Ima Jean asked me to go out on a blind date with the gas man. Nevertheless, I agreed to go out with this man, and she told me his name was Jerry Dowdy.

We set a date and time. We were supposed to go to the movies, but as the day arrived, Ima Jean got sick and told me she did not feel like going. She wanted to know if I would be willing to go ahead and keep the date. She assured me that Jerry was a nice guy. I agreed to go.

Jerry was supposed to come by and pick me up at about 7:00 pm. I got dressed and was ready when there was a knock on the door. I had no idea how this guy looked, how old he was or anything about him.

I opened the door, and there stood Jerry. He had dark brown hair, a round face, and baby soft-looking skin. He was about 5 foot 11 inches, and he looked muscular but, at the same time, a little puffy.

He was wearing a gray wool sport coat with darker gray lines going vertical and horizontal, making broad plaids.

His shirt was pink, starched, and ironed, and he wore a necktie with the outline of a lady's face on it; she was wearing an enormous, brimmed hat. He had on navy dress slacks and black shoes.

Within ten seconds, I had summed up my first impression. Jerry Dowdy seemed neat and clean, and he appeared to have gone to quite a lot of trouble getting dressed. This being June in Texas, the temperature was around 100 degrees, and the wool coat seemed extremely hot. He was a little overdressed compared to the other guys I had been dating.

We exchanged cordial greetings after introducing ourselves. I invited him in, and he mentioned a movie he had in mind for us to see. We went out to the movie and had an uneventful first date. He asked me out again, and we began to date regularly after that.

On our third date, Jerry began talking about his hopes for the future and the kind of house he would like to own. We discussed family and our dreams of what we wanted out of life. Nothing was earth-shaking about our relationship, but we seemed comfortable together. After that third date, when I returned to the apartment, I told Doris and Frances that I was going to marry Jerry Dowdy.

I did not fall madly in love with Jerry, and there was nothing overwhelmingly exciting about him. Marrying Jerry just felt right. We went dancing and to the movies. We got together with George and Ima Jean Angel and went to White Rock Lake for a picnic. Jerry did 50 pushups; I think he was trying to impress me. We lay on the blanket under a shade tree and hugged and kissed for most of the afternoon. The Angels probably thought we were a bit silly, and I guess we were. Jerry certainly was not shy.

We went to all the dance places and danced half the night away and smooched in the front seat of the car for hours, and then Jerry would take me home. One night we drove out Central Expressway, and Jerry stopped at the end of the service road under the bridge, and we talked and talked.

That night Jerry told me that he loved me. We talked about marriage, and I knew that Jerry was going to ask me to marry him. I had not told him I loved him but did nothing to give him the impression that I did not want to marry him.

The radio was playing all the time we were parked, and when we got ready to go home, the car would not start. We walked up on the Expressway and along the side of a long bridge. I remember the big trucks coming by and almost blowing me off the bridge, and I would stop every time I saw a truck coming and hold onto the side railing. Finally, we got across the bridge and made our way to a service station to find a phone.

Jerry said he was going to call his brother Norman. His father would not let Norman come; instead, his dad came. We walked back across the bridge, and it was not long until Jerry's dad came. I felt embarrassed.

On October 3, Jerry wanted to come to the apartment after work. A friend of Frances was cooking dinner for Doris, Frances, and me. I told Jerry I already had other plans, but when he insisted, I told him he could come over after work and stay until it was time for us to go to dinner.

He brought with him a small box and pulled out a white gold ring with one small diamond in the center and two smaller diamonds on either side. I guess Jerry assumed I would accept the ring. So, we became engaged. Somewhere along the way, I'm sure I told Jerry that I loved him. To say "I love you" was not an easy thing for me to do. I had never told anybody that I loved them, so to say "I love you" was not something our family did.

After Jerry gave me the ring, I went ahead and went out to dinner with Doris and Frances as I had planned. Jerry left, and I have no idea what he did or where he went. I had a date or two scheduled with other boys, and I went ahead and kept those dates but told them that we would have to break off seeing each other. Since we did not have a close intimate relationship, there was nothing dramatic.

The only boy I dated from time to time that I cared anything about was Bill Floyd, and we were not dating then. He called one night when I was out with Jerry and Frances or Doris told him I had gotten engaged, so I never heard from him again. It was probably just as well that way, but I feel there should have been a better closure of that on-again-and-off-again relationship. I have thought of him many times and wondered about him, and maybe if I had seen him one last time, I would not have continued to think about him and wonder what happened to him.

———•••———

Once Jerry and I were engaged, I put all my past boyfriends behind me, and I was relieved that hunting for a husband was over. I was tired of going out.

Jerry and I began to make our marriage plans. We set a date, and then we moved it up. Then we set another date and moved up again. We began staying home and watching TV to save money for the honeymoon. We planned a budget and figured out how much money we would have to pay for an apartment, utilities, and expenses.

Jerry had a 1951 maroon Mercury and he had it paid for. He also owned a box full of cooking pots and pans and a record player. I had a set of silverware, some dishes, and a sewing machine. Jerry had about $300.00, and I had saved $1800.00. Except for a few clothes, that pretty much accounts for all our material possessions.

We spent every spare minute together. Jerry was still living at home. Finally, we moved our wedding date to November 25, 1955, so from

October 3 to November 25 did not give us much time to plan a wedding and make all the necessary arrangements.

Mother and I went out to look for fabric for a wedding gown. I had only been to one wedding in my life, but I had seen weddings in movies. I bought an excellent wedding magazine, which told us everything we needed to do. We bought some beautiful white fabric, embroidered all over, and Mother went to work making my wedding gown. She also made me a pale blue robe.

I went shopping for a going-away dress, hat, gloves, purse, and shoes. I selected a turquoise wool knit dress. I bought a black leather pillbox purse, a small black hat with a feather sticking up on one side, and a pair of white gloves.

Jerry's grandparents lived in Denison, which was only about 15 miles from my parents' Southmayd farm. Jerry was born in Denison and lived there until he was a junior in high school, when his parents moved to Dallas.

Jerry graduated from North Dallas High School and attended Texas A&M University for one year.

8 Melding Families & Personalities

Jerry's dad was Arvil Dowdy, who had helped the general locate the site for Perrin Field. Jerry and I had lived within 15 miles of each other for most of our lives but did not know each other.

Because Jerry's dad had managed to get a government job during the depression era, his family had fared better than most. His grandparents, Kyle and Willie Marcene Dowdy, had a mom-and-pop type grocery store. They had a few rental houses and took care of them. They lived a modest lifestyle but had a good old house and lived comfortably.

Kyle Dowdy, Jerry's grandfather, had diabetes, and he had his second leg amputation about the time I met Jerry. As a result, he spent much of his time lying in bed and watching Television. Both Kyle and Willie, Jerry's grandmother, had bought some apartment houses, which they rented.

Willie Dowdy ran the grocery store since Arvil was in high school. Now she had sold the grocery store and retired. Kyle and Willie seemed just to tolerate each other. They kept their money separate and did not seem to desire to do anything together. He slept in one bedroom, and she slept in another. They had worked out their life together with few conflicts, but they shared little. For a woman in that day and time to secure her independence, Willie was a pretty strong-willed woman. She was a good businesswoman.

Willie probably weighed no more than 90 pounds. (She looked a little like "Ma" on The Beverly Hillbillies without the high-top boots.) Both Kyle and Willie adored Jerry, and he had lived with them or just down the street until he moved to Dallas. All the family accused the Dowdys of being partial to Jerry.

———•••———

Connie Dowdy was Jerry's aunt who lived in Wichita Falls. Shortly after our marriage, she came to live with her parents so she could take care of them.

Connie was a colorful character, and about the only thing beautiful about Connie was her fingernails. She always kept them long and painted them bright red. Connie's hair was dyed a reddish brown, and she rarely wore makeup. Her clothing was very modest, and she usually wore a lightweight cotton dress without a slip or bra. Her legs were bowed like she had straddled a horse all her life.

Connie could curse like a sailor and did not hesitate to express herself with explicit language. She went to church every Sunday, and the preacher loved coming by for a frequent visit, a cup of coffee, and a long chat.

Everybody loved to stop by to see Connie and talk. She always had something good to eat. She was not afraid of hard work. After her parents became bedridden, she took care of them. After their death, she took care of the apartments, built another apartment house, and managed everything most economically. She bought herself a good car and a fishing boat, but her life was extremely modest outside of that.

Everybody loved Connie. To know her was to love her. Her first husband had burned to death in an accident while he was working on his car.

Her second husband also had some kind of tragic death. I am unsure what happened to her third husband, but her fourth husband died of a heart attack. Connie had four or five husbands, and now she had none. If she felt any remorse or any regrets, she never showed it.

Connie laughed, talked, smoked cigarettes, told jokes, cooked, and worked. It is hard to describe Connie. She was one of those loveable hillbilly type women who seemed secure and totally happy with herself, but she liked to get her own way.

If you took her out of her element, she was like a fish out of water — her personality changed, and she felt uncomfortable. But as long as she was home, Connie was a bright spot on the corner of the block in Denison.

To be around Connie, one would not think she was religious, but she went to church every Sunday. She would drive around town, pick up all the old widow women, and take them to church with her. When they needed help, she also took them to the doctor. Even when Connie was about 80 herself, she talked about picking up the "old women" and taking them somewhere. She was kind and helpful to everyone.

———•••———

Jerry's parents were Pauline Maness and Arvil Dowdy. They moved to Dallas in 1948, so Jerry's dad could go to work for the Corps of Engineers in Dallas. Arvil had run a service station when Jerry was born. He had ridden his horse, Nellie, into the bank to make deposits for his mother. (He would laugh and say he invented drive-in banking.)

Arvil was a small man, about five foot six inches, with small bones. He only weighed about 135 pounds. He liked to joke and tell stories, and he had friendly mannerisms.

Once before Jerry and I were married, he made a crack about me having "Kildee legs," and I never appreciated that very much. Jerry's family seemed to delight in finding fault with me or saying little things to put me down. I ignored these little insults because I would tell myself that was their way of trying to bring me down to their level. My father had always said insulting remarks to my brothers to try to make himself look more intelligent or better than them. He did this because of his inferiority, so when the Dowdys would make sly remarks, I tried to ignore them, but it hurt.

———•••———

Jerry's Mom, Pauline Maness Dowdy, was a small woman who was very prim and proper. She had been raised on a farm and had worked hard as a young girl. She worked the rest of her life trying to remove that poor farm image from her past. She was a perfectionist and hounded

64

Arvil, trying to make him perfect, but he was reticent to change, although he worked very hard to try to please her. Pauline would tell Arvil when to take a bath, when to change clothes, and what he should wear. (It would not have surprised me to hear her ask him if he had washed behind his ears.)

Pauline kept an immaculate house. She did not want anybody to put a finger on any wooden furniture because it would leave fingerprints. As the years went by, the family was less particular about touching the furniture. She kept herself meticulous all the time. I never saw her with a hair out of place, and she religiously went to the beauty shop every week. She slept in a hair net so her hair would not get mussed.

Most cars did not have an air conditioner when Jerry and I met, so Pauline had a great deal of trouble riding in a car during the summer because the windows had to be down, and the wind would blow into the car and mess up her hair.

Pauline liked good clothes. Even though they did not have a lot of disposable income, she always managed to buy well-tailored dresses and suits that would last from one season to the next. Her shoes and bags matched, and she was always well-coordinated and put together. Because of her petite figure, Pauline always looked like she had "stepped out of a bandbox" (meaning that she was neat, clean, and orderly). She made every effort to be perfect and made every effort to see that her family looked and acted perfect, but because they were not all perfectionists like herself, she encountered many unnecessary heartaches.

Pauline was a brilliant woman who had attended college on a basketball scholarship for one year. She was always interested in college basketball and football. She listened to the games on the radio and had a brilliant memory of players' names; she always remembered who won what game and the final score.

Pauline was never lazy. She kept a perfect house. She cooked good meals for her family and managed her household on whatever money was available. Because Arvil had a good job with the Corp of Engineers, they were able to manage quite well and never lived above their means. They had lived through the depression, and even though they had survived better than most, they still needed to "save some for a rainy day" (meaning they always wanted to be prepared for the unexpected).

Jerry had one younger brother, Norman, and one sister, Jann. Norman came along three years after Jerry, and Jann was born about eleven years after Jerry. In many ways Jann was a surprise to Arvil and Pauline.

Jann was just ten years old when Jerry and I started dating. Jann's dresses always seemed a little long, and when Pauline would buy Jann dresses that fit, she always had to hem them up. Her legs were much larger than my skinny legs. She had thick, light brown hair with lots of curls.

Jann was far from a perfectionist. (Maybe she was messy as a subconscious rebellion, or maybe she was just not motivated.) Jann was also very strong-willed and did not want to mind her parents. One day when the Dowdys invited Jerry and me over for Sunday lunch, Jann got into an argument with her parents, and Arvil took her to the bathroom. I could hear Arvil say, "if you don't mind me, I will stomp your guts out."

By the tone of his voice, I don't think he would have hesitated. However, Jann was not as convinced as I was and continued to talk back to him.

Then Arvil spanked Jann with his hand. He spanked and spanked her, and she cried, screamed, and screamed. The rest of us sat at the dinner table in total silence. (Our family was a bit dysfunctional, too, but we did not dare talk back to our parents.)

When it was all over, Arvil came out of the bathroom looking exhausted, and Jann continued crying. To this day, I am not sure who won the battle. Jann retained her strong will, and Arvil became no less domineering. Jann was determined to do what Jann wanted to do regardless of the consequences.

Norman, Jerry's younger brother, was the only one that Pauline seemed to get along with well. She thought that he was just perfect. Norman was the greatest baseball player on his team to hear Pauline talk. Norman was also the smartest kid in his class, according to his mom.

Norman graduated from North Dallas High School the year Jerry and I met. He seemed to have plenty of friends and to be well-liked. Norman was smaller than Jerry, and he took after his parents when it came to physique. His hair was dark, and his skin had an olive complexion like his mother's.

Pauline said Norman was accepted at the Air Force Academy accidentally but failed his physical due to an obstruction in his nose. Probably a minor surgery would have repaired the nose, but his family was not big on going to the doctor.

They were a very healthy family, and the only thing in the medicine cabinet likely would have been some Campho-Phenique or some aspirin Pauline took from time to time. I don't know if it occurred to the family to consider surgery. It cost money to go to the doctors, and people rarely went except in an emergency.

Then Norman applied at Texas A&M, where two of his uncles had graduated, and he was accepted as a military cadet. Four years later, he graduated as a second lieutenant and entered the army.

By the time Norman graduated, he had left his family behind, only to visit them occasionally.

The Dowdys lived on Lover's Lane in Dallas near Love Field. Arvil would catch the bus to work each morning and return each afternoon on the bus. Their life was simple and orderly. They got up at a specific time, ate their meals at a set time, and went to bed at a set time. Their life was regimented.

From time to time, Arvil would get a wild hare to do something on his own, but Pauline never had the guts to live a little dangerously. Pauline always bragged about Arvil's abilities, but when it came to trusting their income to these abilities, she could never make that commitment and put their lifestyle on the line. Since he had a good job, it was hard to give it up "a bird in hand."

After Norman graduated from High School, the family moved to Beltline Road in Richardson. Jann finished high school in Richardson and went to college for one semester.

9 Wedding Daze

Jerry met my family, and I am not sure what he thought. After I graduated from high school, Mother and Daddy moved to a small apartment in Fort Worth. Then they moved to Greenville, where Daddy worked for Temco Vaught as a painter of airplanes. Part of the time when we were dating, they lived up on the farm.

One weekend before we were married, I wanted to go home to the farm, and Jerry said he would take me home. He would spend the weekend with his grandparents in Denison, and we could still go out together.

So, Jerry picked me up after work, and when we got to Sherman, it had rained, and the roads were muddy. We could go one way, and the road was rocked to within two miles of our house. Or we could go through Southmayd, and there would be five miles of mud. Knowing how bad one mile was in that mud, I opted to go through Southmayd, but Jerry chose the least mud in terms of distance but the worst in terms of spots.

We started on the muddy part, and Jerry was trying to impress me with his expertise in driving on muddy roads. The ruts were so deep that the bottom of the car dragged, but Jerry would gun the car and was able to maneuver on down the road.

Then we looked further down the road, and a car was bogged down right in the middle of the road, so Jerry tried to go around the car. At first, driving out of the deep ruts was difficult, but he managed.

Just as we got around the car and were about to return to the center of the road, the car bottomed out, stuck deep in that mud and refused to budge.

Jerry's ego was shot. He insisted that he could have made it if that other car had not gotten stuck and slowed him down. The truth is that the road was impossible.

Jerry had to get one of the neighbors to come down and pull him out with a tractor. I think he felt embarrassed being a city boy. When he mentioned that incident for years, he would say that the neighbors were probably still laughing at that city boy trying to go down that road and getting stuck. Actually, the neighbors were well-accustomed to getting stuck, and that was just part of life on the farm. Those roads were horrendous when it rained.

The next time Jerry took me home for the weekend, it was raining, and his dad was with us. This time, Jerry opted to go through Southmayd. We still slipped and slid, and the car moaned and groaned, but we finally got to my parents' home. Arvil always laughed at how back in the sticks I lived, and I always felt that he was poking fun at me by equating me with those muddy shoes I had learned to hate as a little girl.

———◆◆◆———

Jerry was not one to be influenced by his family's opinions too much, so he never paid any attention to their remarks. They were his family, and he loved them, and it never occurred to him that I might be offended. My family got offended so easily. We were extremely careful not to say anything about another family member, and Jerry's family never hesitated to say things to cut one another down. This difference was something to which I had to become accustomed. Jerry accepted my family's unusual quirks, and I accepted his family, warts and all.

We planned our wedding for November 25, 1955. We both had turned 21 during the summer and thought we could make it on our own. Jerry had always lived at home except for one year when he went away to Texas A&M University, and even then, his family had paid the tuition. I had been totally on my own for three years.

We mailed out the wedding invitations. We selected our bridesmaids and groomsmen. We planned every detail of the reception. I had asked my Daddy to give me away, and up until the last minute, he said that he would not give me away. Then Mother talked to him and assured him that was the custom, so he agreed to give me away.

On the night of the wedding, a "blue norther" had blown in, and it was bitter cold. Jerry and his family got dressed in Denison at his grandparents' house.

Jerry started to dress in his blue suit pants and could not get his leg into the pants and then realized he was trying to put on the pants belonging to his best, Don Weersing. Finally, Jerry got dressed in his navy-blue suit to match Don's.

Norman and Duane were to light the candles dressed in their navy-blue suits. Doris was my maid of honor, and she was dressed for the occasion in a beautiful pink taffeta dress.

The wedding ceremony was at Southmayd Baptist Church. Jerry, Don, and the Preacher were in the little room where I had taught the little children when I was a child. Daddy and I waited at the other end of the church. People arrived, and the ceremony was about to get underway.

Daddy looked down at my chest and asked what was wrong with me. I looked down to discover big red spots all over my chest. Against my snow-white dress, those red spots made me look like I had a bad case of measles. I assured Daddy that nothing was seriously wrong with me; it was just nerves. He was not so sure. I wondered if he would let me take his arm for fear that I would give him some dreaded disease.

The pianist began to play Felix Mendelssohn's "Wedding March," and the men walked in. Then as she began to play loudly on the piano, "Here Comes the Bride," Daddy and I started walking down the little aisle.

This little church brought back so many memories. It was this aisle I had walked down when I accepted Jesus Christ as my Lord and Savior, and I had walked down this same aisle when I felt God wanted me to be a foreign missionary. This church was one part of my life I had never chosen to share with Jerry.

The church was drafty, people wore their coats, and the ladies wore white gloves and dress hats. There were not a lot of people there. After all, this was not the social event of the year, but many old friends from my childhood were there. Aunt Estelle had made a remarkable effort to find someone to bring her and my Grandma Ray to the wedding. They were living in Dallas at that time.

All the work, planning, and preparation was over within a few short minutes. The preacher began saying the vows and asked us to repeat after him. The traditional ceremony was "Do you Barbara take this man for your lawfully wedded husband, to love, honor, and obey."

During the rehearsal, I had balked at the word "obey," and the preacher said he could change that to "cherish." There was no man alive I could love enough to want to "obey" — "until death do us part."

Little did I realize at the time that "love, honor, and cherish" could be every bit as difficult as "obey." But to me, "obey" meant giving up a certain independence which I did not feel any woman should be demanded to do. All this seemed to go over Jerry's head; he could have cared less. Maybe he was not taking each particular word as seriously.

So, we made it through the part where we both said, "I do," and were pronounced "man and wife."

When we entered the reception room next door, the punch was not on the table. I learned that Eddie Lou Bilger, who was supposed to serve the punch, had missed the wedding because she and her Daddy were cooking the punch on the stove.

It seems that the ice cream was frozen so hard that they could not get it out of the five-gallon container, and it had to be soft enough to mix with ginger ale. With their gallant efforts, they were able to get the ice cream thawed enough to serve. (Since cake and punch were all we were serving, the punch was important!) Frances Bell served the wedding cake, and at last, people could come in out of the cold and go through the receiving line.

I was so frazzled over this unexpected complication that I am not sure I ever thanked Eddie Lou, and I feel certain I never thanked her father. I guess Estelle realized I was not at my most polite best, and she informed me that I should go over and speak to my grandmother, who had made a considerable effort to attend the wedding. Being thoughtful and considerate of others was never one of my strong points, and I still held onto my shy, self-centered self.

I could not wait to get away. My wedding was far from being a fun and pleasant evening, but it was something I felt I had to do to be somebody. In high school, I learned the little poem, "I'm nobody, who are you? Are you nobody, too? Don't tell they'll banish us, you know."

God had given his only Son to die for my sins; you would think that would make me feel like someone special, but I still felt like a nobody.

God had given me this wonderful young man to be my husband, but the truth was I felt like a "nobody," and I was self-centered enough that I was not grateful.

So, Jerry and I were married, and we went to Carlsbad Caverns on our honeymoon.

10 Honeymoon & Early Marriage

By the time the wedding was over, we were probably exhausted, but neither of us felt exhausted. We were anxious to get to the hotel room, at least I was, and I think I can speak for Jerry on this matter.

My experience with sex was limited, to say the least. I had never climbed into bed with a man ready to give myself fully to him. I had desired many young men, but my puritan background and fear of getting pregnant had kept me pretty much on the straight and narrow. Quite frankly, I don't think Jerry was too experienced either, but nature has a way of taking its course.

Our love and sex life had to grow and mature quite a lot before I could allow myself to become completely vulnerable. Jerry knew what he wanted, and fulfilling his needs did not take long. My idea was that a wife scripturally is supposed to "submit" to her husband. To me, that meant that she does not have the right to say "NO." When it came to sex, I never said "NO."

When we got back from our honeymoon, Jerry's Mom made us an appointment so a doctor could fit me with a diaphragm. Jerry bought a large box of condoms before we got married, but neither of us found that an effective method for birth control.

When we went in to see the doctor, for some reason, he examined Jerry first. Then he came in and examined me and fitted me with a diaphragm, the most popular birth control method at that time. The doctor was careful to explain to me how to use it.

He also told me something else that was most helpful. He said, "What you and your husband agree to do behind closed doors is your business." He also explained to me some positions for more enjoyable sex. (I did not request this additional information, but maybe he suspected we needed a little advice.

I was still working for Burroughs Corporation and making about $45.00 weekly. Then about 1.5 percent was taken out for FICA. Virtually nothing was taken out for income tax, and my hospitalization insurance cost about three dollars a week. After all the deductions, I brought home about $38 a week. That was not much, but that was about what office girls made then.

Jerry and I discussed his going back to college. We sat down with a pencil and paper and decided that we could pay the rent, which was $35.00 per month, the utilities, and gasoline from what I made and still have enough left to eat.

Jerry had found this neat little servant's quarters behind one of those fancy houses on Turtle Creek. The place was owned by Mrs. Selcraig, who also owned a few blocks of downtown Dallas. The home was furnished with primitive furniture.

Jerry picked up an old abandoned Universal cook stove at the gas company. We took it apart piece by piece and cleaned it with lye and all kinds of cleaning chemicals. By the time we got it back together, it looked like new. Jerry adjusted the burners and oven so that it cooked perfectly. At least it measured up to our cooking abilities.

The little house had one room that served as living quarters and bedroom, a bathroom, and a kitchen/eating area. I made some curtains, and Jerry's Mom gave us some hook rugs. I did not particularly like the hooked rugs, but they kept the floor from being so cold when we first climbed out of bed. They were lovely rugs, and I am sure she paid a good price for them.

J. T. and Hazel Maness, Pauline's brother, gave us a side of beef. He ran the locker plant down at Granbury, Texas, and the meat came in handy since it lasted for almost a year. With the money that family members had given us and the wedding gifts, we were able to set up housekeeping with all the necessities.

The house being on Turtle Creek gave us a beautiful garden. When the azaleas were in bloom, the entire area was a blaze of pink.

We could not have asked for a nicer place to start our first home.

———•••———

We had not been married too long until the Dowdys blessed us with a duck. Jann had gotten a baby duck named Sam, and it had grown up in their backyard, never seeing so much as a bucket of water. For lack of anything else Sam could do to occupy his days, he would jump up on Pauline's wash hanging on the clothesline, getting things dirty. Sam would also swing on the hems of the sheets, pulling the hems out. With Pauline's perfectionist temperament, this was just too much for her, so they decided to bring Sam over to our house and turn him loose on Turtle Creek with the other ducks that had the run of the creek.

Now, Sam had never seen water or other ducks, so when they turned him loose, he almost beat them back to the car. Then Arvil decided to throw Sam into the middle of the creek and run for the car. Because Sam had never been in the water, as we learned later, he did not have oil in his feathers that would allow him to swim.

Sam did not like the water and almost drowned, so I guess it made him mad. Finally, the Dowdys got in their car and drove away from Sam.

That afternoon, when Mrs. Sailcraig walked down to Turtle Creek to survey her territory and admire her beautiful surroundings, she came across this duck lying up on the hillside, a short distance from the water. When Mrs. Sailcraig tried to shoo the duck back into the water, he attacked her, pecked her hand, and drew blood in several places.

She told us that there was a crazy duck on the creek as she ran in front of our house, broom in hand. When she got to the creek, she beat poor Sam nearly to death. Poor Sam must have wondered what was happening to his life.

We never let on to Mrs. Sailcraig that we had ever seen that duck before. Instead, we made a beeline up to the service station and called the Dowdys and told them they would have to come over and take Sam back.

They came over and retrieved Sam without Mrs. Sailcraig being any the wiser. They took Sam back to their backyard and gave him a tub of water to swim and play in. After a few weeks, they took him to Bachman Lake at the end of Love Field and left him there.

Every time they drove by Bachman Lake, they wondered about whatever had happened to Sam.

———•••———

Jerry and I began to settle into a routine. We did not have a telephone and did not want one, and we were perfectly content to let the world go by and to be left alone.

We would make love all night and at every opportune time during the day. Sometimes Pauline would want to invite us over to lunch on Sunday after church. Since they could not call us, Arvil would drive over to invite us to dinner. We would always be in bed, and the floor would be covered with Kleenex. As soon as we heard the car coming down our driveway, we would jump out of bed and start grabbing Kleenex.

Maybe it was evident to Arvil that he was coming over at an inopportune time. As a result, they decided to have a telephone installed for us. Jerry and I did not appreciate the phone, but we allowed them to have a phone put in, and they paid the minimum bill. They selected a service with a minimum charge where we could receive an unlimited number of calls without additional cost, but we could only make three outgoing calls per month without extra cost. (We never made more than three outgoing calls per month.) This addition did eliminate the Sunday morning disturbance.

———•••———

Mrs. Sailcraig was a small Jewish woman. She was probably in her seventies but still very much independent. Her husband had passed away some years before, leaving her a very wealthy woman.

When Dallas political elections were on the horizon, Joe Pool had placed a political sign in the neighbor's yard across Fitzhugh Street from where we lived. After dark, Mrs. Sailcraig got her paintbrush and some white paint and painted out part of Joe Pool's sign to read "Joe Fool." Mr. Pool won the election, and "Smart," or "Fool," has remained in the political forefront for many years, even having a lake named after him.

One day Mrs. Sailcraig decided to clean out her basement. She had not been down into that basement for a long time. We looked out our window just in time to see big opossums with baby opossums clinging to them, scurrying out of the basement and climbing up the brick wall at the back of her house.

Soon, here came Mrs. Sailcraig up the steps from the basement, broom in hand, yelling, "Get out of here!" Opossums have a way of playing dead to divert danger, so when Mrs. Sailcraig started yelling at the critters, trying to get them to leave her house, the opossums were trying to play dead while hanging onto the back of the wall.

She yelled and yelled, and they relentlessly played dead and would not budge, so she began trying to repair the house so they could not get in. Long after she was gone, the opossums reluctantly came down from the side of the house.

———•••———

Following our November wedding, the next college semester started in early January, and Jerry wanted to go back to college. We decided we could make it on one salary, so Jerry quit his job and enrolled in Arlington State College. He began his classes, and I continued working to support us.

Jerry decided that his Mercury used too much gas, so we began searching for another car. My family had driven Chevrolets in recent years, and I thought that was the best car on the market. We selected a used salmon and silver 1955 Chevrolet Bellaire two-door coupe.

With the trade-in of the Mercury, a lovely car that still looked new, we could take out a loan for $55.00 per month. This additional bill would put a real strain on our budget. However, forgoing any unexpected expenses, we could still make the payments.

Jerry assured me that we would save a lot on gasoline, and with him driving back and forth to college in Arlington every day, this was the right choice. I did not particularly like the Mercury, so I agreed to the used Chevy. This transaction was the beginning of a pattern of rationalizing to trade cars.

Each morning Jerry would drive me to Burroughs at 7:00, and I would sit in the front lobby until some other people would come to work. I had to ask for a key to the building, and they gave me one. Then Jerry would drive to Arlington State College (later, it became the University of Texas at Arlington) for his classes.

In the afternoon, I would catch a ride with one of the other employees who came near my house. When I got home, Jerry would have supper cooking. With the side of beef J. T and Hazel had given us as a wedding present, Jerry would cook chicken fried steak, mashed potatoes, and gravy. I would help him finish supper, and we would clean up the kitchen together. (Jerry had already gained weight between the time we met and married, and he continued to gain; at one point, he got up to 220 pounds.)

After supper, Jerry would study, and I would quiz him, and we would study together. Jerry surprised himself at how well he did in college. He had practically flunked out of Texas A&M and was now making As and enjoying school.

———•••———

Once when I was sick, I ran a very high fever for several days. I was so sick I could not think straight. Jerry continued to have his normal sex drives and would complain because I was so hot and say I was burning him. (I still did not feel I could tell him to leave me alone.) Still, I did not ask to go to the doctor, and Jerry did not take me.

After four days of dangerously high temperatures, Jerry took me to the doctor. It was a Saturday morning. The doctor took one look at me and began to order tests. He determined that I had Diphtheria and shot me full of antitoxin.

By this time, my natural immune system had fought off most of the infection. The health department came to the house and put up a yellow quarantine sign. The doctor came by every day for the next few days and gave me a shot.

Quickly, I began to recover but was very weak. The doctor said I should take another week off from work, and the health department lifted the quarantine. Jerry took me to Greenville to stay with Mother and Daddy. Mother cooked for me and cared for me like a baby, and I regained my strength.

When I returned to Dallas, I went back to see the doctor, and I weighed 108 pounds, which looked fairly skinny on my five-foot-six-inch frame. I am sure Mother had put several pounds on me the previous week. I went back to work.

———•••———

Jerry attended college that semester and continued to make good grades. A friend named Red Cutright approached Jerry and asked if he would like a job at Warren Petroleum.

Jerry had attended North Dallas High School with Red's son. Red said that Warren was installing a service station and some distribution plants in Texas for liquefied petroleum. Jerry decided to quit college again and went to work for Warren Petroleum in Irving.

———•••———

In January 1957, we decided to buy a house at 1320 Ronnie in Irving. The house was 1600 square feet with three bedrooms. The front door opened into a living room/dining room combination. A bar separated the den from the kitchen/breakfast area. There were two small bathrooms, three bedrooms, and a double-car garage.

This house was quite a move up from the little servants' quarters on Turtle Creek, but we had to give up the beautiful Turtle Creek. The kitchen had a dishwasher, which was quite a modern thing for a new home. There was a garbage disposal, too, which was something I had never seen before.

There was no lawn, so we spread Bermuda seed and planted a magnolia tree on the corner and a live oak beside the house. We also planted some shrubs. Of course, things had to be fertilized and watered, and then we needed a lawn mower. There seemed to be no end to the things we needed.

We had borrowed $1,000 from Doris to put with our money to make the $3,500 down payment on our house. We paid $16,700 for the 1600 square foot, new brick home. We conserved every cent so that we could pay Doris back the money which we had borrowed.

———◆••———

We were very happy. We had become good friends with Red and Mary Cutright and Jim and Norma Demitz, who also worked for Warren. We played pinochle and ate meals together. Everything went along pretty well for a year. Then Jerry was notified that he would be losing his job because Warren was going to close down its Irving plant.

Then Jerry applied for a job at National Cash Register. They agreed to hire him as a service trainee, promising to send him to Dayton, Ohio, in six months. At that time, he would become a technician with a considerable salary increase. The trainees were paid very little, but we thought it would be worth working six months there to get training that would lead to a career.

———◆••———

I got pregnant in the summer of 1958. After reviewing our finances and the cost of getting someone to care for the baby, I decided it would be best for me to stay home after the baby was born. We could not live on the trainee salary, but Jerry's six months were up, so he went in to talk to his boss about when he would be sent to Dayton. The boss acted as if he had never made any such promise.

Jerry knew he was doing a good job and had fulfilled all the

80

requirements, so he felt the boss had just outright lied to him. Under these circumstances, the only thing to do was to quit.

Jerry soon found a job at Tex Oil installing gasoline pumps and various similar jobs. It was not a good job, but he would make enough money for us to get by, barring any unforeseen expenses.

During my pregnancy, I would ride to work each morning with Jerry and get sick along the way, and we would have to stop for me to throw up. I would start to brush my teeth, and I would throw up again.

———•••———

We traded the 1955 Chevrolet in for a 1957 Chevy with air conditioning. We had to pay extra, so that meant taking out another loan, but Jerry wanted another car and convinced me that trading cars was what we needed to do.

The older Chevy was not a better car, but the air conditioner did help get me to work feeling better. I would nibble on crackers and finally overcame the morning sickness. Then I was sleepy and could hardly keep my eyes open long enough to get my job done.

Burroughs had a policy that said that when a woman had to start wearing maternity clothes, she would have to quit her job. When I started getting big, I bought three pieces of material, and Mother made me some maternity dresses. Most all maternity dresses then were two-pieced and quite ugly. Mother made me some one-piece, comfortable dresses that camouflaged my bulging belly.

Burroughs allowed me to work until about a month before the baby was born. By that time, I was more than ready to quit.

———•••———

We bought a black Boston rocker with red corduroy cushions. I got Jann's old baby bed from the Dowdys, and we refinished it. We bought a chest of drawers at the unclaimed freight place and picked up a bassinet somewhere. We bought a few essential items for the baby, and with the clothes given to us, we were ready for the baby.

By the time the baby was due, I had become uncomfortable and irritable. Jerry wanted sex all the time and would pout if he did not get everything he wanted. The doctor did not think we should have sex the last two weeks, but since I did not believe I had the right to say "No," he would go ahead and have sex. I would not say anything, but I continued to build up resentment, and I felt this showed a lack of love and respect for my feelings.

———•••———

Finally, the day came. Early in the morning on February 20, 1959, my water broke. This unexpected event gave me the strangest sensation, like I was wetting myself and had no control over my bladder. We called the doctor, who told us to start timing the contractions and when they got five minutes apart to come to the hospital.

We cooked scrambled eggs and bacon and ate a large breakfast. (I didn't know any better.) Then we got dressed and drove over to the Dowdys' house on Lovers Lane so we would be closer to St. Paul Hospital in East Dallas. We waited for a while, and my contractions began to get hard, so I went into the hospital.

They put me in a lovely private room. There was snow on the ground, and it was cold. The nurses prepped me, and the doctor came in to examine me and said that I would have to dilate to five before they could give me any pain medication.

When we first got to the hospital, Jerry came over to my side like he wanted to comfort me, but everything he did made things worse.

I got hot, so he opened the window, sat in the chair next to the window, propped his feet up on the table, and smoked his cigarette. Every little while, he would say, "I am going out to call my mother." This announcement irritated me to death. I thought his place was by my side. I was in terrible pain. I began to pray for God to take my life and spare the baby's life.

Finally, Dr. Donald Fangman, my obstetrician, came in and sat at the end of my bed. I asked him if I had dilated to five yet, and he said, "no." Jerry continued to sit by the window, smoking his cigarettes. I think Dr. Fangman realized that all was not well with us, so he stayed with me, and that was a great comfort, but I continued to pray that I would just die.

Then Jerry got up again and said he was going out to call his mother, and I told him that if he did, he could just go to his mother and not come back.

The doctor was there, and Jerry walked back to his chair and never said another word. He just sat there without speaking to me the entire time I was in labor, and he acted as if it was a real imposition to him and cramped his style. As far as I could see, there was not a twinge of compassion on his part.

Finally, the doctor gave me something for my pain, and shortly after that, I was completely knocked out. When I woke up, I was in the recovery room with Jerry saying, "What's wrong with you? All these other women had babies after you, and you are still here." I was so groggy that I did not know what was wrong with me, and I became scared that something terrible was wrong with me. I sunk back into a deep sleep, and every time I roused a little, Jerry was complaining because I was still in the recovery room.

When I came to, I was in a room, and I was all alone. I could feel something down between my legs sticking me, and being half-conscious, I began to pull at what was sticking me. By the time I had come out from under the anesthetic enough to know what I was doing, I had completely pulled out one of the stitches. I was sore and hurting, and I felt like I was still having labor pains. The nurse told me the pains were just normal after-birth pains.

Jerry came back with his mother. They had been out to get something to eat. It did not occur to either of them that one should have stayed with me until I came out from under the anesthetic. I was angry at Jerry but never said anything. After just three years, the honeymoon was definitely over.

———•••———

The baby was the most beautiful baby boy I had ever seen. We named him Kenneth Wesley. Ironically, I wanted to name my baby boy after my father, with whom I had never had a close relationship. I was learning to love and respect my father.

I tried to nurse Ken but felt totally awkward. I knew nothing of taking care of a baby. There was no way I could position myself that did not hurt. I asked the doctor about the pulled stitch; he said it would allow good drainage. The woman in the bed beside me did not seem to be having near the soreness which I was experiencing.

I stayed in the hospital for five days and still did not feel like caring for a baby, but I dressed my precious son, and we headed home. Mother had come when I had the baby, so she was ready to leave by the time I got ready to go home. I asked her to wait until I got out of the hospital, but nothing would do but for her to come when the baby was born.

I went home without help, and I was so sore I could hardly walk. I was also depressed but did not realize it was depression. I did not like Jerry or anybody else except my baby. I was determined to take good care of him. I felt I had paid a high price for him, and he was worth every pain.

———•••———

Ken started off crying. No matter what I did, he would cry. I was trying to nurse him and could not tell if he was getting enough to eat. I did not know that it mattered what I ate so there is no telling what I might have been eating which would cause him to have a stomachache.

He cried night and day. I walked the floor with him until I thought I would go crazy. We put him in the bassinet and rocked the bassinet. We rocked him in the rocker. Finally, the doctor, who was virtually no help, suggested I give him a bottle. He would suck the bottle and would continue sucking. He would suck and act like he was hungry, but I knew he was not. I would try to burp him, and he would throw up all over everything, and I am sure that was because he was overfed.

Jerry and I both walked him and messed with him, and nothing helped. The most painful part of the situation was that I knew he was in pain. Since I had never been around a baby, I really did not know if it was unusual for a baby to cry so much; I more or less just accepted it as part of having a baby.

———•••———

Ken grew big and strong despite all the crying. He had a nasty diaper rash; the harder I tried to get rid of it, the worse it got. Finally, one day when I was rinsing out one of his many diapers, I noticed a lot of soap in the commode.

We bought a new washing machine before Ken was born to wash the diapers. There was a box of Ivory Flakes in the machine when I bought it, so I used it to wash his diapers. After checking my wash, I found the machine was not getting all the soap out. I had a terrible rash on my bottom, and Jerry had a jockey strap itch. A repair man told me that the Ivory Flakes had ruined the washer by stopping something up.

Ken was several months old by this time, and all three of us were about crazy. A neighbor across the street got some A&D ointment at the hospital where she worked, and we used it on him. Finally, his diaper rash was cured; his colic was over shortly after that.

———••———

On top of the stress of the new baby who cried all the time, when Ken turned six weeks old, Jerry came in and said he had lost his job. I asked him why he was fired.

Jerry said his boss would not tell him, but if he came back in on Monday, he would tell Jerry why he was fired. I thought that was a bit strange, but I believed Jerry.

When Monday came, I asked Jerry if he was going back to Tex Oil to see why he was fired, and he gave some excuse and did not go. I worried about what we would live on. After surveying the situation, we could make it about three months without a paycheck with Jerry signing up for unemployment. We could live off the nominal unemployment check and savings, which would carry us through until Jerry could find another job.

That next week, Jerry went job hunting and applied for a job at Copease Corporation as a warehouseman.

He got the job. He said there was a girl there named Norma who had worked at NCR, and she said that if Jerry had worked for NCR, then he must be all right. Jerry told me he had never met Norma before. It was not until thirty-six years later that I learned that Jerry had met Norma in Greenville, and they had worked at NCR at the same time.

———••———

This job turned out to be a real blessing. Jerry would help Norma with her filing during the day, and we would go down to the warehouse at night and set us an inventory and work in the warehouse. Since I had been an inventory clerk for Burroughs for seven years, this was right down my line. We would tie a string on the end of a cardboard box, crumple some papers up in the bottom of the box, lay Ken in the box, and pull him up and down the aisles with us as we labeled copying paper bins.

The boss who hired Jerry got transferred shortly after that, and Lenton White was brought in as the new Regional Manager. Jerry seemed to get along well with everybody, and soon he had Jerry out servicing machines. Then Jerry would find people who needed a new or different machine, and Jerry would sell them a machine.

———•••———

The copying machine was new to the business world. A few years before, 3M had developed a Thermo-fax device that made copies on onionskin paper. This process was ineffective because the copies would become brittle and were not permanent. Copease sold machines called "photo processing" or "wet" copies.

You would run your original into the machine, and two sheets of paper would come out bonded together. You would then wait a few seconds, peel the two pieces of paper apart, and have a nice, clear picture. Although these were considered "permanent" copies, they would turn brown in time. The paper was thick and heavy and made filing copies bulky. Postage would be expensive because the copies were heavy.

The industry was new, so most people used carbon paper for extra copies. The office clerk would type some more copies if they needed additional invoices. Of course, this was long before computers and word processors and before offices created paper mountains. People depended more on a man's word and did not have to have proof of everything, and they did not have to document everything.

So many things that are commonplace today had yet to be invented.

———•••———

An anonymous person wrote the following for people born before 1945.

86

CONSIDER THE CHANGES WE HAVE WITNESSED

"We were born before television, penicillin, polio shots, frozen foods, Xerox, plastic contact lenses, Frisbees, and the Pill. We were here before radar, credit cards, split atoms, laser beams, and ball-point pens. Before pantyhose, dishwashers, clothes dryers, electric blankets, air-conditioners, drip-dry clothes, and before man walked on the moon.

We got married first and then lived together. How quaint can you be? In our time, closets were for clothes, not "coming out of." Bunnies were small rabbits, and rabbits were not Volkswagens. Designer Jeans were scheming girls named Jean and having a "meaningful relationship" meant getting along with our cousins.

We thought fast food was what you ate during Lent, and Outer Space was the back of the Riviera Theater. We were here before house-husbands, gay rights, computer dating, dual careers, and commuter marriages. We were here before daycare centers, group therapy, and nursing homes. We had never heard of FM radio, tape decks, electronic typewriters, artificial hearts, word processors, yogurt, and guys wearing earrings.

For us, time-sharing meant togetherness — not computers or condominiums. A chip meant a piece of wood, hardware meant hardware, and software wasn't a word.

Back then, 'Made in Japan' meant "junk," and "Making Out" referred to how you did on your exam. Pizzas, McDonald's, and instant coffee were unheard of. We hit the scene when there were 5 & 10 cent stores, and you could really buy things there for five and ten cents. Ice cream cones sold for a nickel or a dime. You could ride a streetcar, make a phone call, buy a Pepsi or enough stamps to mail a letter and two postcards for one nickel. You could buy a new Chevy coupe for $600 — but who could afford one? A pity, too, because gas was just 11 cents a gallon.

In our day, "grass" was something you mowed. "Coke" was a cold drink, and "pot" was something you cooked in. "Rock Music" was a grandma's lullaby, and "AIDS" were helpers in the principal's office. We were certainly not here before the difference between the sexes was discovered, but we were here long before you could change your sex. We made do with what we had. And we were the last generation dumb enough to think you needed a husband to have a baby.

No wonder we are so confused, and there is such a generation gap today. But WE SURVIVED!!! What better reason to celebrate?"

— Author Unknown

At Copease, we were introduced to the Copy Machine Industry. First Jerry worked in the warehouse; then, he was trained as a service technician, and then Lenton asked Jerry if he would take over the Fort Worth office. This promotion was a big jump, even for Jerry. He was about twenty-six years old, and the thought of managing anybody was overwhelming.

By this time, we had gotten to know Lenton White and his wife, Ila Fay, pretty well. Jerry and I discussed this promotion, and Jerry decided he could handle the job. He worked for three months, and then Lenton was transferred. Jerry had hardly gotten into his new sales management position.

11 Church, Children, & Family

Maybe I should back up and catch up on what had happened with our Christian walk. After Jerry and I got married, we went to church fairly regularly. Still, I had not mentioned anything to Jerry about my feeling that God had called me to be a foreign missionary.

When we moved to Irving, Jerry and I had gotten away from attending church. After all, we were busy putting in a new yard, and then Ken came along.

When Ken was only three weeks old, he fell off the bed on a Sunday morning. We felt terrible, and we both felt that if we had gotten up and gone to church, Ken would not have fallen off the bed. We felt so guilty that Ken had fallen — and guilty that we were not in church.

There was an older woman who was mentally challenged, and she would occasionally walk to my house to visit me. She told me often that I should be going to church. She had more influence on getting me back into church than anybody. I would think, God is using this woman who is struggling so much, and here I am with all my facilities, not willing to go witness.

At Jake and Velma Carrol's invitation, we visited Southside Baptist Church, a small church with Brother Emmitt Hunt as its pastor. He and his wife Lucille were dedicated Christians, they had started the church, and Brother Hunt had been its only pastor.

When Jerry went to work for Copease, we returned to church. All these years of wandering from job to job coincided with the years we were out of church. Brother Hunt preached on tithing, and we felt convicted that this was something we should be doing. We gave up cigarettes and vowed not to use any of our money to buy liquor.

Under Brother Hunt's leadership, we grew as Christians. We made a diligent effort to follow the teachings in the Bible. I began teaching a single young women's class, and Jerry taught a men's class. Jerry was ordained a deacon and served as Chairman of the Deacons and Finance Chairman. I served as Women's Missionary Union President. For all our years in Irving, we attended Southside Baptist Church and made lifelong friends.

One couple we knew, Donna and Lawrence Weir, moved away and eventually divorced. If you were basing temperaments on Hippocrates, Donna was Mrs. Sanguine. She was warm, buoyant, and lively. Her decisions were spontaneous, with no thought of consequence tomorrow. While we were in Irving, she was Jerry's bowling partner, and I would stay at home and keep the kids because I did not want to pay for bowling and a babysitter, too.

———•••———

Returning to the job situation, the long and the short of it was that God blessed us materially once we got our relationship right with Him. The more obedient we were with our tithes and giving and willingness to help others, the more God blessed us materially.

The Bible tells us, "In tithes and offerings...Test me in this, 'says the Lord Almighty, and see if I will not throw open the floodgates of heaven and pour out so much blessing that you will not have room enough for it." (Malachi 3:8b-10.) It seemed that this verse was written just for us.

Within a short period of time, Jerry had acquired a great deal of experience, and when Lenton White was transferred, he recommended Jerry as the new regional manager.

It had only been two or three years since Jerry worked as an NCR trainee for about $55 a month. Suddenly he had the opportunity to be the regional manager of four states.

I did not know what this would mean regarding responsibilities and the travel required. Jerry accepted the job and was supervising men much older than himself. He hired people to run branch offices in three states.

———•••———

When Ken was eight months and three days old, he began to walk. He learned to walk young, and he learned to talk young. When the other children his age were still saying "Mamma" and "Dada," Ken was making complete sentences. He was an absolute delight, and I thought he was the cutest and smartest child who ever lived.

I bought him some little knee-length black and white striped pants and a black short-sleeved shirt that was top-stitched with white thread. The pants had a white cord that tied through the belt loops. He was beyond description when I dressed him in this shirt and pants with white shoes and socks.

We had a long-haired beagle we called "Frisky," and everywhere Ken went, Frisky followed. When Ken was a baby lying on a blanket on the den floor, Frisky would crawl up and lie beside him. If Ken pulled Friskie's hair, there was never a growl, but Ken learned the meaning of "NO!" quickly, and Frisky did not have to endure much pain.

One Christmas, someone gave Ken a toy chicken that cackled. Jerry tied that chicken to the back of Ken's tricycle, and he would ride around and around the table with that chicken cackling — or he would go through the house like the wind with the chicken cackling. That was enough to drive any mother crazy, and it did not bother me for a long time, but eventually, that chicken had to go.

———•••———

I got pregnant again, and this time the morning sickness was not so bad, partly because I did not have to get up early, rush around getting dressed, and go off to work. I had some difficulties, but basically, this was a happy pregnancy. I was excited about the coming of a new baby.

People would say, "Do you want a boy or a girl?"

I would say, "It really does not matter," but in my heart, I really wanted a little girl.

Ever since I was a teenager, I had said I wanted to get married at twenty-one, three years later to have a baby boy, and then two years later to have a baby girl. This schedule, to me, was the perfect way to do things.

So far, my life was pretty much on the perfect schedule. There would be three years difference between the kids instead of two.

After Ken was born, when he was having his crying problems, I thought I was pregnant, and then I began to have severe cramps and began to pass clots of blood. I called Doctor Fangman and told him what was happening.

"Go to bed immediately," he said.

"I don't think you understand," I said, "I don't want another baby now. I simply cannot handle it emotionally."

Anyway, I lay down on the couch and continued to pass blood. Dr. Fangman asked me to come in for an examination and bring the clots with me.

Sure enough, I had miscarried, and he had me go to the hospital for a D&C. It should have been a traumatic thing to lose a baby, but I could not feel that I had lost a baby. I felt relieved that I would not have another baby just yet.

By the time I got pregnant again, I was delighted. It was time for Ken to have a little baby brother or sister.

———••————

The time seemed to pass fast.

Then the time came for my delivery. I had fixed up the baby's room and had some old baby clothes and a few new ones.

Jerry and I were happier together.

Again, my water broke, and I prayed I would not have to endure such a painful labor this time. With Ken, I was in labor only three hours after I got to the hospital, but still, I did not like all that pain.

A young woman told me the baby would come faster if you did two or three knee bends when your water breaks. I went into the bathroom with water streaming down my legs and did my knee bends.

I had not even awakened Jerry yet. I prayed that my labor would be short and that I would not have to suffer. When I rose from my knee bends, my labor pains started. Instinctively I knew God had answered my prayer.

I yelled at Jerry to get up because it was time for me to go to the hospital. Jerry calmly climbed out of bed, acting miffed at being awakened from a sound sleep.

I rushed around and got my clothes on. I got Ken's things ready to take him and his things over to Jake and Velma Carrol's house. (They had agreed to keep Ken while I was in the hospital.) My labor pains were hard and constant. I tried to rush Jerry, and he finally got into the car.

We drove over to the Carrols in silence. Jerry took Ken up to their door and rang the doorbell. It seemed to take an eternity for them to get to the door, and then Jerry stood there and talked and talked. Finally, I rolled the window down and hollered for him to come on.

This was December 10, 1961, and the roads had snow on them. It was unusual for there to be such an early snow in North Texas.

When Jerry strolled back to the car, I said, "Jerry, we'd better hurry."

He did not speed up one little bit. In fact, it seemed to me that he intentionally drove more slowly. (He would disagree with this part, but this is how I felt and what I remember.)

When we got to the edge of Dallas, I said, "I have got to lie down."

This news shook him into reality. He took one look at me and stuck out his arm to hold me up so that I could not lie down.

"I'm having this baby," I said.

Jerry put his foot on the accelerator and sped up as fast as it was safe to travel.

"Cross your legs!" he said.

I continued to insist that I had to lie down, and Jerry continued to insist that I not lie down, holding out his arm so I couldn't.

When Jerry drove up to the emergency room, I got out quickly and walked into the hospital, bent over, and holding my stomach in support.

The nurse took one look at me, grabbed a wheelchair, and whisked me up to the labor room. Another nurse scurried in to help me get undressed. After a quick assessment, she laid me down on the bed and dashed out of the room.

A moment later, a whole crew of nurses came in, removed my clothes, shaved me, and gave me a shot.

I asked if the shot would put me to sleep.

"Oh, no," the nurse said.

That is the last thing I remember until I awoke in the recovery room.

I preregistered with the hospital, but Jerry had to go to the office to let them know we had arrived. By the time he got upstairs, the doctor was bringing the baby out. (We learned later that the doctor had an auto accident on the way to the hospital, and we are sure the nurses delivered our baby.)

Sure enough, this time, it was a baby girl. This time Dr. Fangman kept me so knocked out that I did nothing but sleep for 48 hours. I was so sleepy I could not stay awake when the nurses tried to bring her to me, so they would just have to take her back. When visitors came to see me, I could only open my eyes but could not talk to them. Finally, I became conscious enough to tell the nurse I did not want another shot, and she said I did not have to take it.

At last, I woke up enough to see that I had a beautiful baby girl. When they brought her to me, she was sleeping. She had all her fingers and toes, and Dr. Fangman said she was healthy. I was happy to have a girl but even happier that God had blessed me with a healthy baby.

We had picked out the name Peggy Karen before she was born, and I had planned to call her Karen, but when I looked at her the first time, Karen just didn't fit. So, she was Peggy.

———••———

From the moment we took Peggy home from the hospital, she was a perfect baby. There was no problem with diaper rash or anything else. She was very calm, easygoing, and happy. She ate and slept like babies are supposed to do. We did change doctors, and I told the doctor I could not handle another colic baby. He gave me some red drops, and that probably had something to do with her temperament.

Mother made Peggy pale pink and yellow diaper sets, and then she bought her a couple of cute, frilly tops with plastic-lined diaper covers with ruffles on the bottom. Peggy seemed so tiny and fragile, but she weighed seven pounds and nine ounces, only one ounce less than Ken weighed as a newborn. Her hair was light brown and slightly curly. Ken was so sweet to Peggy; he loved getting me a diaper or holding and talking to her.

———••———

With Peggy not quite a month old, we decided to move to 1001 Sleepy Hollow, across town from our first home in Irving. This house had about 2100 square feet. It was built from burnt brick, and the trim was painted white. The yard was filled with oak trees. The roofline was tall, as if it was two stories. (It could have had an ample finished space upstairs, but we didn't need that upper area.)

There were four bedrooms, a living room/dining room combination, a large den with a fireplace, and a large kitchen with an eating area. The bathrooms were quite large compared to our other house.

The house was carpeted, and that made a great deal of difference. We thought the house was quite pretty, and it was my favorite of all the homes I have lived in.

We packed, loaded, and moved ourselves, which was not unusual for us. (We were always doing things for ourselves because it was cheaper.) We just set up the furniture in the house, and Jerry had to go off on a business trip. (He was now traveling 50,000-plus miles by car every year.)

I found myself with an almost-three-year-old active boy, a brand-new baby, and a house full of boxes. It never occurred to me that I probably should not be picking up heavy boxes; I had always picked up anything and everything, often helping Jerry by picking up one side of anything he needed help picking up.

The cabinets were covered in sawdust, and the den and kitchen floors had black streaks from old work shoes' skid marks. I began to wash everything and put in shelf paper. Mrs. Dowdy came out, and the two of us got on our hands and knees and scrubbed up the skid marks off the floor, and then she went back home.

I unpacked boxes between taking care of the kids and the dog. By the time Jerry got home the following weekend, I had the house all straightened up.

———•••———

The furniture looked much better in this house on the carpet. In the last house, I had bought a sofa, chair, end table, and coffee table for the living room. When Jerry returned home, he put the living room drapes from our previous house in the den, and they looked really good.

We then had a living room and dining room without drapes, so I called Sears to come out and measure, and they made some drapes for those bare windows, and quickly the house came together.

We did have to put in another lawn, and with so many trees, we had to set out sprigs of St. Augustine as soon as the winter freeze was over.

One day, Mr. Davis from our church came out to talk to me about planting some shrubs. I had just put on a pot of pinto beans on the stove with the burner on high. I thought I would have just enough time to talk to him and get back in to check on my beans before they boiled over. I guess I got to talking to him and lost track of time, because when I walked back into the house, it was filled with black smoke. I felt sure I had ruined everything, but after airing the place out, you could not tell where the soot had settled.

————•••————

Not long after we moved into the house, Daddy learned that he had cancer of the lungs and that it possibly had spread, so they did not know if they could remove it through surgery. The doctors recommended that the surgery be performed in Dallas, so Mother and Daddy came down and stayed with us for a couple of days before Daddy was admitted to the hospital for surgery.

They rolled Daddy into the operating room, and when the doctor came out after the surgery, he told us he was not sure he had gotten all of it. He said that Daddy would have to have radiation and there would be quite an extended recovery period if he even recovered, but hopefully, the cancer was contained.

I stayed up at the hospital with Daddy quite a bit; I was their only child who was not working, and I lived pretty close. Sometimes Mother would keep the kids while I stayed with Daddy. They had sawed his ribs apart and made an incision down his back and around his side so they could lay his back open and remove his lung.

Obviously, Daddy was in a lot of pain after this surgery. Still, he seemed to recover as well as could be expected. When Daddy was dismissed from the hospital, Daddy and Mother came to stay with us. Daddy could not drive, and Mother had never learned how to drive. When he started his radiation treatments, they painted red dashes and dots to mark the spots for radiation.

They would give him the maximum dosage, and he complained that he could taste burnt flesh in his mouth. I guess they almost burnt him up trying to eradicate the cancer the doctor could not get with the surgery.

At first, Daddy seemed to be getting along pretty well. By summer, he was walking out in the backyard and watching Ken and Peggy play in a little plastic swimming pool. Peggy would be dressed in a little designer swimsuit that was salmon colored with a small white design. Ken was a husky little boy who would run, jump, and splash.

Ken and Peggy had such a good time together, just playing, but I had little time to enjoy them. By the time I did the things that needed to be done, I was always worn out.

———•••———

With Jerry gone all the time, I was entirely responsible for the house and the children, cooking and dishwashing, washing and ironing, errands and grocery shopping, paying bills and taxes, plus whatever else anyone needed. There was little free time.

Peggy and Ken were good to sleep in during the morning but were a mess to get to bed at night. Ken was never ready for bed, and when I would get him down, he could think of a dozen things to ask for. I liked to sleep late, so it also made it nice for them to sleep late.

Some mornings I would hear Peggy awake in her bed, and she would coo and talk to herself. She could always find things to entertain herself, like playing with her fingers or toes, and then she would go back to sleep until I would get up with her.

One Sunday morning, I had gotten up as usual and dressed the kids for Sunday School and church. I laid Peggy down in her baby bed while I got dressed. When I walked back to check on her, she had found something new to play with. She had a touch of diarrhea, and it had squirted out of her diaper and plastic diaper cover and onto the sheet beside her. She had squirmed around, played in her pooh, and made a terrible mess. She had it all over her hair, socks, and pretty little dress. I had to undress her completely, give her another bath, and start all over.

———•••———

Daddy did not like for me just to let Peggy lay in bed and play. He would tell Mother, "Rube (short for Ruby), "go change that baby's britches and bring her in here."

Mother would get up, change Peggy's diaper, and take her to bed with them. Daddy would bounce her up and down, and they really grew attached to these duties.

Mother was good with both of the kids. She would get down on her hands and knees and play with Ken. He would scream with delight, crawl, hide, and want her to look for him.

Even though Daddy was sick, this was a good time with all of us together.

———•••———

When Daddy completed his radiation, he and Mother returned to Greenville. At first, we thought he was doing better, and mother waited on him hand and foot as she always had. Despite the few years of infidelity, Mother deeply loved Daddy, and they enjoyed a good life together.

From the time I had gotten out of school, Daddy had a pretty good job at one of the airplane plants. He was looking forward to retiring the following year. Daddy was tired and ready to retire, but he wondered whether to quit because neither of his boys had a very good job. He wanted to be able to help them if they needed help. He loved his family even though he kept his emotions well concealed.

Daddy had mellowed in his later years. He and Mother had gone to church on a fairly regular basis. They had deep convictions regarding his relationship with God. He never talked about religion or the Bible, nor did he ever pray out loud. When we were there at mealtimes, he always wanted Jerry to pray before we ate.

Mother and Daddy had both grown to appreciate Jerry. At first, Jerry was not Mother's first choice, but Daddy told her she would wind up depending on Jerry. Sure enough, that was the case.

———•••———

On December 31, 1961, Daddy went to be with the Lord. He had lost so much weight he was skin and bones. He spent his last month in a nursing home hooked up to needles and unable to swallow. Cancer had gone to his brain and affected some of his motor skills.

We buried Daddy on a cold January 2. We returned his body to Sherman for the funeral and buried him at Cedar Lawn. He had lost so much weight that lying in the casket, he looked like someone else. Of course, both of my brothers and their wives and my sister Doris and her husband were at the funeral. The grandchildren were there except for Peggy, who stayed with Aunt Connie.

Mother was all alone. She went home and tried to die. Daddy had always written all the checks and paid the bills. If Mother needed to buy something with a check, she would ask the salesclerk to write out the check, and then she would sign it. The very thought of taking care of any financial matters terrified her.

Mother was just sixty-one, but I thought she was an old woman. Mother did not look particularly old. She took good care of her skin, went to the beauty shop each week, and was fleshy enough to stretch out the wrinkles. But, after Daddy's death, she was devastated and could not adjust to being alone. She sometimes called us late at night and asked if Jerry could come to get her.

―――――•••―――――

After a few months, Mother decided to sell her house in Greenville and move into a government housing development in Howe, Texas. Daddy had a sister, Josie Enloe, who lived there, and Mother moved to be near them. She still called us to come and get her, even after she moved to Howe.

No matter how tired Jerry was or where he might have driven in from that day, Jerry would climb out of bed without a single complaint or any inkling of resentment, put on his clothes, and go to Greenville or Howe. He would get Mother and bring her back to our house, and within four hours, he would be back in bed as if that was no trouble at all.

Of course, the kids would be delighted to find Mammaw at the house the next morning. She would stay a few days, and we would take her back home, or Doris and her husband, Lindy, would take her back.

Doris worked for Republic National Life Insurance, and taking on much additional responsibility was hard for her.

Doris and Lindy had a baby boy, Roger, who was six months older than Ken. Lindy had a good job but had recently lost his job and started working in Dallas. They were living in Euless in a new home they had bought before Lindy lost his job.

Roger was their delight. He was a sweet, easygoing little boy. He had been chunky as a baby but had soon lost that baby fat once he started walking. Roger was an easy baby to handle, but between working outside the home, housework, and Roger, Doris more than had her hands full.

My brother Duane had married Marie, and they had lived up at our family's farm for a while, and then they moved to Fort Worth. Marie was a good cook. At times, she cooked for restaurants, or she and Duane worked in a nursing home, and she cooked, and Duane worked with the patients or managed administrative details that required attention. Marie had several older children from a previous marriage, and they became Duane's family; they did not have any children of their own.

My brother Bobby had married Lue Combs of Denison. Lue had Delaine, a beautiful little dark-complected girl when they got married. Delaine's eyes were dark brown, and her hair was dark and naturally curly. She was petite and dainty. She was a precious little girl, one of those children who was so pretty you wanted to take a second look. Shortly after Bob and Lue married, they had another baby girl they named Marsha. Marsha was a beautiful little girl also, and just the opposite of Delaine in looks. Her skin was fair, and her hair was blond and curly. Her bone structure was large, her face was round, and she tended to be more active than Delaine.

Shortly after Marsha was born, Lue got pregnant again. This time they had another baby girl they named Monica. I went up to help Lue when Monica was born, but Lue would not tell me what to do, so I was

100

little help. I only stayed a couple of days. Monica was a good baby and also pretty.

They lived at the family farm where Bob had spent most of his life. The only job he could get was manual labor which he did not mind, but the pay was minimal. Somehow, they were managing to make ends meet. But the stress of past experiences, a hard life, and three baby girls was more than Lue could handle emotionally. Lue tended to internalize everything and eventually had a nervous breakdown.

Bob called one day and said Lue was sick and wanted to stay with us for a few days. The doctor thought maybe if we pampered her for a few days, she might snap out of her problem.

So, one of Lue's sisters in Denison took Delaine, one sister in Irving took Monica, and I took Marsha and Lue. Bob brought them to our house. We kept Lue for just a few days, and she did not seem to get any better. She decided she wanted to go home; she went home, and I kept Marsha.

It became apparent that Lue was going to need some additional help, and the doctor suggested she be taken to Wichita Falls to the mental hospital. Lue was there for a few months, and we kept Marsha, and Lue's sisters kept the other two girls.

Marsha had big boils on her little legs, and we would mash those boils and sit her in the bathtub with a tiny bit of Purex. This process was excruciating, but we finally got rid of those boils. Marsha and Ken played together really well, and she was an absolute delight to have around. Together they were not as much trouble as Ken was alone because he needed someone to keep him company and share his ideas. (This was before Peggy was born.)

After a while, Lue got out of the hospital and was able to take the girls back and take care of them. It was not easy, but she had a strong will and determination to be OK — and somehow, she managed to care for the girls. At first, she was really quiet but slowly returned to herself.

Mother was having medical and emotional problems after Daddy's death. Mother wanted to sell the farm because she got upset dealing with taxes and any business matters that came up relating to the farm. Bob, Lue, and the girls were living in the old farmhouse, and if she sold the place, that would put them out of a home. So, when she set a price for how much she wanted to sell the place, Jerry and I decided we had the money and would just buy it.

With Jerry's job at Copease, he was making good money. Not that he was making so much, but it was more than we ever dreamed he would make. (When he brought in a check for $1000, it was unimaginable!) From the time we decided to start tithing, God had blessed us financially.

We had made every effort to remain faithful and good stewards of our time, talents, and money. God gave us resources and opportunities to be helpful to family members. He gave us resources and opportunities to lend money to people in the church who were in need. (Most repaid us, and a few were never able to repay, but we looked at our money as a special blessing from God.) We would not have had it if He had not blessed us with it, so it was our responsibility to use it wisely.

Jerry and I were getting along wonderfully. We never fussed about anything. Our friends were going through adjustments over the use of money, the children, time, or something else. Jerry was gone most of the time, so I did whatever I wanted. I continued with my church work, and when Jerry was home, he served in various positions.

We did have some sexual problems. Jerry tended to think he knew what I wanted or needed, and I would say, "I would rather you didn't do that" or "Please don't do that." Still, I did not think I had the right to say "NO" and make it stick. In later years, I learned this is not what the Bible teaches.

I still handled all the money and bought anything I wanted without Jerry complaining or disapproving. When he had started traveling so much, it was not practical to keep Jerry's expense money with personal money, so Jerry set up a separate bank account.

Jerry was buying one or two new cars a year because he was traveling so much, and he liked new cars; in fact, he just liked cars. He did not get attached to them; he always wanted new ones. That was all right because he bought them out of his expense money.

Once, Jerry asked me to travel with him to Altus, Oklahoma. He had a big account at some defense plant there. He had made regular trips there, but he wanted me to go with him this time for some reason. I bundled the kids up and packed our bags, and at about four in the morning, we headed for Altus. When we arrived, Jerry got us settled into a motel and then went on to call on his customer.

At lunchtime, I walked with the kids down the street to get us a bite of lunch, and we looked around town for a few minutes and then walked back to the motel. There was no swimming pool or anything for the kids to do but sit in the room.

By five o'clock in the afternoon, I was ready for Jerry to be back. By six, he was still not back, and I was hungry, and the kids were hungry. I began to get worried that something had gone wrong. By seven o'clock, I did not know whether to be mad or concerned. Shortly after that, Jerry came dragging in as if nothing had happened, and he acted as if I should not have been concerned.

Jerry was always free to come and go any time of the night or day, and I had never questioned his coming home late before. I did not say much, but the experience was not a joyful one. He did not explain being so late other than that he was working. I did not question his "working" at that time, but I did wonder why they did not quit working out there at five, as was the custom. I was hungry and ready to get the kids something to eat, and we just did not argue about things.

When I was a little girl, I vowed that I would not remain married if I had to argue as my mother and daddy had argued. As a result of this vow, I simply did not argue with Jerry. As far as I was concerned, God had placed him as the head of our household, and that was that. If I disagreed, I could leave, never to remarry. That was my interpretation of the scriptures at that time.

———◆◆———

Peggy and Ken grew strong and healthy. Other than the expected childhood diseases and an occasional skinned knee, they were unusually healthy.

When Ken was five, we started him in Little League baseball. The boys were so cute. When they first started playing, one little boy stood up to the batter's box, and when the umpire said, "strike three," the little boy just stood there. Finally, the umpire said, "That means you go back over there." Ken did pretty well in baseball, especially considering he had nobody to practice with; Jerry was still traveling most of the time.

Then when football season began that same year, we bought Ken shoulder pads, a helmet, and a uniform — all the needed equipment. The Dowdys thought that the sun rose and set on football, so it was just a foregone conclusion that Ken would play. I had never been to more than two or three games in my life, so I knew virtually nothing about the game and certainly knew none of the pitfalls of injury.

Ken also went to a private kindergarten and did really well. They had plays for the parents, and when Christmas came around, they did a Christmas program, and Ken was Santa Clause. (He was one of the largest children in the class, which may be why he was chosen for that part.) I was just as proud as if he had been elected president of the United States.

12 Starting Our Business

In 1964 the copy machine business began to change. Electrostatic machines had come on the market, and the photocopiers like Jerry was selling were becoming obsolete. The sales dropped off, and business did not look promising.

Jerry was going to New York and wanted me to go along with him. I had never been to New York and wanted to go with him.

I had traveled with Jerry a few times, and it was never very pleasant, but I thought this would be different. I asked Mother to come to keep the kids. So, I went.

Jerry had bought a first-class ticket, and the wife could fly free. We should pay the difference in airfare and hotel costs for me to go along. I did not expect Copease to be out anything extra, especially now that their business was not doing well.

The next day we arrived in New York. We went to the Copease office, and I went into the big boss's office with Jerry. Immediately, he began questioning Jerry about his expenses, renting a "double" room, and about me traveling with Jerry. I did not understand that at all, and he was looking straight at me.

I became defensive and told him that I had a baby and did not travel with Jerry. He could tell that he had stepped on the cat's tail, so they escorted me out of the office, and he continued to talk with Jerry. Ironically, I never asked Jerry what they had said or anything about the double motel room. It did not seem to be an issue.

That night they invited me to go out to dinner with several men who were there, and everything went well. But I think Jerry could see that this was the beginning of the end at Copease, even though nothing was said.

———•••———

When sales continued to decline, Jerry came home one day and said he thought we should go into business for ourselves. He felt that if he could make a living for someone else, he could make a living for himself.

We had about $1500 saved up. We sat down and determined the bare minimum we needed to get by. I was driving a 1962 Buick that we had paid for, and Jerry said he would sell the little station wagon he was driving. With a giant leap of faith, we borrowed $1000 from the Dowdys to buy some inventory.

Then Jerry went to Copease and asked them for the Fort Worth Copease office. As luck would have it (or as God would bless us), they agreed to give us the office. We would just have to buy the inventory. Of course, they would get the accounts receivable, and we would get any repeat business from existing customers. There was very little business there, but there was some, which was a tremendous help. Jerry knew many people in the industry, and their support and advice were invaluable.

Jerry traded his car to a Copease salesman in Houston for an old white 1955 Chevrolet the salesman had been driving. This car was worn out, but Jerry worked on it and got it back into reasonable condition with minimal cost. He took the seats out of the inside except for the driver's seat and set the car up so that he could deliver supplies with it. We got a desk for the garage, and I bought the necessary office supplies to set up an office: staples, a stapler, invoices, letterhead, business cards, etc.

On October 1, 1964, we started Copy & Litho. Little did we know what the future would hold!

I was looking in a magazine one day and saw a picture of a 55-year-old man retiring. Retiring so young was unheard of to me, and I mentioned it to Jerry. He said that when the kids get out of school, he would like to retire and go into mission work.

This was the first time Jerry had said anything about going into mission work. I had never told him that I felt that God had called me to be a foreign missionary when I was just a teenager. I was thrilled at the prospect of us starting our business and making enough money to retire at 55 — and then we could become missionaries. We filed this thought in the backs of our minds but did not forget.

Jerry would load up the car at night with any orders we had so he could deliver them the next morning. As he delivered our orders of paper or toner, he would also call on prospective customers nearby. I would take care of the house and kids during the day, and as time permitted, I would do office work, usually at night.

There were often things for Jerry to do at night, so I would type letters, type up bids and invoices, or do whatever other office work needed to be done. Soon, checks began to come in for the supplies we were selling, and occasionally, Jerry was able to sell a machine. Little by little, our business began to grow.

The office work got heavier and heavier. Mrs. Dowdy would look at the garage we had converted into our warehouse and say, "What part of this belongs to us?" That would just goad me to no end.

Within six months, we paid the Dowdys back their thousand dollars so that there was no doubt what belonged to whom. I am sure Mrs. Dowdy did not mean anything about the statement, but it really bothered me.

First, we had an answering service in Fort Worth and a garage to keep a few supplies. Then Jerry was able to take on the Savin line, and he began to sell the Savin 220 Electrostatic Copier. He said that we really needed an office with a showroom. We decided to get a babysitter to keep Peggy, and the same lady agreed to keep Ken after school.

We set up an office on Lancaster Avenue in Fort Worth, Texas, with a sign, phone, and everything we needed. Granted, it was one 12-by-15-foot room with a small closet. I started going into the office every morning with Jerry, and we would drive Highway 183 between Fort Worth and Irving.

At that time, the highway was one lane going in each direction and had no divider in the middle. It was considered the most dangerous piece of highway in Texas.

This danger was all right, but I was not too pleased with the babysitter. She had a boy a few years older than Ken, and one day they tied Ken to a tree and left him. That did not go over too well with me at all.

We were getting paranoid driving and seeing so many accidents and decided that maybe we should move to Fort Worth. The Irving Schools were excellent, and Ken was doing well, but we decided to move anyway.

———•••———

We put our house on the market, and virtually nobody even looked at the house. I had to have it clean and straight every morning before going to work, which became a hassle. We had the house on the market for almost a year, and nobody was interested.

This home was beautiful, and I could not understand why it had not sold. We decided that God just was not ready for us to move. Southside Baptist Church was struggling to pay the pastor's salary and its bills. We agreed that God wanted us to stay at Southside so that we could give our tithe there and continue to work in the church.

We said, "God, if you want us to sell this house, you will have to sell it." We took the house off the market. Six months later, a lady called and wanted to look at the house, and we set a time for her to come by the next day.

Before she hung up, I said, "By the way, how did you know that we wanted to sell the house?"

"I saw the sign in your yard," she said.

I told her we had the house up for sale, but we had not had a sign in the yard for six months.

She paused and then said, "No, I saw that sign yesterday when I was driving by, and I got the phone number off the sign."

"Was that at 1001 Sleepy Hollow?" I asked.

"Yes," she said.

When Jerry came home, I told him about the woman calling, and he said, "Go ahead and show it to her."

She came by at the appointed time the next day, and I showed her the house. She was a Jewish lady, and this was her first trip to Texas. She said she wanted to purchase the house and wrote me a check as a deposit.

When Jerry came home that night, I told him I had sold the house. We just looked at each other in awe, remembering what we had said about God selling the house. The only thing was that she wanted the house in 30 days.

We had not had a vacation for ages, and someone else had called the house earlier and said that if we agreed to look at some property in Florida that they would pay our airfare and put us up in a hotel for three nights. We had taken them up on the offer, and we were supposed to go on this trip the following week. That would throw a hitch in our house hunting, but we decided to go ahead and take the trip anyway.

We set up a time with the woman that following weekend to close the papers on the house. Everything went through without a hitch. They wrote a check for the entire amount, and we would be out of the house in 30 days.

Jerry and I boarded the plane for our free trip to Miami, Florida. When we got there, we got to this old hotel with a lot of character. It was quite pretty, and there was quite a lot of gold glitter and gleaming chandeliers.

We sat in the sitting room/lobby, about 15 feet wide and 35 feet long.

There was houndstooth woodwork around the ceiling area with wide molding. Sofas and chairs were scattered around, with pretty tables and a piano at one end of the room.

Jerry and I sat in the room and began talking about what we would do about a house. And the subject came up of what kind of house we would like to have. I laughingly said I wanted a place where the living room looked just like the room we were sitting in. Jerry said, "Oh, sure." And we both laughed. The room was really beautiful to both of us.

We decided that we probably should try to buy a very inexpensive house so that we would not have such expensive house payments. We looked at the property we agreed to see and walked on the beaches. We marveled at how many older adults were walking on the streets and how sad they looked.

We talked about the old wealthy Jewish people coming there for the summer. We wondered why, if they were so rich, they looked so unhappy. We had so little, and we were "as happy as if we had good sense." We had a wonderful time doing nothing in particular and spent virtually no money.

After our little vacation was over, we headed back to Dallas. Mrs. Dowdy had agreed to keep Ken and Peggy for us so we were anxious to get back and see if all their skin had been washed off. (Mrs. Dowdy always kept the kids meticulously clean when she kept them, and the kids complained about her washing their ears.)

It had not been long since Jann was small, so I asked her to keep the kids no more than three or four times. I appreciated her caring for them and knew they were in good hands.

13 Family Life in Ryan Place

As soon as we returned home and unpacked our bags, we began to put our plans into action. We went to Fort Worth and began to look for a house. We wanted to keep the cost down, so first, we looked at a little frame house in a rundown area of town.

We had hired Charles Nelson, a young man from Southside Church, to help deliver or run errands or do whatever else we needed to be done. Charles went with us to look at the house. He said, "You do not want this house." It was a considerable come down from what we had grown accustomed to. It was considerably less than anything that Charles had lived in.

I will have to admit, it was not much. Besides being small, the floors were uneven, and you felt you needed to hold your arms out to help you balance as you walked across the floor. The place was dirty, and the bathroom was unspeakable. We decided maybe we should consider a step up.

———◆◆◆———

We went to the real estate agent and told her we did not want to buy anything that cost more than the amount we sold our house for. We looked at several homes on the Southside of Fort Worth, and none seemed to be what we wanted.

We looked at one that overlooked Forrest Park, which was nice, and it had a swimming pool with a pool house in the back. The only problem was that there were only two bedrooms in the house and we needed three.

We returned to the real estate agent's office and looked at the picture book of listings. We came across a picture of one stately house, a big two-story home, which looked impressive.

Jokingly, I said, "That would be a nice house to buy."

As I had assumed, the agent informed me that the house was out of our price range. We continued to look in the book, and the agent left the room.

The agent returned in a few minutes and told us that the house's price had dropped $10,000, or about 25 percent, the day before. The house had been on the market for a long time, and there had been no interest.

Since it was late in the afternoon, the agent suggested she arrange to show the house to Jerry the next day. (I was not planning to return to Fort Worth the next day.) We agreed that would be fine but never really thought that we would be able to buy the house.

The next day, Jerry looked at the house and was impressed, so the day after, I went to Fort Worth, and we both looked at the house. We decided to try to purchase it.

———◆•◆———

The house was red brick with solid exterior walls almost a foot thick. The roofline was trimmed with wide facia boards and dentil molding. There were also impressive semicircle trimmings above the front windows and door. The front door was unusually wide, tall, and made from fine grain mahogany with massive doorknobs. The roof had fancy green slate tiles.

A wealthy oil tycoon had built the house in 1923, and a servant's quarter in the back contained a double-car garage underneath. The narrow garage door openings would accommodate the small Model T Ford but barely allow for modern cars.

The right side of the house had a driveway covered by the upstairs side balcony. A side door with a built-up porch would have accommodated a horse-drawn carriage.

Across the front of the house and going down the other end was a wide concrete porch surrounded by a banister made from concrete pedestal posts. On the upper level was a balcony porch with a wrought iron banister and fencing. At center front was a small round balcony that protected the front entrance. The sidewalk up the front lawn was unusually wide. Everything about the house was stately and massive.

From the exterior, we were impressed, but once we walked through the front door, we were even more impressed. There was a Venetian crystal chandelier hanging in the entry hall. Around the entry hall and living room ceiling was gold leaf about eight inches wide, set off by white dentil molding. Crystal sconces hung on the wall below the massive molding in the living room and dining room. There was a lot of molding, giving it immense character.

When we walked into the living room, the similarities between it and that hotel lobby in Miami were uncanny — almost frightening. Jerry and I both knew that this was the house that God had chosen for us, and the timing of lowering the price was just for us. We felt so sure that this was the house that we hardly needed to look at the rest.

We walked up the spiral staircase that overlooked the entry hall. There were three bedrooms and a sitting room, and two baths upstairs. A laundry chute went from upstairs to the basement, and a dumbwaiter went from upstairs to the hall off of the kitchen.

One of the bathrooms was modern, with a pink square tub. The other bath had an old porcelain pedestal wash basin and a footed bathtub. Both bathrooms had tile floors. There was a cedar-lined closet off the upper hallway, and the dressing room off the master bath had a safe and many doors and drawers.

The house also needed a lot of work. The carpet and living room drapes were a "dusty rose" color. The lined drapes had heavy cornices, swags, and "sheers" beneath them. Both carpet and drapes were quite old and needed to be replaced, but I felt I could live with them because I knew it would cost a fortune to carpet and drape the entire house.

There was a full basement with one room finished with a beautiful marble fireplace with funny characters on each side mantel. There was a large room for washing, suitable for hanging clothes to dry on a rainy day. A furnace room and another room opened to the outside with a little door for dumping coal into that room. (A gas furnace had updated the coal furnace years before.) Another room in the basement was used like a cellar to hold canned goods, fruits, and vegetables. I had never seen anything like it.

We signed the contract for the house that afternoon and gave a deposit as earnest money. We later learned that a local banker had looked at the house that same day, and he called his real estate agent and told her he wanted to buy the house. His agent was sick and asked him to come to the office the next day to sign the contract. He was heartbroken that he missed out on the house. Evidently, he had considered the house before, and when the price dropped, he jumped at the opportunity.

To us, this was no coincidence; it was God's hand at work in our lives. He had sold our house and had another one picked out for us.

<hr>

So, on October 31, 1967, we moved from Irving to Fort Worth — and into the house at 2516 Ryan Place Drive. It was Halloween night, and over a hundred children came by trick or treating. Poor Ken and Peggy did not get much opportunity to trick or treat. Still, I had managed to throw costumes together for them, and Jerry took them out to a few neighbors' homes while I handled the home front.

On Monday morning, the kids and I went to Daggett Elementary school to enroll them. Peggy was starting kindergarten, and Ken went into the third grade. They had been in Plymouth Park Elementary School in Irving, where all the children were all well-dressed and well-fed. Their families had money to buy school supplies (and anything their children needed), and the school was well-equipped with books and teaching materials.

One look at Daggett, and you could easily see the disparity. The school was old, and many children were from the lowest-income families. Some children looked ill-cared for, but a few looked more like the children in Irving. I could look at the school and immediately knew that the kids would not get the academic education they would have received in Irving. I told myself they would get an inferior academic education, but they would get a far better education in people's lives.

There was a broad spectrum of backgrounds. There were Hispanic children, quite a few black children, and fewer Anglo children. Some children were from wealthy families, some from middle-income families, and the vast majority were from families below the poverty line. Many of the children's families were on welfare and had very little to offer their children monetarily.

Ken and Peggy quickly saw and began to understand the "haves" and the "have-nots." Ken tried to "dress down" by wearing a dirty white sailor hat all the time, but Peggy did not seem to pay that much attention since she had not attended school before. I did not have a sitter lined up to care for the kids after school, so Mother came down to stay with the kids.

The house needed painting, so we got a crew of painters in there, and we set up our camping stove and electric skillet in the basement. Mother would try to wash out some clothes for me, and when she would go out of the basement to the upstairs, she would get confused and have to tell the painters that she was lost.

The house was not that large, but with all the ladders and drop cloths, navigating it was confusing to Mother. The painters would point her to the steps that led to the basement. When the children came in from school, she made them a special little snack and played with them.

One of their games was for the kids to pile toys on the floor near their doors and call Mother to come into their rooms. Mother would go in there and pretend to fall over the toys, which would delight them. They would then crawl around on the floor together and laugh and giggle.

———•••———

When Pauline and Arvil came to see the house, they thought we had lost our minds. They were not impressed at all. All Pauline could see was all the wood trim — and anticipate all the dust that would accumulate and require dusting. Arvil could see all the electrical and plumbing problems. They did not say much else and gave us three hundred dollars to put in on the painting.

I will admit the house was a bit of a mess. The plumbing did have more than a few difficulties. Evidently, whoever installed the new upstairs commode did not connect the pipes well, and a leak had dripped through the living room's ceiling. (The prior tenants must have avoided using that commode in place of repair.) It appeared that the upstairs commode was rarely, if ever, used.

When Jerry started to repair this leak, he found that the pipes ran through a one-foot-thick poured concrete floor. With jackhammers, chisels, and hammers, the leak was at last located and repaired. (This leak was just the beginning of seemingly minor problems that became major difficulties.) Because its previous owners had not maintained the house's 40-year-old plumbing very well, invariably, we would get up on Sunday Mornings to find a small flood running down some wall.

Then there was the electrical wiring which was a severe hazard, and it was a wonder that the house did not burn down. It probably would have caught fire but for the nine-inch-thick concrete and brick interior walls.

Then there were those slate tiles on the roof. We learned that the felt liner underneath the slate lasted only thirty years, so we needed to remove all the tiles and install new felt.

The kitchen looked like something from some war movie. The rusted-out holes in the tops and sides of the metal cabinets made it obvious that we would have to tear them out and replace them.

With all diligence, we started working on the house every spare minute, but this only lasted a few months before the new wore off. Jerry became more disinterested in the house and more interested in other things. He would repair things when we had a real problem, but everything else stood status quo. Due to a shortage of money, this was about all we could do for a while. The house looked pretty good.

———◆◆◆———

We got up and headed out to look for a new church home on the first Sunday we were there. Our banker told us that all the influential businesspeople attended Broadway Baptist Church, but we simply could not see going to a church because maybe it would help us in our business.

We were more interested in a church where we could serve the Lord. And we wanted to attend a church that was nearby.

There were only three churches near, so that would limit our choices. We first visited College Avenue Church. It was old, and it certainly looked as if it could use some help. We questioned whether the children would get a good religious education there, which was a genuine concern.

That same Sunday night, we attended Travis Avenue Baptist Church, a huge church. (There had been only one hundred or so people at

Southside Church on a good Sunday.) The sanctuary at Travis would hold three thousand three hundred. I thought I might never be able to find my way around. (It looked more like a college campus, and I had never been to college.) Although it was a little overwhelming, we thought Travis would have a good children's program for Ken and Peggy.

Because Travis was beginning a "visitation revival" that Sunday, on Monday afternoon, we had a group of people come to visit. On Monday night, Bill Pearson, the music director, and his wife, Pat, came to visit. On their way out, Bernie Spooner, the educational director, and his wife, also named Pat, were coming up the sidewalk. We enjoyed short visits with all of them.

Jerry had sung in the choir, and on a rare occasion, he would sing a solo, so Bill assured Jerry that there would be a spot for him in the choir at Travis. We shared with Bernie that we had both taught Sunday School, and Bernie said he needed a director for the young married couples department. He offered Jerry that position that night without really knowing us.

I was amazed that a big church like Travis would allow us to start working in the church without first proving ourselves or calling for references. I would have thought they would have plenty of teachers and workers, and we would have to stand in line.

The next day here came the pastor, Dr. James Coggin. This impressed us. (Who were we that the pastor should come for a visit?) We had such a steady stream of people from the church coming for a visit I could hardly unpack the boxes. We told them we had promised our banker we would visit Broadway but promised that we would be back to Travis the following Sunday morning.

We attended Broadway and were very favorably impressed, but we still felt we could not join there because it might look like we were joining for our own gain rather than to serve the Lord.

———••◆••———

The following Sunday, we did attend Travis as promised — and joined. Sure enough, Bernie Spooner was not joking. He put Jerry to work as the director of the Married Young Peoples Department. Martin and Shirley Jetton, the department's previous directors who had been telling Bernie they wanted to give the department up, stayed on and acted as secretary and helped with visitation, hosting parties at their home, or whatever else needed to be done.

Charles and Sue Ann Layton were teaching, as well as Jewel Medford and Jane Basden. About twenty-five people attended each Sunday. Jane Basden quit teaching after a couple of Sundays. I started teaching but only taught briefly before the department was restructured.

Martin had contended that you could not mix married young couples with young seminary couples. Bernie wanted to include the Southwestern Seminary couples with those couples who were lay people. Martin said that if we mixed the department, it would very quickly become all Seminary.

Jerry had no experience with this and, like Bernie, did not see why the non-seminary couples would feel threatened or stop attending as long as the seminary students did not use Sunday School to expound on everything they were being taught. With proper teacher control, these two should mix.

Some couples in that department included Pete and Patsy Dwight, Don and Becca Williams, Bill and Celia Rice (Bill was in the service), and Mike and Sue Tripp. These were some quality young people. We were given names of new Seminary students, and the teachers, Jerry and I, and some of the young couples would show up each Tuesday night and go out visiting those in our age group regardless of what they were doing in Fort Worth.

The department grew and grew. We had a Valentine's party at our house and had 75 for a sit-down dinner. As Martin predicted, it was not long until there was more Seminary folk than non-Seminary, and all the couples mentioned above left the department to work in another department. Within three years, no matter how hard the teachers tried or how hard we worked to get non-Seminary couples into the department, the department became a Seminary Department.

We attended church on Tuesday nights for visitation, Wednesday nights for prayer meetings, and Sunday morning and night. Then Jerry and I were appointed to serve on the Baptismal committee, and before long, Jerry was elected deacon. Some years later, he was elected to the finance committee and then served as chairman of the deacons. I served on the nominating committee, and then something happened; I began to rebel and almost dropped out of church altogether.

Besides our church activities, we were both working at the office. We hired a couple of service technicians and a couple of salesmen. One of the salesmen we hired was Mickey Lewis.

Mickey was a big talker and dreamer, and Jerry was a talker and dreamer, so the two of them loved to get together and talk and dream and talk and dream. Where one went, the other went. (All this talking and dreaming resulted in Jerry not selling anything and Mickey not selling anything.) I suggested we let Mickey go because he was nonproductive.

Then Mickey and Jerry had the brilliant idea (according to their way of thinking) that installing coin machines was the way to make a "fortune." I sat down with a pencil and figured out the cost of the machines, supplies, and manpower, and I could not see that this would be very profitable — and possibly we would lose money unless the machines made a lot of copies.

We were selling (or trying to sell) Ankin 124 Copiers, and some dealers were installing coin boxes on these machines and putting them in grocery stores, shopping malls, department stores, or anywhere else for public use. Some dealers were pretty successful at this, but most were probably not reporting all their income and paying taxes. This was not our way of doing business. (Putting money in the trunk of the car was not my idea of what Christians should do.) Jerry and Mickey put out two or three machines that year, but we had not made enough to live on by the end of the year when I figured out our profits.

----•••----

One day a doctor called and wanted to talk to Mickey, and I told him that he was out with Jerry. The doctor became irate. (I will just call him Doctor X, whom Mickey said bought season tickets to Casa Manana Theater for Mickey each year)

That day, Dr. X went into a jealous tirade. It seems that Mickey had a date with him and had stood him up. I did not know what to say to Dr. X that day or when he continued to call on rare occasions and wanted to talk to Mickey. (Many years later, I heard that Mickey died of AIDS.)

At the end of the year, when I began to evaluate the profits, it was apparent to me that Mickey was not pulling his weight and that Jerry had become nonproductive with Mickey around. I told Jerry that the business was going under if he did not let Mickey go, and he had to get out and start selling machines and calling on customers again.

We let Mickey go, but we continued to put out some coin machines, mainly in Fort Worth Public Libraries and Southwestern Seminary. These were good, productive customers, but the grocery store copiers were a total loss. Coin copiers were still a part of the business, but a small part.

We moved our office from our one-room space on Lancaster to Boston Street and then to Oakland Street. With each move, we increased in business and employees.

Jerry helped Ken Parma start a business in Waco, and Ken did well in his business. Later Ken wanted to put in a business in Temple, and somehow, Jerry and Ken got together and set up a partnership in Temple that covered Temple, Belton, Killeen, and the area in central Texas. We also set up an office in Wichita Falls that became an extension of our Fort Worth Office.

While we were in the office on Boston Street, I decided that if I was ever going to quit working, the time had come. Jerry hired a young woman at the recommendation of an insurance man. That girl was on drugs or something and had too many problems; she would not show up for work, and in a one-girl office, that did not work. I went back into the office.

I interviewed another young woman named Linda Sisk, and then Jerry interviewed and hired her. She was tall, skinny, had black hair, and seemed very capable. So, Linda went to work in the office, and I began staying home.

When we moved to Fort Worth, I hired Donzel Colton, a 35-year-old black woman, to care for the house and the kids when they were not in school. Donzel was considerably overweight, and she brought a brown paper bag to work with her every morning and took her bag home with her every night.

One day I asked Donzel what was in her bag, and she told me she was afraid — and she carried a knife in the sack for protection. She said, "People are bad in my part of town."

———•••———

Once when we were taking a trip, I asked Donzel if she would keep our dog, a miniature black and white spotted poodle named MacTavish Poinyee. We kept the dog well-groomed, never allowing the hair on his ears to be trimmed, and there was always a pom-pom on the end of MacTavish Poinyee's tail. MacTavish was the cutest poodle. He would run down the stairs, and in the process, he learned to run on his front two paws.

Donzel agreed to keep MacTavish while we were gone on vacation. I told Donzel I would pay her the same, but it would be fine if she wanted to take the dog to her house. That way, she would not have to pay the bus fare and would be free to do whatever she wanted.

When we returned to Fort Worth, we did not even go by our house first. We were so anxious to see MacTavish that we went straight to Donzel's house.

She met us at the car in tears. "Oh! Miss, a terrible thing has happened," she said. "My husband got drunk and cut MacTavish's hair. He also bathed him and rubbed him down with Vaseline. Then MacTavish got outside, rolled in the grass, and he's a terrible mess. He tucked his tail, crawled under the bed, and won't come out." Donzel was crying and carrying on.

Donzel had been a faithful worker. She was sure that I was going to fire her. She cried and carried on so much that I think she was as upset over the horror of MacTavish as she was about losing her job. She had grown attached to that little poodle as well as to the kids.

Ken and Peggy both puckered up, and then Peggy began to cry. This situation seemed like such a terrible thing for poor little MacTavish, whom we had always treated like "a people."

Donzel did not want me to enter the house, but I barreled in anyway. I went into their bedroom with Donzel to try to coax MacTavish out from under the bed. Her husband lay sprawled out across the bed with just his pants on. He was dead drunk, and I was glad he was not awake.

I got down on my hands and knees and called MacTavish to come out from under the bed. He came out with his tail between his legs and looked so embarrassed. His eyes were droopy, and his hair was sticky with Vaseline and badly botched. There was no hair on his tail or ears, and the grass stuck to the Vaseline. As MacTavish crawled out from under the bed, it was easy to see in his hunched posture that MacTavish might never run like a proud stallion again.

We took Mac home with us, bathed and bathed him, and finally removed the Vaseline, but still, he walked hunched down and cowered at every sound. Somehow, he knew that he was not pretty anymore. He was still our dog, the same dog, and we loved him just as much.

We showered him with hugs and kisses, talked to him, and gave him even more attention. Within a couple of weeks, he began to act like himself. Poor Mac had a terrible vacation.

With Jerry working and becoming more involved in church, there was less and less time to spend with the family. After we hired Linda, I started staying at home. After a while, I felt nonproductive and decided to let Donzel go because I saw no reason to keep paying her for things I then had the time to do. I stayed at home to take care of the house and the kids.

14 Ryan Place: The Dark Years

I was in my mid to late thirties, which should have been a wonderful period. The business was going well. We were not getting rich, but it looked like Jerry would make a go of Copy & Litho. Our name was becoming recognizable to our competitors and prospective customers.

Ken and Peggy were doing well in school, Ken was involved in various sports, and Peggy was singing with The Texas Girls' Choir.

I could now stay home and didn't have to work at the office except occasionally. I continued to work with the accountants, reviewing the financial statements monthly, asking questions, and having them make corrections as needed.

We were very involved in church, but we had not made any close friends. We had a lot of acquaintances but no close friends. I had nobody I felt free to talk to or call to go out to lunch. I had always been so closed that I never thought I could open up to anybody. I guess I did not trust them to keep a confidence, or maybe I felt they would not like me if I really let them know who I was, or perhaps it was just my nature to turn inward.

A few years before, Jerry's grandfather, Papaw Maness, had passed away; now, Mammaw Maness became ill and passed away. After Jerry's grandmother Maness died, Jerry and I got in his pickup and drove to Stephenville, Texas, where she had been living. The family was going down there to dispose of her household effects, and we thought the pickup would come in handy for moving furniture. I don't know whether Jerry's Mother had asked him to help, but I felt like maybe I could help.

When we got down there, Pauline was going through things. She pointed out the couch and lamps and said some elderly relative might be able to use them. We loaded the couch, chairs, and lamps from the living room onto our pickup, and Jerry delivered them wherever requested. Other items were sorted through and given away.

Pauline then went through the linens and sent many of those to Johnny Ruth, a granddaughter living in Alexander, Louisiana. I did not think Johnny Ruth would want many of those things, but I did not make any comment about anything.

I'd simply ask, "what do you want me to do with this or that?"

She asked if I wanted Mammaw's overnight case, and I said "yes."

A pillow in the closet had Jerry's name on it, so I took it. There was a small silver-colored pin that was costume jewelry, and I said I would like to have the pin.

We continued to sort through things, and I guess some things were given to Mammaw's brother and sister-in-law, J.T. and Hazel Maness, as well as her sister and brother-in-law, Zelma and Estell Ammons. Zelma, J.T., and Pauline were Mammaw's only living children.

Bessie Crump, her other daughter, had passed away a short time earlier, and Bessie's only child was her daughter, Johnny Ruth Nabors. These were Mammaw's sole heirs.

By the end of the day, most things had been disposed of. Pauline had our pickup loaded with a bedroom suite and the only good chair from Mammaw's living room. Pauline had put all the China, crystal, and many other items in boxes, which were also loaded onto our truck. The pickup was totally packed as we pulled out of the driveway. We drove straight to Richardson and unloaded everything at Pauline's house.

The only thing I kept was a pan, plus the overnight case, pillow, and pin.

I was tired and ready to go home. Arvil offered to pay some for the gasoline, but Jerry would not take any money to cover our expenses, which were more than the items we were taking away. We had not gone there to get anything — that had never crossed my mind.

Little did I know that this would be the beginning of many years of heartache and pain. I could not have guessed that this day of work would wind up changing my life forever.

———••———

The Vietnam War was going on, and Norman, Jerry's brother, could not come home for his grandmother's funeral. There was a small white book in the overnight case. (There was also a spoon and a package of douche powder; that was all in the case.) I took the little white book, put it in a letter, and mailed it to Norman because I felt bad he could not be with the family during this time.

When Norman returned from Vietnam, he, Arvil, Pauline, and Jann came over for lunch. Norman commented that he did not get anything when his grandmother died except the little white book I sent him. He said someone in the family had told him that "Barbara" got everything.

I was absolutely speechless, appalled that someone would make such an untruthful statement. I did not comment, thinking Jerry would come to my defense. However, he did not attempt to clarify the situation or inform Norman that I was not a grave robber.

Norman went back into active service, and when we saw him the next time, he made the same statement about what "someone" said about me. Still, neither Pauline, Arvil, Jann, nor Jerry set him straight. I was furious but said nothing, thinking I should not have to defend myself.

After all, they knew the truth. Why didn't they tell Norman that Pauline and Jann had gotten the bedroom suite, the good chair, the crystal, and whatever else they had gotten?

After they left that day, I told Jerry I was very disappointed in him. I told him I felt he should have defended me if he loved me. My family would not have allowed someone to say such a terrible thing without supporting the family member. If someone had told a terrible lie about Jerry, I would have been quick to come to his defense. Still, Jerry never went to Norman and told him the truth. I was angry, hurt, and disappointed, and the more I thought about it, the angrier I got.

This response was so opposite to my nature; I rarely got angry. The only plausible answer I could come up with was that Jerry did not love me. This realization was the real beginning of my problems. Or maybe it was the thing that brought to the surface all of the issues I had overlooked and not faced.

Instead of opening up and telling Jerry what I was thinking, I kept everything bottled up inside of me and began to think about everything that had taken place in our marriage. I began to look at things differently.

———•••———

The next time we saw Norman, he made the same statement. Again, Jerry, Norman, Arvil, Pauline, and Jann were there. Again, they said nothing to correct Norman's inaccuracy.

I blew my top. I had told myself that if Norman ever again said that "someone" said "Barbara got everything," I would set him straight in no uncertain terms.

So, I did. I told Norman precisely what I got, and I did not attempt to tell him where everything else had gone. (I did not think it was my place to explain that). I was so mad I could hardly talk. Jerry had never seen me angry like this before.

None of the family had ever seen me lose my temper, and I had not lost my composure since I was a senior in high school. When Jerry saw how mad I was, he tried to defend me, but it was too late. I had already decided that this conversation would not have been necessary if Jerry had loved me. It was of no consolation that Jerry had come to my defense only after I defended myself.

The family sat in awe. They had never seen me act like this.

I went upstairs and got the pin, the night case, and the pan and offered them to Norman. "If this is "everything," I said, "then you are welcome to it."

Norman did not take anything and was rather cool toward me for the rest of the day. I never felt the same about the Dowdy family or Jerry after that. To me, this was just unforgivable.

———•••———

126

I closed my mind off from the rest of the world and stayed closed up in my thoughts. I cleaned the house, washed the clothes, and ironed. I continued to cook, wash dishes, buy groceries, and do everything else I had taken on as my responsibility. But I spent most of my days just lying on the couch in the basement watching television. I had no energy, no hope, and no drive. I continued to attend church but had no interest in it, and I had no friends.

Jerry was busy with his work and at church, and he had very little time for the kids or me. He began to stay at the office later in the evening. (Unless Ken had a football game, we seldom saw him.) It seemed to me that he would come home, change clothes go to work, go to church, go to Ken's games, sleep, eat, and have sex.

Our life had become nothing but a ritual. I felt no love for Jerry and was sure he did not love me.

———••••———

I began thinking back over our marriage. I began to wonder about things I had never questioned before. I had trusted Jerry completely, but now I looked at things differently.

Why did Copease question him about renting "double" hotel rooms and assume he had been taking me along on trips? Why had he become so sexed up after bowling so many years before? Why had Donna made so many passes at Jerry in my presence?

Our Irving friends had always gotten together on New Year's Eve, and we went out to eat. One year Donna had fallen all over Jerry. She had drunk too much, talked too much, and been too friendly with Jerry. Usually, our group never drank, but Gay Phariss's boss had ordered champagne for our group, and a few in the group drank a glass. Jerry and I did not drink any, so there was more than enough for Donna Weir.

Once, Donna had taken up reading people's handwriting. She looked at Jerry's handwriting and said, "Ooh-la-la!" and giggled and would not make any other comment. Once in later years, when we had not seen her for a long time, she told Jerry that she would have lost weight if she had known she was going to see him.

And there were other things, as well.

Then I wondered about Mickey Lewis and Dr. X. Had something been going on between Mickey and Jerry when neither of them was selling anything but spending all their time together? When Dr. X got jealous, should I have been a little less trusting, myself? I had never considered that maybe they were doing something less than honorable.

Then I remembered when we lived in Irving, and I got sick and went to the doctor. Dr. Irving (in Irving) sent me for a blood test and told me that I had low blood pressure, and then he proceeded to give me a shot each week for six weeks. It was not until about this time that I learned that you do not give shots for low blood pressure, but you do give shots for venereal disease.

I tried to contact Dr. Irving to find out what was really wrong with me. Unfortunately, he had died, and his wife said she had destroyed all the records.

Once, about the time I was getting those shots, I went in to see Dr. Irving, and when I got there, the receptionist could not find my file. Dr. Irving stuck his head in the door, and the girl told him she could not find my file.

Dr. Irving told her he had put my file inside Jerry's file because Jerry told the doctor he was moving to New York City, and Dr. Irving assumed I would move with him.

Jerry had never mentioned anything to me about moving to New York City. Had he planned on leaving me, years before, when we were living in Irving? Why had he told Dr. Irving that he was moving?

Why had he not told me the complete truth about getting fired from his job at Tex Oil? Was it because he was messing around with the girls in the cafe across the street? After all, he had insisted on taking me and Ken to that dumpy little cafe just after he got fired. What was the real truth about that?

Then there were all those trips to Altus, Oklahoma. Where had he really been when he left us all day and evening in the motel — after he had insisted on taking us to Altus with him? Was he seeing another woman there and wanted us there so he could break off their relationship? With Ken and me waiting in the hotel, it would make it easier for him, I thought.

What had really been going on in our marriage all those years? Was it my imagination? Was it because my father chased around on my mother that caused me to distrust Jerry now? Was my bad experience with my uncle what caused me to distrust men in general? Was I making all this up — or was there something to all my thoughts?

The more I thought about all this, without realizing it, I went into a deep depression. For about three years, every day, I would try to decide whether I wanted to leave Jerry or commit suicide. I wanted to die but didn't even have the courage to do that.

For that matter, I did not have the courage to live, either. I felt defeated and hopeless, and I did not think there was anybody I could turn to.

I would not turn to the pastor because I did not trust him to understand my point of view. After all, I had no concrete evidence, and Jerry was a deacon and a department director. He would never believe me, I thought.

If Jerry and I got a divorce, what effect would this have on the church?

I searched the Bible and decided that suicide would be wrong. Divorce would be OK if Jerry had indeed committed adultery. I felt he had undoubtedly been unfaithful in his heart, and he probably had been with other women — and maybe even other men.

———

Then I got sick. I had been having dizzy spells, and then I awoke one morning and could not move my arm. It was totally numb. Blood seemed to be cut off from my brain. I took one hand and picked up the numb arm, and when I released it, it plopped onto my chest like a cold piece of meat that was not a part of my body. Blood began to rush from the base of my skull to the top of my head. It felt like a blood vessel had broken, and the blood was spreading.

I went to see Dr. Rose in Fort Worth and told him about my symptoms, never mentioning the mental anguish also taking place. He sent me to the hospital and laboratories for tests, and they did all kinds of brain scans, stomach tests, and blood tests.

When I mentioned to Jerry, I was having some medical problems, he did not comment. He showed no concern for me. He never asked me about the results of any of the tests, and he never asked me how I was feeling. It was just as if I had never mentioned anything to him. Obviously, Jerry did not love me and cared not whether I lived or died.

Dr. Rose wanted to do some stomach tests on me and said I would need someone to drive me home after the test. I had fasted, drank medication, and cleaned myself out before they could run the test. I asked Jerry if he would go with me. He willingly took me to the hospital, and afterward, we went out to lunch together as if nothing was wrong, and then Jerry took me on home.

We never argued. We talked to each other when we needed to, but usually, when Jerry was home, we just watched TV. I lived in my little world, and he lived in his.

I had told Jerry that they were going to run tests on me for a brain tumor, too, which they did. I was having trouble with memory and had a strong sex drive, both of which I have since learned can be symptoms of depression.

I would think that Jerry would surely be a little concerned about me if the doctor was running tests on me for a brain tumor, but still, he never asked me the results. He continued to work and showed no interest in me.

When the results came back, Dr. Rose said he could find nothing wrong with me. If I had just told him what was going on in my marriage, maybe he could have helped me. I told Dr. Rose I thought perhaps I was starting through menopause.

He just smiled and said, "No, you are not."

But actually, I was going into menopause. I don't know if the marital problems had caused me to go into early menopause or if my going into early menopause was contributing to my marriage problems. Whatever the case, I was going through hell mentally.

———◦•◦———

Finally, I decided I could not go on that way any longer. Emotionally, I was in the pits. I felt dumb, ugly, and unlovable. I did not feel I had the sense to go out and get a job. I felt useless. Yet, I had two children who had to be cared for.

Ken was starting the eighth grade, and Peggy was entering the fifth. Since I could not kill myself, I decided I would just leave Jerry.

We were living in this big, old house, and I figured out how much it cost us to live there. The monthly payments were minimal, but we were spending $6000.00 per year for upkeep and repairs, which was a lot of money then.

I had asked Ken and Peggy to help me sweep the driveway and do some work around the yard, and neither wanted to help. At that time, I told myself, "I will leave Jerry, buy a small house, and move."

I told Jerry I wanted to sell the house, and Jerry said, "Fine."

I called the realtor who had sold us the house, and we signed a contract so that she could list it. Immediately, she called the man who had wanted the house when we initially purchased it.

The next day he said he wanted the house sight unseen. He signed a contract, and we sold the house. I had not yet looked for another house, and this man wanted it in 30 days.

The following day, Dr. Fred McCaulley called Jerry and said he had a house he wanted us to look at. He said he had been up most of the night praying about this house, and our name kept coming into his mind. We asked him if he knew we had sold our home. He said he had no idea. He just knew he had prayed and thought about us.

Even without looking at the house, I felt sure this was the house God had prepared for us. It was ironic how God had worked in our lives regarding housing, and I felt this was no coincidence, and it was just too bizarre.

I was mad at God because women must be submissive to their husbands. I thought the Bible taught that women have to give up being themselves to be submissive. I had tried to do that but found that it was impossible for me to play this role any longer.

I had given up my name; I had given up my identity, and I blamed God. I thought that God was unfair to women. Yet, at the same time, I still believed in God and desired to follow His leadership.

Occasionally I would wonder how my life had gotten so far off the right path. What happened to that call I had as a girl to become a foreign missionary? I was the farthest thing from being a missionary; I was no good to my family, myself, or God.

Anyway, Jerry and I went over to look at Dr. McCaulley's house, knowing before we went that we would probably buy the house no matter what it looked like. The house, located at 3747 Bellaire Circle in Fort Worth, was in a good part of town. It was well constructed, with about 1800 square feet, three bedrooms, and two baths — considerably smaller than the 7000-square-foot house we were living in.

It was a house I saw as manageable financially if Jerry and I got a divorce.

I still fully intended to tell Jerry I wanted a divorce. I hated the thought of returning to work, but I felt sure it would be necessary to make a living.

My self-image was so low I did not think anybody would hire me. I did not know what I could do, but at least this would be a step in the right direction.

We signed a contract on the house and purchased it. It turned out that everybody who had ever lived in the house had been a full-time Christian worker, either a preacher or a missionary. Southwestern Baptist Theological Seminary even carried the loan on the house. We assumed the loan and moved into the house.

———•••———

Immediately, Jerry started remodeling the kitchen. There was no built-in stove, so we bought another used stove and cleaned it up. It reminded us of that old stove we cleaned up when we first got married.

We removed the cabinet doors, installed a new garbage disposal and dishwasher, hung new doors, and installed a built-in stove, countertops, and new cabinets. We also tore out the bar and installed a new floor covering.

Rita Bristow (however, this was before she married Earl Bristow) came over and helped me to wallpaper the kitchen. She knew how to hang wallpaper, and I just helped her. I really appreciated her help.

Getting out of that dark basement made life seem brighter, and things seemed to improve. I got my mind off of myself and on to something else.

———•••———

We had met JD and Gypsy Kelly at church, and Gypsy had passed away. Then J. D. married Joani Bodine from down in the Valley, and we immediately became friends. Joani was lonely and having some difficulty adjusting to living in Fort Worth.

Joani had two daughters from a previous marriage and had a very close relationship with her daughters. I watched how she related to Leslie, her daughter the same age as Peggy.

Peggy started attending Bluebonnet Elementary School. She did not know anybody, and I had let her wardrobe become shabby. This had not mattered when she attended Daggett, but these Bluebonnet children judged a person by the kinds of clothes they wore.

Joani shopped a lot for herself and her girls, and they dressed nicely. I began to take a new interest in Peggy.

Peggy had started sucking her lips until they looked like someone had hit her in the mouth, and I realized that Peggy had a problem and needed some help. I took her shopping and bought her some new clothes. I joined the PTA and tried to befriend some of the mothers. I looked for someone who wanted to be friends with Peggy.

Little by little, Peggy began to come out of her shell, and by the time she was ready for middle school, she had slimmed down and really looked pretty. She stopped sucking her lips, and I knew she was developing a better self-image.

In the meantime, I had begun to make friends, too. In addition to Joani Kelly, I became friends with Sandra Taylor, Billie Keeton, and Bobbie Roberts (her name was not Roberts then).

Jerry and I were beginning to learn to play bridge. We played bridge with other couples, went out to eat together, and enjoyed these times.

Because things looked so different, I had given up on the idea of divorce and thought maybe I should just stay with Jerry. I rarely thought of suicide and felt like I was getting a new lease on life. Perhaps I should say I was getting a life.

We had not been in the Bellaire Circle house but a few months when Jerry and Ken began complaining about the house being too small. Jerry decided he would add on a den.

That "den" turned into a 2000-square-foot addition. I was very irritated with Jerry, but I got out there and helped with the construction. We hired most of the work but did much of it ourselves. I had not left Jerry when I got the chance, so maybe I really did not want to leave.

———◆••———

The years on Bellaire were pretty uneventful. I still was not cured of my depression, but I started playing bridge with Sandra, Joani, Billie, and Bobbie. Bobbie was going through a divorce, and she was really open about it and talked freely about her problems. I admired her ability to openly share intimate little things about how she felt.

133

Billie and Jerry Keeton had a beautiful home in Ridglea Country Club Estates, but when Jerry's business went sour, they sold their house and moved into a smaller place. Joani was still trying to adjust to her new marriage. As time passed, Joani shared some of her problems with me.

If there were ever an opportunity to share my problems, it would have been at that time, but I simply could not open up to anybody. The only problem I was experiencing then was the same sexual problems that developed about eight or ten years into our marriage. This issue was too private and personal to share, and I did not think anybody would understand.

———•••———

Ken began experiencing some difficulties. I had raised the kids alone, as far as discipline was concerned, and Jerry had shown no interest in correcting or teaching, leaving all this up to me. Now that Ken was almost grown, he needed his father to show interest in him beyond just watching him play ball.

One night Ken was required to be home by 10:00 pm, and he came in and went upstairs like he was going to bed. All the rest of the family went to bed.

Then I heard Ken tiptoeing down the stairs and heading across the den; I caught him just as he got to the front door. He was slipping out of the house, so I told him to come back in and go to bed.

I asked Jerry to start assuming some responsibility for raising the kids. I wanted him to talk to Ken and to do more things with him. We had taken a trip with the kids each year, but now Ken needed more.

I was disappointed in Jerry's lack of responsibility for the kids. They loved, respected, and admired their dad, and I had never told them a bad word about him. I always praised their dad, regardless of how I really felt, and I even made excuses when he was not around.

Ken played football at Paschal and was a star player. He was very popular and good-looking. We bought him a Porsche 914 for his graduation present and had always furnished him with a car.

He thought colleges would be standing in line to sign him on the dotted line, but nobody was interested. His playing had deteriorated during his senior year.

He began cutting classes, his girlfriend broke up with him, and all of a sudden, his world fell apart — and he fell apart. It took him several years of wandering before he got both feet on the ground again.

Peggy then changed roles with Ken; now, she was popular. We had bought her a car when she turned sixteen, and she would get her girlfriends in her car on the weekends, and they would go out and have a good time. She had a boyfriend when she needed one to take her to the school dances. She was having a good time, and the future looked bright for her.

I had finally taken a genuine interest in church again. I was not teaching or assuming any area of responsibility. I was attending Carolyn Coggin's Sunday School Class. She is an excellent teacher, and I enjoyed sitting and listening to her.

From time to time through the years, I would mention something to Jerry about becoming a missionary, and he would assure me that he still planned to follow through with that plan.

Our life together was pretty good, even though it was not perfect.

15 The Call Finally Answered

It was December 1978. Jerry and I had, since 1964, planned to go into foreign mission work . . . someday. We had planned to leave our business and change our career, and Jerry had in his mind that we would make this change when the kids got out of college.

Since we started our business in 1964, we knew that if we went into business for ourselves, we would have to plan our own retirement. We had always lived comfortable but conservative lives. I tried to save everything I could out of our personal money so that we would have a little nest egg.

The business had done very well, and we had worked hard and allowed it to grow without taking too many risks. Since we were always under-capitalized, we always had to walk a fine line between success and failure.

———◆◆◆———

We had told the kids that we planned to go into mission work one day, but it never sunk in. They did not understand the impact this decision would have on their lives. We had brought Ken and Peggy up in the church, and they were both Christians but very little different from most other kids.

We had never mentioned our desire to be missionaries to our friends, and they had no idea we had any plans to do anything different with our lives.

We were settled into our home at 3747 Bellaire Circle and attended Travis Avenue Baptist Church in Fort Worth, Texas. Dr. James Coggin was the pastor, and Jerry was serving as Chairman of the deacons. I was president of the Downtown Lady Lions Club. We were heavily involved with church, business, and community activities.

<hr />

On the first Sunday of December, Travis Church always has the Parade of Flags, a service where the missionaries of the Foreign Mission Board are honored, and many flags from all kinds of faraway places our Foreign Mission Board of the Southern Baptist Convention (FMB) missionaries served are paraded in front of the church. Derwood Rowell read the names of the different countries where the FMB had missionaries serving, and there was a flag for each country.

This was always my favorite service, and I wondered if we would ever be serving in one of those countries. We certainly had made little preparation for going.

Then that Sunday morning, after Dr. Coggin concluded his preaching, he asked if anybody in the congregation felt God was calling them into mission work. He asked anybody who felt this "Call" to please come forward and make it public.

When I was 16, I felt this call and always remembered the occasion well. Jerry had never felt a "call" per se; it was just his desire to go.

Something different was happening to us that Sunday morning. I felt this was the right time to go forward and make my commitment public. At the same time, Jerry felt God was calling him to commit, too.

Much to Dr. Coggin's surprise, we both went forward. Our friends were shocked and did not understand, and they could not believe that we would give up our business to go to the mission field.

Jerry felt sure this was our time.

First thing Monday morning, he got on the phone and called the FMB and said, "Where do you want me to go?" They did not know what to say, so they transferred him to someone in the enlistment department. They asked Jerry many questions, then explained that he had to follow specific procedures before being allowed to go with the FMB.

First, Jerry had to have a degree, and I had to have about 60 hours of college credit. Jerry did not have a degree, and I did not have any college credit. Then they said we would have to write our life history. We would have to pass a physical and a psychological analysis. We would have to furnish a lot of references. We would have to go to orientation, and the list went on and on.

By the time Jerry got off the phone, he was frustrated. All he wanted to do was go to some foreign country, obey God's call, and serve him. Why was the FMB making such a fuss? Hadn't his successful business career counted for anything? Hadn't his years of faithful service in the church counted for anything? He was totally opposed to what the FMB was trying to do. After all, we were not a couple of kids just starting out.

The FMB told us about their "Associate Plan" for people over 39. This plan was the same as the "Career Plan," with a few exceptions. There were no benefits for the children of Associates, and Associates would not be required to have the same foreign language proficiency.

Jerry talked to several board members and let them know he did not like their plan and didn't want to have to go back to college. After all, we were both 44 years old!

Peggy was a senior in high school, and Ken was in college. The kids made few comments regarding our decision; we did not ask what they thought, and they did not volunteer their feelings.

A few days after talking to the board, Jerry went to Dr. Coggin with his complaint. Dr. Coggin then called Dr. Baker James Cauthin, President of the FMB. Then Dr. Cauthin called Jerry and told him that the board would waive the request for a college degree.

Then they began to talk to us about where we wanted to go. We learned that Ethiopia, Ivory Coast, and Malawi all needed business managers.

For some reason, we zeroed in on Malawi. We had never heard of Malawi and could not locate it in our old-world books. Then we learned that it was the former Nyasaland of Africa. We talked more to the board about Malawi.

Jerry had jokingly told our friends that he heard God calling him to Switzerland, where he could ski. (The Encyclopedia Britannica referred to Malawi as "the Switzerland of Africa.") We felt that, in some way, God had a sense of humor. And at the same time, Malawi seemed to be where we were supposed to go.

They were asking us to go as business managers, but Malawi had a request for a printer, and they kept asking Jerry about printing. Since our company name was Copy & Litho, they thought Jerry was a printer.

Then Jerry would ask them what kind of printing equipment they had in Malawi, and the board did not have the faintest idea what they used in Malawi. Then Jerry got very insulting and criticized them for not knowing about their assets.

Finally, Jerry said, "I will just go to Malawi and find out what printing equipment you own. This declaration took them completely by surprise. We had already gotten out of the normal loop of things, and this was just too much.

The board told Jerry that such a visit would be impossible because it would require a visa and airline ticket — and the missionaries would have to be notified and agree to his coming.

Jerry said, "OK! I will take care of the visa and airline ticket, and you take care of the missionaries." So, within a week, we booked the ticket and got a visa from the Malawian Embassy in Washington, DC.

Jerry called the board back and said, "I have the tickets and visa in hand. Do you have approval from the mission?"

There was dead silence from the other end of the line. Obviously, they had not taken Jerry seriously — it had never been done that way. After a long pause, they told Jerry they would get on it.

By the time the board called back with our approval to visit Malawi, Jerry had begun to have second thoughts. What if the mission felt Jerry had to pull strings to get there, and we had come in the back door? The more he thought about it, the more he realized he was probably making a mistake.

In the meantime, we had already checked with Texas Christian University and Tarrant County Junior College, both in Fort Worth. And we had checked with Dallas Baptist University about enrolling in their schools.

We learned that Dallas Baptist University had a plan where you could take a four-hour course and write your life experience with documentation proving that you had specific abilities. Then the college would give you up to 30 hours of credit for work experience. This sounded like an excellent idea because we had acquired a lot of work experience.

Jerry then called the board back and said we needed to cancel our trip to Malawi. He had decided we should go to college, and if we went to Malawi, we would not return in time to start classes. (The last thing we needed to do was start classes a week late after not being in school for over 20 years.) So, we started college.

At the same time, the board put us in the loop so that we could go through the normal channels to be appointed associate missionaries. Occasionally, they would send us the paperwork, and we would fill it out and return it.

———•••———

Only my trust in God gave me the self-confidence to go to college. We each enrolled in about 21 hours. We were to write this book on our experiences that said, "I have the ability, knowledge, and skills" to do certain things that could be applied to specific college courses. Besides that, we enrolled in a couple of classes at Tarrant County Jr. College.

We indeed must have been crazy.

Jerry was determined to get his degree in one year, and I was to get 72 hours in a year. Dallas Baptist University (DBU) accepted 26 hours of credit from Jerry's previous college experience. Jerry felt sure that if we went to DBU day and night school and Tarrant County Junior College (TCJC), we could fulfill our requirements in one year.

Jerry promoted a sales employee to be the new manager of Copy & Litho. Jerry would go in on Friday afternoons and sign checks and answer questions; other than that, Copy & Litho would be the manager's.

———•••———

We started college in January 1979. On Saturdays, I would wash, iron, clean the house, and cook casseroles so that Peggy and Ken could warm things up when they wanted something to eat.

We would get up early in the morning and study on our way to school. We would attend classes, then stay at school and study until our next class. Then we would attend our night classes and get home at about 10:00 pm most every night.

We would write and take our papers to a typist, Vickie Kindig. She was excellent. She would type, we would make our corrections, she would retype, and we would turn in our work. Without Vickie, we would not have been able to get through all that work. We kept her busy almost full-time. She was indeed a gift from heaven, and we never gave her full credit for all her expert assistance.

Peggy was left alone but was busy with school activities and not at home much anyway. She never complained and did not seem to mind that we were gone so much.

We were credited 30 hours for our "work experience," but that was no "gimme." Since my work at Copy & Litho was as an owner, there was no "employer" to write the required letters of recommendation to describe my abilities. I wound up asking lawyers, suppliers, accountants, and associates to write letters about their work with me on specific projects and situations.

I was able to locate a man I had worked closely with at Burroughs Corporation, and he was willing to write a letter for me. I am not sure he remembered me, but I told him what I did, how long I worked for Burroughs, and who I worked with, and he wrote this documentation.

Some people from Travis Church also wrote documentation regarding certain books I had studied. Bro. Emmett Hunt, our former pastor, wrote a letter regarding my completed study materials. Dr. Coggin wrote letters for both of us.

I asked for credit on everything from sewing to accounting. I completed my notebook and filled it with many pages, including all kinds of reports I did at Copy & Litho and copies of the financial statements I compiled. I had wracked my brain to collect all the knowledge I had acquired since graduating from high school.

After Jerry and I completed our notebooks, we learned the name of the man who would review them. We took them to him personally and shared with him what we had done in our lives so far — and our plans for the future. When his evaluation came back, he gave each of us the crucial 30 hours of credit we hoped and prayed for.

———•••———

I remember the first test I took after starting college. It was in Miss Bumgarner's business correspondence class. She was a genuine "Old Maid Teacher" in every way. She had a sense of humor but was very serious about perfection.

When I went in to take the test, I thought I was prepared. It was not a very long test; we had only been in college for about a week. After I walked out of the class, I could not remember a question on the test, and I could not remember what I answered when Jerry quizzed me about my answers. I blanked out and was sure I had failed the test.

When I attended the following few classes, Miss Bumgarner did not look at me. I was sure she was embarrassed for me because I had done so poorly on the test. I became quite upset.

Jerry said I was being ridiculous and suggested (or I should say he insisted) I go see Miss Bumgarner and find out about the test. So, I did.

I asked Miss Bumgarner if she had graded the paper and explained my feelings. She said she had graded the paper but did not recall me making a bad grade. She then looked up the grade, and I missed only one question! I was so relieved. That was the last time I blanked out on a test, and I am sure the Holy Spirit must have helped me through it.

We finished Spring Semester and signed up for summer classes, including a speech class at Tarrant County Junior College. The teacher, Mr. Willkie, had an unusually deep voice, and he was quite small, so it was always a surprise to look at him and then hear such a resounding voice.

Mr. Willkie gave us several different topics for the different types of speeches we were to give. Then one day, he told us that we were also to give a speech about anything we desired.

Young people of many nationalities comprised our class; Jerry and I were the only old folks. We sat close to the front because we both had hearing loss and didn't want to miss anything said.

Several black students gave speeches about witchcraft, which I found very interesting. I did not know that anybody really believed in poking needles in dolls and witchcraft, so this was a real eye-opener. (I would have expected this in Malawi but not the USA!)

Then a lovely black girl came forward, stood right in front of me, and laid a small brown paper bag on my desk. (I had to look straight up at her because she was so close.) She proceeded to say that she wanted to give her speech on the proper use of condoms.

Several people in the class snickered, but she never cracked a smile — she was dead serious. She first explained why condoms should be used, then explained how they should be used, and went into great detail.

Then she reached over and picked up the little brown paper bag from my desk and pulled a long, unrolled condom from the bag. (I think I gasped, even though I was trying very hard to stay objective.) She exhibited the condom, rolled it up, and talked more about how it must be used properly and why it must be used.

To wrap things up, she showed all the different kinds of condoms available, including red, gold, iridescent, and even some that glowed in the dark, called "The Glow Worm." (And I thought they were all just plain white!) Boy, did I get an education. She gave an excellent speech and held my attention as well as everybody else's in the class.

At the end of her speech, she opened it up for discussion, and the next lesson I learned came when all the girls in the class opened their purses and pulled out the condoms they carried around with them. Most of the boys remained relatively quiet, but the girls were happy to announce their preparedness.

I had never carried a condom in my life, and I had no idea girls carried such things — I thought boys carried them. I'm sure I sat there with my eyes bugged out as I learned this lesson on American culture.

That speech class turned out to be the most interesting class I took, and I learned more about American young people from that class than I could have imagined. I taught young people and worked with them in church —and I had two teenage children myself— so I thought I was pretty savvy. However, I learned quickly that I was like a turtle with its head in its shell — I was totally ignorant of my surroundings.

We had a psychology class at TCJC. Our teacher was a woman, and it was evident from the beginning that she was pulling for me. I enjoyed psychology, read everything in detail, and tried to remember everything. Jerry was not as interested in psychology, but he studied just as hard because he said he did not know how hard to study to get a "C" instead of an "A."

When we went to the room to take our final exam, three classes of first-year psychology students filled the large room. The three teachers sat at the front of the room. As we walked into the room, our teacher motioned for us to come over to where she was sitting. She said if we brought our tests to her when we finished, she would grade them and let us know our grade.

When we finished, we took our papers to our teacher. That afternoon we went by her office, and sure enough, she had our papers graded. Jerry had a 97, and I had a 98. (I could see she was delighted I had made a better grade than Jerry.) I am sure if Jerry's paper had been better than mine, she would have tried to find a way to grade his paper down.

We had a history teacher who supported us, but it was easy to see that he wanted Jerry to beat me. Jerry and I would just laugh. I never felt competitive with Jerry, and I don't think he competed with me, but for some reason, some of the teachers liked to pit us against each other.

By the end of the year, I had 76 hours of credit, and Jerry had 96 hours. He had "clepped out" of about 14 hours that I had not been able to do, and he took a couple of extra courses (on Revelations and something else) that made the difference.

We could never have completed those 76 or 96 hours on our own. We truly give God all the credit for helping us. I made an "A" in every subject except for a "B" in English, even though I made a 29 (out of a possible 30) on the final exam. I had trouble with the nervousness of the teacher, who talked non-stop when we were writing or taking a test — I could not listen to him and take a test at the same time.

Jerry made an "A" in everything except Revelation (he made a "B" in that subject) because he and his teacher had different perspectives and beliefs in the interpretation. It was hard for Jerry to answer questions the way the professor believed.

All in all, we had no right to complain. We worked hard, and it paid off. We were pretty proud of ourselves. (I even got a certificate for being Summa Cum Laude.)

Jerry had one more class to complete before graduating, so the next semester, he signed up for that class. At last, he had the hours required for a degree. It was all a miracle.

———•••———

On the night of Jerry's graduation, several of our friends went to watch him walk across the platform and move his hat's tassel from one side to the other. They told us not to applaud as the students crossed the platform, but our friends decided that when Jerry walked across, we would applaud anyway.

The school president called out "Jerry Dowdy," and I stood and applauded — but nobody else stood or applauded with me. (The president just grinned and went on.) It was a long time coming, but Jerry finally had his degree, and we were both proud of it.

This little piece of paper says so much about our society. It confirmed Jerry's accomplishment and declared him "educated." Whether he had learned anything new or not, he had validation that now he was educated.

Our education made us officially acceptable to the FMB and to the countries that might choose to grant us a work permit (or decide to deny the request). This little piece of paper was proof that we could help their people.

———•••———

During that year, we sent names to the FMB as references, wrote our entire life history — and then tore it up and told the FMB only what we wanted them to know.

Writing things from our past was a real eye-opener. Jerry wrote about many hurtful things from his childhood that he had not considered in years. As he wrote these personal and private things he had never shared with anybody, he cried several times. Even though the board never received these details, this experience was very cleansing for us.

They only wanted five pages, but it is hard to condense your life into five pages when you are 44 years old. Jerry had written six pages by the time he was six, so it became apparent that he would have to condense things considerably.

I was not quite so long-winded with all the details; still, it was difficult even to hit the high points in just five pages. They had five different topics which we were to write about, one page each.

We had completed our education and fulfilled all the FMB requirements, and at last, we were ready to go. However, God knew that some things would happen to keep us in the States a little longer — and that the kids needed us to be at home with them for another year.

16 New Building for Copy & Litho

Copy & Litho was located on Chambers Street at the Old Dallas/ Fort Worth Turnpike. The location was great in many ways, but it left much to be desired in other ways.

It was near downtown Fort Worth and convenient to all the freeways. It was near the "Mixmaster" interchange at the east end of Fort Worth, so the service technicians could quickly reach most of our customers.

This part of town was run down, and that was a problem. A rescue mission had been built on the corner one block away, and many of Fort Worth's down-and-out people stayed nearby. There was a black church across the street, and they were always good neighbors.

If we went by our office at night, finding a group of call girls gathered on our front porch was not unusual. This use of our property after hours did not sit well with me. It did not seem right for our property to be part of the solicitation of prostitution.

Nevertheless, we decided to double our space because we needed additional space, and the building had 3,500 square feet. We also bought the five connecting lots, also terribly run down, strewn with old tires and rubbish. Despite the drawbacks, we purchased the lots, hired a builder, and began construction on the additional space.

This unexpected project all happened about the same time we decided to go into missions and leave Copy & Litho. We initially thought Copy & Litho would not need additional space with us gone. Little did we know what was going on.

When the construction was coming to its final stage, and just before making the last payment to the contractor, the Texas Highway Department sent a notice stating that a new freeway interchange was about to replace the old "Mix Master," and this construction would require our property. Our building was condemned.

We were up to our eyeballs with college and getting paperwork for the FMB. We could not believe we would be out of an office building, but we knew fighting the Highway Department was no use.

We hurriedly contacted the Highway Department to determine the procedures for collecting damages and reimbursement. We knew buying other property would cost more than we had invested in our current location.

The biggest hurdle was exorbitant interest rates. (This was 1980, and interest rates were around 20%)

We set out looking for a building that already existed. We looked and looked but could not find anything suitable. We found 4 1/2 lots on the Airport Freeway. The location was great, but the cost was considerably more than the value of our current property.

While reading through the papers from the Highway Department regarding condemnation rights, I noticed it said we would be entitled to a loan with a lower interest rate from the Small Business Administration.

Jerry called a friend who had been dealing with the Highway Department regarding Forrest Park being closed for so long in front of his steak house.

He told Jerry he had dealt with a man in Congressman Jim Wright's office, and he gave Jerry a lot of helpful information for knowing how to get started.

After receiving our guidelines for getting a loan (The new building could only be 20% larger than the condemned property), we learned we should qualify. We contacted an architect and got him busy creating drawings. The building would be limited to the two lots facing Highway 121. Jerry wanted to construct the largest building the lot would hold because the property was valuable. The architect came up with a two-story building that had 15,000 square feet.

148

We had to negotiate with the highway department regarding the costs of reprinting our stationery showing a new address and notifying customers of our change of location. Then our phone system seemed expensive and complicated — it had come a long way from the single line we started with in 1964.

Jerry continued to work with Jim Wright's Office, and they were extremely helpful in getting what we needed. The Lord had led us to the information we needed and the people we needed to talk to. It was an additional problem, but we knew this new location would be considerably better.

It all worked out beautifully. The Small Business Administration approved the loan that allowed us to double the size of our building. We scraped together every cent we could come up with to purchase the property and pay for one-third of the building's construction cost. (We even got the cash value from our insurance policies and cashed in Certificates of Deposit.) When we got every cent compiled, we had exactly enough money; we did not have a thousand dollars left over.

It took everything we had, but Copy & Litho was still intact. We had never gotten personal business mixed with corporate business. The building belonged to us personally, and we wanted the new building to belong to us personally. We got everything approved and were ready to start construction by mid-1981. (Jerry finished college in 1980.)

———•••———

After Jerry graduated, he did not want to remain in Fort Worth, where he would be too close to Copy & Litho, since he had already turned the day-to-day operations over to the manager.

Our home on Bellaire Circle was up for sale, but nobody was interested in purchasing it. (The way we added to the property did not make it any more saleable.) Property in Fort Worth was selling for a premium, but with high interest rates, real estate was moving slowly.

We decided to move to the farm. We read in the paper about a house in Denison for sale, and we surmised that we could move it to the farm and live in it for the next year until we were ready to go to the mission field.

We did not give much thought to all that would be required. (Having a house on the farm instead of town is quite different.) If "ignorance is bliss," then we were truly blissful.

First, there had to be a foundation for the house and then underpinning once the house was set on the foundation. Then we had to build and rock a road to the house. We had to run almost half a mile of electric lines to get electricity to the house. Then there would need to be a septic tank, a butane tank, and a water well with a pump.

Before moving the house, they removed the bricks from the fireplace, so we had to construct a new fireplace. And, of course, there was no front or back porch, so we had a cement front porch and steps built — and enough cement poured in the back to accommodate a two-car garage.

The house was in fairly rough condition — added onto at least three times. The first section was constructed in 1923. So, with all this construction going on in Fort Worth and all our money tied up, we were more or less camping in a frame 1923 house.

Jerry said that he would do most of the work himself. So, we put a mattress on the floor and camped out in the house. One morning before I climbed out of bed, I found a dead mouse in the bed with me. Then another morning, the telephone man came and was going to install a phone right where we had the mattress thrown on the floor.

Just as I squatted down to the floor where the phone man was working, a mouse ran across the bed and across the phone man's foot. I did not say a word, and he didn't either. I told Jerry I felt we needed to close the hole in the floor and wall the brick fireplace once covered. Jerry got some plywood and covered the holes in the floor and wall so maybe the mice could not get in.

I cooked using only a griddle, a crock pot, and an electric skillet. (If I could survive this, I surmised, the mission field should be a snap.) We first did not have running water hooked up to the house, so we took our baths with the water hose out on the back drive. The water coming from 185 feet underground was ice cold. (We waited until nightfall so the neighbors would not be exposed to our nudity.) I learned to lay out a length of water hose during the day so it would get hot in the sun, and as soon as possible in the evenings, I would bathe so that the water would warm up a little in the hose.

Little by little, we got the house into livable condition. It seemed that working on houses was our forte. First, the Ryan Place house, then the Bellaire Circle house addition, and now this farmhouse. (How in the world did I allow myself to get into these messes?)

150

This is taken from a letter I wrote Peggy on September 5, 1980.

"Dear Peggy,
Here is more exciting farm news.
The Moore's dog killed a coon. Your Daddy beat a tarantula to death
with a broom.
We poured poison into another big red ant bed, and we saw a
coyote, five rabbits, and an armadillo.
Every afternoon it sounds like war just broke out. Dove and quail
season opened this week, and hunters are everywhere. So much for
the animal kingdom.
Is God preparing me for Africa or what?"

———•••———

I painted the inside of the house and made drapes for the windows.
Jerry worked on the plumbing and electrical wiring. Jerry did not like the
squeaking floors, so he spent days under the house redoing the flooring.

The bathroom was a mess, but little could be done to it short of
tearing it all out and starting over, so I just painted it, and we made do.

When we got the house to the point where we could move our
furniture in, we decided what we wanted to take to Africa, and that is
what we moved to the farm. Peggy had graduated from high school and
got an apartment with Allison Hahnfeld, so she took some furniture. We
helped Ken with a down payment on a house, and he took some of the
furniture, too. Getting rid of all our furniture seemed to work out pretty
well, and we did not have to dispose of too many things. By the time we
got the house fixed up, it was almost time for us to go to orientation.

———•••———

They continued the construction on the Office Building while we
were living up at the farm and during the time we were at orientation.
The building was actually finished after we went to Malawi, but I think
the office, inventory, and business moved into the new building on the
first weekend in January 1982, just as we were getting ready to leave.

Although the open house event was several months after we left, we saw the building almost completed before we left. We were delighted with its appearance.

When we left for Malawi, we asked our neighbor, Bob Moore, if he would look after our farmhouse. He said he would try to rent it out and keep it rented for us while we were gone. As it turned out, he kept the house rented almost all the whole time. It did not bring in much money, but enough to keep it from completely falling down or deteriorating as empty houses tend to do. The rental of the farmhouse worked out fine. Even though it was probably a mistake, it seemed to turn out OK.

So, the Copy & Litho building construction turned out fine, even though we had to stay in the States for an additional year. As it turned out, God knew that the kids were not ready for us to leave, and they needed us to be at home for another year. This delay helped them get settled and adjust to the idea that we would not be around to help them.

17 Orienting for Mission

During the year, we had time to reflect on our world and our universe and the significance of God. As we thought of the expanse of God's creation, we tended to feel small and insignificant. We knew this feeling was a cop-out if we allowed it to rob us of the joys of service and the love of God.

While on the farm, we could see the stars and moon shining brightly. We could hear the coyotes howl at night and the birds singing in the morning. Jerry bought an old bulldozer and worked the land. He smoothed the erosion, planted grass, and fertilized the ground, and we could see God's handy work. As the rains came, the earth was refreshed, and when spring arrived, Indian Paintbrush carpeted the field. What once was brown became a lush green.

We had time to get in touch with our feelings. We attended Sadler Baptist Church, which has such a rich heritage. Many of its leaders were once on the staff at Sadler Baptist Church. Jerry and Bobbie Rankin, president of the Foreign Mission Board, once pastored the little congregation. We got back to the grassroots of God's leadership in that small Baptist Congregation. The people at Sadler were warm and friendly, and it turned out to be a blessed year.

It was August 1981, and the time had come for us to attend Orientation. We were accepted and appointed as missionaries in June 1981.

We packed the few belongings we wanted to take to Malawi, and they were in storage crates, ready for us to approve shipping. Because shipping approval required our work permit, we knew it would probably be nine months before we saw our belongings again. Little did we realize it would be 16 months. (Had I known that, I would not have packed oatmeal for the weevils.)

After packing, we headed for Calloway Gardens in Georgia for Orientation. I had driven a Cadillac for years; that was our only car. We felt a little self-conscious going to Orientation in a Cadillac, but I don't think anybody noticed except us.

We were the next to last group to go to Calloway Gardens for a 13-week orientation. (After us, they decided 13 weeks was too long and unnecessary, and I wholeheartedly agreed.)

While at Orientation, we read books about our country, Malawi. We studied its culture, and we learned everything possible about the people. We watched movies about other missionaries' lives and analyzed the possible mistakes we might make.

One thing we did was play games to teach us how to get along with the other missionaries. One game was supposed to teach us about mission meetings, and what I got from that was that if you wanted anything, you better go prepared to fight for it. This game did us a great disservice because the Malawi mission did not bicker or fight at mission meetings. (I always laughingly said they did not have enough money to fight over.!)

We took a linguistics class that everybody thought was ridiculous. We learned what a bi-labial-fricative is (you put your two lips together and blow until your lips flap together; we actually learned this at six months of age — we just did not know what to call it.)

We stayed in a little A-Frame house made of cedar or pine. Tall pine trees overpowered and engulfed our surroundings. Magnolia trees grew wild with wild holly shrubs as tall as trees. Two thousand acres provided adequate space. The colorful fall leaves fell around the lake, which reflected a rainbow of colors.

Two new missionaries were riding their bicycles on the little road before daylight, and they collided and were injured. The men enjoyed the three golf courses; Jerry even found time to play regularly.

Charles and Gayla Corley were at Orientation with us. We met them at the candidate conference and saw them at the appointment service, but at Orientation, we became very close friends. They also played bridge, so we got together frequently on the weekends for bridge or meals.

Tom and Jeanie Eliff, who later became president of the Southern Baptist Convention, were in our orientation group. Although everybody was expected to be there for every session, Tom had a lot of other commitments. (He stayed busy preaching and speaking in different churches.) When Tom returned to Orientation, he worked hard to catch up. (He did not like linguistics any better than anybody else.)

The Eliffs, the Corleys, Nancy Carley, and Pam King were all appointed to Zimbabwe, and Janie House was appointed to Zambia. Since all of us were going to the same part of Africa, we made friends.

Our orientation group of 185 was the largest group ever appointed up to that time. We had people going worldwide to share the love of Jesus Christ. In all, the FMB had about 3,300 Career and Associate missionaries serving, the largest Protestant mission force in the world at that time. (Since then, a few larger groups have been appointed at one time, however.) We had a good time at Orientation, and I suppose it prepared us for missionary life. We came home for about a week and Thanksgiving and then drove back to Pine Mountain, Georgia, to our Calloway Garden home.

The week before we were to complete our Orientation, we had Princess, our dog, flown out to see us. We were not supposed to have pets, so we had to keep her hidden. We wanted to see how she would fare riding an airplane, and we hated to fly her all the way to Malawi without trying her out on a short flight first. (I guess this was silly, but I really loved Princess.)

She was a small mixed Terrier with short hair that was mostly tan with some white areas. Her eyes bulged out just a little, and her tail made a full curl. We got her at the Fort Worth City Pound. When we went to the pound to look at dogs, she barked and begged us so desperately to take her home with us, and we could not resist her. She was Peggy's dog, but Princess and I were best buddies.

Princess stayed by my side during the good times and the bad times. She slept by my side when I was depressed and felt like I did not have a friend in the world. When I felt like nobody in my family loved me, Princess wagged her tail, kissed me on the face at every opportunity, and was my shadow.

She arrived from her flight just fine. She was so glad to see us. Gayla and Charles would sneak her leftovers. Others would bring food over for her, and she became Queen of the Household in no time, even though she was smuggled in.

18 Into Africa

With our 13-week orientation behind us, we packed up and returned to Fort Worth for our last Christmas in the States with the family. We stayed with Ken for a few days and had Christmas at his house.

On January 13, 1982, with all the requirements completed for the Foreign Mission Board of the Southern Baptist Convention, we were prepared and ready for departure. With our bags packed into the car, Ken, Jerry, Princess, and I climbed in and headed to the Dallas/Fort Worth International Airport. We were exceptionally quiet.

We checked our bags and kept Princess in her kennel with us. Arvil and Pauline came to the airport to say goodbye. Pauline could hardly hold back the tears and was not a woman to show her emotions very often. Peggy was there, as well.

We were supposed to fly into Chicago, but the airport was snowed in. We were supposed to leave at about 8:00 am. We eventually learned we would be rerouted to fly directly into New York to connect to South African Airways.

After waiting with us at the airport for several hours, the family started to leave. It was late afternoon when we finally departed, and they needed to de-ice our plane's wings before we could go.

We had mixed feeling about leaving. On the one hand, we were excited and glad; on the other, we hated leaving our family, especially Ken and Peggy.

———•••———

Peering out the window, we watched as we left Texas, and soon we were flying over Lake Texoma and Oklahoma. A blanket of snow covered the area, and our emotions tumbled as we sat quietly. We checked Princess to go to New York, and from there, we would pick her up and pay her way to Malawi.

Our flight arrived in New York in the worst snowstorm of the season. We were in one terminal and had to double back to South Africa's Terminal. I stayed and collected Princess while Jerry went upstairs to hail a cab. Jerry stuck a twenty-dollar bill into the driver's hand, and he jumped out of his car, raised the hood, and told Jerry to hurry.

Jerry came rushing back down to me as I was collecting Princess. The taxi jumped the median strip as soon as we were loaded and headed back to the terminal just across the bridge. We were in the South Africa terminal within five minutes, trying to check in. The attendant said they already gave our seats away, but there was one seat up front and one in the back. She said that she would take the dog and get her on the plane and that we could pay for her when we got to Malawi.

We dashed onto the plane, and the door shut behind us. Snow was everywhere. We located our seats and then started looking for Charles and Gayla Corley. They feared we would not make the flight, and we were exhausted and relieved. Then the plane sat there and sat there. The snow was three feet deep on the wings, so they had to de-ice them. (If I had known then what I know now, I would have climbed off the plane and waited for the weather to change.) Finally, we began taxiing down the runway and were off for an 18-hour flight.

The only stop we made was on the Cape Verde islands to refuel. We were able to stretch our legs and use the bathroom. I don't think there was anything to buy, not even candy or a drink. We got back on the plane, and after a few hours, we landed in Johannesburg, South Africa. We went through immigration, and as we went by the carrousel, there was Princess, going around. She saw us, and we went over and collected her, even though she was checked straight through to Malawi.

The Corleys arranged to stay at a Baptist guest home, and we booked a hotel room. We tried to get Princess to relieve herself when we arrived, but she refused. She had not dirtied her cage, and it had been almost 24 hours since she had taken care of her business. Jerry tucked her under his coat, and we rushed up the elevator to our room.

After we were in the room for a couple of hours, Princess needed to go outside, so Jerry dressed and walked her down the street until they found a little grass, and she finally went. The street was dark, and Jerry did not know if it was safe for him to be out in the middle of the night walking around; he felt apprehensive, to say the least. The bed was a welcome sight, and we slept soundly.

Jean Frank took us to the airport the next day. When we got to the check-in, lights began to go off, and bells began to ring. We were already jumpy and still had not paid Princess' airfare. What in the world had happened?

Everybody stepped back from us like we were criminals. A man who looked very official came up to us and said, "I am very sorry, madam, but we have lost your dog."

I felt so relieved. "Oh! No," I said, "we have our dog. We saw her going round and round, so we took her with us."

The man looked mad at us for getting the dog. "We have been looking for that dog all night," he said.

I apologized profusely. He was so mad at us. He told us that we would have to take the dog over to the veterinary terminal and check her in there so they could put her on the plane.

Jerry took Princess, caught a taxi, checked her in, grabbed another cab, and headed back to our departure terminal. (I began to wonder if he would get back in time.) We had left frigid cold weather and a snow-blanketed America, and when we arrived in South Africa, it was mid-summer. At last, Jerry got back, wringing wet with sweat.

Within three or four hours, we were landing in Blantyre, Malawi. Jerry Spires and Van Thompson met us at the airport and took us to the Baptist guest house.

Malawi looked pretty nice. The rains had everything lush green, and the hot pink Bougainvillea and other flowers were in full bloom everywhere.

On the way from the airport, people were walking beside the road. Some were carrying bundles of wood and other things on their heads. People kicked up dust as they walked barefoot. Most of the women had babies on their backs, and another one by the hand, and other children were trailing. Young men, older men, and all ages in between walked. There were also several cars on the road.

We rested in our apartment for a while, and then we were picked up and taken to Ernest and Audie Sibley's house for dinner. All the Blantyre missionaries were there. Besides the Sibleys, the Spires, the Thompsons, we met Doris and Carl Houston, Mary Ann Chandler, and a young male volunteer.

We felt welcomed into the Mission, and everybody seemed really nice. We got back to our apartment and went to bed. Within a couple of hours, we were awakened by a knock on our door and all this shouting in another language. (We could not understand a single word!) They were dressed in green uniforms; we thought they were probably the police or military. We sent them across the courtyard to the house where the volunteer lived.

The next morning, we learned what happened. The volunteer came to the guest house gate, and the night watchman was asleep, and the volunteer took his stick away from him, and he never woke up. When the inspector came by, the watchman did not have his stick; he was in big trouble because he was caught sleeping on the job. Someone told a story that once a volunteer came in and took the pants off of the watchman, and he never awoke. This was our introduction to our new country.

———••———

We learned that our bags had not made it onto the plane in New York due to the lack of time, but Princess had arrived in Malawi just fine. On the way back to Lilongwe, we stopped in Zomba, and a man got into the car. He needed a ride to Lilongwe, and Gerald Workman, our advisor, knew him. His name was Fletcher Kaiya, and he was nice-looking, well-dressed, and spoke English perfectly.

Jerry and I arrived at the apartment where we would live until Jerry could build us a house. We thought we would spend one year studying the language, but the Mission assumed we would not want to learn Chichewa.

———•••———

We soon learned that Jerry (Dowdy) would be the business manager in Lilongwe, and Jerry Spires, would be the business manager in Blantyre. We were expected to run Baptist Printing and Publications (referred to as "Publications"). This was the first we had heard about our assignment, but we didn't question it — we just decided to try to be cooperative with the Mission. Also, during the first three months, we were to visit the six mission stations.

Jerry and I had terrible jet lag and could hardly stay awake in the afternoon. Gerald started teaching us Chichewa in the morning. Then he took us around to the different stations to meet all the missionaries.

One day, a young little Malawian man came by and said he was hungry and wanted a job. He looked like he needed work. I was not responsible for the grass, but I hired him to cut grass. One of the workers came to me and said that "Godfrey" could not cut grass because he was too weak. So, I gave him something to eat and told him he could help me in the house.

After lunch one day, I sat on the couch to study my Chichewa and asked Godfrey to sit beside me and help me read. It was hot and I began to get sleepy and would stretch and yawn. I told Godfrey I was sleepy. We started studying again, and Godfrey scooted a little closer to me. (I just thought that he wanted to see the book better.) Again, I yawned, and Godfrey scooted a little closer. I told him I would have to stop studying and go to bed.

He scooted even nearer me.

This time my eyes flew wide open, and I jumped up off the couch, realizing that what Godfrey thought was not what I was thinking. I looked at him and said," I think you better go home." I thought, Oh my gosh. I haven't been in the country for a month, and they will send me home for sexual immorality.

The next morning, Godfrey came in and began to apologize.

I stopped him and said, "No, it was my fault. I stepped across a cultural barrier, which was my fault."

He seemed so relieved.
We never mentioned this incident again.

———•••———

J.R. and Georgia Heriford were volunteers who lived in the duplex beside us. J.R. was a printer, but he did not know much about business. He also helped work on the cars. The Malawian people seemed to really love J.R. and Georgia.

I started riding to Publications with J.R. each morning to work. J.R. had tried to make a financial statement, giving me a pretty good idea of Publications' financial situation. I started by taking an inventory, setting up the accounts payable and receivable, and signing onto the bank account.

Publications had a debt of about $3,000, which was a lot. I presented the bankrupt financial statement to the Mission, and they were unsurprised. I watched everything J.R. did as far as the printing. (I knew nothing about printing; printing is very different from copy machines. Nevertheless, they expected us to know about printing.) Jerry had a three-week course on printing in New York, so he understood the fundamentals. We also sold some little printing presses at one time.

The printer that J.R. had worked with for a year came into the office, drunk as a skunk. He was falling around and shooting off his mouth. Gerald Workman told him he was fired, which made J.R. angry because he had put a year of training into the man and now there was no experienced printer.

Barnwell Chakawanira was already working for us, so J.R. began to train him. There was no translator, so no new books could be printed until someone translated them. Fletcher Kayia, who had quit working for the French embassy, came by and wanted a job, so Gerald hired him as a translator. He was excellent.

I had just got my teeth into my work. When typing on my electric typewriter, my fingers were sweating so badly that they slid off the keys. (I set up a small fan, which helped a little.) I had assumed the responsibility of being the Publications advisor until Jerry could spend more time helping out. (He was busy building us a house.)

———•••———

162

Then, when things were working smoothly again, trouble popped up. I walked into the room where Fletcher was supposed to be translating, but he was not there. I asked some of the employees where he was. They told me he was over at the Bible School translating for Sam Upton, one of the other missionaries. The Bible School and Publications were on the same compound, only about 100 yards apart.

Sam came up to Publications, and I asked him about taking Fletcher. I told him that Fletcher worked for me, and I did not appreciate him taking him. After all, his salary was being paid by Publications. Sam got red-faced and really mad at me. He was not accustomed to being confronted by another missionary, especially one who had only been there a few months.

I told him his actions were worse than those in the business world.

"I will report you to the Executive Committee," he said.

"I hope you do," I replied. "I think they will understand my position."

He stomped out of my office.

The next morning, Sam returned to my office and apologized. (I don't know if he reported me to the E. C., but he probably did.)

Sam said he wanted to use Fletcher for half a day, and I could use him for half a day.

"No," I said, "I need a translator all day."

As it turned out, Sam got Fletcher all day and started paying him, which meant we were out of a translator again.

I don't know what Gerald thought about this, but he got busy and found another translator who was not as good as Fletcher. (Occasionally, the missionaries would complain about our translation, but Sam never did.)

After this was over, it was over. I had no hard feelings toward Sam, and Sam always treated me with respect. When I think of my and Jerry's business background, we were a different breed of missionary. They learned right off the bat that Jerry and I knew how to hold our ground, and we were not afraid of the E.C. or any missionaries. We wanted to do what was right and tried to get along with everybody. So, I did the best I could with the printing and publishing. We printed thousands and thousands of "tracts" (pocket-sized pamphlets sharing the gospel message), Women's Books, Sunday School Books, Bible Way Books, and Theological Education Books. We even started printing for Government agencies. Soon Baptist Printing and

Publications got its operation making money. Jerry was responsible for getting many government jobs that paid well.

19 Building Our Malawi Home

We were assigned a plot of land, almost an acre, purchased in Lilongwe City Center, Area 43, to build ourselves a house. The houses in front, across the street, were lovely small-brick homes.

The land had been open terrain, never cultivated. There were several trees — some nice and large, and others created thick underbrush. The lot was on the high side of the street, and it was a lovely place for us to make our nest.

Jerry had applied for building permits — and now they had been granted — so there were many things to do. Jerry would act as the contractor. He began by hiring a supervisor to oversee the details. (Since Jerry's Chichewa was limited, someone had to give the workers instructions they understood.)

Wayne and Bertie Paul were construction volunteers. Jerry and Wayne located the brick material. Wayne was also in charge of the Singa Bay Medical Clinic, which was also under construction. The Clinic was quite a large project, and Wayne had acquired good experience in getting construction work done in Malawi.

Bricks are made by hand. One man sits in a little pit of mud. Girls carry water in buckets on their heads and pour the water into the hole.

The man mixes the water and clay dirt to make it the right consistency. The man is usually dressed in a towsack and is barefoot.

The "brick man" will pick the mud up by the handfuls and put it into little wooden boxes shaped like two bricks. He will fill both sides of the brick mold with this mud and smooth it off with a little stick.

Once the wooden mold is packed with mud, the brick man hands it to a young girl, and she carries it to a smooth, level area covered with straw. Then the girl turns the mold upside down, and the freshly molded clay falls onto the straw. Then she carries her mold back to fill again, and the process starts again. Several girls carry water and bricks.

The sun begins to dry the bricks; when completely dry, they are stacked into a rectangular pile with a hole in its center so firewood can be crammed into it.

After a waiting period, the workers smeared wet mud all over the brick stack to seal off the air and keep the heat from escaping. They then lit the firewood inside the brick stack and kept it burning for several days until the bricks were thoroughly heated. During this heating process, the clay hardened into brick.

This process was amazing to watch. It was arduous work, and sometimes the girls had to carry water on their heads for more than two or three miles. It took a lot of time to make one brick.

Life was tough in Malawi. They worked so hard for so few rewards. Almost everything had to be done by hand; little was mechanized. There were upsides as well as downsides to doing everything by hand. Because many people were without work and had a hard time just having enough to eat, making everything by hand offered employment so some could make a little money.

There was no such thing as government unemployment compensation or welfare. If you didn't work, you didn't eat. Most of the people were willing to work hard, and they understood that it was necessary to survive.

Jerry continued to pull transmissions and engines from those old Volkswagen Kombis and rebuild the engines. (Jerry grew to hate the thought of a Kombi, a type of minivan taxi.)

Problems at Publications still existed. Jerry insisted that if he were to run the Publications, he would have to have the authority commensurate with this responsibility, including the power to hire and fire at will. He was perfectly willing to listen to the Committee's recommendations, but recommendations would be all it could be.

If saddled with this responsibility Jerry wanted ultimate authority.

The employees could only grasp a minimal amount of training. They were slow, understandably so. It was their culture and background. Trying as hard as they would, they were still limited. Some of the 13 employees had walked 10 miles to work. Their diet was very poor. Their formal education was almost nonexistent.

———•••———

I started attending a Ladies' Bible Study Group at Linda Meachem's house. Linda and her husband, Don, were Church of Christ missionaries. Don was busy getting building materials to build churches, and we had a lot in common with them. It was good for me to get together with a group of ladies for Bible Study. The fellowship was really important to me.

In the meantime, Jerry was getting a driveway put in with a culvert at the street to enable cars and trucks to get in to unload building materials. We also had a fence built so things would not be stolen.

———•••———

Jerry went to the sawmill at Dedza, a good two-hour drive from us, and ordered lumber for the house. As we traveled from place to place, it was customary to stop in at other missionaries' homes to go to the bathroom. If it was mealtime, they usually invited travelers to stay for a meal. As we went to Dedza, we stopped at Darrell and Judy Garner's farm in Balaka. Judy gave us some coffee and cake. We had a pleasant visit with them, and this became a regular pit stop for us anytime that we drove from Lilongwe to Blantyre.

We went on down to Blantyre and had dinner at Mount Sochi Hotel and tried to buy a sink for the Garners' house. Jerry also had some shopping we needed for Publications. We headed back the next day, stopped in at the Garners again, and, since it was late in the afternoon, we spent the night.

On the way back, we stopped to check whether a carver had carvings ready for Sherry Collier. Sherry and Ross Collier, with their two sons, Bryan and David, arrived shortly after we did. They were living in a three-bedroom house in the Guest Compound.

David was hardly more than a baby, a chubby little cotton-headed boy. He would wake up in the mornings, before Ross and Sherry had gotten up, and begin to yell, "Nanna! Nanna!" calling for a banana. That little boy loved bananas and ate so many that I thought he might become a banana.

Ross was in the country to do Sunday School training work. Sherry's interest lay in women's work.

Rebecca Phifer's water heater wouldn't work, so Jerry went to her house and worked on the heater. With Rebecca and all four of her children at home, it was very difficult to shower and wash clothes without hot water. That heater had been a constant problem until Jerry took the time to make some significant adjustments in the pipe routing. Then Rebecca could depend on hot water.

———•••———

Every day seemed to bring unexpected guests for meals. Trying to juggle work, meals, and our social lives was a constant struggle. One day after an especially hectic day of people coming and going since 5:30 a.m., Jerry said, "let's eat supper before somebody else comes by."

The next morning, I got up, and as I took the mustard from the refrigerator and looked for the mayonnaise, the phone rang. I stopped dead still as I listened to Jerry say, "Sure enough," and "Where are you?"

I knew there was a problem. It was the Herifords. They had been to Zomba, and the gas stations were closed because it was a holiday, so they ran out of gas just outside Lilongwe.

As Jerry headed out the door, he asked, "Do you have enough for the Herifords to have something to eat?" We both knew that they would not have had anything to eat. So, Jerry took the Herifords some gas and brought them home with him for something to eat.

We all spent a lot of time taking care of ourselves and other missionaries' needs. That same day we also took Pastor Banda to the hospital, and I attended Bible Study at Jo Ann Clark's, where Linda Meacham taught a good lesson.

We learned that evening that three British people had been murdered in Zimbabwe, and there was fighting on the streets of Nairobi, Kenya.

———————

I couldn't figure out what gifts God had blessed me with, but after some consideration, I figured it must be hospitality. I have cooked so many meals.

Godfrey was still helping me in the kitchen. He couldn't read English very well, so he could not use a recipe. I taught him how to use a measuring cup and measuring spoons, and little by little, he became more helpful.

By August, our house was coming along pretty well. Publications seemed to have settled down a little, and I was getting some of the bills paid off. I had the books in order. J. R. was still there helping with the printing and teaching the employees.

Our thoughts turned to other matters. Once when we were taking Bro. Kanowa, The Convention Chairman, to Blantyre, he said, "it will be over my dead body before there is another English-speaking Baptist Church in Malawi. (There was already an English-speaking Baptist church in Blantyre, and the convention did not like it.)

Still, we hoped and prayed we could start an English-Speaking Baptist Church in Lilongwe despite Brother Kanowa's attitude. So, we prayed that God would guide and direct us into creating a church if it was his will.

———————

Jerry and I had been meeting on Sunday mornings at Andrew and Rose Mary Kingston's house for Bible Study. The Westons from New

Zealand and Jim and Liz Parrish from England were also attending. Some others attended occasionally.

Andrew Kingston was an accountant from England, and Rose Mary's father was a preacher. Both the Kingstons and the Westons were from Baptist backgrounds. The Parrishes were of Methodist background, and Jim was an accountant with the British Commonwealth. Liz was actively helping people in need. These were three wonderful Christian couples.

The eight of us talked of starting an English-speaking church in Lilongwe. Some missionaries supported starting an English language church, but some were completely against it.

Land was available, and we had the money for the development fee. We just needed to be sure of God's leadership and get the missionaries to move off dead center. The Capital City Development Center (CCDC) said we could have the $6000.00 lot for $2000.00. It was a perfect lot, but not all the missionaries were sure the location was right.

———•••———

We were beginning to get to know some of the English-speaking Malawian Christians.

We had Harry and Rhoda Tambuli over for dinner. Harry was working for Manica Freight, and Harry shared his Christian testimony with us, and this is what he said:

"My sister had written me several times, sharing her Christian faith with me. I didn't pay any attention until I got a letter that I couldn't stop thinking about. She said I should read the Bible and pray, which I had never done. I was raised a Muslim and had never had any reason to think about Christianity. But still, I couldn't get my sister's words out of my mind.

I found a few tracts that a little cousin had left at my house after someone gave them to him. I began reading them. I didn't have a Bible but found one in a bag of clothes and belongings I was keeping for a friend.

I read the tract over and over. I fell to my knees and, with tears rolling down my cheeks, gave my life to Jesus.

170

I prayed the simple prayer suggested at the end of the tract.

I laboriously looked through the Bible until I found the scripture verse on the tract and began reading."

Harry said that after that, he heard about a Bible Study that Mike Canady was having at his house and began attending it. He asked Mike to baptize him and was baptized into the Baptist Church. He was the Sunday School Superintendent at Falls Baptist Church in Lilongwe.

He said, "since that day when I gave my life to Jesus Christ, I have not taken another drink of alcohol."

When a friend asked Harry one day, "Why do you smoke? Don't you know your body is the temple of the Lord? Harry said he had never really thought about not smoking. That night, he decided to stop smoking and hasn't smoked since.

We had a lovely evening visiting with Rhoda and Harry Tambuli. It blessed my heart to see how God changed his life and placed a new importance on the distribution of tracts.

Tracts in the States take a low level of importance, but in Malawi, they are essential. People will read them and pass them on to seven or ten other people to read.

We had a letter from Pauline and Arvil, and they said that Jann, Jerry's sister, had surgery. When the doctor sewed her up, he got three stitches too near her kidney, so they had to go back in and operate again. It sounded like Jann had been really sick. We kept up with the family through letters, and I wrote Ken, Peggy, my mother, and Jerry's parents every week.

20 Settling into Lilongwe Life

Ngombi's wife Mayi (all wives are called "Mayi" in Malawi) is still sick. She cried all night, so Ngombi put her on his bicycle and pumped her the five miles to the nearest clinic. Mayi was not doing well. Ngombi, our janitor, usually sang choruses around Publications, but he didn't sing anymore.

"I don't smile much anymore," he said when I asked him about this. My heart just went out to him and all the people here.

Ngombi is so thin. He never wears socks with his shabby black shoes, long ago worn out. He just doesn't have the money to buy new things.

There were so many needs around us that it was challenging to maintain a balance between a compassionate heart and a cold heart with blind eyes. If you are too compassionate, you couldn't stand to be around so many problems, yet if you are blind to the needs - we might as well pack up and go home. We continue to try to hold this balance.

It was a tremendous encouragement to know that we had friends from Travis Avenue Baptist Church in Fort Worth who regularly lifted us up in their prayers. Monte Clendinning had worked with Ray and Sandra Taylor in setting up a prayer group for us back home, and each month we would write them and give them a list of prayer requests. Then J. D. Kelly would call us just before the meeting to see what we needed.

This group became our lifeline. Sandra put a little rope in her window to remind her to pray for us. She was holding the rope for us, and I am sure we would have failed or sunk if she had not been holding the line.

Over time this group became so dear to us. They enjoyed meeting, praying for each other, and visiting with each other.

Jim and Jewel Medford were part of the prayer group even though they had moved to Dallas and had become a part of First Baptist Dallas. One weekend they were hosting the meeting, and it was raining and a bit hectic for all the Fort Worth folks to make their way over to the Medford's house. On the way home after the meeting, Dr. Coggin began to laugh, which was a little out of character. Others in the car asked him what was going on. He said, "We had such a good time that we forgot to pray." I think that is the last time they forgot to pray.

We were so grateful to have such prayer warriors as Dr. James and Carolyn Coggin in our prayer group. We were thankful for Sandra and Ray keeping the group going. We were grateful for J. D. Kelly faithfully calling us each month for the ten years we spent in Malawi to get our prayer requests.

I want to describe all those wonderful people. I want to mention each one by name individually, but God knows them by name, and they will be blessed and rewarded for all their prayers. Without their prayers, we would have never been as effective as we were. We love and appreciate every one of them. Though miles may separate us, God connected our hearts.

———— •••• ————

By August 13, our house plans were finally approved so actual construction could begin. Jerry hired people and they began to dig the foundation — by hand, of course.

We needed something to put the tools and supplies in each night so they could remain on the building site without being stolen. A container at the Salima Clinic was used for that purpose. Now that the Clinic was almost finished, Ed Barnes said we could have this container if we would come and get it. (Little did we know how much trouble it would be to move a container.)

The Mission had an old flatbed truck we would use during the construction. So, Jerry decided to go and get the container himself.

Ed said that he and some of his helpers would help load it. These steel containers weigh several thousand pounds, even when they are empty. Somehow, Ed, Jerry, and many men took poles and loaded the container onto the truck. It was a miracle that it did not turn over on some of the men and crush them.

I think God looks down on His people and helps them in their ignorance. Many missionaries attempt the impossible and succeed. Only with God's help can they accomplish some things, and this was one of those accomplishments.

Once the container was loaded, we thought the worst was over. We headed out in the truck. Every time we hit a little bump, the tires rubbed against the truck and made a terrible squeaking noise. Jerry realized the container was too heavy for the truck, but he was determined to get it to Lilongwe now that they had gone to so much trouble getting it loaded.

We headed out of the driveway with it squealing and squeaking most of the way. As we leveled off on the road, it settled down and did not squeak so often.

The road was narrow and bumpy. Usually, when a vehicle meets a car, each vehicle moves halfway off the road. As we met the first car, we pulled over but soon realized that we would be unable to pull off lest we turn the truck over and blow out the tires.

So, after that, whenever we met a car or truck, we just hogged the road and prayed that the other vehicle would pull off entirely and allow us to use the road. At times, deep trenches would be beside the road, making it virtually impossible for cars to pull off.

The people who drove Mercedes tended to think that they owned the road. We learned that when driving our car, we would have to give right of way to these discourteous Mercedes drivers who would fly down the road, and everybody would scatter like chickens.

Now that we were in this overloaded truck, we wondered what would happen when we met someone in a Mercedes. Sure enough, along came a Mercedes, and we held our ground. They almost turned over when they pulled off the road because they had not slowed down enough.

The real problem would come when we met another truck. If they were also loaded, they had the same difficulty pulling off. Sometimes, there would be a smooth area on our side of the road, and we could nudge our truck off slowly and allow the other truck to go by.

At turtle speed, we inched our way along the road. We came upon a young boy pumping a bicycle with what looked like his grandmother on its handlebars. (He was probably taking her to the doctor or hospital.)

When we were a short distance behind the bicycle, the truck hit a little chug hole in the road and roared like a lion. The young boy quickly turned his handlebars, and down into the ditch he went.

The grandmother went tumbling, headfirst, rolling down into the ditch. By the time we got to where she was lying, she began trying to get up. The poor boy looked like he was in a state of shock as he looked up and saw the yellow truck hauling a container.

Because we were headed up a hill, Jerry was afraid that if he stopped, he would not be able to get the truck started again. We eyed the two as we drove by, and they did not look seriously hurt. We both felt terrible but did not attempt to assist or make right what had happened.

It took four hours to travel the 30 miles to Lilongwe and area 43. Under the circumstances, we felt we had made remarkably good time.

Jerry and the workers had laid a brick foundation and a concrete floor to hold the container. They slid the container onto its new foundation without incident.

The following year, someone in the Mission decided it was unfair for us to have a container at our house, and they had no place to store their things. (The container leaked a little and was unsuitable for storing furniture or anything for a long time.) This small group of complainers approached us and said we would have to give up the container. Jerry said he used the container to hold mostly personal tools for Mission work. (He had brought a lot of tools from home to work on cars and houses.) However, he told them that he understood, and we would be more than happy to relinquish the storage container.

But he was not willing to move the container. Whoever wanted the container would have to come to get it. Also, he felt that if they tore our driveway up, which we had paid for out of personal money, we would expect them to repair any damage. Nine years later, when we moved out of the house, the container was still there, and we never heard another word about it.

So, the construction got underway, and the container was put to good use during our home construction. Men mixed concrete and hauled it in wheelbarrows. Jerry had repaired an old concrete mixer that would mix one or two wheelbarrow loads at a time, and men would move it over to the foundation. Remarkably, the concrete was mixed little by little, and the foundation was finished. It looked amazingly good, considering the crude construction methods.

The bricks began to go up, and before long, you could make out how the house would look. All the interior and exterior walls were made of solid brick because the termites would eat anything from wood. (Jerry poured a lot of chemicals on the ground before construction began to try to deter these little hungry critters.

At first, the bricks did not look good — the bricklayer would just dab a bit of mortar between the bricks and then leave it all rough and jagged. The workers assured me someone would come back later and "point" the brick and make them look good, and sure enough, they did.

We ordered the lumber from Dedza, and when Jerry went to pick it up and bring it back to Lilongwe, we planned to have dinner with the Messers, so I went over to the Messers' house to wait for him. We waited for a while for him, and Jerry still had not returned home, we began supper.

Just then, the phone rang, and it was Jerry saying the truck had broken down. Don left to get Jerry and bring him back to Lilongwe. (They left the truck in a man's yard alongside the highway.)

Jerry said he was driving down the highway and heard a loud "ping" sound, stopped the truck, and walked around it. He saw nothing wrong, so he started driving down the highway. He only went a short distance and heard the "ping" sound again — and then another, louder "ping," more like a gunshot.

He stopped the truck again, determined to locate the problem. He walked around the truck, stooped over, and looked under the truck. Then he began to check the wheels and found that one of the wheels only had

176

two nuts left holding the wheel. Because the truck was so heavily loaded with lumber, the nuts had just shot off the wheel.

When Don and Jerry got back, they finished supper, and the next day after looking for hours, they finally found some nuts that would fit the truck. They repaired the truck and brought it, still loaded with our lumber, to Lilongwe.

———•••———

With the framing going up, we ordered the trusses, lovely wooden window frames, and kitchen cabinets — and things were taking shape. When the windows were delivered, and the men put the first window up to where it was supposed to go, it would not fit. There seemed to be some mix-up in the measurement, and the window was six inches wider than the hole.

They checked another window, and it was too large also. The foreman assured Jerry they could chisel the bricks to make the windows fit.

Jerry did not want jagged edges around all the windows. Since the bricks were soft anyway, Jerry had a different idea. He got his saber saw with a concrete blade and began to saw away. All the workers stopped what they were doing. They were amazed — they had never seen an electric saw before.

The brick dust from all the sawing created a fog, and the red dust covered Jerry. Within a few hours, all the windows were widened by six inches. Very little other work was done while the sawing was happening because everybody was so excited. They applauded and cheered as each window was sawed out.

———•••———

There were so many problems. The major one was a shortage of cement. Jerry would take the truck to the cement factory and leave it all night to be in line by 6:00 a.m. the next morning — so he had to get up by 5:00 a.m. each morning and go immediately to the cement plant. If any cement was available, he would get some — and even then, they would only let him have ten bags. The cement work was a long process.

Then there was a gasoline shortage. When Jerry was not sitting in line to get cement, he would be in line to get a little gas. Once, when the President came to town, and the government officials didn't want him to know that there was a gasoline shortage, all the service stations suddenly had plenty of gas. That is about the only time during the construction that Jerry could get a full tank of gas.

Then there was the water problem. There was supposed to be water in Area 43, but there was not enough water to supply all the houses built. (Also, the entire town was experiencing water shortages.)

We would have a little water between 10:00 p.m. and 6:00 a.m. So, we got a supply of 55-gallon drums, and during the night, we would fill the drums. (This is how we got water to make concrete or extra water for anything else.)

Then there was the cabinet problem. The cabinets arrived and looked good, but the doors were not ready. (We were anxious to complete the house because Arvil, Pauline, Peggy, and Ken were coming for Christmas, and we needed to be in the house before they arrived.) When the cabinet doors came, there was another problem. Somehow all the doors were too narrow and too short — they looked great but didn't fit.

The family would be there within a week, and now there were no doors for the cabinet. It was very disappointing, but there was nothing we could do about it. We would just have to move into the house, fill the cabinets, and then install the doors after they were re-made. In the States, not having doors on your cabinets would not be a big problem, but it is a big problem in Malawi. Everything was so dusty that the house needed to be swept and dusted daily.

Building the house consumed most of Jerry's time, leaving me with Publications. Somehow during the last half of the year, we managed to print over 200,000 tracts, the Theological Education by Extension Books, The Women's Books, and the Sunday School Books.

We studied Chichewa and learned enough to get around without too much difficulty. We visited all the different mission stations and met all the missionaries.

Jerry built our house in record time by pushing the workers to their limit.

Everybody assured us we would not be in the house by the end of the year, but Jerry was determined to be in the house by Christmas. Jerry pushed the workers, and with lots of prayers, we completed the house and driveway.

So, on December 14, 1982, two trucks were supposed to be at Kanengo to get our crates along with the Colliers' crates. We had packed our crates 18 months before and had been living out of our suitcases ever since. I had almost forgotten what I had packed and was eager to get my pictures and personal things. It was such a busy year that I had not missed my possessions much.

When they got to Kanengo, only one truck was there, so Jerry told Ross to go ahead and get his things loaded. Jerry would get the old yellow building truck and load our things onto it. Bambo Robert, Bambo Peter, and Rebecca's Bambo loaded our crates onto the truck.

Jerry drove the truck to our new house as Godfrey and I cleaned the cabinets, floors, and bathrooms. They arrived about noon, and we were both too tired to be excited.

We started unpacking and setting things in place. All went reasonably well. One box was sitting on top of the freezer, and Jerry pushed it off. This box was filled with our most treasured pieces — Mammaw Dowdy's butter dish, the little blue vase Pat Bradshaw gave me for keeping her kids once when our kids were really small, several special glasses and bowls — all broken.

The fruit bowl I got when Mother broke up housekeeping was also in there. My heart sank when I saw it; I feared its feet would be broken. Fortunately, it was not broken. I thought Jerry would cry when he saw the shattered pieces of his grandmother's butter dish lying in the box.

The next day we continued to unpack and put things into the closets, cabinets, and drawers. Jerry put the beds together, the desk, and my sewing machine. Jerry took a lot of furniture apart to fit more in the crate. Somehow, Jerry got everything back together.

On December 15, we had to move our things out of the guest house. We had been living there for the past year, and now some new missionaries, Howard and Belinda Rhodes, Jim and Patsy Parker, and their families were soon to arrive in Lilongwe.

So, I packed up everything we had brought with us, plus all the food and newly accumulated items. It took two Kombi loads to carry all the "Katundu" (as they would say in Malawi.)

While Jerry loaded the Kombi, I cleaned the little duplex that had been our home for the past year. It was quite comfortable, but I hoped I would never have to live in another house with red concrete floors.

———••———

In the middle of this move, I made an appointment at the hospital to have a dark-colored mole removed from my back. My bra would rub it, and it would get sore, and I was afraid it might be something more serious than just a little benign mole.

This was my first trip to the Kamuzu Central Hospital as a patient. There was a Dr. Magda there, a Catholic Sister with a good reputation, who agreed to remove the mole.

I got up at 4:00 a.m. that morning and packed as much as I could, so by 11:00 a.m., when I arrived at the hospital, I was tired and hungry — and more than a little nervous.

I sat down on a little wooden bench just outside the doctor's office, glad for the opportunity to rest for a moment. I couldn't relax because I thought the nurse had sent me to the wrong place; I sat there until 11:45, and nobody showed up. I asked a man about Dr. Magda, and sure enough, I was in the wrong place. He directed me to the recovery room.

I entered the recovery room, and a nurse directed me to remove my clothes. Standing there barefoot and naked, I was glad when the nurse gave me a sheet to cover myself.

We walked through the recovery room among the patients, through another room, and then into the operating room. I saw big pans of bloody tissue (I assumed that maybe it was afterbirth) and other pans with bloody stuff in them. I tiptoed across the floor, trying to miss the drops of blood on the floor.

When Dr. Magda saw me, she complained to the nurse, "You let them walk in here, and then we wheel them out on a stretcher."

The nurse said nothing.

I climbed onto the operating table, and a nurse brought out what looked like a sterile green pack. It looked clean, and I assumed that it was the sterilized instruments.

Dr. Magda was cordial and asked me to roll onto my stomach, and she deadened the spot where she would cut. Nurses peered at me with

180

big black eyes from behind their green masks. Very efficiently, Dr. Magda removed the mole and put a few stitches in my back. She assured me it was nothing to be concerned about, and I am sure the tissue was not sent off to be analyzed, but I was glad to have it removed.

Sure enough, they rolled me onto a stretcher and back out to the room where my clothes lay. Still a little shaken up, I dressed and went home to continue my packing and unpacking.

That night I fell into bed in my new home, too tired to appreciate it. The next day the family was to arrive, and as hard as we had worked, we were not ready.

21 Family Visit: Christmas in Malawi

We got up the next morning at about 4:30 a.m., which had become our usual time of getting up. We climbed out of bed just 15 minutes before the plane was to arrive. Jerry put the screws in the last towel rack, and then we headed for the airport.

Excitedly and hurriedly, we drove to the airport. The plane touched down about 5 minutes past schedule, and we got there in time to see the family climb from the plane.

Pauline was very nervous about going through customs and immigration. We had told them to keep their mouths shut and answer any questions directly without volunteering any additional information.

We told them to say they did not have any gifts, or they would have to pay 100% duty on any Christmas gift. We told them if they decided to give us something after they got into the country, that would be all right but don't bring us any gifts.

After hugs, kisses, and tears, we took Ken, Peggy, Arvil, and Pauline to our new home.

We thought it looked pretty good, but they didn't make many comments. We had taken drapery lining and hung it over the windows for privacy, so maybe it lacked a little to be desirable.

They were tired from the long trip, and there had been no air-conditioning on Air Malawi from Blantyre to Lilongwe. We had not seen any family for a year except Peggy, and it was so good to see them again.

We just visited and let them rest for the remainder of the day. They gave us a lot of things we had asked them to bring and that our prayer group had bought for us. Now my pantry was packed with American goodies like chocolate chips, Jell-O, and pecans.

The next day we went to Kawali Baptist Church, and Fletcher Kayia's Choir sang a couple of Christmas Carols in English. They asked our family to stand in the back of the church, and everybody came by and shook hands with them. Everybody was so friendly even though they could not communicate a word.

Peggy had learned the greetings in Chichewa, and she tried them out on the people — and they would smile at her attempt to communicate with them. Arvil and Pauline were very impressed with the people, and both had tears in their eyes throughout the service.

The next day I packed enough food for us to have sandwiches for two days, and we headed for Kasungu Game Park. We were eager to show them the African animals.

Arvil had caught a cold on the plane, which developed into bronchitis. When he began to run a fever, we headed back to Lilongwe after one night. They had seen quite a few animals and seemed to have seen enough to realize they were in Africa. We took Arvil to the doctor and got some medicine for him.

There was a Christmas Party over at Sam and Marlyn Upton's house for all the Baptist missionaries in town. I made two batches of pralines, two batches of sugar cookies, and some brownies to take. (Providing the deserts seemed to be what I did best.)

We had Mexican Food for our Christmas dinner, which seemed very strange to me, but all the other missionaries seemed to think nothing about having Mexican Food.

We drew names and took a gift.

But almost all the missionaries had given us a gift, and I had not taken any of them a gift.

The next day was December 25, and I was going to make a more traditional Christmas dinner with Chicken and Dressing, but I couldn't find the cornmeal, so it turned out to be Chicken and Rice.

I had not had time to go shopping for the family, so I wrapped up a few Malawian artifacts I had lying around and gave them as our gifts. I think Ken and Peggy were disappointed.

With Ken and Peggy both in college, it had cost us about $12,000 each that year. Then there were their airline tickets and trip costs. We did not give them anything else, and we probably should have, but we didn't.

It was almost a full-time job trying to keep water boiled. Jerry and I were drinking water from the tap by then, but I didn't want our family to drink it.

———•••———

Arvil and Pauline had always heard of Victoria Falls, and they wanted to see it. So, the next day they packed up and headed to Zambia. Peggy and I stayed home. We had already seen the Falls.

Peggy was making plans to marry Bruce Lawson. We took this time to be alone and talk about the wedding. I told Peggy I would give her a certain amount of money for the wedding. We planned their wedding while we were on our hands and knees with Brillo pads cleaning the kitchen floor.

We made a list of everything she would need and discussed how much each should cost. We talked about where she would have the wedding cake made, who would officiate, and where to go to buy things.

After being gone for four days, the rest of the family returned from Victoria Falls. They were tired. The roads had been rough and bumpy. Traveling in a car without air conditioning had been sweltering, and the wind would blow in the windows and burn their skin. They were stopped several times by armed military men, which was stressful. Arvil still was not feeling well. They enjoyed the falls but understood for the first time the difficulty of travel.

———•••———

They still had not been to a traditional village, and their trip would not be complete without that. We took them out to Ngombiaria's village. (I took Ng'ombe a pair of pants and a shirt and Mayi a blouse.)

When we arrived, we parked the car on the road and walked through the little houses until we came to Ngombi's house. They welcomed us and shook hands with each of us. Then they began to go throughout the village trying to find enough chairs so that the six of us would have a chair. We insisted that we did not need a chair, but they felt we must have a chair or stool.

The Mayi began to boil some water so she could serve tea. They took their guests into their house and proudly showed the pictures on the wall. They talked of God's love for them.

This pride and hospitality really touched Pauline, and she could hardly keep from crying (she was not a woman given to tears). The loving Malawian people touched our family's hearts.

Later, Pauline would say she could stand in the middle of the living room and touch all the walls. The houses were mud with a thatch roof, and cow dung was mixed with water and then rubbed on the floor to make it smooth. With so little, they were still thankful to God.

This village had an impact on Ken and Peggy's life.

Somehow, they felt guilty when complaining when they did not have everything they thought they needed.

With us gone, it had not been easy on Ken or Peggy. They had to assume a lot of responsibility, that had we been home, they would not have felt they had to accept. They also moved from a big house to a smaller residence. They did not have their mother cooking them three meals a day, nor was I around to wash and iron their clothes as I had always done. Then there was a shortage of money.

Jerry's and my life changed out of our choice, but our children's lives had changed not out of their own choice but out of ours. They wanted to be supportive of what we were doing, but I think that deep down, they resented being abandoned.

We sat outside on the chairs and stools and enjoyed tea together.

As we left the Ngombiyera's house, they gave us a sack of fruit. We shook hands, and they walked us back to our car. Many village children also crowded around us and walked with us back to the car.

We drove back to Kawali and had a coke with Mayi Lydia Kolako. She had invited us over. Since she had no refrigerator to get the Cokes cold, she placed them in red clay pots filled with water to keep them cool.

Mayi Kolako lived in a nice little house with a metal roof, windows, and doors. Several of her children were home. We sat on a couch and chairs, and some sat on a straw mat on the floor. Mayi Kolako spoke very good English, so she could converse well.

She talked about her church and her work, and her family. She wore the traditional wrap (a piece of two-meter-long fabric) all the women wear at home even if they work out of the home and wear Western attire.

———•••———

Their visit was coming to an end. We wanted the last night to be special, so we made reservations at the Capital Hotel dining room. The Hotel called during the afternoon and said they would not be open for dinner, so we decided to go to the Lilongwe Hotel. There were only two hotels in Lilongwe.

Our meal was delicious, and the service was impeccable. The dinner was served on tables covered with starched tablecloths and starched napkins. Pauline could hardly eat, and every time I looked at her, she had tears in her eyes. It was an emotional evening. We knew it would be another year before we saw each other.

Early the next morning, we took them to the airport and said our goodbyes several times before they entered the international departure area. It was far more difficult for them to say goodbye this time than when we had come to Malawi a year earlier, and it was also hard for us to see them go.

We stood on the observation deck and waved as long as there was hope they could see us. Jerry and I held hands and watched the plane through blurred eyes until it disappeared. There was nothing left but an empty feeling. My heart felt empty, and I felt so alone.

As we drove back to the house quietly, we knew there were a million things that we needed to do. But when we got home, we just pulled off our clothes, climbed into bed, and held each other for a long time without saying a word. We were tired, and we felt so empty.

It was January 4, 1983, and we had completed our house and our first year on the mission field. What a busy, educational, and interesting year it had been.

22 Navigating Sensitive Issues

It is 6:15 a.m. on a Saturday, and nobody has knocked on the door or stood at the gate calling, "Odi." I wonder if this is going to be our usual Saturday. Maybe today will be calm; it can't compare with last Saturday's activity.

The sun was shining, with a slight breeze rustling the trees. I hear a church bell ring in the distance, and several roosters are taking turns crowing. The little travel clock ticks beside my bed while Princess, my trusted companion, snuggles against my feet as I lay propped up in bed reading my Bible.

Jerry brought me some coffee. I stay in bed, sipping my coffee and writing in my journal. My children and family had gone home after the Christmas holidays, and I felt lower than a polecat.

Then these words came to me:

COMMUNICATION

From America to Africa,
From Cadillac to Kombi,

From business to missions,
But still in God's will.

From left-hand drive to right-hand drive,
From hood and trunk to boot and bonnet,
From windshields to the windscreen,
From wipers to twitters,
From canned food to fresh food,
But God remains constant.

From biscuits to scones,
From cookies to biscuits,
From rags to waste,
From alcohol to spirits,
From pick-up to box-body,
From horn to hooter,
From yard to garden,
My vocabulary keeps changing,
But God does not change.

Do I speak American or British?
From a two-story apartment to a flat,
From natural family to mission family,
But God remains unchanged.

From cold to hot weather,
From arid to tropical,
From Fort Worth, Texas, U.S.A to
Lilongwe, Malawi, Africa,
From road-side park to layby,
From yield to giveaway,
From bump to dip,
From watching out for deer,
To watching for elephants,
But it doesn't matter where I come from or
Where I am going, God goes with me.

There were joyful days and days when I had to pull myself out of bed. The many interruptions made it virtually impossible to stay down and out for very long.

I climbed out of bed, dressed, grabbed my basket, and headed for the market. People lumber along the road: mothers with their babies tied on their backs, women struggling under the weight of firewood piled high on their heads, and children following along.

And I think to myself, how fortunate I am to have a car to ride. What if I had been born a Black African Woman? Why had God chosen for me to have so many comforts and these women so few? I could not help but feel the pain of those women, but at the same time, I thanked God that he had made me who I am. He had made me "who I am" because he is "I AM."

When I returned from the market, it took me the rest of the morning to soak my fruits and vegetables. I laid the meat on my kitchen cabinet and dissected it into pieces small enough to fit into the refrigerator and cooking pot.

Godfrey, my cook, came into the house and helped clean and prepare meals. I had so many visitors this past year that I don't know what I would have done without him.

Jerry was working on a sermon he would preach at Kawali Church the next day.

———•••———

We took Godfrey and his family to church with us. After sharing our faith with them, Godfrey and Beatrice Poundi made professions of faith in Christ during the year. We also picked up Mr. Mkandawire and his family for church. He was not a Christian but said he would join the church. People often tell us what they think we want to hear.

For example, you take your car into the shop and ask when it will be ready. They say, "This afternoon." You go back "this afternoon," and it is not ready. You are irritated because you know they did not plan to have it ready. They say, "This afternoon" because they think that will please you.

If you have someone giving you directions, you ask, "How far is it?" They will say, "Pafupi," which means "nearby."

You ask again.

Again they say, "Pafupi."

After driving for an hour, you understand that they cannot tell you what they think you will not want to hear. This cultural quirk takes some flexibility.

Anyway, the church services were good; Jerry did a good job preaching, as he always does.

After we got home from church, I called Mother because all the family was supposed to be with her. I talked to Mother, Doris, Duane, Bobby, Marie, and Ken. They all seemed to be doing pretty well. Ken was just doing odd jobs, and I couldn't keep from worrying about him.

Bobby was having some dizziness but has been able to work. Doris had given Marsha a baby shower. Mother is now 80 and staying with Doris but wants to move to a retirement home.

Duane got on the phone and cried so hard that he could not talk. Mother was not crying but sounded like she was fighting back the tears. Telephones are a blessing when you are far from home. It was nice to get to say hello to everyone, but disappointing that Peggy was not there.

By Monday, our week started all over again. I worked at the Baptist Printing and Publishing house most of the time, and I pretty much had a system worked out.

I was training Bambo Mkaka to keep up with the inventory. Bambo Mkaka's English was good, and he counted and added well. He is a deacon in his church and preaches and has worked for the Baptist Mission for about 18 years.

The Singa Bay Medical Clinic was complete. All the Lilongwe missionaries filled their cars with people and took them to Salima for the clinic's dedication. The Minister of Health, Mr. J. T. Sangala, attended and spoke. About 100 dancing women attended, attired in their traditional government dresses.

They danced for about 15 minutes. As they circled and danced in a small circle, then spread out into a larger circle, you could see the picture of President Banda around their buttocks. They were all draped in chirundu cloth with images of the President's picture on the fabric. It made for a strange sight. But it was beautiful.

Bill Wester gave the history of the clinic, and Ed Barnes spoke. Both gave God the glory for all that he had done. The theme was "To God Be the Glory."

Before Christmas, the pressure had been on us to complete the house before the family and the new missionary couples arrived. Jerry had been unusually grumpy, and I was having difficulties with some of the missionaries.

Maybe we were experiencing culture shock. However, if this was a culture shock, it certainly was not what I had expected.

We had a little party when the roof was on our house, and several missionaries came to look at the house. Barbara Workman just seemed to turn up her nose and made no comments, either good or bad. Beverly Kingsley found nothing good to say about the house, but she found a considerable number of faults. She thought we should have done a lot of things differently.

I tried to ignore Beverly because we had come in and taken over her husband's job. But it was becoming increasingly difficult. Beverly and Gene had lost a son some years before. Some missionaries told us that Beverly would never allow herself to go through the grieving process. She just went about with a Pollyanna attitude.

I felt she had an emotional problem that she needed to deal with. She had developed a tick in her eye and had a severe twitch on one side of her face. If she openly discussed how she felt with a psychologist, she could be helped. Jerry and I were concerned about her, even though she bugged us sometimes.

Once, Jerry asked her if she thought her problems could be emotionally related, and she almost went into a tirade. Somehow, she felt that having an emotional issue would reflect her faith in God.

So, we never mentioned that to her again. However, we felt that going to a doctor for a mental problem is no different than going to a doctor with a physical problem.

To break up some of the tension, we went to see a George Burns movie that was very light-hearted and funny. Lilongwe had one walk-in theatre that was really in disrepair. They also had one drive-in movie that was pretty good if you could find a speaker that worked. Taking a little time off and doing something by ourselves was helpful.

I was secretary of the program planning committee. After I typed up some minutes, we went to the Uptons' house to discuss an upcoming meeting in Blantyre. We were to discuss relations between the Lilongwe missionaries and the Blantyre missionaries.

We prayed about the upcoming meeting because we saw it as potentially tricky. We were going to try to iron out some difficulties. The Lilongwe missionaries seemed to get along much better with the Nationals than the Blantyre missionaries. We had different philosophies.

Also, there was another BIG topic we had to discuss. Some of the National Convention officers had asked Bill Wester to leave Malawi. Some of the missionaries disagreed over this issue. Some thought that since Bill's churches still wanted to work with him, the Mission should stand behind him and stand up to the Convention Officers. Others believed Bill should leave.

I could not understand some of the missionaries' rationale. What were the charges? They seemed so vague. With some of the missionaries' dogmatic attitudes, I thought, well, maybe Bill has committed some immoral act that the missionaries don't want to talk about.

So, I came right out and asked, "Has he committed some immoral act which is some deep dark secret?"

They said emphatically that Bill had committed no immoral act.

The problem was that he had not sent any of his men to the Bible School for training, then that was unusual, if that was true. But it should not be such a big issue that it could not be rectified. When the Bible School opened for the next session, why not just send some men to school?

Next, they accused him of being "selfish." It seemed that when he had training sessions with his pastors, he would cut a bar of soap in half and give the men half a bar of soap instead of a whole bar. Nothing said that he needed to provide them with any soap. He had more churches than any of the other church developers and a minimal budget to work with. He had to be conservative.

I knew he had gone out of his way to get clothes for his people. He had bought bundles of clothes and sold them for just what he had paid. The Catholic Church had donated bundles of used clothes to Malawi. We had to pay for the freight for the clothes, and the Malawian people in Bill's area did not even have the freight money. So, Bill would buy

192

bundles of coats and help the people to get a coat so they could keep warm. (It got cold up on Zomba Mountain in Bill's area.)

Then there was the charge that Blanche had helped the women make some cloth bags, and there seemed to be some squabble about that. Blanche said that she remembered helping the women learn to sew and make the bags. Blanche said the women were so proud of their bags after finishing them. She had no idea what had been wrong.

These are all the charges I can remember. I thought, if this is all, we should discuss the issues with the Convention Officers and get to the bottom of the problem. Other missionaries felt we should make Bill and Blanche leave.

It was inconceivable to Jerry and me to ask Bill to leave when he would retire in a few years. But more than that, they had given their lives to these people. They loved these people, Zomba Mountain, and their home there.

At the meeting, Sam Upton said, "I will not abide by the democratic process if the mission votes to stand behind Bill all the way, even if it means leaving Malawi." Then Sam and Gerald said they would not abide by the majority vote. Beverly was very vocal and thought the Westers should leave and eliminate the Mission from dealing with the problem.

There was still the issue of the Convention usurping authority over the churches. Then I mentioned that according to the bylaws, the chain of command flows up from the Churches to the Convention. Then I said the word "autonomous," and I could feel the hair on the back of Gerald's and Sam's necks raise.

Gerald said that the bylaws were written by a bunch of Americans and signed by Malawians who did not understand them. I felt that if the bylaws are not worth standing on, we can't be a democratic body and have no forum on which to base a stand.

I couldn't believe that Gerald understood the significance of what he had said. It was as if he felt no responsibility to the Southern Baptist Convention, his sending body. He also seemingly felt no obligation to teach the Baptist doctrine.

It was apparent to me that there indeed was potential for difficulties at the December meeting. The Lilongwe Station seemed to have a good enough relationship to disagree and still not get angry, but all the missionaries did not hold the same mutual understanding and respect.

I had not gotten the least bit upset at the meeting, but Marlyn and Rebecca cried. I understood the sensitivity of this issue. It meant all the missionaries might get thrown out of the country if we stood behind Bill. We had not been here long enough to have the same feeling about Malawi as they had. But to me, right is right, and wrong is wrong. Just throwing Bill out after all his years of service for no reason at all would simply and plainly be wrong.

At the end of the meeting, we all knelt and prayed about the upcoming conference in Blantyre. We discussed fasting and praying.

Jerry and I were still hoping and praying about an English-speaking Baptist church, but this was not a good time to bring it up with the missionaries or the Convention Officers.

23 Connections & Common Ground

We continued to meet fine Malawian couples who were good prospects for an English-speaking church. Dan and Wendy Sherman with Young Life were in Malawi. They were a great couple, and Dan wanted us to start a church. He was working with many English-speaking men and wished he had a church to send them to.

One of the men Dan was working with was appointed to his position with the government by President Banda. I thought Bro. Galatia and Bro. Kanowa might think twice before they come up against someone like him.

We met Dunstan and Gladys Mwangulu, who had recently moved to Lilongwe from Mzuzu.

Mike Canady had worked with them in Mzuzu, Dunstan was a judge in Lilongwe, and Gladys worked at the Reserve Bank. Both were very capable young people. They would not fit into and be fed spiritually, like they needed, in one of the Chichewa Baptist churches. They spoke Chichewa, although it was not their mother tongue.

They had studied in English, were educated in English, and preferred to worship in English instead of Chichewa.

One day, I rushed home from work and prepared a vegetable dish to take over to the Uptons' house to celebrate Rebecca's birthday. After dinner, we played 84. (This was the second time I had played 84.)

I sat next to Sam. Once, I was trying to figure out if we had lost enough so that we had gone down; I thought we had, but Sam said we had not. I was talking and figuring in my head when Sam sarcastically said, "Well, I'm not going to argue with you." A hush fell around the table. I had no idea that I was arguing.

Delis Brown from Zambia was there, and he said the bid was 55, not 59, which I thought. I simply ignored Sam at the time, but I thought he was rude. I decided it would be best to stay clear of Sam; he obviously did not like me. I wondered if he was suffering from a guilty conscience about how he had proselyted Fletcher to work for him and if he was just trying to relieve his conscience by finding fault with me. That's his problem, and I would not allow it to interfere with my ministry or service.

We continued to get together with the Lilongwe missionaries, and I didn't notice hard feelings toward anyone. We played Mexican Dominoes with some of them, and I won by a big score. Jerry said I should be ashamed and embarrassed for winning by such a significant margin, and I am not sure he was joking. We seemed to have a good time together.

We continued to go to Kawali church and took more and more Malawians with us. Several members of the church were a result of our ministry.

Sam Upton, Van Thompson, and Carl Houston conducted a training session in Lilongwe for some National Leaders. Bro. Kanowa said they did not want missionaries in the country who were unwilling to teach. Gerald said that great strides had been made in the meeting.

Bro. Kanowa said that he had a new vision. I had been praying that the leaders would get a new idea regarding reaching all the people of Malawi — not just the down and out but the up and out. All people who do not know Jesus Christ need him, whether rich or poor, educated or uneducated, black or white. I prayed that this was the vision he had. I had the National leader Van and Carl to dinner after the meeting.

———•••———

Malcolm Judge was the music teacher at Kamuzu Academy. Kamuzu Academy was a very elite high school, designed for the brightest young people of Malawi. They take only the students with the highest grades and put the children through a rigorous education.

Malcolm Judge had invited Jerry to speak at the Student Christian Organization. We got our car loaded and headed to Kasungu. The school is in the village area of Kasungu, and we had never been out there before.

We drove to Kasungu and then down a rub-board type dirt road for 15 miles through villages and down narrow winding roads. Then from amidst the back woods of Africa, up jumped a beautiful, modern campus filled with grassy, well-manicured lawns, plush flower gardens, a beautiful reflecting lake, paved roads, and gorgeous brick buildings.

It was absolutely breathtaking — and such a contrast. About 350 of Malawi's most intelligent students attend, and this year would be the first graduating class. The boys wore dress trousers, a white shirt, and a tie, and the girls wore a gray jumper, a white blouse, white socks, and black shoes.

They all looked immaculate. They were laughing and talking as they walked along.

We stayed with the Judges, and I did not think they were Christians. That night Jerry spoke to a group of about 150 to 175 students. Jerry had completed the most spirit-filled speech I had ever heard him give. The Mission had been praying for him, and God obviously answered their prayers.

Students began to ask thought-provoking questions about Jesus Christ and salvation. Jerry answered all the questions without wavering. At 9:15, he had to stop with the students still going strong. (The lights went out at 9:30, and the students had to be in bed.)

We handed out tracts. We met Harold Kachaje, who was the leader of the leaders. He was a young man with a lot of potential — intelligent, good-looking, and he seemed to have plenty of common sense. He said he hoped Jerry would be able to come back.

The next day the students were in class, and Malcolm Judge was teaching, so we looked around the school and had lunch in the cafeteria with the students.

That night we showed a Billy Graham film about a young man that was a race car driver. The young man was having some difficulties with his father. The students began to roar when the young man went to the refrigerator and took a drink from a half-gallon milk carton.

They were laughing so we felt we should stop the film and explain something. The students thought the boy had gone to the refrigerator and drank beer. In Malawi, beer was sold in half-gallon paper cartons, not milk. Their milk is sold in pint-size soft plastic bags.

After making this clarification, we resumed the film. The students seemed to enjoy the movie, and it was a good time with them. We drove back to Lilongwe and had a five-course dinner at the Capitol Hotel; it was the climax of a lovely weekend.

We continued to learn about international economics. We had Mr. Akers from Nelo Tear over for dinner. He said Malawi had over-extended itself and would have to devalue the Kwacha again, maybe as much as 40%. This would be disastrous for the people.

He said the U.S. had an agreement with Malawi for their tea and sugar for the next ten years. He told us Malawi used its tobacco income to pay back debts, to build the Lilongwe airport, several homes for the President, and Kamuzu Academy. I didn't fully understand how all this fit together. Anyway, we had a great dinner and visit with Mr. Akers.

———•••———

Since our arrival in Malawi, we shared our residence with geckos. Geckos are little lizards that would run all over the walls, on the furniture, and anyplace else they wanted to go. We did not kill them because people said they ate mosquitoes — and mosquitos carry malaria, so we accepted the lesser of two evils. This little monster had watched me every day as I prepared dinner.

We knew there were crocodiles in the river, but it seemed like all of a sudden, they had begun to attack people with a vengeance. One man who worked on our house had been attacked. Then we heard that crocodiles had attacked two men right there in town. (One of the men died, and the other man had serious leg injuries.) Another crocodile attack happened when a local woman was washing her clothes down by the Old Town Bridge, and a crocodile grabbed her child. She was able to pull her child from the mouth of the crocodile, and the child was not injured badly. Nobody had to tell me to stay away from the river, and yet, when we drove across the bridge, we would see women washing their clothes.

———•••———

Jerry and Joyce Spires, and their two children, had come up from Blantyre. Joyce had been through surgery and did not seem to be healing and recovering well. She also appeared to be on the verge of a nervous breakdown. They had dinner with us, and the kids went to the Workmans to play Canasta. Joyce said she was ready to throw up her hands and quit.

The next morning, they had breakfast with us, and we took them on a tour of the railroad station and around town. We stopped at the Capitol Hotel for coffee. The Messers had all of us over for lunch, and then all the missionaries took a covered dish over to the Workmans for dinner so everybody could visit with the Spires. (Years later Joyce learned they stitched her up improperly.)

After Joyce had a good night's sleep and everybody was very friendly to them, she seemed like a different person. Things were falling into their proper perspective for them. Everyone seemed to have a good time over at the Workmans, including all the Spires.

Then the Spires came over for breakfast of hot biscuits, gravy, eggs, and bacon. It was delicious. Joyce expressed how much she had enjoyed the weekend, and I think they left with a new hope for the mission/ convention relations.

———•••———

We had hired Dyton Kagwa as a fulltime mechanic. There were so many vehicle problems that Jerry could no longer do so much of the work himself. The places in town that serviced the Kombis just did not seem to do a very good job. Lilongwe Mechanical was good at pounding out dents and some problems, but when it came to the engine, it was hopeless.

Dyton was a real Godsend. But, as would be expected, some people in the Mission did not think he should have been hired.

Since we were handling the expenses, it was obvious to us that it would save the Mission a lot of money, and the downtime would be significantly reduced.

Hiring Dyton took a lot of pressure off Jerry and freed him up to do other things. He could schedule repairs, buy and keep the parts we needed on hand, and supervise Dyton, who was already a trained mechanic. So, with just a little supervision, vehicle servicing was greatly enhanced.

24 Nerve Jangling Shortages

Besides Missionary, Convention, and relationship problems, the shortages were beginning to worry the missionaries. There were still cement and petrol shortages. There was no fertilizer for the farmers. There was no cooking oil, black pepper, diesel, or paraffin (coal oil), and any time you went to look for any specific item, you would be told they were out of it.

I seemed to still be getting into other missionaries' hair. Gene Kingsley had come over to Publications and been doing some personal work in the darkroom. Somehow, he had taken over the supervision of printing the women's books.

Gene supervised the layout of the book and pulled the paper from the inventory to print the book. Upon checking the book, the layout was incorrect (Page number 23 followed page 17), and Gene got really upset with himself. He felt so bad about the error because they had already run quite a few pages before he caught it.

Then I became involved. I knew very little about printing, but I was learning fast because I was exposed to so much so quickly. And basically, it was my responsibility because Jerry had spent most of his time at the house construction.

Then Gene corrected the problem and went to pull more paper. He and I started arguing over how much paper it would take. So right in front of all the employees, we had it out. I insisted that it would not take as much paper as Gene wanted to pull, and I had already figured out how much paper it should take and allowed 10 percent for wastage.

Gene insisted it would take him 20 percent more paper than I had calculated. Since I was having a hard time controlling the inventory and getting the print shop to stay on a break-even basis, I was not about to let him pull the additional paper.

After a heated discussion and putting a pencil to the figures, we learned that if we had pulled the additional paper, there would have been enough to have 17 blank pages in the book. The book called for no blank pages, but sometimes you have a blank page at the front or back. The ultimate decision had to be mine since it was my responsibility.

I think this was the last time Gene tried to help. It was a real shame because he knew ten times as much about the darkroom and printing as we did. However, we had the management and accounting skills that Gene needed to run Publications. I sincerely liked Gene and really hated that his job turned out as it did.

A jeep came by Publications, with loudspeakers on top of the jeep. A voice bellowed out that the President was coming to town, and all the businesses would have to close. When the President came to town, it was customary that the stores would close and let their employees off so that they could go out beside the street to wave at him when he drove by.

Sometimes the people would stand out in the hot sun waiting half a day for him. Sometimes the streets would be closed for hours. You could get caught in one part of town and could not go anywhere until after the President went by. Sometimes you did not mind too much, but other times this just added to the stress when you were hurrying and trying to accomplish something. It required an unbelievable amount of patience to live under these circumstances.

I was in hot water again. Jerry was in charge of houses and cars as the business manager, and somehow, I always had to make decisions that really were not mine to have to make. One day during a severe petrol (gasoline) shortage, J. R. Heriford came to me and wanted the keys to the emergency petrol drum. He wanted to go out to some village on some worthwhile mission but needed more petrol.

I told him the petrol was for emergency use, and I could not let him have the keys because I did not consider this an emergency. J. R. got really mad at me but did not say a lot.

When Jerry came home, I told him J. R. was mad at me because I would not give him petrol. Jerry said he would get a ruling and guidelines on what constitutes an "emergency."

So, at the next appropriate meeting, Jerry said he needed some guidelines. The committee ruled that the drum of emergency petrol be used for medical emergencies, life and death situations of both missionaries and nationals, and, if necessary, we were to give Mike Canady enough petrol to get from Lilongwe to Blantyre the next week because he, Linda, and their family were going on furlough. This ruling helped to alleviate that problem.

The petrol shortages continued, and it was amazing how this shortage coincided with short tempers. (And not just mine.) There had been no chickens in the stores on a regular basis since we came to Malawi.

Now there was also a shortage of beef.

We were told that cows were being driven down from Mzuzu and Kasungu. (The cows were naturally skinny anyway, and I could just imagine how skinny the poor cows would get on a cattle drive.) They were moving these cows just 10 miles a day, so I primed myself for a long wait before we would have beef again. (We'd better learn to enjoy beans because no meat was available.)

There was also a shortage of paper at Publications for printing our literature. We had been getting our paper from the Catholics in Blantyre. (It seems they were the only ones in the country who could get a license to import paper, other than the government.) For three weeks, Blantyre Print promised they would send us some paper. Maybe they were running short, too; I didn't know what the problem was.

We asked Jerry Spires to go out there and talk to them and see if he could determine why they would not send us some paper. Jerry Spires went out to Blantyre Print and called and said they would ship the paper the next day. I thought, yes, I have heard that before. But sure enough, they sent the paper, we got it the next day, and we were back in the printing business.

———•••———

Janie House came by for a short visit and brought me a few goodies from the Corleys. Janie had been to Zimbabwe, and the Corleys sent me some chocolate-covered peanuts. They were a welcome sight. With my love of chocolate, especially chocolate-covered peanuts, it was like I had died and gone to heaven. Little thoughtful things can mean so much when you are having a bad day.

There was another adjustment that I was experiencing. Each mission family was issued "one" car, and all the other families managed with that one mission vehicle. The problem was that our family vehicle was Jerry's personal vehicle. (He had never had to share a car with anybody.)

I had to hitch a ride to work every morning and back home in the evening. I had my own car in the States for the past twenty-four years, but now, I was completely without wheels. I had a hard time getting to the market, and I could never just go someplace on my own. Of all the adjustments, this was the most difficult for me.

When we came to the mission field, we agreed we would try to live on our missionary salary just like everybody else. We had been paying about $500 a month for the excess shipment in our crates. With this expense paid off, we should be able to buy me a car. Being without a car was one problem I refused to endure any longer. So, Jerry made plans to have a rebuilt car shipped from Japan for me. (He wanted to try one of these cars out and thought that if it worked out well, he might order some for the Mission.)

He ordered a Toyota Corolla Station Wagon. When it arrived, it was yellow and about four years old but looked almost new. We were really pleased with the appearance, and it ran well. It felt wonderful to have my own car again.

———•••———

I was still feeling moody, and Jerry seemed irritable. We would get into arguments over the simplest things. The pressure over the attitude of Bro. Kanowa regarding starting an English-speaking church bothered me. The Convention's attitude toward Bill Wester was boiling at a fevered pitch. Publication always had a problem. (If not problems with the work, it was the employees sitting around and not working.) Gerald Workman was not feeling good, and I figured it was nothing more than the stress of Mission/Convention relational problems.

All my visions, dreams, and hopes for an English-speaking church got pushed aside by house building and publications. I didn't possess the slightest inkling of feeling like a missionary with a burning desire to share the gospel. I hoped desperately to climb out of this pit of despair.

A verse from the hymn "Showers of Blessings" came to mind: "Showers of blessing/Showers of blessing we need;/Mercy-drops round us are falling,/But for the showers we plead."

I don't think I had ever understood this song until then. We plead for blessings, but they are all around us.

God is great, and He has been so good to us that it is ridiculous to become so uptight about things that are in God's hands anyway. He must see me much like he saw the Children of Israel in the wilderness.

He had done so much for them, yet they grumbled and grumbled. And there I sat in my easy bed with all the comforts and necessities. Instead of praising God for all His marvelous handiwork and love for me, I grumbled.

I will praise the Lord and thank him for Jesus. I will take care of today's problems, for they are indeed plenty. I will commit tomorrow to the Lord and trust all the Publications and Mission problems to His care.

On December first of last year, James Hampton with the Foreign Mission Board came into Blantyre to meet with the missionaries, and we attended that meeting. The missionaries spoke freely about some of the things that were bothering them among themselves, and some of the pressure between the Blantyre and Lilongwe missionaries was released. It was a smooth meeting. Because Jerry and I could not vote and we needed to return to Lilongwe to work, we left early.

However, after the meeting, the Spires, the Sibleys, and Mary Ann Chandler all received letters from the Blantyre Association asking them to leave Blantyre. One translation of this letter, written in Chechewa, said they were to leave. The missionaries could not decide whether the intent was for them to leave Blantyre — or the country.

What had seemed to be a good, productive meeting had turned into a truly sad experience. I did not know what the Mission would do, and I did not know how this would affect Jerry and me. Joyce seemed to be taking it very hard. (Joyce had not been feeling well anyway.) I felt sure they would leave the country no matter what the Mission decided. Since Jerry Spires had been the Business Manager, this would directly affect the takeover of Jerry Dowdy's business work.

Jerry Dowdy called Jerry Spires and offered our help in any way possible. Joyce seemed to have gotten a grip on her nerves and was handling the problem much better than expected.

25 Convention & Relationships

Dr. Saunders, the director of the Southern Baptist Convention over mission work in Southern Africa, came to Malawi. He had met with some of the National Leaders. The Lilongwe missionaries got together for dinner at the home of Sam and Marlyn Upton. Dr. Saunders expressed his concern regarding relationships. He said serious problems existed between some of the National Baptist Leadership and some of the missionaries.

The Mission Meeting was when the missionaries got together to discuss their budget and make plans for the upcoming year. We elected Bill Wester as Chairman at the time, and Bill declined. At first, we did not understand why.

Later, Bro. Galatia told Jerry and me that the Nationals couldn't work with Bill Wester and would not allow him to have a leadership role. We had difficulty understanding their position since the Mission had no official input into who the National Convention would elect as their officers.

Bill and Blanche Wester lived in Zomba. They were the first Baptist missionaries to come to Malawi and arrived in 1964. By coincidence, that was the year Jerry and I started our business and decided to go into full mission work.

Bill and Blanche were loved dearly by the Malawi people, and maybe some of the National leaders were jealous of them. Also, two church leaders in their area were having difficulties. One group of Bill's churches followed one leader, and one group followed the other. This division of loyalty put Bill in the middle of a squabble, and no matter what he said, somebody would not accept his decisions.

For clarification, The Mission is made up of missionaries from America. The National Convention is made up of Malawian nationals. The two work together for the glory of the Lord. The two are separate entities but work together hand in hand, hopefully in complete harmony under the leadership of the Holy Spirit. Because the Mission supplemented the Convention budget, they had a little input where money was concerned. The Mission audited Convention expenditures to be sure they used the money as voted on by the National Convention. We suspected there might be some Mission-Convention problems, and we were still trying to understand precisely what was happening.

The next day, we had the opportunity to be alone with Dr. Saunders. We probably spoke out of turn (and partly out of ignorance), but we approached Dr. Saunders about the amount of capital that would be budgeted for the Malawi Mission.

Dr. Saunders was the one from Richmond, Virginia who divided up the money, and then it was approved by a higher board.

I told him that Malawi got $30,000 in capital and that would purchase one and one-half cars per year. Malawi had to pay 100% duty on each vehicle they brought into the country. With 18 cars in the Mission, I explained that we could replace the cars every 12 years. This estimate did not consider trade-in, but at the end of 12 years, the vehicles would have very little value.

Jerry was in charge of the Mission's cars and had spent an enormous amount of time trying to keep them repaired. I could see a lot of unproductive downtime with the missionaries unable to get around. This was Jerry's area of responsibility, but that did not keep me from jumping in with both feet — sink or swim. I told him that considering the country's roads and lack of parts and service, I felt $30,000 in Capital was unrealistic.

The $30,000 was not explicitly allocated just for cars but for all capital expenditures. That did not give us one cent to build churches or put roofs on churches. Through the years, the missionaries donated their tithes for such projects — at least some missionaries did. This provision did not give us a cent for missionary housing (at that time, I did not know that special funds would be appropriated for missionary housing).

He did not defend giving Malawi such a small amount of capital; however, he did share a little story about something that had happened to him many years before, and I fully understood why Malawi got what it got.

Dr. Saunders said that he had flown into the airport in Blantyre. He was exhausted and expected someone to meet him at the airport and take him to Mission Meeting at Chongoni.

When he arrived at the airport, nobody was there to meet him. He was given a note and a set of car keys. The note said for him to find his own way to Chongoni and Mission Meeting. Even though this was many years earlier, his voice cracked as he came to this part of his story. It was easy to see that he was still angry with how the Malawi Mission treated him.

(Later, I asked a couple of missionaries about the incident, and neither even remembered it.) But Dr. Saunders certainly had not forgotten. Although he did not say so, I concluded that this is the reason Malawi was in such bad shape with automobiles. I said nothing further about Malawi and the capital. Dr. Saunders left Malawi and went on to one of the other countries in Southern Africa under his leadership.

———•••———

Jerry and I needed to go to Blantyre on business. Bro. Chisi and Bro. Galatia rode part of the way with us. They were making the rounds campaigning to get reelected to the National Convention.

For some reason, they felt threatened by some of the young, trained leaders in some of the churches. Bro. Galatia said that the Convention was ready to have all the missionaries thrown out of the country if the Convention didn't get its way.

The National Convention officers wanted to tell the churches what to do, how much they should donate (or pay) to the Convention, and dictate which preachers could baptize. The Convention wanted to boss the churches, whereas, in the States, the churches tell the Convention what to do.

It seemed that if the National leaders did not get their way, they thought the missionaries were putting thoughts into the heads of the young men. So, there were some problems that had no easy answers, and the missionaries were caught in the middle. Issues with the Convention seemed to have been brewing for a long time, and now they had surfaced.

While in Blantyre, we had dinner with the Spires. Mike Canady was there and reported on Davis Saunder's recent visit and meeting with the Nationals. Van Thompson was put in charge of mass media during our mission meeting. The media building was on the same compound, in Blantyre, with the Business Manager/Treasurer Office. Jerry Spires was the Business Manager/Treasurer. Jerry Dowdy had been assigned to Malawi as the Business Manager to take some of the work and pressure from Jerry Spires.

Jerry Spires said he was fed up with responsibility and lack of authority to hire and fire. He was referring to what was happening at the Mass Media Building. He said people were coming in late or sometimes out for a week without any excuse.

The Mission didn't think he should be reprimanded. Also, some men had been using the media building to "entertain" women. With Malaboyna, the son-n-law of Bro. Galatia — and a convention officer — now working in mass media, this situation was explosive.

We had given Malaboyna material to translate for Publications about three months prior, and it still was not translated. Jerry told him three weeks ago he had to have the materials translated immediately to get them printed in time to distribute to the churchcs.

Before we left the States, Dr. Saunders told us there were two things he wanted us to do when we got to Malawi. First, he wanted us to evaluate the publishing house and determine whether it should be closed. Second, he wanted us to start an English-Speaking Baptist Church in the Capital City of Lilongwe.

————••••————

Dr. Davis Saunders, the area director for Southern Africa, came to Malawi. He had met with some of the National Leaders.

The Lilongwe missionaries got together for dinner at the home of Sam and Marlyn Upton. Dr. Saunders expressed his concern regarding relationships, saying there were serious problems between some of the National Baptist Leadership and some missionaries.

Earlier, we had concluded our annual mission meeting. The Mission Meeting was a time when the missionaries got together to discuss their budget and make plans for the upcoming year. At that time, we elected Bill Wester as Chairman, and Bill declined. At first, we did not understand why.

Later, Bro. Galatia told Jerry and me that the Nationals couldn't work with Bill Wester and would not allow him to have a place of leadership. We had difficulty understanding their position since the Mission had no official input into who the National Convention would elect as their officers.

Bill and Blanche Wester lived in Zomba. They were the first Baptist missionaries to come to Malawi; they arrived in 1964. (By coincidence, that was the year that Jerry and I had started our business and decided we wanted to go into full-time mission work.)

The people loved Bill and Blanche dearly, and maybe some of the National leaders were jealous of them. Also, two church leaders in their area were having difficulties. One group of Bill's churches followed one leader, and one group followed the other. This division put Bill in the middle of a squabble, and no matter what he said, somebody would not accept his decisions.

For clarification, let me explain:

The Mission is made up of missionaries from America.

The National Convention is made up of Malawian nationals.

The two work together for the glory of the Lord. The two are separate entities but work together hand in hand, hopefully in complete harmony under the leadership of the Holy Spirit. Because the Mission supplemented the convention budget, they had a little input where money was concerned. The Mission audited the convention expenditures to be sure the money was used as voted on by the National Convention.

We had suspected there might be some Mission/Convention problems, but we were still trying to understand exactly what was going on.

———•••———

So, when Jerry was asked to take over the publication of all the Sunday School literature, tracts, women's books, TEE books, Bible Way books, and all other mission printing, he felt somewhat obligated to accept. Dr. Saunders indicated that the Publication House was experiencing difficulties and had a history of problems. He did not elaborate on what kind of problems. This involvement connected Jerry and me with the Mass Media Committee because the Publishing House fell under Media.

When Jerry went into the Media building in Blantyre to pick up the translated material, Malaboyna still hadn't translated it, so he picked up the English version while Malaboyna was not in his office. (Nobody knew where Malaboyna was or when he planned to return.) Jerry told Van Thompson that if there was any problem, Jerry Spires was holding the English copy for a few days. Malaboyna was gone all week. Jerry did not hear anything, so he assumed there was no problem.

We went back to Blantyre again to meet with the Mission Support Committee, which was standard policy for new missionaries. The Spires invited us to stay with them, and they built a fire in the fireplace. It was damp and cooler in Blantyre than in Lilongwe. The weather had been lovely since our arrival, and the tropical flowers were spectacular.

We met with the Mission Support Committee, and Bill Wester was the chairman since this committee deals with missionaries. Bill said that Malaboyna had "blown up" because Jerry had come in and taken the Sunday School Material that needed to be translated. (What really bothered me was that Bill said he had not intended to mention this "blowup" to us.)

Bill said he felt that Jerry had a big problem with Malaboyna, even though we assumed there were no problems; Van Thompson had not mentioned any problem to Jerry. (Jerry was on the mass media committee with Van.)

The way I saw it, the Mission Support Committee was not even going to allow Jerry to tell them his side of the situation, and if Jerry didn't know a problem existed, then how could he possibly make things right with Malaboyna?

Naturally, I had to let the committee know that it aggravated me that they were not going to mention this to us. It seems to me that the missionaries are afraid to say things to one another for fear of hurting feelings.

So, they say nothing, and problems with the Nationals that could be worked out are not. Then problems grow because the missionaries will not confront an issue. (They would rather find someone guilty in their own mind than confront an issue and discover the whole truth.) Missionaries must then make decisions based on half-truths.

This impasse was not the first time I felt the missionaries were a bit like ostriches. (They stuck their heads in the sand and hoped the problem would disappear.) Instead, these issues escalated to explosions.

———•••———

Back in Lilongwe, we had a prayer meeting at our house. Sam mentioned that he had taken Bro. Chisi's two children, who were very sick, to the hospital for treatment. Jerry and I had been to see the children and asked Bro. Chisi if there was anything that we could do. Bro. Chisi said he wanted to take the children to the clinic, but he did not have the money, so Jerry gave him K12.00, which was more than the clinic and medicine would cost.

Jerry mentioned at the prayer meeting that he wondered why Bro. Chisi had taken the children to the hospital since he had given him money for them to go to a clinic. Gerald and Sam agreed that it was best not to mention it to Bro. Chisi. (I felt that in both their minds, they had found Bro. Chisi guilty of taking money deceitfully — just another case of finding someone guilty without hearing both sides of the story.)

Jerry agreed that Bro Chisi would think he was being accused of misconduct if asked about the K12.00.

This prediction may be accurate, but I wonder if we'll tuck this memory away along with many similar incidents. Is this fair? Won't somebody explode someday and recall all these incidents?

Bro. Galatia had just brought up something to the missionaries that happened to him 18 years ago. When we do not confront issues as they happen, a giant wall of distrust is building between the Nationals and the Missionaries. Each misunderstanding adds a brick to the wall rather than facing the issue and correcting the problem when it occurs. I had been through this and knew full well. Nonconfrontation just does not work.

Sam said, "You just have to forget these little things."

But neither the missionaries nor the nationals forget, and each one bases today's decisions on yesterday's experiences.

Verbally, they say, "I forgive and forget; yet, they cannot forget, nor do they forgive.

I felt good about my missionary experience despite everything that was going on. On June 2, in my privacy, I prayed, "God will you lead me and direct me in how I should deal with people? Maybe you will use me to start tearing down the brick wall."

———————

Our work was becoming more varied, and there were just not enough hours in a day. Jerry had to get several visas from the South African and American Embassies.

We took Ngombiaria to Likuni Hospital to visit his wife. Mayi had been sick with a fever for three weeks. Likuni Hospital was one of the best in the country. Her mother had come to stay with her. Mayi was so weak that she could hardly move her legs. I gave her mother some money for food to supplement her diet.

Since she had a sore throat, Mayi would not eat. I told her mother to make a thin porridge supplemented with powdered milk and ground peanuts so she could drink it. I insisted that she had to drink water. In a couple of days, I heard that Mayi was eating and feeling better.

When Jerry and I got home after work, two young men and a young girl were waiting for us. I started cooking supper, and Jerry talked to the young people. Jerry witnessed and read Bible verses with them, and the girl accepted Jesus as her Lord and Savior. The girl was a second-year student at the nursing college.

When they left, we had supper and went to the Collier's house, where the missionaries had a birthday party for me. It was very nice, and the missionaries gave me some very nice presents.

Malawi did not have many things to buy, so it always amazed me what the missionaries could find to give as birthday gifts.

———————

Peggy called at about 10:30 and said that she had moved into her new house at Texas A&M. She was all excited. We had authorized her to buy a house so she could have a dog. She was so lonely after we left; we felt that maybe a dog would help.

She brought me up to date on the family. After Jerry's aunt Connie died, Ken went up there, got the refrigerator, and took it to Peggy's new house. Ken had also helped the Dowdys remove an awning from their back porch so they could have a room added onto their house. She said Ken was doing lawn work and cutting grass for a living. (We always paid their college expenses and gave them a few hundred dollars a month.)

Arvil and Pauline celebrated their 50th wedding anniversary with a Caribbean Cruise, even though Pauline had not been feeling well. The family also gave them a party to celebrate their anniversary. Peggy hired a trained chimpanzee to help entertain them. The chimpanzee, dressed like a woman, had climbed up in Arvil's lap and given him a big kiss.

It was wonderful to talk to Peggy. Because of cost, we only called home a few times, and rarely did any of the family call us.

Peggy was also planning a trip to Malawi. It would be so nice to see her again and to be able to sit face to face and catch up on all that had taken place since our departure.

One Sunday, we went to Kawali Church and picked up Bro Chisi and many others from the church. Godfrey and Beatrice were with us. (Godfrey was our cook/housekeeper.) After our Kombi was utterly jam-packed, we headed out to Chisapo Village.

The people went through the village witnessing to people and telling them about Jesus and telling them we were going to have a church service there.

On Sundays, we would frequently take a group of people out to different villages. Sometimes there would not be a church in the village, and sometimes they already had a church, and we encouraged them. (If it was a little congregation, the women would cook lunch for us, and it would turn into an all-day affair.)

On June 16, 1982, with our new office building complete and the office moved in, Copy & Litho had its grand opening. They had a caterer from one of the local country clubs cater. It would have been nice to be there, but surprisingly, we had no regrets. We were just thankful that God had helped us work out all the necessary details to complete this building.

That same day, Peggy left the States for a month's visit with us. Two days later, we drove to Blantyre to pick her up.

She had flown from Houston to Amsterdam, to Nairobi, Kenya, and then on to Malawi. We were thankful she traveled with few problems. She was a little apprehensive since she had never traveled outside the States alone. She brought me some tuna fish and pantyhose.

We spent the next day in Blantyre so Peggy could rest up a little before we started back to Lilongwe. On the way back, we took her up Zomba Mountain, but it was cloudy, and we could not see much.

Blanche and Bill Wester had us over to their house for lunch. When we got into Lilongwe, Marlyn and Sam Upton had us and a few others over for dinner. The next night, I invited all the missionaries over for dessert and coffee so they could meet Peggy. We were so glad to be with her and have her meet our friends.

We wanted to show her some of Africa, so we went on an eleven-day trip to Zambia and Zimbabwe. We stayed with some missionaries, and other missionaries had us over to their houses for meals. We headed down to Harare (Salisbury) and Zimbabwe (Rhodesia) to visit Charles, Gayla, and Chip Corley.

Gayla had drawn us a map of how to find their house. Because Zimbabwe was in the midst of changing names from English to African, Gayla's map did not match the street signs when we got into town, and we could not follow her map.

On the way into town, we were stopped several times by armed military personnel, but we did not find this unusual. There were a lot of armored vehicles driving on the streets, and we did not think much about it.

When we did not know which street to take, we just took one that looked wide and went in the direction indicated on Gayla's map.

As we got down one street a few blocks, it became too narrow, and we pulled up in a driveway. We immediately realized we were in a place where we should not be.

The big white house sat behind a high, white fence with large metal gates. Two armed guards were standing at the entrance, and Jerry knew it was too late to turn around; that would arouse suspicion. So, he took the little map Gayla had drawn, got out of the car, and walked up to the gate.

Another armed guard (with a machine gun with a bayonet affixed) approached Jerry and asked what he wanted. Jerry showed them the map and told them he could not find the street names on the map.

The guard said the streets were renamed that week and gave him directions.

Jerry, who was ready to get out of there, quickly turned around to leave.

"Do you know where you are?" the guard called after Jerry.

"No."

"The President's Palace."

Jerry thanked him and hurried into the car.

Once we found our way out to the Corley's house and greeted them, Jerry told them what had happened. Charles picked up the daily paper and showed us the headlines that revealed that the Prime Minister's House, across the street from the President's Palace, had been blown up the night before — and white South Africans were suspected of the bombing.

We breathed a sigh of relief and had a good visit with the Corleys.

We played bridge and talked. They told us that a laboratory white mouse was loose in their house. Then Gayla talked about a chicken someone had given her, and she was trying to figure out what to do with this chicken.

We went to bed, and I had bombings, guns, mice, and chicken on my mind. Sometime during the night, I felt something under the mattress, and whatever it was, it raised me up.

I jumped out of bed and yelled and awoke everybody in the household.

Charles and Gayla came running in.

Jerry climbed out of bed in a stupor.

I explained that something was in bed with us and thought it was a big rat. Gayla got the broom, and Jerry took it. Charles raised the mattress up to find the cat trapped in the hide-a-bed where I was sleeping. Charles helped release the cat as we all had a big laugh and then went back to bed.

After two or three days, we headed back out on our sightseeing adventure. For the remainder of this trip, we were stopped many times by guards with machine guns and asked questions. We had difficulty getting across the border. (They did not want to let Peggy cross the border because she had not brought her airline ticket with her.)

We stopped to spend the night with Steve and Shirley Taylor. Steve had been hunting and shot several kudu, reedbuck, and other deer-like animals. Shirley cooked some of the wild animals for dinner, and we enjoyed a lovely visit.

We headed on to Bulawayo and spent the next night with Tom and Jeanie Elliff. The military continued to stop us frequently. Once we arrived, Jerry went out of town with Tom to deliver some Bibles. The military stopped them and physically searched them and searched the car. Tom gave them some Bibles, and they were allowed to leave. (I think it shook both of them up just a little.)

Wankie Game Park was where we saw some elephants, baboons, and monkeys. We spent the night in the game park but did not see as many animals as I expected. It was rustic but so lovely. We had two bedrooms, a kitchen, a dining room, and a living area.

The facility provided a cook to prepare meals with the food we brought along. (We had reedbuck, baked potatoes, and salad.) We had passes through the park. The cost was about $24 Zimbabwe dollars, equal to about U.S. $33.

We left our cabin just before dark and saw elephants, giraffes, zebra, and warthogs, all very close. It was lovely, just like something you might see in a movie.

We drove to Victoria Falls the next day and spent the night in another game park. We walked along the paths that overlooked the spectacular Victoria Falls. There was so much water, and the spray fogged up from the falls, so you could not see the bottom. There were no guardrails to prevent you from falling in, never to be seen again. (It was all I could do to keep from pulling Peggy back from the edge.)

It was hard to imagine that much water could spill over, day after day, year after year. We were wearing raincoats, and the spray was so heavy it felt like it was raining. Without our raincoats, we would have been drenched!

Driving across the bridge from the Zimbabwe side of the falls to the Zambia side provided a different view. The next day, we had one last look at the falls, drove on into Lusaka, and spent the night again with Janie House.

Nelson and Sandra Hiachita had us over to their house for dinner. Lusaka was without milk, so we drove over to Franklin Kilpatrick's house to get some milk. These countries seemed to run out of some of the strangest things, and Zambia seemed to be in worse shape than Malawi.

We had a lot of shortages, and there were many things we could never buy. But Zambia was worse.

———•••———

We were grateful to all the missionaries who had been so hospitable to us on the trip. This culture of hospitality is the way it was. We stayed with one another and ate with one another whenever and wherever we traveled. This practice was far better and safer than staying in hotels.

The trip was good without any medical problems, except Peggy got a stomachache. I think it was because she was so tired; she was exhausted when she left home.

Peggy had difficulty getting the utilities turned on in her new house, problems with the builders finishing everything, and then her check from us got delayed and she did not have any money. She had really gotten an education, but with everything going on it was just too much.

Because she did not feel well, we slowed down a little to try to let her rest some. We just wanted Peggy to experience everything during the month she was there.

Showing her the village where Barnwell Chacwanira and Mbusa (Pastor) Sandalamu lived was a pleasure that turned into an all-day affair. We ate goat with Barnwell and his family, and then when we left, Barnwell told us that we were to go by Sandalamu's house.

When we got there, they had planned for us to eat with them. We explained that we had eaten with Barnwell but could tell they would be offended if we did not eat with them. We said that we would eat with them under one condition. We wanted to watch Mayi Sandalamu cook the nsima, and they thought that was so funny but agreed.

She cooked in a little, open, straw-covered hut out behind their house. She built a little fire in the center of the hut, and smoke traveled upward and through the straw roof. She heated the water on the fire, and when it was hot, she added some corn flour. She stirred and stirred and continued to add more corn flour. Finally, when she had added all she felt like she needed, she continued to cook and stir the nsima. When it was thick, she took it off the open fire.

In a small pan, she scrambled a few eggs in a bit of oil. Then she took a broad wooden spoon, dipped it into the water, and put it into the nsima. She dipped out a little nsima and turned it upside down into a metal bowl. She continued to dip the spoon in water, dip out nsima, and turn it upside down into the bowl until the bowl was full of little nsima patties and the pan where she had cooked the nsima was empty.

She had squatted the entire time near the little fire. Smoke had gotten in her face, so it was difficult for her to breathe, yet she continued to stir the nsima. Although this was a common, daily occurrence for her, I had never before watched anyone prepare a Malawian meal; this was also the first cooking lesson she had ever given.

We could not eat much because we had already eaten, but we still had a pleasant visit with them, even though their English was limited, and our Chichewa was extremely limited.

The following week allowed Peggy to rest. We went shopping for ivory bracelets and wooden necklaces. She bought some wooden animals and a small ear of corn made from malachite. She also claimed some things I had previously purchased, including a favorite Malawian artifact, a train of 12 elephants carved of wood. (The ones with their legs in a walking position were especially popular with the missionaries.)

John Burroughs was the newly appointed American Ambassador, and we went to the Ambassador's residence for a July 4th celebration. The Lilongwe missionaries sang a medley of patriotic songs. (I thought we sounded awful.)

We had hot dogs and hamburgers — the wieners were flown in from South Africa. We had cold drinks, and the children played games. They sold the main course, and the guests brought desserts and chips to share.

All Americans living in Malawi were invited, and we had a wonderful time. It was so nice to be with Americans, sing American songs, and see the American flag flying. It brought tears to our eyes.

During Peggy's visit, we found a little time to work at Publications and study some Chichewa, but this was our vacation time, also. To round out Peggy's trip, a group including Rebecca, Melanie, and Kirk Phifer, along with a guest of Rebecca's and Harold and Jimmie Fitzhugh from Marlin, Texas, loaded into our Kombi, and we headed for Kasungu Game Park, one of my favorite places in Malawi. We spent the next two nights in the park's "round ovals." We saw a lot of elephants, a fox, some wild dogs, a hyena, and many deer-like animals.

During the night, the hippopotamus woke us up, snorting and playing around our cabins. We saw several grazing outside our window,

219

and sometimes they would scratch their backs on our round ovals. One night Peggy, Jerry, and I played Uno. Everyone in our group played the next night and had a wonderful time.

When we returned to Lilongwe, I went to Publications and rushed through some paperwork. Gene and Beverly Kingsley, some of the first missionaries to Malawi, had returned from their furlough, and they wanted us to come to dinner, so we accepted. She served elegant shish kabobs with rice.

Both Gene and Beverly spoke Chichewa very well. Beverly had approached me about Jerry now running Publications, and I told her we had not wanted nor asked for the job. I shared with her some of the things Davis Saunders told us before we left the States. The decision for Jerry to take charge of Publications was a Mission decision, not ours.

She was not too happy with how I explained the situation to her, but there was nothing else I could say. She did not allow this little problem to keep us from being friends.

Peggy was supposed to leave Lilongwe Airport at 10:30 the next morning.

We took her to the airport, and when she entered the International Departures area, we left the airport. (We had a lot of things to catch up with.) Peggy was to fly to Blantyre, and at 4:00 p.m., she was to board her plane to the States.

At 12:05, she called and said they had been allowed onto the plane two times, but the plane had not yet taken off. She was afraid she would miss her Blantyre connection. Jerry got in the car to pick her up and drive her to Blantyre, but the plane was gone when he got to the airport.

Then at about 6:00 p.m., Peggy called again to say she was back at Lilongwe Airport. She had flown to Blantyre, and now they had flown her back to Lilongwe. She said, "I have been flying all day and am back where I started." Eventually, Peggy was on her plane for the States, and that was the end of her trip.

That is the way it is in Africa. You have to hang loose and have a lot of patience. Things usually work out, but frequently, not in any way you expect.

———•••———

When Peggy left, we felt so lonely. Then we began to have people over, people had us over, we got neck-deep in our work, and there was no time to miss the family.

We went to the Capital Hotel for a lovely Sunday Buffet for $7.75 per person. The Capital Hotel is lovely for Malawi. Everything is very formal and proper — typical English style — with meals served on white, starched tablecloths.

The countries around Malawi continued to make headline news with the wars and battles in their country. The U. S. Army & Navy radio station reported that a tour bus had been hijacked outside Bulawayo, Zimbabwe. Six people were held hostage: two Americans, two British, and two Australians. They were being held for ransom by some of Mugabe's leaders imprisoned under the new Zimbabwe leadership.

Mugabe's men were charged with trying to overthrow the government, and arms were supposedly found in their possession. Constant fighting was going on in Mozambique, and Zambia was not fighting, but a threat lay just under the surface, and their economy was declining. There were so many shortages and there was a lot of unrest.

Malawi was faring better than most of her neighbors. They were the most successful at putting up a smokescreen to foreign governments. They had mastered the game of collecting foreign aid. If not for this aid, Malawi would have been in terrible condition. It was still considered one of the five poorest countries in the world.

Jerry wrote a letter to the Mass Media Committee and signed his name, "Publications Director." We attended Kawali Baptist church, where Bro. Chisi was pastor; he was also chairman of the Mass Media committee. After church, he cornered Jerry and quizzed him about how he had signed his name.

It seems that at a meeting Jerry missed, the committee spent an hour discussing his title. The committee thought Jerry was trying to pull a fast one over them. The "director" title was supposed to be reserved for a National.

Jerry had not given the title a second thought when he wrote the letter, and this reprimand really irritated him. Jerry told Bro. Chisi he did not come to Malawi to run publications, and he didn't even want the job. He said he would give it to the committee right then if they wanted it.

Jerry did not think that he made Bro. Chisi angry, but he said he was pretty sure he had gotten his point across. There had been a constant squabble ever since we took over Publications. It was given to us bankrupt, with immoral employees, a former missionary who resented us taking his job, and a committee who squabbled over every decision.

I wrote in my journal about this time, "Life is interesting in Malawi. It has its problems and rewards, and we are loving every minute of it. All in all, everything seems to be going well."

————•••————

Georgia Heriford and I went out to see Mayi Ngombiaria. Her blood pressure was very low, and Georgia thought she should return to the hospital. She was weak, but Bambo Ngombiaria would not let her return to the hospital.

He said there was nobody else to take care of the kids. He complained because Mayi would not get out in the fields and plant the crops. He seemed more interested in the fields than he was in his wife. This outlook was understandable because if the fields did not produce crops, the people would go hungry or starve.

I gave Bambo Ngombiara $15 to hire someone to work in the fields so he would not make Mayi work. Giving money was a way of life for the missionaries. Some people were in such desperate situations that we felt we had to do something. It only takes a little to help a lot. We constantly had people coming by our gate requesting food. They would say they were hungry, or they wanted someone to take them back to their families.

26 Capital City Baptist Church

Jerry and I attended an informal Bible study on Sunday mornings at Andrew and Rose Mary Kingston's home. The Kingstons were from England, and they had one son, Mark, who was about ten. Neil and Glenda Weston and their children, Craig and Lisa, were attending, as well as Jim and Liz Parrish. The Westons were from New Zealand, and the Parrishes were from England.

The Kingstons and Westons had a Baptist background. The Parrishes were Methodist but had attended different denominations through the years.

We began to talk about starting an English-speaking Church. There seemed to be a need. (There was one at the Presbyterian Church, but people who attended did not seem particularly impressed.) Because starting a church was one of the primary reasons for our going to Malawi, I was very excited at the prospect of starting a church.

On June 7, 1983, we met at our house and had our first serious discussion about starting a church. There was talk about making it inter-denominational. Jerry and I explained that we were Baptist missionaries sent to Malawi by the Baptist Convention. If we were to be deeply involved in the church, it had to be a Baptist church.

We all desired to minister to the needs of the ex-patriot community and the English-speaking Malawians. The ex-patriots came from all different churches, so how would they mesh into a Baptist Church?

We had several meetings in June and July and began ironing out some details. Jerry and I said we would need a church covenant and bylaws, which would become our church guidelines.

Andrew Kingston did not understand why we needed a constitution. He insisted that their home church did not have a constitution. I insisted they probably had one, but maybe he was unfamiliar with it. After discussing this for about an hour, I suggested he write his church and ask if they had a constitution, and if they did, to ask them to send him a copy.

In the meantime, we secured a copy of Blantyre Baptist Church's constitution. We also had them from a couple of other Baptist Churches in the States. We got copies of "The Baptist Faith and Message." Jim Parrish stayed pretty non-committal. Neil Weston thought their church had a constitution but was unfamiliar with it.

It was only a few weeks later when Andrew produced a copy of his home church's constitution. He was very surprised, but since they had a constitution, it must be satisfactory for us to draw one up and create bylaws.

We compared the constitutions and reviewed the "Baptist Faith and Message." Some items in both documents were inappropriate for our church, and we did not want to include anything related to war.

One Saturday morning, Jerry and I went to the Lilongwe County Club swimming pool. Andrew and Rose Mary joined us. Jerry and Andrew drew up a tentative constitution, and there were no differences in beliefs to reconcile.

We then presented it to the Sunday Morning Bible study group. We tentatively adopted the constitution. So, Jerry and I felt confident that we wanted to join this nucleus to start a new church.

We jumped in with both feet. We made plans of where we would meet. Andrew and Jim were both accountants, but I think it was Neil who knew something about the Malawi School of Accountancy at City Center.

We contacted the school to find out if we could use two of their rooms to hold church on Sunday morning. They agreed.

These rooms were just classrooms and would not hold very many people, but we thought they would be large enough.

On Sunday, September 25, 1983, Capital City Baptist Church conducted its first service. (We chose this name at one of our meetings.) We planned for this first Sunday to be just a "dry run" of the service to see how it would go, and we did not invite anybody.

Thirteen people were present, including three visitors: George Hall from Arizona and two American doctors who were agriculture specialists. Jerry preached, and Andrew Kingston was in charge of the music. Rose Mary played a little electric organ that belonged to the Parrishes. Neil Weston took care of two children and had a Sunday school for them, and I took refreshments for a little social time afterward.

Jerry and I were quite nervous, but it went very well. I never did know how the visitors had learned about the service. We were so excited. We said, "Yes! We can do this! (Of course, we meant with help from the Lord).

On Saturday, I gathered up things for hospitality time, and I took one of my bread baskets to use for the offering plate. (We did not have one the first Sunday.) Jerry had been working off and on all week on his sermon. (A called meeting during the week selected who would do that.)

Our first official service was on October 2, 1983. Jerry preached and did an excellent job. Rose Mary played the organ again, and Jim Parrish led the singing. This Sunday, we had 16 people there, four of which were Malawian.

We were off and running now. I began to invite everybody I came in contact with. I told people at the hospital when I went to the doctor. I told people at the airport, my hairdresser, and everywhere I went. I was so excited; I just wanted everybody to know. (I am sure the others were just as excited as me, and they were doing the same thing.)

We met each Tuesday night to discuss the previous Sunday and plan for the next one. Everyone was coming over to our house. Jerry had gone to Blantyre for a Mission Support Meeting. I made copies of the church covenant and Baptist Faith and Message and presented them to the group. We had a prayer time, and the covenant was adopted as presented.

During the next week, Neil Weston had a little framed sign made that we could set up each Sunday out near the sidewalk, and then we could take it down after the service. Neil and Glenda brought it to our house, and it looked great.

Light Chiwanda, my cook, had gone to church with me the previous Sunday, but he wanted his wife to go also, and she did not speak English.

So, the following Sunday, I took Light and his wife to Kawali Baptist Church, and he made his profession of faith.

Over the next six Sundays, Jerry did the preaching, and I continued to provide refreshments. Sometimes Neil would lead the singing, and he was outstanding. He would sing choruses. We would clap our hands and stand up and lift our hands and praise the Lord. We had a wonderful time. It was less formal than the American churches. It was a cross between Malawi and America and England and New Zealand. I loved it!

Jerry and I started going to church in separate cars. (We were taking some people to our church and some to Kawali church and could not transport everybody in one car.) At Capital City Baptist Church (CCBC), I guess we did not have enough faith. We also ran out of paper and material for children, songbooks, cups, and glasses,

Instead of getting together so much with missionaries, we began to have prospects for CCBC over for tea and meals. I had a little welcome-home party for Elizabeth Parrish, who was returning from England. I pulled out my China and silver and tried to make it as special as possible.

We talked to Dunstan and Gladys Mwangulu about joining the church. Dunstan was ready, but Gladys had been" sprinkled" as a child and was not ready to be baptized by immersion. However, they attended the church regularly. I visited with Jean Ndjovu and shared the plan of salvation with her, and she accepted Christ.

Big tears ran down Jean's cheeks as she shared with me that she had been trying to find Jesus ever since last May when her five-year-old son drowned. She said that she was afraid she would never see her son again. She wanted to be baptized and join the church. This intimate conversation felt so special to me.

I got to church the following Sunday in time to help set up tables and chairs. We had to move chairs out each Sunday and transform the space from schoolroom to sanctuary.

Church started, and Jean Ndjovu was supposed to be there. I waited on her and became disappointed. Then about halfway through the service, she arrived, perspiration running down her face and her two-year-old son on her back. The bus had not come, and she had walked the entire way. (I don't know how many miles it was, but it was several.)

Jerry preached on the responsibility of Christians once they are born again. Dunstan and Gladys Mwangulu said they had decided to join the church. Roseby Muntali said she had been a Christian for many years but was never baptized. She wanted to be baptized and join the church. Jean Ndjvou also wanted to join. We were all ready to shout with joy! (I cannot explain how exciting this was. How can I express it other than saying we praised the Lord?)

<hr />

In the midst of all this excitement, we continued our work in Publications. Jerry was doing the business work and caring for cars and houses, and I worked at Publications.

Then we had a call from Peggy with even more exciting news. Bruce Lawson, her fiancé, had accepted Jesus as his savior, and he planned to be baptized soon.

We were planning to return to the States in December for Peggy and Bruce's wedding on January 7, 1984. We were thrilled that Bruce had made this decision.

I bought a dress for the wedding on our trip to South Africa. Peggy had made all the wedding plans alone, and Pauline, Jerry's mother, had gone with her to look at dresses and veils. The only thing I had done was to help with the initial plans and money — and supplied a list of people's names and addresses. I regretted that my only daughter was getting married, and I was not there to be involved. I was not worried about the wedding; I knew Peggy could handle everything.

Bruce, who played football for Texas A&M, had injured his knee in a game, and he would have to be in a knee brace for thirteen weeks and might require surgery. Peggy said that he might be unable to play ball again. I hated to hear that. Ken had also messed his knees up playing football, and now Bruce had messed his knee up. Bruce was in school on an athletic scholarship, and I didn't know what effect the knee injury would have on his scholarship.

When Peggy selected Bruce, she picked a lot of man. Bruce was about 6'6" and weighed almost 300 pounds — big enough to protect her. She had her little house, which we had bought, and Buster, her dog. Bruce would move in with her until they finished their degrees.

<hr />

Meanwhile, back in Africa, CCBC continued to progress. After six weeks of assembling, our attendance was between 40 and 50 people each Sunday. We had put all the chairs in the room that it would hold, and we arranged to move benches in so some people could sit along the wall. We figured the children could sit on the floor down front, Malawian style, and we could cram a few more people in, but it was apparent we would soon outgrow this place.

At the same time, we talked to Bro. Kanowa, and he seemed to have softened his attitude towards another English-speaking church in Malawi. Bro. Kapalamula Banda of Falls Baptist Church said something about his desire to start an English service at his church. We had been faithful members at Kawali Baptist Church, where Bro Chisi was a pastor, and we continued to go there on Sundays after CCBC let out. (And we took people to that church almost every Sunday.)

With a little softening from the Nationals, the missionaries were beginning to come around also. They had only opposed the English-speaking church because they were afraid it would stir up a problem. (And we did not need any more Missionary/Convention problems.)

Our Dowdy Prayer Group, led by Ray and Sandra Taylor, prayed about us starting the church. God would (and did) work out the details if we were faithful to follow His leadership. We felt that God had been at work in the hearts and lives of Nationals and Missionaries, and He was working everything out to His honor and glory.

———◆◆———

By the end of October, we had everybody to sign who wanted to join the church, and these became our charter members. Then on November 6, we had our first baptism service. Capital Hotel was under construction, and they had a vat they used to cure brick. We asked if we could use it, and they agreed.

On Sunday, we took Jean Ndjovu, Roseby Muntali, and the entire congregation to the hotel for baptism. The vat was about three-and-a-half feet wide and five feet long. It was not large enough for Jerry to get in, too, so he stood beside the vat and baptized the two women. It was a moving experience as the congregation stood under the big shade tree.

These were the charter members:

Jerry Dowdy
Barbara Dowdy
Andrew Kingston
Rosemary Kingston
Neil Weston
Glenda Weston
Jim Parrish
Elizabeth Parrish
Judith Spears
Roseby Muntali
Keith Varnham (but needs to be baptized by emersion)
Rebecca Palmer
Michael Palmer
Jean Ndjvou

Then Tony and Betty Kabayi moved their letter from Blantyre Baptist, and Dunstan and Gladys joined, and from there, we became a church.

———•••———

We had a dedication service. Carl and Doris Houston had been a pastor in Clearwater, Florida, for many years. He was the pastor of Blantyre Baptist Church and preached the dedication sermon. Gene Kingsley led the call to worship, and Sam Upton said the prayer of dedication. (They are both Baptist missionaries.) Rev. W.A.C. Chisi conducted The Lord's Supper. Jerry acted as the master of ceremonies. Neil Weston led some choruses. Rosemary played the little organ. Glenda Weston, Roseby Muntali, Marlyn Upton, and Sherry Collier made up a quartet and sang.

My part was getting everything ready for The Lord's Supper, and I took a lot of things for the reception and toilet tissue for the bathroom. Elizabeth Parrish was in charge of the reception, and she furnished most of the items needed for the reception.

For a bunch of novices, we felt that the service was beautiful and thought it went off without a hitch. It was indeed a mixture of people from 13 different countries.

Since we did not have an adult Sunday School as we know it in the States, we decided to include an adult bible study on Tuesday nights with our planning meeting, and I prepared and led the first lesson. All the responsibilities were related to our "Spiritual Gifts."

We concentrated on Spiritual Gifts and tried to discern which spiritual gifts each of us possessed. Then we tried to plug into these gifts and utilize them. We believed that God would give us who we needed, and He intended us to use everybody for His service. As time went by, it was beautiful to see how God sent people just at the right time.

At that same time, Capital City Development Corporation (CCDC) had been managing the property in Lilongwe but was planning to turn it over to the Malawian Government. Some of our men went to CCDC to check what would happen when the property changed management. After talking with them, we decided we should try to secure some property before the change of management.

CCDC said they had a lovely three or four-acre plot right on Presidential Drive we could have. They would give us the land if we put in a paved road to come around to the back of the property. We learned that this road would cost about $6000, and that was a lot of money for our little congregation.

We began to meet and pray about that land. We decided that if we wanted this land, we'd better do our best to raise the money. It was the last week in November, and the management would change at the end of December. That did not give us much time.

We began to fast and pray. We called everybody we knew and asked them to pray. We had people all over the world praying.

Jerry and I had to leave for the States, but I knew there was no way I would allow this opportunity to pass us by, even if it meant that Jerry and I had to pay for the property ourselves. We did not tell anybody that because we wanted everybody to have the opportunity to give whatever they wanted to give. Jerry and I set a figure that we would plan to give.

We returned to Texas and continued to join our hearts and lives in prayer with the people of Malawi and prayed for the money. When the deadline was up, we called Andrew Kingston, and he was on cloud nine.

The church had raised the money! (Without anything from us, I might add.) Andrew considered this a miracle of miracles because he thought it was impossible. After that, members began to believe that anything was possible with God.

We told Andrew what we intended to give and said we would make our gift the first toward the building fund. And so, God was victorious. Because they had stepped out on faith and accepted the challenge to raise so much money, the people's faith was strengthened.

The property was on the most prestigious road in Lilongwe, situated on a hill near City Center. It was absolutely perfect, and so much more than we had ever hoped for or dreamed was possible.

———•••———

CCBC continued to grow and prosper. It called Van Thompson, a Baptist Missionary, to be its first pastor. Van was only allowed to pastor the church for a short time because the Area Office did not like for a missionary to pastor a church and told Van that he ultimately had to give the church up. He had no choice.

The building fund grew, and people packed the school rooms. Then in 1986, we had raised enough money to build our church building. Peter Palmer, who designed and built the Presidential Palace in Lilongwe, volunteered his expertise with architectural plans.

A church member, Derrick Ledsom, from England, was a builder in Lilongwe who agreed to build the church for a minimal fee. We had to have a licensed landscape person design the plan. A young man was walking down the road on Sunday and heard the singing from our congregation and came in. He was heading to another church. It just so happened that he had the experience to do the landscaping. He became a member of the church and gave his service. (This was another one of those "God things.")

We went on Furlough in 1986, and when we got back, the church was built. Then we started raising funds for an educational wing. Once the church raised the money, construction began and was soon completed.

The congregation had grown immensely, and they called a man from England to be the church pastor. Then we needed a place for him to stay, so we raised the money for a parsonage, and soon it was built. We even replaced our little organ and got a more significant electronic organ.

God provided a doctor, Andrew Mortimer, who was a pianist. Andrew's wife's name was Fiona, and they had several children.

God also provided a music teacher, Matthew Raymond, who played beautifully and was able to help with our music program. His wife's name was Allison, and they had three children. (Leading the music continued to be passed around, but I preferred the service when Neil Weston led us.)

By the time we left Malawi at the end of 1991, we had poured our hearts and lives into that congregation. It was not without struggles and conflicts. Trying to mold so many people from so many different countries, with so many religious backgrounds, into one Holy Spirit-led congregation was not easy.

Sometimes I would get so upset with different personalities that I would want to cry or quit going to business meetings. I tried to keep my mouth shut, but a lot of times, I had to bite my tongue. (Sometimes, the people from England had a hard time getting along with the Americans and vice versa.)

Somehow out of brotherly and sisterly love, and mutual respect, we worked through our differences and resolved them. It was a struggle to keep the church Baptist, and we read the church covenant many times.

Oh, how my heart yearns to go back and see what our church has become. I will not be disappointed. Helping to start Capital City Baptist Church was the most fulfilling and rewarding experience of my entire missionary life.

27 At Home in Lilongwe

Thirty-two years ago, I felt God's leadership calling me to Africa. Like in Pilgrim's Progress, had I taken the wrong path? Had I followed in the way God planned?

Had I taken a wrong turn somewhere along the way?

I recalled the night when I was 16 and praying to God, "Just test me." Had I failed His test?

To this day, I do not know. It seems strange that God would call me to Africa, yet it would take me 32 years to get there. I understand that God's timing is different from our timing.

From time to time, I still ponder all of this in my heart.

Just like the children of Israel who wandered in the desert for 40 years, had I been wandering for 30? If I took the wrong path, God made an alternate route for me. He understood and forgave me and certainly had not punished me. My life had been good.

Jerry and I busied ourselves with language study and visiting missionaries. I cooked meal after meal and had missionaries, committees, and friends over. Jerry taught a weekly Family Relations class at Kawali Church, and he was extremely well-received.

In Malawi, having two wives was common. Jerry had not gotten into his teaching very far before someone asked, "If a man becomes a Christian and has two wives, what does he do? Does he put the last wife away, or can he choose which wife he wants to keep?"

Jerry knew that "putting one wife away" meant that the man felt no further responsibility to that wife and any children they had together. Jerry shocked that class when he asked, "Is the church in business promoting prostitution?"

They immediately knew what he meant. If the man "puts the wife away," how else can the woman make a living for herself and her children besides prostitution? (That usually is what happens.)

They proceeded to investigate what should be done. Once sin came into the picture, there is never a perfect plan. We have to take into account the best alternative under each circumstance.

The class decided that the man must keep the first wife if she was willing to stay. The second wife would have to bear some responsibility for what happened. She would have to live without a husband, but the husband was responsible for the welfare of the second wife and her children.

———◆●●———

Arvil, Jerry's dad, called to say that Connie Dowdy, Jerry's favorite aunt, had passed away. Connie had been like a second mother to Jerry and always good to our children and me. Our hearts felt heavy, mainly because we were separated from our family during this time.

Oh, how we wanted to attend the funeral. We treasured the memory of those last days we spent with Connie when she was so ill. We could not go home to the funeral, so we sent flowers.

Our life had to go on, so I made a chocolate cake and took it to the prayer meeting at the Heriford's house for Barbara Workman's birthday.

———◆●●———

We had one last station we had not visited. Don and Barbara Messer were Nazarene missionaries, and all the Baptist missionaries loved them. They were like our own mission family. Barbara played the piano beautifully and played for the interdenominational service we held at the church every Sunday night. Don helped to start Nazarene churches and worked with their pastors and leaders.

Don invited us to ride to Mzuzu with him. Our missionaries, Gary and Carolyn Swafford and Mike and Linda Canady, lived in Mzuzu. We agreed to go.

Don came to our house to pick us up early in the morning, driving an old Land Rover. I had never ridden in a Land Rover. I climbed in the back seat with our luggage, lunches, and drinking water. The backseat was covered, but there were no springs. (It felt like I was sitting on a board.)

Jerry and Don climbed into the front seat and bumped out of the driveway. The first 30 miles were bearable as we were on a paved highway. Then we hit the gravel road. I began to bump from one side of the car to the other. As I looked at one arm for bruises, we would hit another bump, and my other arm would hit the other side of the car.

Don told a story about an old Malawian woman walking down the road, carrying a heavy bundle on her head, and could hardly walk. The driver of a Land Rover stopped and offered the woman a ride, and she accepted. After they traveled a short distance, the driver stopped to check his tires. The old woman grabbed her bundle, jumped out of the car, and started walking down the road, saying she preferred walking.

By the time we stopped for lunch, I felt much like that woman. I was ready to get out and walk, but I didn't. We found a rock to sit on, sat beside the road, ate lunch, and drank some water. (This gave my eyeballs a chance to stop jumping.)

We finally arrived in Mzuzu in the middle of the afternoon. Don dropped us off at the Swafford's house, and Carolyn showed us to the guest house, which doubled as their school classroom.

I was glad to get my dusty clothes off, shower, and wash the sand from my eyes and hair. We stretched out on the bed and rested.

Carolyn Swafford had invited us to supper. She was an excellent cook, probably the best in the mission. She cooked on a wood-burning stove on the back porch. She made her own fires and had learned to cook on a wood stove since coming to Malawi many years before.

The Swafford's home was lovely, and their yard was beautiful. Their house was on a hill that overlooked a military installation. (They had planted a row of cedar trees around their yard to help obscure the view of the military base.) It was cooler there than in Lilongwe.

They told us that sometimes, snakes would get into the cedar trees, and they had to call the police to come to shoot the snakes. They told a story about one of these incidents in which they called the police, and sure enough, it was only a few minutes before a jeep filled with police came. They got out of the jeep, and their sharpshooter had a gun. (The other police had no weapons.) A snake was spotted, and the sharpshooter took aim and shot.

He missed the snake. Because he had only been issued one bullet, they were out of luck.

I think the story goes that they went back to the police station and came back with about three bullets. This time he took aim and shot, and by the time his three bullets were gone, three dead cobras were lying on the ground, and everybody was excited.

The next morning, we attended church with the Saffords and went to Mike and Linda Canady's house for midafternoon "Teatime." Linda's house was lovely also; it was relatively new and on a steep hill just up the road from the Swafford's.

The floors of the Canadys' house were highly polished wood. The furniture was modest, with a nice wooden dining room table and chairs. The couch and chairs were wicker or cane, painted white with soft cushions. Both the Swaffords and Canadys treated us very nicely, and we enjoyed getting to know them and seeing where they lived.

Then on Monday, Don came by, and we piled into the Land Rover for the dreaded ride back. My eyes had stopped jumping, and the bruises on my arms were no longer hurting. Maybe I was numb or just had prayed harder about the trip. Whatever the reason, traveling back to Lilongwe did not seem quite as rigorous.

———•••———

Then the following weekend, we planned to go south — in the opposite direction. Malawi had one paved highway that ran to the South but did not go all the way. We were assigned a Volkswagen Kombi that was probably no more than ten years old, but it had seen better days, and Malawi roads had beaten and shaken it to pieces. Every time someone opened the back side door, I had to jump out and close the door from the outside. (If closed from the inside, it would jump off its track and fall completely to the ground.)

We loaded our baggage, or "Katundu" as we called anything carried along with us, into the Kombi. We were going to spend the weekend with Ron and Delinda Miller.

That night, with Delinda, Ron, their daughter, Renita, and their son, James, we all had a pleasant visit. James had been playing ball with a group of Malawian boys when we arrived. Ron had arranged for us to go to a village the next afternoon to show a Biblical film. But the generator was broken, so Jerry's first job was to repair it.

On Saturday afternoon, we took our Kombi, Ron, and his two kids in his Kombi and headed for Balaka Baptist Church. Once there, we loaded our two vehicles with Brother Kanowa, young people, and adults. We headed out to a village road which was to be a five-mile trip that turned into the wildest trip I had ever experienced — and I never experienced anything like it in the ten years that followed.

We drove out a muddy road that turned into a path across a cornfield. We were chugging along, gunning the engine, twisting, and churning through the mud. We came upon a Land Rover sunk into the mud up to its frame. Because it was so heavy, the people could not push it out.

If we planned to continue, there was nothing we could do except go around. First, Ron headed out across the hand-plowed rows of corn, and he did not get more than his front tires off the road when his Kombi became buried in the cornfield mud. Stalks of corn lay on both sides of the car.

Everybody, including me, got out of the two vehicles, and we began to push Ron's Kombi through the mud. There were so many people that we could almost pick up the vehicle. (I had learned as a child not to stand behind the rear tires, so I picked me a nice place on the side of the car where I could push and push.)

Once Ron got back onto the road in front of the Land Rover, it was Jerry's turn. Jerry gunned the car and slung mud 50 feet behind him as he wrestled the steering wheel. Everybody strained as we pushed our Kombi past the Land Rover.

Once our Kombi was clear of both mud and the stuck Land Rover, we all climbed back into our two Kombies with mud up to our knees.

We began singing Christian songs, laughing, talking, and having the best time. (The singing and clapping of hands were deafening!) We tried to sing along with everybody and struggled over every word, trying to understand their pronunciation (even though I could not grasp the meaning, either). Occasionally, someone would explain in English what we were singing about.

It was a real treat for these young people to get to ride in the car. They were excited about going someplace, and they were excited that they were going to see a motion picture. This experience was a real adventure for them as well as for us.

We did not travel much further when we got stuck again — and again, everybody jumped out and pushed the vehicles out. Then we came to a riverbed with just a trickle of water running between steep banks. Ron got across the river, but when he was halfway up the bank on the far side, he got stuck, so everybody got out and pushed again.

Everybody stayed on the riverbank as Jerry got into his Kombi and gunned that poor Kombi across the riverbed. When it started up the embankment, it chugged, the wheels turned, and I knew Jerry was determined not to get stuck.

But that Kombi just could not make it to the top on its own power. Just before it reached the crest, it bogged down. Everybody ran over to the Kombi and gave it a hearty push, and up it went to the top. Everybody, including me, was giggling and chattering.

By then, the car was two inches deep with mud on the inside, but nobody seemed to mind. One good thing about the Kombi was that you could take a water hose and hose it down inside and out — and within minutes, even the worst mud could be washed away.

When we got to the village, it was beginning to get dark. No village was in sight when we stopped, and there was only a water well in the middle of a cornfield. Two women were drawing water from the well, and then they put the filled buckets on their heads and faded into the cornfield.

Bro. Kanowa used a megaphone and announced that we would show a movie, and everybody was invited. Ron, Jerry, and some men began to clear the area so people could sit down. They set up the generator, a light, and a screen to show the movie.

By this time, it was pitch dark. There was no moon and no stars. Darkness surrounded us. We dug our flashlights out as some men from the nearby village escorted us through the cornfield until we came upon some houses. Several little fires gave some light.

The women had cooked a meal for us. We sat on straw mats. When Jerry turned his flashlight off, I could only feel him next to me. A Malawian woman sat on my right side, but I could not distinguish her features. She was joining the others as they sang choruses.

Then someone set two bowls on the ground in front of us. (The fire on the ground made the bowls visible.) After we washed our hands in a pan passed through the crowd, Jerry and I took some of the nsima and rolled it into balls, and then we dipped the nsima in a bowl of something with a foul odor.

I took the nsima and dipped it into the bowl with the aroma. I brought the nsima up and put it in my mouth. That was my last bite. (It was so dark I knew I wouldn't offend anybody if I didn't eat anything else.)

Jerry realized that this was something strange. He picked up his flashlight and shone it into the bowl. Then he lay the flashlight down. He later said it was better sometimes if you do not see what you are eating.

It was some kind of dried fish — and really nasty tasting.

This meal was the only food in Malawi that we could not eat at least a little. People had supplied us with the best they had to offer, and it saddened us to think they had nothing better to eat. But soon, the corn would come in, and they would have some to sell, and maybe they could buy something. Or we hoped perhaps they had some beans planted.

After a while, we returned to where we had put the lights. Much to our surprise, when we got back, there must have been 500 people gathered and sitting on the ground. When we had taken our respective spots, Ron had the film ready to roll. Some of the young people from the Balaka church sang Christian choruses; they clapped their hands, stomped their feet, and danced around in front of the people. They were praising God.

The village chief got up and told the people how to act while they watched the film. (They had never seen a movie before, and Ron said the chief told him I was the first "white woman" to ever come to that village.)

Then they began to show the film. It was in English, so they cut the sound off, and Brother Kanowa spoke all the parts in Chichewa. His expression and enunciation were fantastic. As the characters got excited, Brother Kanowa would also get excited. Then when it was a sad scene, you could tell it by the tone of his voice. His narration was perfect.

Once the people began to stand up on the West side, they would sit down. They got up and sat down like a wave. The wave was coming closer to me as the chatter got louder.

"Oh, my gosh, there is a snake!" I thought.

Nobody had to tell me to get up when the people around me arose, and I strained my eyes to see what was causing the commotion. When everybody else sat down, so did I. Then the wave ended on the East side of the group of people. Later, I learned that a mouse had run straight across where the people were sitting.

After the film's first reel was over, and while Ron and Jerry changed reels, a group of young people acted out a skit about a man, the village drunk, who had two wives. Everybody seemed to enjoy the performance, and even I could understand what was happening. The people seemed to have a natural talent for acting and music. There was not a hint of intimidation or inhabitation.

They started to play the film again, and just as we got into the story, a man walked between the screen and the projector. He wobbled and weaved back and forth. He stumbled and fell and got up. Some men got up and escorted him into the cornfield. It was like a real-life reenactment of the play that the young people had just put on to depict what happens to people when they drink too much.

When the film was over, Brother Kanowa talked to the people. Several people came forward, and Brother Kanowa spoke to them. Ron had some tracts to hand out, and I got some of them and helped.

Then we were ready to put the generator, equipment, and people back into the Kombis. At about midnight, we headed back to Balaka. I felt tired and exhilarated; it had been a fun and exciting trip.

But now, for the drive back to Balaka. At least we knew what to expect and where the bad mud holes were. The people jumped out of the car, pushed, and climbed back into the Kombi. I closed the door so it would not fall off, and we went on our merry way.

The next morning, Jerry preached at Balaka Baptist Church. He really had given a good message in English, and Brother Kanowa translated with lots of expressions and excitement. After the service, a woman came forward with one of the tracts we had passed out the night before in her hand, and she wanted to know more about Jesus. Another

240

man from the village came forward and wanted to trust Jesus as his Lord and Savior.

The Balaka Church women presented me with a polished wooden bowl. The congregation shook hands with Jerry and me and seemed so pleased that we were with them. Ron and Delinda were surprised that they gave us a bowl, saying that the congregation had never given anybody a bowl before when they visited the church.

We felt good about the weekend. This place was home, and these were our people. We had only been in Malawi for a short while, yet we had already learned to love and appreciate them.

During my childhood, God had prepared me for these muddy roads. He had prepared me to push cars out of the mud. Somehow, now I accepted the people's plight and could relate to them. I understood the difficulties of their lives better than most young Americans could understand. I could relate to how they felt, even though my life had never been as challenging.

I better understood that sometimes the difficult times in our lives are necessary to prepare us for our future. We do not understand "why" at the time. How much easier our lives would be if we could accept the bad that comes our way as quickly as the good. *All things work together for good, for those who love the Lord.*

28 Ministry & Culture

The name Malawi means "fire flames." Even today, Malawians use fire for both practical and ritual purposes. Malawi is a small, landlocked country in Southeastern Africa, equidistant to Nairobi, Kenya, and Johannesburg, South Africa.

About one-fifth of the country is covered by Lake Malawi, the southernmost lake in the chain of the Great Rift Valley. The country is about the size of Tennessee, and when we arrived, the population was about seven and a half million people.

Primarily, three groups of people make up the population. About 90 percent of the people's ancestry goes back to the Bantu people, who came to the area during the third century AD. Next were the white Portuguese, Arabs, and Asian Indians who arrived in the mid-1800s as slave traders. Then came a host of other people to live there, such as missionaries, government aid people, advisers, workers to help develop the country, and some foreign businesses.

In 1891, the country became a British Protectorate. David Livingstone, a Scottish missionary, had explored "Nyasaland," as it was called in those days. The slave trade was in full swing, and Livingstone went back to Scotland and encouraged people to go to Malawi to spread Christianity and to also go in search of hard cash. So, hand in hand, Christianity and industry came to Malawi.

Malawi remained a British Protectorate until 1959 when she gained independence, and Dr. H. Kamuzu Banda was elected president. (There was a minor skirmish between England and the Malawian people before they were granted their freedom.)

President Banda was a medical doctor educated in England and the United States. At the time of his election, he was an older man, but he had lived outside Malawi since he was young.

For more than 100 years, white men from Europe and others from India and Asia have resided in Malawi. Many people came and never returned to their homeland, thus, making some of the people five generations away from their roots. (That's why only about 95 percent of Malawians are black.)

Malawi has three major religions: Traditional, Islamic (Muslim), and Christianity. Almost all the people of Malawi believe to some degree in "traditional religion." When they become Muslims or Christians, their ancestry is so saturated in animistic beliefs (the belief that objects, places, and creatures all possess a distinct spiritual essence) that it affects their lifestyle, home, and work.

———•••———

Traditional religion is shrouded in mysticism. (Some might describe traditional Malawian doctors as "witch doctors.") These "medicine men" learned their trade from their fathers; this is a belief system and tradition passed down from one generation to the next.

The medicine men have the power to cast a spell on someone, and bad things will happen, or they can cast a spell to make someone befriend you. They can explain what has happened in the past or foretell the future.

People can go to the medicine man for a small fee, and he will perform all kinds of services. If someone's cow dies, the owner can go to the medicine man, and he can reveal who poisoned or put a curse on the cow.

Mayi Laddi worked at publications with me. She had a headache one day, and the next day she came in with a gash cut into her neck, just

243

at the base of the skull. I asked about the incision, and she said she had been to the medicine man, and he had cut her neck to drain blood so the evil spirits would come out.

Another day, she had a headache and wanted me to take her to the medicine man. I told her I would take her to the medical doctor, but I did not believe in the medicine man's medicine and refused to take her.

Malawians believe you can have a curse put on someone for a fee, and it works. The affected person believes so strongly that they've been cursed that they may become sick and die or are literally scared to death. Witnesses have seen people die from a curse, so it is hard for them not to believe in the power of a curse. (Even though it is really fear that causes these bad things to happen.)

When a baby is born, the grandmother ties a string around the baby's waist to ward off evil spirits that can make the baby sick. Sometimes a fetish is tied to the string. Sometimes strings are tied around the baby's neck. Some Christian women will say they do not believe in the string but allow their babies to wear the fetish because they do not want to offend the grandmother.

We had some employees at the publishing house steal some inventory, but everyone was afraid to talk — to tell us what was happening — for fear that the thief would have their children poisoned.

When I asked them, "What about white people?" they would say the medicine does not work for white people because they do not believe in it. I could never help them to understand that if they, too, refuse to believe, a curse could not be put on them. (Fear and belief in the medicine man were the actual curses.)

If someone makes an enemy, they might fear that their house could be burned, their children poisoned or drowned, or medicine put into their food to make them crazy. These are real things that happened (probably with some assistance from the medicine man), so people had a right to be afraid.

One morning, I looked out my bedroom window as Light Chiwanda, my cook, was coming to work. He stopped at the flower bed, picked up a small bottle, took a drink, and placed the bottle back in the flower bed.

I got up, got dressed, and went out to find the bottle. It was a clear bottle with liquid about the color of whiskey with some little sticks in it. When I asked Light about the bottle, he said the medicine man had given it to him to make me like him better, which changed our relationship. Maybe, subconsciously, I did not want it to appear that the medicine was working.

There was a potion for almost any ailment that you had. (Some of the medicine made from roots actually worked.) They even had a potion to improve their sex lives.

A woman came to me one day complaining about one of the pastors sexually assaulting some of the women. The pastor was forcing the women to have sex with him, and then he would tell them that if they told anybody, he would report them to the medicine man. They were scared almost to death and would not allow me to tell anybody, so my hands were tied. I left Malawi ten years later, and that pastor was still abusing women, but he had lost favor in his church (and he certainly had lost favor with me.) Some church leaders knew this abuse was happening, and the pastor also lost favor with them.

Sometimes, there would be all-night ritualistic ceremonial dances, and all kinds of activities took place at these dances. One man wanted his mother-in-law to like him, so the drums began to beat. Amid chants and songs, the man walked around in a circle with a goat until he became worked up into a semiconscious state. Then he sat down and put the goat's nose and mouth in his mouth. Two or three men helped hold the goat until the goat suffocated. Then they slit the goat's neck and drained the blood into a pan.

The medicine man mixed something white with the blood, and while the man was still in this semiconscious state, he consumed the blood. He smeared the blood on his head and face, and then he literally licked the bowl clean with his tongue. At the same time, other people were dancing around, killing chickens, and doing unthinkable things.

I saw this all-night affair on a video taken by a young man from Europe in Malawi to do a documentary. He had lived in the village with the people for months, and then they allowed him to make the video.

Several people were invited to the USAID director's home to view the video. (I would have given anything to obtain a copy.) Gene and Beverly Kingsley were there with Jerry and me to view the film. When it got so gory, Beverly got sick to her stomach and had to leave.

The room had a strange, mystic feeling while we watched the video. The medicine man had used parts of the Bible in his presentation, and he had used them in the name of Jesus. The man who made and narrated the film was obviously not a Christian, so most of the religious innuendoes had eluded him.

They served refreshments after we finished the film, but nobody was interested in eating or drinking anything. However, all of us missionaries made a beeline to the young man and began to talk to him about Christianity. In the film, he commented that this ritual was no different from traditional Christianity. We set him straight on any number of things he believed. We tried to be a good witness for Christ, but too many people were around. He was returning to Europe the next day, so we never had an opportunity to see him again.

Then there was the Islamic religion. Muslims and Christians came to Malawi about the same time, and both continued to play an essential part in the life of Malawi. There is a lot of ceremony in the Islamic religion. The people from India and Arabic countries constitute the real Islamic strength, but a lot of black Malawians converted to Islam.

Most Muslims are businesspeople, and they own and operate most stores. Each day at noon, the stores are closed, and the people are called to prayer by a voice blasted over the loudspeaker at the mosque. The men and boys are called to prayer several times throughout the day. (The women are not allowed to attend.) On Fridays, the store owners are compelled to give something to anybody who asks, so they keep a sack full of tambalas (one-cent pieces) to give to each beggar who comes by.

When Kuwait adopted Malawi, the Kuwaiti government made long-range plans to build a mosque every five miles, crisscrossing the country. Walking or driving down any road results in spotting a mosque.

Many schools are built in conjunction with the mosque. They plan to educate their own and get them into high places in the government to run the government. They see government and religion as synonymous, as it is in most Islamic countries throughout the world. They are very dedicated and evangelistic.

When we were in Malawi, no Baptist Missionary was working with the Muslims. However, five young Muslim men at CCBC converted to Christianity.

One young Malawian lay preacher, Bambo Chilombo did a fantastic job converting many Muslims. Bambo Chilombo was a well-paid mechanic who wanted to serve Christ more directly. He was very active in Kawali Baptist Church, and our Salima medical clinic hired him to be the ambulance driver of our mobile medical clinic.

While the nurses conducted pre-natal clinics, Bombo Chilombo sat under the trees with the men, read tracts and his Bible, and preached and taught. Through this approach, he started six churches in the first year. Because this medical service was predominately in a Muslim area, hundreds of people accepted Christ, were baptized, and are now active church members. They are hungry to hear more about Christ.

On the Christian front, Presbyterians, Anglicans, and Catholics came to Malawi in 1859 and continued after that. The Presbyterian group is the strongest of the three; two groups of Presbyterians originally came and eventually merged. Southern Baptists sent their first missionaries, Bill and Blanche Wester, in 1959.

In 1983, we had 21 missionary families:
Howard and Belinda Rhodes
Ernest and Auttie Sibley
Carl and Doris Houston
Gary and Carolyn Swafford
Hermon and Joy Russell
Rendell and Teresa Day
Ed and Judy Barnes
Jim and Patsy Parker
Ron and Delinda Miller
Darrell and Judy Garner
Mary Ann Chandler
Jerry and Joyce Spires
Hermon and Joy Russell
Mike and Linda Canady
Sam and Marlyn Upton
Gerald and Barbara Workman
Rebecca Phifer
Gene and Beverly Kingsley
Ross and Sherry Collier
Jerry and Barbara Dowdy

There were a few small Baptist groups as well. Also, there were Nazarene, the Church of Christ, the Assembly of God, several other denominations, and numerous para-church groups.

All the Christians worked together very well. Each had its own focus, but there was plenty of work to go around. I estimate that there were 400,000 people per Baptist missionary unit. The people were amicable and receptive to the gospel, so working in Malawi was a pleasure.

29 Malawi Lens of Tradition

Some of the articles in the newspaper would be hilarious. One report told of an elephant that wandered off the game preserve and began to trample the people's corn and terrorize the people, so the elephant was shot.

The article stated that the government men who killed the elephant took some meat but left the larger portion at Khutamaji Village. The elephant meat was sold for 33t (about 36 cents) per kilogram (2.2 pounds).

I figured that elephant meat sold for about 17 cents per pound. I wondered if it was worth that.

They proudly announced, "We have realized K41 out of the portion sold here." That meant that they sold the elephant meat for about $45. They did not say what they did with the tusk or the feet, but I am sure the government took those.

Then there was the day that we read a long article about a "jigger epidemic." Jerry asked, "What is a jigger?"

He continued reading the lengthy article that went into great detail about the problem. Then, at the end of the article, they mentioned that a jigger is a flea that burrows into the skin of its host to lay its eggs.

We were always reading and hearing elephant stories. The Workmans went to Kasungu Game Park and stayed in a tent when an elephant began terrorizing them. Somehow, Barbara and Debra got out and went to a little cookhouse, and the elephant followed them. He would stick his trunk into the cookhouse, make strange noises, breathe, and blow, which scared them terribly. They spent the rest of the night in the cook house.

At a park in Zambia, two young men and one young girl spent the night in a tent. The girl was lying between the men. A lion appeared, pulled the girl out of the tent, and mauled her to death. Women must be cautious during their period because the animals can smell blood very well and will attack.

———•••———

One day when I was at Kasungu Game Park, I walked around the end of one of the buildings and was looking down, not paying attention. I walked about thirty feet, and when I looked up, I was almost face-to-face with an elephant. The elephant was about 30 feet away, just grazing and walking toward me. I stopped, backed up quietly until I got further away, and then I ran as fast as I could to the first open door I found. I ran into a little room and closed the door until the elephant was gone. As you enter Kasungu Game Park, a sign says, "Elephants have the right of way." (Believe me, I didn't want to challenge that information when I came face-to-face with an elephant!)

———•••———

There were many Malawian cultural things I found of interest.

One practice is for the wife to shave her husband's genital area, which is done for cleanliness. The wife also shaves herself, and sometimes the husband shaves his wife.

Before her marriage, the young girl is taught how to do this. She is told to make nice warm water with soap, soap the area well, and then shave. (I never asked how often this is done.)

250

Another practice is on the girl's first menstrual period, the mother of the girl gives her a chain of solid white beads to wear around her waist. Then, on her second period, the mother gives the young girl a chain of beads of different colors. Then, when the girl is married and is on her period, she lays the colored beads on her bed; when she is not having her period, she lays the white beads on her bed. The husband and wife never discuss the menstrual period, but he automatically knows and does not have sex with her.

Another practice, the people up north, the Tambuka people, put a lot of emphasis on virginity. The young girls are taken to a stream each month to determine whether they have had sex. The girl lies down at the stream without underwear and spreads her legs apart. Then a woman pours cold water on the genital area, and if the water goes in, the woman determines that the girl has had sex. The girl's mother is then shamed and blamed for not raising the girl properly.

Another thing they do is to place a white cloth under the girl on the first night of her marriage, and if she bleeds, then she is a virgin; if she doesn't bleed, the man may ask for some of his money back.

Part of the society in Malawi is matriarchal, and part is patriarchal. Therefore, sometimes the man has to pay a dowry for the bride, and other times they do not.

Another thing a girl is taught to do before marriage is to "dance in motion," which means she dances in such a way that the couple experiences sex while dancing. (It is said that if a Malawian man marries a white woman — which rarely happens — the man is teased by the other men, who laugh and say, "She can't even dance in motion."

If a family all lives in one room, they will hang a cloth across the room to divide it. Rarely will any village people have a bed; they sleep on a straw mat. If they have a bed, it will be tiny, and the man will get it. (In all my years of going to villages, I only saw one bed in any village home.)

Women carry the katundu (belongings). Katundu is a beautiful catch-all word. (I wish we had it in our English language.) It can be anything from your house full of furniture to a can of water.

The women carry on their heads water, firewood, clay pots, and bundles of items wrapped in a cloth. I have even seen two men lift a 220-pound sack of corn and put it on a woman's head, and I once saw a woman carrying a 55-gallon drum on her head. All of this is called "katundu." The women have very strong necks, but many also have back trouble.

The women also carry the children on their backs until they are two or three years of age. They take two meters of cloth and wrap it around their bodies and then tuck the ends in front. Sometimes when the child is very large, they will take another cloth, wrap it around their bottom, and then tie it across their shoulders.

Little girls start carrying their siblings on their backs when they are very young. Once in a while, the boys will carry a baby on their backs also. One day, I looked out my window and saw my cook's little two-year-old boy picking up a string and placing it on his head. He would stand very straight and walk with the string on his head.

Then the wind would blow it off, and he would pick it up and put it back on his head, and the process would start all over. The child was so intent on learning to carry something on his head.

———◆◆◆———

Women do most of the farming. If it is virgin land, the man will clear the field the first time, then tending crops is primarily up to the woman. The woman takes a little short-handled hoe and tills the soil into rows. Then they punch a hole in the ground with a stick and drop two seeds. Then, she takes the back of her heel and mashes dirt on the seed.

Then she keeps her garden clean and harvests the crop. The man then takes the produce to market if they have excess to sell.

He gets the money and may buy his wife a piece of cloth for a new chirundu or a small piece of fabric for her head. Hopefully, the man will also buy salt, matches, and cooking oil. He may also buy tea, sugar, and milk if they have a good crop.

I read that the Yao people, down on Lake Malawi, would smear cow manure on the newborn babies' umbilical cords when they are born. I wondered if this was still the practice. Since my cook, Godfrey was a Yao, I asked him about this, and he said, "They don't do that much anymore."

———•••———

Malawian villages were comprised of one family and the extended family for generations. Everybody tended to watch the children, and even though each family planted and harvested their own crops, they also tended to oversee everything belonging to the village. You could not say no if someone was in need and asked you for something. (This concept was beginning to break down.)

One of the Publications employees lost corn and peanuts from their field while his wife was sick. Then, after the peanuts were harvested, someone broke into his house and took some of them. The employee was very upset — so mad that he moved into town against his uncle's wishes.

———•••———

If you ask Malawians about their mother, they may say they have several mothers. After quizzing them, they may say, "The one who born me" or "My big mother." (Many times, the aunts are also considered their mothers.)

Beer parties are big occasions among most Malawians (but Baptist Malawians are supposed to abstain from drinking beer), and beer is served at most weddings. After the women finish working in the fields, they may "cook beer" by digging a pit in the ground and brewing beer in the pit.

———•••———

Corn and greens are staple crops in Malawi. Once the corn is harvested, the women shuck it, remove the silks, and clean it through a lengthy process. Then the women dry the corn and pound it with a stick in a rounded-out tree, called a "mtondo."

The women prepare the meal from beginning to end. First, they carry the water on their heads from the well, river, or creek. Then they gather the wood to build a fire. Once the fire is ready, they make patties of the ground corn, cook it over the fire, and then put it into a bowl. The woman first takes the man a pan of hot water to wash his hands and then serves him the food. Sometimes the woman will crawl into the room to the man with her head ducked down to show respect. Then she will crawl out of the room backward, always with her head down. (I think maybe some of this crawling and bowing may now be going away.)

Usually, the boys eat with the men. Afterward, the women and the girls eat. I had some difficulty accepting this system. I did not openly try to change cultural things unless they conflicted with the Bible. Through teaching the woman about their place in the Kingdom of God and God's love for them, sometimes they would begin, little by little, to assert themselves. If the husband was a Christian, he would make some changes, too. I noticed that as people accepted Christian principles, women were being elevated.

———————

The men will sit around and weave baskets, talking together while they work. The men are also the tailors. (Some of them even learn to use the sewing machine.) Walking through a village, you might see a young man mending the knee or seat of his pants. Often men sitting at sewing machines are lined up along the city sidewalks, where they may make suits or dresses.

The chief is considered the protectorate of his village. If a stranger shows up in a village, the chief is notified. When someone dies, the death notification goes first to the village chief.

When the chief dies, his brother usually becomes the chief.

———————

Since we left Malawi at the end of 1991, many changes have occurred. Some changes have been for good — and some have not been good.

There is more of a concept of "ownership." A particular hen running in the village might belong to a certain family, and they may have private herds of cattle or goats. Villages are getting smaller as people flood into the towns, and life in the village continues to be hard.

———•••———

Malawians usually put little emphasis on Christmas celebrations, partly because Christianity is relatively new and partially because the lack of disposable income removes the commercial aspects of Christmas.

This is how some Christians told me that they celebrate Christmas.

During the afternoon on December 24, people go to church and have prayer, a devotional, and maybe a little drama depicting the birth of Christ.

Then they go home and perhaps get together with some of their family. They might drink Orange Fanta or Coke Cola. (These drinks would not be very cool.) Then they would eat their customary meal of nsima and indwo. The nsima is made from finely ground white corn stirred into water and cooked until it is a consistency that will hold together in a little patty. People with more money might substitute rice for the nsima.

The indwo is a meat dish made from chicken, beef, or goat, provided meat is available. The meat would be boiled in salt water with maybe a few tomatoes and onions added, then cooked on an open fire until it falls apart.

Before eating, hands are washed in warm water but not dried, and eating is with the right hand only. To eat, one pinches off small pieces of nsima with their fingers and dips it into the meat or vegetable indwo. (One chicken could feed at least eight people.) After this meal, the people would go home.

On Christmas morning at about 9:00, the people would attend church for a two-to-three-hour service. Flowers in cans, clay pots, or maybe even plastic glasses adorn the church, and baskets of flowers might be hung on the wall. Reeds or banana leaves might be placed in the corner. Pictures of Mary and the baby Jesus might be affixed to the church walls, along with a sign that says, "Merry Christmas."

The sermon would always be the story of the birth of Jesus. Songs that might be sung include "Yesu Wa Badwa" (Jesus is Born) and "Onane Mwana Wa Badwa Ku Mzinda Wa Bethlehem" (A Child is Born in Bethlehem).

In a Malawian Christmas, there is a total absence of Santa and no decorated tree. The people say, "God gave Jesus, so we must also give." Due to the limited amount of money, however, it is challenging to buy things. Sometimes gifts are exchanged between husband and wife, children and parents — and sometimes brothers, sisters, uncles, or aunts.

It is most important that the gift is new. "Since Christ was a new child, the gift must be new," said Bambo Mkaka.

Gifts might include candy, corn, peanuts, sugar, bananas, tea, a chicken, or even two tambalas (two cents). The husband might give his wife a new cloth, and the children might get five or ten marbles or a small ball.

A real gift should be wrapped or in a sack. It can be wrapped in any kind of paper, which is important since paper is very scarce in villages; wrapping paper can be as challenging to come by as the gift.

Wrapping paper is saved and used over and over, and plastic bags are washed and saved and used repeatedly. The missionaries treasure their little boxes that can be used over and over.

The children and wife will expect some kind of a gift. Bambo Mkaka said, "There are other things which a husband might give his wife:

Chirundu — two meters of cloth to wrap around her.

Zipatso — shoes

Duku — headdress (a piece of cloth for her head)

Mpango — headdress

Msuko — pot in which food is cooked

On Christmas Day, you might go to somebody's house for a visit, or you might go to the hospital to visit. "Christmas Day is to be a happy day," said Bambo Mkaka.

I asked my gardener about Christmas, and he was so embarrassed that I could hardly get answers from him. Yobi said, "Last Christmas, I gave my family bread, sugar, and bananas for the children."

He was not embarrassed because he felt he had given them so little; he was embarrassed because he had given them something and then revealed that to me about it.

30 Stateside for Peggy's Wedding

After our first two years in Malawi, Peggy was having her wedding, and the Mission voted to allow us to go home. It is recommended by the Foreign Mission Board, at least at that time, that the missionaries stay in their assigned country for four years before they return home.

Since Malawi is so far and the expense is so great, Malawi did not have any problem with the missionaries jumping up and going home for just a visit.

Missionaries are allowed to return home for their children's weddings and the death of children or parents, and the Mission may approve other visits when necessary. These un-designated trips are at one's own expense.

Besides going to the wedding, there were several other things we wanted to do while we were in the States.

The business was not doing very well. The manager and Pete Dwight had talked to Jerry for a long time on the phone and assured him they would turn the business around. They said Copy & Litho would do great things selling word-processing equipment.

We told the manager we needed a car to use while at home. (We probably owned about 30 cars at that time that the service technicians were using.) The manager said he would have a car for us when we got home.

We wrote Peggy that we might want to drive her car since we were flying into Houston, and we were anxious to see the house we had bought for her, Bruce, and Buster, her dog.

Peggy had decided to have her wedding in Fort Worth at Travis Avenue Baptist Church. The reception would also be at the church. Dr. Coggin would officiate. Jo Ann Morgan would help Peggy with who does what and when at the wedding. Jo Ann had done this many times; she was a real pro.

We wrote the Wicks and asked if we could spend the month with them. Dorothy and Warner Wicks had a lovely two-story home in the Ridgle area of Fort Worth. They wrote back that they would be delighted for us to stay with them and would turn the upstairs over to us.

Richardson Heights Baptist Church had asked Jerry to speak on December 18th. Travis Avenue Church was busy planning Dr. Coggin's retirement parties. We had accepted a couple of their speaking engagements, as well.

We would have Christmas with the family, and there would be plenty to keep us busy.

———◆◆◆———

Our minds switched to plans of going home. We also had to arrange for different people to cover our work in Malawi while we were home. Publications could be closed most of the time since Christmas and New Year's holidays fell during that time.

We went to the airlines, made reservations, and got our tickets. We could not obtain reservations to depart and return exactly when we wanted to, but we were able to make adequate arrangements.

As we began to plan on going home, we got excited. We had not thought much of home because we had been so busy, but as time passed, we could hardly wait.

Then panic struck. There was so much to do before we could get away that we wondered if we could pull everything together. We had Mission money and a list of things we would need to buy for Mission business while in the States. Five or six missionaries had given us a list of a few things they wanted us to bring back to them. Each of them had also given us a check.

Then we decided to drive to South Africa so we could pack our car with Mission things when we got back to Johannesburg. This trip was at our expense, but there were a lot of Mission things we would be doing just because we could save the Mission money. So that meant that we would have Malawi, Zambia, Zimbabwe, South African, and American money to keep up with. We had to get proper papers to take the car out of the country.

Jerry bought a python snakeskin on the street in Blantyre, and I had to secure authorization to export it out of Malawi. I rolled the 18-foot skin, put it in my shopping basket, and took it to the authorities. When I arrived, a man asked, "Where did you get that?"

"My husband bought it on the street in Blantyre," I replied.

"That skin belongs to the government!" He said, and he grabbed hold of my basket and tried to confiscate my skin. I did not release the basket and explained that I did not know it was an illegal skin. They were selling it in broad daylight, and we had assumed there was nothing wrong with us buying it.

He tugged on one side of the basket, and I tugged on the other. After arguing over who owned the skin, the man said I would have to buy it from the government.

"How much will that be?" I said.

He released the basket and said he would have to find out, so we walked back through the building to another man's office.

I waited in the hall for an answer.

He came back out and said it would be about $4.

"Fine," I said, "I will take it."

After I purchased the skin, they said I would have to secure a veterinary doctor to authenticate that the snake was healthy. So, then I went to a veterinary doctor, and he approved my skin.

I went back to the authorities to get my permit, and they were out of forms, so I had to return the next week and get export papers. Altogether this took an entire day. (This was so typical of getting anything done there!)

259

I kept trying to think of what I could give Peggy and Bruce as a wedding present. There was nothing for sale in Malawi that I wanted to give. Then I decided to type up all my favorite recipes and make her a recipe box. (She had previously asked me how to cook oatmeal and cream gravy.) So, I began to type cards, and I included those things for which you do not usually need a recipe. I did not know how much time this would take. I typed off and on for several days and finally went through my files. This gift would be something personal and useful, I thought.

Finally, the date of our departure arrived. It was the end of November, and we packed our car and headed out. Rebecca Phifer had agreed to keep Princess, our dog. We drove through Zambia, the Zambezi Valley, Zimbabwe, and on to South Africa. The temperature was around 100 degrees, with no air conditioner in the car.

After a few days' travel, we arrived in Houston, Texas, to find the onset of one of the coldest winters in history. It was snowing in Houston, and that was almost unheard of. Thousands of water mains broke in the Dallas/Fort Worth area. We had two or three snows that left Fort Worth covered in a blanket of snow that lasted for days.

Almost every day while home, the temperature ranged from 8 to 32 degrees. This cold was a shock to our systems, and I thought I might freeze to death. Jerry went to College Station to check on Peggy's house since she had not turned the water off to her house. Three pipes had frozen and burst, but very little water had entered the house. When Jerry was trying to help a neighbor with a frozen pipe, the neighbor's dog bit Jerry's leg. (That took over a month to heal completely.)

Arvil and Pauline, Jerry's parents, met us in Houston with their camper, and we headed for a restaurant immediately. It was so nice to be back where you could order anything on the menu and get it without someone saying, "We don't have any today."

Peggy had taken care of everything regarding the wedding. She and I went around to different places, and I paid the bills and made sure everything was scheduled correctly. We went to College Station and attended church with Peggy and Bruce, and we got to be there for Bruce's baptism. That was a special occasion.

Sandra and Ray Taylor had scheduled a dinner party for us and invited the entire Dowdy Prayer Group. It was so wonderful to see everybody again. We hugged and kissed everybody, and I was so gregarious that probably everybody thought I was a little silly. Sandra had served an excellent meal; she is the best cook I know, so that was not surprising.

Ray led the meeting and prayer time that followed. Almost everyone in the group was there, and I had brought everyone a little ivory elephant. I was one short and gave Jo Ann and Bill Morgan a little wooden train of elephants instead. They are very popular in Malawi, but I felt terrible that I never gave her an ivory elephant.

Jerry spoke at Richardson Heights Baptist Church, and I wore wool twill pants. (This was before women wore pants to church, and I felt so self-conscious, but it was so cold I just did not think I could wear a skirt.)

We had the rehearsal dinner the night before, and I had the opportunity to meet Bruce's mother and daddy. They seemed very nice, and Bruce acted very calm.

Peggy and I spent the entire wedding day lying around at the Wick's house and talking. The only problem we experienced was the cake was late getting delivered to the church. After several phone calls to the bakery, two men came wandering in with French fries and cold drinks in their hands. Then they brought the cake in, and it was leaning sideways. (I wound up putting something under the tablecloth to raise the bottom of the cake so that it would not look like the Leaning Tower of Pisa.)

Jerry was to give the bride away, so he wore a tuxedo, and Ken was one of the best men, and he looked terrific in his tuxedo, too. Bruce also looked great, all dressed up, but I could tell he felt uncomfortable.

Peggy had asked a friend of Bruce's family to sing, and she had a beautiful voice. Dr. Coggin performed the service, and Jo Ann got us going and coming at the right time.

Soon the wedding ceremony was over, and we were all relieved. Dorothy and Warner Wicks were terrific hosts, and their house was a perfect place for us to stay.

They had a big closet for Peggy's dress and everything she needed for the wedding. They had gone on about their work and business and had left us to do our own thing. Everything was just fantastic.

Mother was feeling pretty good and was able to get around okay, too. She was so cute at the wedding. Two young men picked her up and carried her up on the platform at church so she could get her pictures made. (I think it hurt her pretty badly, but she was not one to complain.) She was just excited to be involved in Peggy's wedding. Since we were gone, Mother had moved into a senior citizen and nursing home. She was adjusting to it and tried to act like she liked it.

All my brothers and sister and their families were there. Pauline, Arvil, and all of Jerry's family were there, too, so we got to see everyone.

Even the snow was nice. The first morning we were at the Wick's house, Jerry went out to get me some donuts, and he started down the street in the car. When he reached the intersection, he realized he was driving on the wrong side of the street. After that, he was more careful and mindful of his driving.

We had been extremely busy with shopping. We had accumulated two television sets, one for the Barnes's and one to replace the one stolen from us. We had a video player/recorder and got a lot of tapes that Jann and Peggy had made for us. Jerry exchanged ten carburetors that we had brought with us. We got Lord's Supper plates and trays for CCBC.

The end of our month's stay came way too quickly. Arvil and Pauline drove us back to Houston in their camper. We caught South African Airways and flew directly to Johannesburg, RSA. We checked seven large boxes and our suitcases.

I carried one suitcase, a hanging bag, and my purse stuffed with U. S. magazines, passports, tickets, and all those necessities on the plane. Then Jerry had two carry-on bags, his shaving kit, a shoe box packed with auto parts, and a video camera strapped around his neck. One of Jerry's bags was full of auto parts and was so heavy that one strap broke and almost pulled Jerry's arm out of the socket. (We looked like we had forgotten to check our luggage.) Fortunately, nobody stopped us, and we had no difficulty getting on the plane. Once on the packed plane, we managed to find a few little cubby holes to secure all our goodies.

We picked up additional auto parts, printing material, and other items when we got to South Africa. We had to unpack the seven boxes we had brought on the plane to stuff everything into our little Toyota. (I had also bought 15 cans of ham to have on hand when people showed up unexpectedly.)

Then we headed back on the 1550-mile drive to Lilongwe, across the Zambezi River, and through all the heat. It was even hotter than when we had been through there a few weeks earlier. We crossed the borders without any unexpected difficulties and arrived home, happy to be back but very tired.

Our dog, Princess, had done fine with Rebecca, who said that Princess had slept on her pillow during the day and slept with her at night. The moment she saw me, though, Princess would not have a thing to do with Rebecca. (This made Rebecca angry, I think.)

We were thrilled to see Publications was operational, even though they were not accomplishing very much. We had a lot of things to do to catch up. We used the new Lord's Supper trays the first Sunday back. (I made the bread before we went to church.) It was so special, and everybody was praising God for raising the money for the road so they could get the land.

Peggy called and said that she had tried to prepare a special dinner for her and Bruce, and she would use her new China and make everything nice. Then she cut her finger and had to have stitches, which messed up their special meal.

Ken figured that he would graduate from TCU in about a year. Ken still had not taken accounting and was scared to take it, so he changed his major. Bruce and Peggy planned to graduate from Texas A&M in about one and one-half years. Ken had a new girlfriend, and her name was Suzanne Sellers. She was very pretty, and they seemed very fond of each other.

It had been good to see the kids, family, and friends. But now, we had to change gears; we were back home.

For a long time, we would say "home" and were not sure if our home was in Africa or America. We loved our American friends and family, but Malawi was now our home. My house even looked good to me, and my garden (yard) looked absolutely beautiful, like something out of a magazine.

I jumped in and got caught up on the paperwork at Publications and at home. Jerry worked diligently on cars and his work. We were beginning to see the light at the end of the tunnel when we were notified that the cars Jerry had ordered from Japan would be coming into Tanzania, so someone would need to go to Tanzania to get the cars.

The mission agreed for Mike Canady, Ross Collier, and Jerry Dowdy to fly to Dar Es Salaam, Tanzania, and drive the cars back. I left them at the airport at 6:30 a.m. when their plane was supposed to depart.

I went over to Peter and Rebecca Palmers for dinner. When I returned home about 10:00 p.m., here came the men.

Jerry said that Air Tanzania could not see the runway because it was raining. It had come in, missed the runway, and almost crashed into the terminal. After the pilot pulled up, he radioed back that he did not have enough fuel to make another pass. After a while, they learned they would not be able to fly out.

Air Tanzania told them they could fly to Nairobi, Kenya, and catch a flight from Nairobi to Dar Es Salaam the next day. Nairobi was in the wrong direction — it was only an hour's flight from Lilongwe to Dar Es Salaam, but there was only one flight per week.

So, the men returned to our house, Ross spent the night at home, and Mike and Jerry stayed at our house. Sherry Collier had made fried chicken for them to take on the trip, and they had already eaten most of their chicken and had not even gotten out of the country. They departed for Nairobi at 10:30 a.m. the next morning.

When they got to Nairobi, they learned that the connecting flight to Dar Es Salaam was the plane's maiden voyage. The border had been closed between Tanzania and Kenya, and this would be their first flight — so it was packed with diplomats. There was no way they were going to make that flight.

The men cornered the Air Tanzania man that had directed them to Kenya. The man tried to get away from them without doing anything. Jerry stood in front of his gate and would not let him pass until he promised to do something. Jerry said that if he did not give them hotel and meal vouchers, they would go home with him and stay until they could get on a flight.

There were 13 people in all in this same situation. They elected three spokesmen to deal with the problem, and Jerry was selected. (He told me later that he stuck to that Air Tanzania man "Like a flea on a dog's back."

Finally, the man gave them vouchers for a downtown hotel and provided a bus for them to drive there. He told them he would "work something out," so they went to bed. Their phone rang at about 1: 00 a.m., and they learned some food was ready for them. (They had not had any supper, but now they were more interested in sleep than food.) Some of the people ate anyway.

The next morning, they learned there was no flight after all, but the man from Air Tanzania had booked passage for them on a bus across the border. From there, they would catch another bus to Moshi, and from Moshi, they could fly to Dar Es Salaam.

When this bus arrived, they were reluctant to get on it. It was old, crammed with people, goats, chickens, and dead fish. They were unsure this bus would even make it to the border, quite a few hours away.

With no other option, they climbed aboard, pushed the animals aside, and squeezed into a seat. Jerry told me later that every time they would come to a hill, the bus would chug and rattle its way to the top. Then they reached one hill too many, and the engine gave up — and a thick fog covered the inside of the bus.

Everybody scurried off the bus, coughing and rubbing their eyes. They found a bucket and a little stream and dipped enough water to fill the radiator, and then they climbed back on the bus and headed down the road. They would run out of water every few miles — and go through the same process — until they finally reached the border.

They got off the bus and started the border-crossing process. (Because this was the first day in several years that the border was open between these two countries, this process promised to be interesting, if not dicey.)

Our three men got their bags and headed for immigration and customs. They filled out the required papers and got through immigration. Then they started through customs. The agents there wanted to look at their underwear, socks, and everything, and they wanted to ask them all kinds of questions. It was unclear what they were looking for, but the agents were curious about everything.

Once through the border crossing process, the men got aboard another bus (which was only a little better than the first one) to go to the airport, where they finally caught a flight into Dar Es Salaam.

Because they were so late, the missionary who was supposed to meet them was gone. (He did not know what had happened to them.)

Eventually, they learned of another Baptist missionary in the area who retrieved them from the airport. This missionary helped them locate the business manager who had met their plane two days earlier.

There was a severe petrol shortage there, but the business manager had saved enough petrol for them to get to the next Baptist mission station, and that station had enough petrol to get the three new Nissans out of Tanzania.

They spent the night in Dar Es Salom, Tanzania, got up early the next morning, and headed back to Lilongwe. They drove all day, spent the night on the road, and arrived safely back in Lilongwe the following day. It was one of those trips Jerry always vividly remembered but did not want to experience again.

This was the first time the Mission had ordered cars from Japan and picked them up in Tanzania. Jerry had talked to the Secretary of the Treasury and was trying to get the government to lower the duty on the vehicles we imported. Jerry got them to provide us with a better rate, and he was allowed to take some off the value because the cars had several miles on the speedometer, classifying it as used. He saved about $15,000 by ordering these cars, which made the rough trip worthwhile.

31 Work & Strife

Our sins, mistakes, and good can be used for the Glory of God because, as the famous inspirational author Catherine Marshall put it:

"The cross stands as the final symbol that no evil exists that God cannot turn into a blessing. He is the living Alchemist who can take the dregs from the slagheaps of life – disappointment, frustration, sorrow, disease, death, economic loss, heartache – and transform the dregs into gold."

When she calls Jesus the Alchemist by which *"all things work together for good to them that love God. . ."* I think Marshall means that even amidst our helplessness, we can glory in the Lord and know that God can use the good and the bad that comes our way for His glory.

So, pick up the pieces where you are and begin to build with what you have, and God will add, multiply, and bless. The dregs of life are sure to come our way, and how we handle these dregs is what makes the difference in the Lord's work — as well as in our own peace of mind, joy, and happiness.

There is no place in the Lord's work for hatred. If there were any room for hate, Jesus would have hated the people who crucified him. But he didn't. He was willing to forgive and die regardless of anything they did or didn't do.

If we are His and He is our example - where is our love? Are we willing to die for those who hate us? Are we willing to love those who hate us? Are we willing to *live* for those who hate us? Are we willing to *work hand in hand* with those who hate us?

We are responsible for our own actions. Whether we feel love or hate, bitterness or kindness, we are responsible. If Christ lives in us and through us, then there is no place for hatred and anger because love and kindness are what Jesus stood for on the cross — and He stands for love and kindness today.

Catherine Marshall's thoughtful words about the "living Alchemist" got me thinking, and her writings undoubtedly related to all that was happening between Missionary/Convention relationships. Maybe "hatred" is too strong a word, but many times Christ's love was not coming across, and somebody was not in the center of Christ's will.

———◆◆———

Jerry had headed out to South Africa to teach the Master Life workshop. I was not particularly afraid to stay alone in our new house, but I felt uncomfortable. I made plans to have a more positive attitude and not allow my anger or ill feelings toward anybody to sap my energy.

That evening I had served dinner to the Sibleys, Spires, Mary Ann, Carl Houston, and the Westers. They were to have a showdown meeting with the National Leaders over the Blantyre Association asking some of them to leave and the National Officers asking Bill Wester to leave. The meeting had gone on from 7:00 to 11:00 p.m. and had not gone well.

At 12:55 a.m., Princess woke me with sudden growling and snarling. I knew something was wrong, and I jumped up and grabbed a spear from under the bed.

I couldn't hear anything. The phone was in the living room, and as I started through the living room door, it sounded like someone was in the kitchen.

"Get out of here!" I yelled, and Princess let out her most vicious bark as I turned on the light. No one was there.

I called Gerald Workman's phone number, and there was no answer. The only other number I could remember was our phone number when we lived in the guest house duplex. So, I dialed it.

Auttie Sibley answered the phone. She held on while I checked the house. Nobody had been in the kitchen after all; they were tearing the screen off the kitchen window and must have run away when I hollered.

I told Auttie that all seemed okay, and we returned to bed.

I said a little prayer of, "Thank you, Lord, for protecting me." I asked Him to continue to protect me — and I went back to sleep.

———•••———

I went to publication the next morning but could not get anything done. The big stapler we used to staple books and tracts was broken. The presses were down, and Jerry took a press part to South Africa to replace or repair it. He was also going to buy a part for the stapler.

The meeting resumed between some of the missionaries and some of the National Officers. The results were that Mary Ann and the Spires could stay in Blantyre and continue their work. The Sibleys could no longer do church development work in the Blantyre Association.

After working in Malawi since 1959, Bill and Blanche Wester were asked to leave the country. Charlotte and Jimmie Walker, who had just returned from furlough, were also asked to leave.

It was truly a dark day in the life of Missionaries in Malawi. I still had not heard all the gory details, but even the bare facts were hard to take.

———•••———

I worked at the office setting up my books, doing payroll, and taking care of the essentials. Then I did my civic duty and went to the police station to report my attempted robbery.

The officer on duty escorted me across a courtyard into a small, dark room filled with police detectives. A detective got out the needed form and began to ask me questions, and I gave my name, address, and phone, and then he asked me the name of my tribe.

269

I balked, and I told him I was not sure. After a lengthy discussion, we decided my tribe was "American."

———•••———

I set out to buy grass and flowers for my new yard. I hired a night watchman to protect the house until Jerry returned home. I took Beatrice around town looking for "ufa" (the corn flour used to make nsima). There was a shortage.

I witnessed to a girl named Loveness with Godfrey trying to translate. Loveness said that she understood and wanted to accept Christ. She wanted to go to church at Kawali with me so that she could join the church.

While Jerry was gone, I bought a little buffet and a piece of carpet for the living area, made drapes, and got a lot of yard work done with Yobi, my gardener, assisting me. Yobi lived in a nearby village and was a good worker.

I stayed busy while Jerry was gone, but I sure was anxious for him to return. I drove to the airport in the blinding rain to pick him up. I grabbed my umbrella, locked the car door, and as I slammed the door, I realized I had left the keys in the ignition. Fortunately, I had left one of the back doors open, so I got into the back, climbed over the seats, and with my feet sticking up in the air, I retrieved my keys and started out in the rain again.

Jerry got in about 6:25 p.m. with Ross Collier, who had also been teaching. They went through customs and immigration. Trying to get all their luggage into my little Toyota was a puzzle.

We took Ross home. I was happy to see Jerry. He had been shopping and brought back candy, green and black olives, shower curtain hangers, and several little goodies I had requested.

———•••———

On Wednesday night, we had the prayer meeting at our house. It was a very good meeting. People were hurting but were genuinely seeking God's leadership in dealing with the problem of some of our missionaries being asked to leave.

Beverly Kingsley came over to witness to Loveness; she lived across the street from us. I was unsure whether Loveness understood what I had tried to tell her. Since Beverly's Chichewa was good, she was the ideal person to ask. She knew all the witnessing scriptures by heart.

Loveness accepted Christ.

———•••———

I had started attending the American Women's Association and was elected Secretary. I met some AWA women at Bottom Hospital, and the hospital nurse gave us a tour.

I had never seen so many tiny, premature babies. One was less than two pounds and had been born the month before. That child and several others were in incubators, and some of the incubators held two babies in them.

The mothers were sitting on the floor holding their babies, and some mothers were outside holding their babies. We walked right into the area that held about 30 premature babies and mothers. We stepped across the mother's legs as we tried to find our way across the floor. It was so full of little beds and women that there was no place for us to walk.

We were there trying to determine how the AWA could help the hospital. We saw one set of twins; the mother had died in childbirth. There was also another set of twins. If all the babies had been in a bassinet, there would have easily been two or three babies in each bed.

We took a long list of needs back with us to present to the AWA, and over time, we supplied many things on that list. I made 17 little baby gowns, and we gave several hundred gowns and blankets to the hospital.

———•••———

Jerry took a sick little girl and her father to see a private doctor and got some X-rays made. The little girl was at Kamuzu Hospital but was not doing well, and Jerry paid for the little girl's medical cost, which was minimal.

I took Mariam, Godfrey's little girl, to Kamuzu Hospital for malaria medicine. It seems we took three to four people to the hospital per week, a ministry all the missionaries took part in.

32 Eslet Chacwanira

Barnwell Chakwanira worked at the publishing house, and J. R. had taught him how to run the press. He had a little girl who was sick. Her name was Eslet, and she was three years old. She was a beautiful little girl, but she did not have any hair.

Eslet, her father Barnwell, her mother Katherine, and her baby sister Annie lived in Sandalamu's Village. Eslet's family did not have much food to eat; that is why Eslet did not have any hair.

Eslet had done pretty well as a baby because she had nursed her mother's breast, but now the new baby Anne got to nurse, and Eslet no longer had any milk to drink.

The main thing Eslet had to eat was a little nsima; Katherine would cook some greens, similar to spinach, mixed with tomatoes. Eslet would dip her nsima patty into the spinach and try to get enough to eat, but she could not eat enough to stay healthy. Eslet had a banana tree just outside her front door, so sometimes she had bananas to eat.

Eslet had gotten so weak that she would not go outside to play. She began just to lie around, and then her parents noticed that her stomach began to swell, and it got bigger and bigger. Her parents took her to the clinic, and the doctors did not know what was wrong with her.

Then they took her to Kamuzu Hospital.

All the beds in the Kamuzu Hospital children's ward had three children assigned to each, so the nurse assigned Eslet a place to sleep underneath one of the beds. Eslet's mother, Katherine, stayed with her night and day.

Because the baby, Annie, was still nursing, she also had to stay at the hospital. The hospital was very crowded with people. The doctors and nurses were very good, but they were so busy that they did not have the time to take good care of all the children.

The doctor looked at Eslet, and he did not know what was wrong with her. I went to the hospital to visit Eslet and saw that her stomach was getting bigger, and she was getting sicker by the day. Soon, Katherine became very tired, baby Annie got sick, and Eslet was getting weaker.

Then one day, Barnwell called me and said he had taken Eslet out of the hospital. "We have decided to take Eslet back to the village and just let her die," he said. "If we don't, we are afraid we will lose both Eslet and Annie."

I got into my car and went to get Eslet and her family. I brought them back to our house. Eslet's family had always slept on the floor. I asked Katherine to take a bath and told her she might feel better after a hot bath. She had always gone down to the water well and taken her baths out of a bucket, so she did not know how to take a bath in the tub.

I ran some bathwater and gave her some soap and a washcloth. After her bath, I turned the crisp, clean sheets down on our bed and asked her to lay down with the girls and go to sleep. Since she had always slept on the floor, she was afraid to sleep on the bed. Finally, she lay down but left one foot on the floor, afraid she would fall off. They went sound asleep with Annie nursing. Then all three slept soundly.

While Katherine was asleep, we talked with Barnwell. He cried because he felt so helpless. He was afraid his precious little girl was going to die. He had no money, he had no food, and he didn't know what to do other than go back to the village and let Eslet die.

We told Barnwell about a hospital in another village, Nkhoma, that was run by Presbyterian Christians. We asked him if we could take Eslet to that hospital, and maybe they could find out what was causing her sickness. We prayed with Barnwell and asked God to guide us in making the right decision.

I cooked a good, nutritious meal, and when Katherine, Eslet, and Annie awoke, we ate together and thanked God for our food. Katherine felt better after her bath, sleep, and food, and she agreed that we could all go to the Christian Hospital.

She would try one more time. We went to bed and slept well, and I prayed that Eslet would make it through the night. Her stomach was so swollen that she looked like she might explode at any moment. It was swollen down into her legs, and her legs were so swollen she could barely walk.

Early the next morning, we got up, prayed again, got into the car, and headed for the hospital.

God had heard our prayers and answered them in a beautiful way. When we got to the hospital, the nurse who met us was a friend. After taking one look at Eslet, she said, "I think she has intestinal tuberculosis."

Soon the doctor came in and agreed with this diagnosis. Eslet was assigned to a bed all her own, and Katherine and Annie had plenty of room to sleep on the floor near Eslet.

Eslet, Annie, and Katherine had to stay in the hospital for a long time. Eslet started taking medicine and food, and soon her stomach swelling began to go down. We all thanked God for answering our prayers and making Eslet well again.

Because we heard God speak to us and asked us to go to Malawi, and because our Dowdy Prayer Group from Travis Avenue Church, family, and friends prayed and gave to the Foreign Mission Board and the Southern Baptist Convention, Eslet went on to become a healthy teenage girl who was able to thank God for what He had done for her.

Our time in Malawi vacillated between emotional and spiritual highs and lows. We would experience situations like helping Eslet or leading Loveness to the Lord. Then we would deal with the relational problems.

———◆◆◆———

I had a very sad phone call from Zimbabwe. Our very dear friends Charles and Gayla Corley called to let us know that their son was riding his bicycle across the street, and a car hit him, and he was killed. He was their only child.

Gayla seemed to be handling it better than one would expect. She was probably still in shock. They were making all the necessary arrangements to take the body home for a funeral and burial. She said he just looked the wrong way. There was a lot of traffic, and he just got hit. It was so hard to become accustomed to watching for traffic on the opposite side from what we did in the States.

I felt so terrible for Charles and Gayla, but I am no good at times like that. I was not there to cry with them, and I could not think of anything to say over the phone to console them. I just felt devastated.

Then we learned in a phone call from Peggy that she had been in the hospital for three days with gastritis. She had been very sick but assured me she was feeling better. The doctor had put her on a strict diet, and she said that every time she got off the diet, she got sick again.

I felt so sorry for her. Again, there was nothing that I could do from Africa. I told her to go to a specialist in Dallas or Fort Worth if she did not recover quickly. Maybe she was reacting to the Malaria prophylactic that she took before coming to Malawi. Perhaps she had gotten some strange African amoeba or tropical disease with which the doctors in the States are unfamiliar. I felt that she was so alone.

Then I called Ken, and he, too, was having problems. I asked him about his job, and he began to cry. I pray that God will help him to get his life straight and happy. I pray that Peggy will completely recover. I am deeply concerned about both of them.

We continued to have numerous people over for meals, and many spent the night with us. It was "committee week" when all the missionaries were in Lilongwe for a called meeting to decide how they would deal with the Wester, Walker, and Sibley problems. I felt that the missionaries were following the Holy Spirit's leadership.

The group decided that the missionaries would support the Westers, Walkers, and Sibleys in their work until charges, evidence, and accusers made their complaints to the Mission. Then the Mission would choose how the missionaries should be reprimanded or disciplined if necessary.

Jerry Dowdy, Carl Houston, and Sam Upton were appointed to draft the letter the missionaries would send to the Nationals. When they presented their draft to the Mission, we went through the letter sentence by sentence, making whatever changes they felt necessary.

Then Gene Kingsley took the letter to translate, and the Mission decided it would go out to the Blantyre Association, The Zomba Association, the Salima Association, and the National Convention Officers.

Each recipient would get a copy in English and one in Chichewa. After tending to a few other business items, the Mission Support Committee began drawing up "Guidelines" for dealing with grievances. After the meeting the next morning, everybody went home except Mary Ann, who had a women's meeting, so she spent another night with us.

———••———

So much had been going on that very little had been done to our house since we moved in. After months of waiting, the cabinet doors finally came in, and I helped Jerry put them on the cabinet. A man came over and finished putting the baseboards down. The workers finished the driveway. I had a "honey do" list of 16 things on it for Jerry, and he got everything done except hook up the dryer. Mkwichi came over and repainted the entire inside. The house was just about as finished as it was going to be.

———••———

After the Mission decided how to handle the missionaries' problems, people began to calm down. My disagreements with the other missionaries also seemed to melt away, and it was just as if we were just one big happy family again.

We went to Kazambala Village with the Uptons. A 23-year-old man had accepted Christ during a visit to Kasungu last August. Then he went back to his village. Since then, he led about 30 people to the Lord, and they were baptized.

They held the church service in Kasungu under a cluster of shade trees. There must have been 150 adults in attendance, and this was another one of those all-day affairs. Sam and the Kasungu pastor preached, we walked half a mile to baptize six or eight people, and then we walked back and had the Lord's Supper. After more preaching, we finally wound things down and returned home at about 6:00 p.m.

———•••———

I started a literacy class for women at our house. I employed Bambo Sanje to teach. On the first day, five women showed up, and then the next day, twelve came. The classes lasted three and a half hours each.

This class taught reading, writing, and simple math. The learning was slow, but the women were working hard.

At the end of four months, about ten women had worked diligently, and it was amazing how much they learned. Bambo Sanje was also teaching them some scripture verses, and they were already very good at memory work.

When it came time for the class to dismiss for a couple of months, I went out, and they showed me their work. They recited their scripture verses, and they were very pleased with themselves. They deserved to be proud — they had done very well.

I continued these classes off and on for about a year, and the women were beginning to know how to make change at the market, write their names, and understand some words.

———•••———

My old distrust of Jerry still resurfaced from time to time. Jerry often would get up at 5:30 and leave to sit in a gas or cement line or go to pick up electricians or workers. I could not understand why he would drive himself so hard. Then I would wonder if he was really doing what he said.

On one holiday, we let the employees off for the day. Jerry was going to play golf with Don Messer, Gene Kingsley, and Bud Pazley, an American government employee. So, Jerry got up at 5:15 a.m. and said he wanted to hit balls from 6:00 to 8:00 a.m. before the others arrived.

I decided rather than not knowing what was going on, I would do the proper thing and check it out. We got to the golf club at 6:10 a.m. Jerry was to meet Maxwell, a caddy, there at 6:00. Nobody was there when we arrived.

When the caddy master came up, I said, "There is the caddy master."

"No," Jerry said, "he is just a guard." As he came closer, Jerry asked him about Maxwell, and he said he would be there soon.

At 6:30, someone else started caddying for Jerry. (Jerry was just hitting practice balls.) When the golfers showed up at 8:00, another caddy worked for Jerry.

My "checking it out" had not shed any light on my distrust, and we were so busy that there was little time to question anything. Our lives continued as if I had no problem with suspicion (or Jerry) anymore. I guess it just goes to show that we never know what is really going on in the heart and lives of other people.

33 Yet Another Robbery

The Spires came up to spend the night. We had dinner and talked for a while and went to bed. Jerry Spires had bought airline tickets for some of the missionary kids returning to Rift Valley Academy in Kenya. He also had several different people's passports in his briefcase. Jerry left his briefcase in our living room when he went to bed.

At about 4:30 a.m., Princess growled, and Jerry told her to be quiet. Then she growled again . . . and again. This time Jerry realized something was wrong. He bounded out of bed, grabbed his pants, and slipped them on as he headed out the bedroom door. As he rounded the corner, a man stood in the middle of our floor holding several of our video tapes.

When the man saw Jerry, he turned around and headed for the open front door. As the thief ran down the porch, he yelled at a man who had his head tucked into the back end of my Toyota. The second thief saw Jerry coming, so he started following the first thief with Jerry in hot pursuit.

Jerry yelled for Jerry Spires to get up, and everybody in the household got up. Jerry let out his loudest Tarzan yell as he rounded the end of the house, and it scared one of the men so badly that he ran right out of his shoes.

As the men headed for the back fence, Jerry continued to give chase. It was dark, and Jerry could not see very well. He later said that he thought, *either they have cut a hole in the fence, or I will catch them at the fence.*

When they approached the fence, the men just kept going. Jerry later said that he thought, *if they can get through the fence, I can, too!* Once the men got beyond our yard, they were in tall grass and no longer visible. Jerry continued to wander in the tall grass, trying to catch them. (I suspect he was probably a little bit relieved not to catch them.)

Godfrey was awakened and came to the house with only his wife's chirundu wrapped around him. I grabbed my car keys and asked Godfrey to come with me.

We headed out of the driveway to see if we could spot them or a car parked beside the road. We drove around the block, and nobody was in sight. When we returned to the house, we began to collect our thoughts and see what the man had stolen.

Jerry Spires's briefcase was gone. Our console television and videos, stereo, speakers, tape recorder, burglar alarm, one set of drapes, tablecloth, and a few small items were missing.

When Jerry returned to the house, his pants were still undone, and he did not have shoes on. His feet were jabbed, blistered, and messed up pretty badly from chasing after the thieves and tromping around barefoot in the tall grass.

We were very thankful that nobody was injured. Douglas Spires, who had been sleeping on the couch in the living room, said that he had opened his eyes and saw someone in the room — and the television sitting in the middle of the room — but he thought he was dreaming and went back to sleep.

The robbers had torn off a screen, three burglar bars, and the window glass to enter the house through a small dining room window. We had left the front door key in the door because, with guests in the house, we wanted them to be able to get out in case of fire. We had quit using the burglar alarm because the little geckos scurrying around would set the alarm off.

The robbers had removed the back window glass from my car. Jerry's golf shoes were gone. The man hanging in the rear car window opening was trying to untie the towel on the golf bag. (I guess he had no use for the clubs.)

We went down to the police station and brought some of the police officers back to the house. They pointed out piles of rocks on the front porch and piles of rocks on my blue living room chair.

The police said it appeared to have been eight or ten people — and we were probably fortunate that we had not gotten up when they first arrived. The original group must have parked their car on the street behind our house because we found our hoe on the ground, and the grass was stomped down. The two men we encountered had likely returned to get a few extra things for themselves.

More police came and fingerprinted the place. We answered questions and filled out reports. The police told us we needed to get a gun.

A few nights later, we heard a gunshot. It seems that the man who lives on the road behind our house had a burglar, and he shot at him and hit him, but he got away. Another time we heard a gunshot across the street from our house, and Jerry and I both rolled out of bed onto the floor for fear of being accidentally shot.

During those few months, our night watchman found the fence cut so often that when Jerry called the fence company and said, "This is Mr. Dowdy," the fence people would not even wait for him to say what he wanted. They just said they would be right out to repair the fence.

For some reason, we had given the watchman the night off on that particular night when the Spires were staying with us. While it may sound like maybe the watchman had set up the burglary, I never believed he was involved. The police questioned all our employees, and I assured them I did not think they were involved.

It was a lot of work for Jerry Spires to get new airline tickets and clean up the mess from having his briefcase stolen. Because Jerry Dowdy's passport was also in the briefcase, he had to go to the American Embassy to get a new passport. Everybody else who lost their passport in this robbery had to get a new one, too.

On the following Monday morning, Jerry made another maiden voyage — with malaria. His temperature came up and did not go down until the next Saturday. He took all the medicine he could take, and he was really sick.

The week Jerry was so sick, Jerry Spires and Darrel Garner came to spend a couple of nights. On Wednesday morning, Bill and Blanche Wester came out to the house. They just wanted to talk to Jerry and went to his bedside.

There had been a problem at the Bible School. It seems that Sam was to teach a T.E.E. class, and Bill was going to sit in on the class, along with several other missionaries. The Nationals said they would not sit in the classroom with Bill, so Bill left — along with all the other missionaries except Sam.

Naturally, Bill and Blanch were all broken up. They just wanted Jerry to know what had happened. Jerry was so sick he could hardly sit up. Then Ross Collier came by to check on Jerry. They all left shortly.

I medicated Jerry all week for malaria and put medicine on his feet, and he got better.

Our regular Wednesday night prayer meeting was at the Kingsley's house, and we had invited all the National Leaders. Bill did not know if he and Blanche should attend the prayer meeting.

It seemed to me that the missionaries had given Bill and Blanche a vote of confidence to stand behind them, and they should have all stayed at the Bible School. (If the Nationals choose to get up and leave, then let them go!)

Afterthought is always clearer. I was very proud of the missionaries for getting up and leaving with Bill. Sam was in a difficult position, so I won't criticize him for his decision. At least Bill did not have to stand alone.

The Nationals were having dinner with the Kingsleys before the prayer meeting. They had just finished dinner when Sam and Marlyn came in. Then Bill and Blanche walked in, and a hush fell across the room. All eyes were on them, and Blanche casually spoke and found a seat. With a big smile, Bill began to speak and shake hands with the Nationals near the entrance. They coldly spoke and shook hands with

Bill. Howard Rhodes, one of the new missionaries, jumped up and offered them a seat.

Bill and Blanche sat on either side of Bro. Galatia. Bro. Kanowa was not there because his stepmother had died. I saw Bill trying to be friendly with Bro. Galatia, but they exchanged very few words.

It took a lot of courage for Bill and Blanche to walk into that room. The prayer meeting continued, and we could have chiseled the ice from the walls.

Praise items were asked for; at first, only missionaries responded, seemingly even more than usual. We prayed for good meetings together. We prayed for several Nationals recovery from illnesses. You could tell we had been praying for several of these Nationals before. The praise items grew spontaneously — there was a sincere concern for the people of Malawi.

Finally, I think it was Bro. Chisi, a National, who spoke up and mentioned a praise item. Casually, a few others chimed in during the praise time and prayer request time. The meeting continued without incident, and everyone seemed to scurry away once the meeting was over. (I assumed Sam took the Nationals back to the Bible School to spend the night.)

It was only a couple of weeks later when the Executive Committee was to meet with an equal number of National Leaders. (The Mission Support Committee had passed the responsibility for "Dealing with Grievances" up to the Executive Committee).

Gerald Workman called the meeting to order. (Neither Jerry nor I were on the Executive Committee) First rattle out of the box, Mary Ann Chandler pointed out that there were three Nationals present who were not invited and not supposed to be there. The tone of her voice was evidently very sharp, as one of the men there was the one she had a problem with in Blantyre. (She was right to mention this, but she maybe should have done it in a more loving way.)

Bro. Kanowa said the three men were Seminary graduates and would not leave, so Mary Ann walked out of the meeting. Rebecca cried. The Convention Officers and men got angry and walked out too.

The Mission had been very clear on an equal number of people at these meetings. Gerald wrote the letter inviting the Nationals to this meeting. (I would have loved to have seen the invitation letter to see if Gerald had clarified this balance in his letter, but now the damage was done.)

Anyway, before the Nationals walked out, Bro. Kanowa said, "When the Westers leave, all the missionaries will leave." This was his threat. Since we were not at the meeting, this was the account gleaned by Jerry Spires, Darrel Garner, and Rebecca Phifer:

Rebecca blamed Mary Ann, and I think Gerald would have to share some of the blame because of how he handled the situation. Jerry Spires said he thought they came looking for an excuse not to meet. Everybody sees things from their own perspective, so it was hard to know where we were.

Bill Wester resigned as Chairman of Mission Support, and Joyce Spires also resigned. Jerry Dowdy was elected to the Mission Support Committee on the first round of ballots, and Sam Upton was elected in the second round. (This is not to be construed as a popularity contest.)

All in all, this past month has been interesting. We had two robberies in our car, one robbery in our house, two fiasco meetings with the Convention, Jerry's bout with malaria and sore feet, our freezer went out, and a swarm of bees invaded our attic.

Oh well! We seem as happy as ever.

When Zeb Moss came to Malawi from South Africa, he brought a gasket so we could install a new back window into our car. He wanted to see the publication house, so we showed him around.

Then the Corleys came to visit for a week. We went to Lake Malawi for a few days, played bridge, and relaxed. We enjoyed seeing them and visiting with them. They did a little curio shopping, and before we knew it, they had to go home.

284

In July, we had the annual Mission meeting at Chongoni. I was partly responsible for the food. We needed 30 dozen eggs; as usual, they were in short supply. Jerry went out to the cold storage plant, and they sold him the eggs. At the last minute, the manager of Chongoni called and needed a long list of things. We were running late, but I managed to get all the items he had requested.

Gary Swafford was elected Chairman of this meeting. Then the National Leaders came for the last two days. The Mission had notified them of their conclusion that they stood behind Bill Wester because they could find no fault with him. Bro. Chisi, Bro. Galatia, and Bro. Kanowa blew up. We told them that we would come to a compromise with them. The Westers would have to leave Zomba, but they would not leave the country.

This idea did not sit well with them, but they realized that the Mission had made its decision and planned to stand behind it. They left the meeting without us knowing where they stood. (They would not have made a decision for the Convention Officers.) So, it got left like that.

34 First Johannesburg Trip

Jerry and I decided to make a business trip to Johannesburg. We had Kombi motors we could exchange, and we needed a lot of auto parts as well as supplies for Publications. We decided we could save the mission a lot of money by driving to Johannesburg and bringing things back with us.

The Mission approved the trip, and we collected shopping lists from most of the missionaries. The rule was, mission items would come first, and, time and space permitting, we could purchase personal items requested.

We removed all the seats from our old Kombi, except the two in front, for extra space. We loaded four Kombi motors, several transmissions, a typewriter, and several other items for repair and headed out for Lusaka, Zambia at 4:00 a.m.

We arrived just before dark with little difficulty crossing the border. We spent the night in the Baptist Guest House that Dan and Mary Robinson, volunteer builders, had finished a short time earlier.

Early the next morning we headed for Harare, Zimbabwe, by way of Lake Kariba. We arrived at Lake Kariba in time for lunch overlooking this beautiful lake. We walked around and looked at crocheted bedspreads and tablecloths. After enjoying the lovely view a bit more, we headed on our way.

We spent the next night in Harare with the Corleys and learned that Gayla wanted to go to Johannesburg, too, so we invited her to join us. There were only two seats, so Jerry put a board across the motors, and we made a little bed. Gayla and I took turns lying in the bed.

Oddly, from the time we left the Corley's, every time we turned a corner our car's horn would blow. (We probably woke all their neighbors.)

We saw a lot of animals during the early morning drive. We arrived in Johannesburg about 6:00 p.m., but it was already dark.

We missed our turn into Edenvale, where our guest house was located, and wound up in downtown Johannesburg. It was like driving into Chicago or Dallas, with high rise buildings, freeways, and fast traffic. It was just like going back to the States. We had not seen anything like this in two years. We marveled — and got so lost it took us an hour and a half to find the guest house.

For the next two weeks we shopped for the missionaries, Publications, and auto parts. We purchased a car and got the little items repaired. The Rhodes were down there, so they drove the new car back to Malawi. Gayla, who became sick on the way to Johannesburg, had been a real trooper, but she finally had to give up and say that she needed to stay in her room. Jerry took her to the hospital, she got some medicine, and returned to her room.

Each day, we shopped from the time the stores opened until dark. Then we would take everything we bought and put it in storage in the BIMS building. Once Gayla recovered, we got a rental car and headed for Hyperrama and Macro's and bought food and personal items for the missionaries. (I had a separate envelope for each of their money.) We would shop for one family, pay for them, take their items to the car, mark their name on the items, and go back into the store and shop for the next family. By the end of each day, I was ready to fall into bed without supper, but we went somewhere nice for dinner three times during those two weeks.

Jerry bought a small freezer, a motor to repair one that was in Malawi, and he got about $2000 for auto parts we could no longer use.

With all our business taken care of, Jerry began to pack the Kombi. It was unbelievable all the things we had bought — and it took Jerry twelve hours of hard work to get the packing accomplished. (He got everything in there except a case of diet drinks for Gayla and a basket I had brought with us.) We had even bought a little television for Janie

House, a missionary to Zambia, and we somehow managed to get it tucked in. Once he finished packing the car, Jerry hired two night-watchmen to watch it. He parked it right outside our bedroom window.

Early on the morning of September 10th, we pulled out of the drive. Neither Jerry nor I had slept all night because we were afraid someone would steal the car. When we got into the car, items were packed all around us — with just little pockets for the three of us to sit in or lie in. The car was so overloaded it would hardly pull out of the driveway. We had our doubts whether it would make it up the mountain at Louis Truccard.

We called our Mission in Malawi and asked them to pray for us. We also called Charles before we left. Then, gradually, and cautiously we moved down the road. (To this day, I am sure it was a miracle that moved that car down the road.)

A flat tire stopped us just outside Petersburg, and Jerry used the truck jack and spare tire he brought to change the tire. The spare tire did not have any air in it, but Jerry also had a small pump that plugged into the cigarette lighter, so he was able to air the tire.

Heading across the first mountain range, we knew this would be the test — if we could make it through the first mountain range, we could probably make it through the Zambia Mountain range. We did not drive over 35 miles per hour on the return trip, and I sat silently praying for most of the trip.

We were also concerned about terrorists. Janie House had been attacked the week before —her car was stolen and she was thrown into the ditch — so we were fully aware of the dangers lurking along our path back to Malawi.

The mountains were steep and rugged. While the scenery was lovely as you looked out across the valley, this was not a time to even appreciate the beauty. Jerry put the car in its lowest gear and we just creaked along. The car — and the tires — kept getting hot, so every hour we had to stop and let the car cool. And each time we had to stop, we knew we were sitting ducks for terrorists or thieves.

Somehow, we arrived at the border just before dark. We had all our paperwork in order, got through South Africa's border check with no issues. When we approached the Zimbabwe border, we were told we would have to see the supervisor.

Jerry showed them where we had taken all the motors out of the country and how many other items were just being returned. We showed the supervisor where we had declared about $25,000 worth of goods. He just looked at us and our overloaded Kombi and stamped our paper for us to go on.

"Two down, four more to go," was said, breathing out a sigh of relief as we passed through the gate. It was dark. We were tired and hungry. We found a little hamburger stand that was just closing. They scrambled us an egg and cooked us some French fries and put them in a paper "to-go" cup for us. We were grateful for anything.

We spent that night at a missionary house in Bulawayo. The missionaries were not home, but there were clean sheets on the beds, ready for our arrival.

The next morning, we headed out about 9:00 a.m. Gayla bought some coffee and rolls, and we ate breakfast as we drove down the road.

It was almost dark when we pulled into the Corley's driveway. Charles came running out to the car — and this was one of the few times I ever saw Charles angry. He was so worried and wanted to know where we had been. He said he had felt sure something terrible had happened to us.

We explained that the car's top speed had been 35 miles an hour. He had difficulty believing that it had taken us that long to get to Harare, but he quickly cooled down and was relieved that we had not had any trouble. He had cooked chicken and dressing for us — and we enjoyed this wonderful meal together as we told him of our adventures.

Jerry and I stayed with the Corleys a couple of nights and then headed on home. On the way up the Zambia Mountains, the car got hot. The left back tire also kept getting hot. Jerry would stop to feel the tire every few miles, and if it was too hot to the touch, he determined that we needed to stop. He had blisters all over his hands from feeling the tires, fighting the steering wheel and wind.

Our money situation was a constant shuffle. Each country had different currency. We carried travelers checks and went to each country's bank to get enough currency to buy petrol to get us across that country. We had to make sure that we did not have too much local currency when we left a country, and we also had to keep up with the total money spent for our books. It was an accounting nightmare.

It was almost dark when we got into Lusaka, and Mrs. Franklin Kilpatrick met us at the gate to give us the keys to Janie House's home. Janie was gone to a meeting but had left food for us to eat.

We left Janie's house about 5:00 a.m. the next morning. Jerry wanted to leave earlier but was afraid it would be unsafe — we had already been stopped in Zambia seven times by soldiers carrying machine guns. They wanted to know what we were transporting. They really wanted a bribe, but we just gave them a tract. (They did not like that, but they let us go.)

The Zambia Bridge took us over the Zambezi River. The security around this bridge was very tight because if someone blew it up, it could cut off their supply lines. When we first arrived, the guard acted like they normally did. Then I noticed something different — a man had walked almost all the way across the bridge from the other end. Once he saw us, he waved to a uniformed soldier up on the side of the hill overlooking the bridge. I think someone must have spotted us moving so slowly that it aroused their suspicion, and he was checking to see that we did not stop anywhere near the bridge to do something subversive.

After the soldier waved in return, the man headed back across the bridge at the posted speed limit of 5 miles per hour. When we got to the other side, there was a truck halfway up the hill that had broken down. Someone else had backed his truck into the side of the mountain and it turned over. Then, further along the road we saw another truck that had hit a dip too fast and turned over. The Zambia road was filled with big potholes — better named washtub holes with some rub board areas.

We stopped in Petauke and picked up three gas cans that belonged to Rebecca Phifer. We put two where we had removed Janie's television and I put one under my feet.

At last, we approached the Zambia/Malawi border — the one I was both looking forward to and dreading. (Malawi could give us a real hassle about bringing this much stuff into the country.) The Zambia border was a breeze — we had the same guard we had talked to three weeks earlier and told him we were going to South Africa shopping.

We got to the Malawi border at 4:50 p.m. and it closes at 5:00 p.m. for trucks with goods, and 6:00 p.m. for cars. We arrived at the perfect time. A Malawi customs man said the person who needed to approve our entry was at his house. The customs officer was home, so Jerry went with a custom man to get the officer. Because there was only room for two people in the car now, I got out of the car and stayed at the border crossing.

I waited and waited. It got later and later. I began to think, what if he does not come back tonight and I have to stay here all night? I did not have a sweater, blanket, or anything. I just sat there at the gateway to "the warm heart of Africa," hoping to get in.

At last Jerry returned with permission to enter. By this time ten trucks had lined up at the border, and they would have to wait until morning to get approval to enter. The agent started filling out the paperwork, but then Jerry got the pad and began to list invoice numbers, prices, and descriptions of the items. Once the paperwork was filled out, the agent said Jerry would have to declare and pay customs when he got back into Lilongwe — and then the young officer stamped the papers, barely even looking at them.

Jerry pulled up to the exit gate, which was closed and locked for the night, and a man came out with a key, unlocked the gate, and allowed us to enter Malawi. After we had driven a couple of miles, we began to shout and praise and thank God for helping us on this journey in an overloaded vehicle across six border crossings without a problem — a true miracle to arrive home safely.

The next day we began to unload the car, and I made separate piles of things for each of the missionaries. I had 25 1/2 pounds of raisins, gallons and gallons of instant coffee, toys, and candy! We also had many auto parts and supplies for Publications. It was like Christmas for everybody.

It was so exciting, but we were so tired. The other missionaries seemed to think we had been on a three-week holiday, but it was anything but that! (Those who thought this usually got invited on the next one of these little shopping expeditions with Jerry.) Once they went, they never wanted to go again — they would come back with their tails dragging and their tongues hanging out.

This was the first of many such shopping trips. Jerry probably saved the Mission between 40 and 50 thousand dollars on cost and custom charges. This was the first new car the Mission had purchased in South Africa, and our bringing it back saved a lot of money. Then getting the engines rebuilt and purchasing needed auto parts brought the biggest savings and was the most help to Jerry.

Back from "the land of plenty," shopping felt very different in Malawi. I bought bananas from a lady at the gate, bread at the Capitol Hotel, cabbage from a truck parked beside the road, potatoes from a peddler in the parking lot, eggs at the Catholic Church, and wood carvings from young men in front of the Post Office. (This all happened the next day after we returned and was standard shopping procedure.)

35 Group Dynamics

Many exciting things were happening. Malawi Baptists were in the middle of Malawian Bold Mission Emphasis meetings, and every week there were reports from villages that between 25-50 people had accepted Jesus Christ as their Savior and were ready for baptism.

Despite Missionary/Convention relationship problems, they were all working together and staying busy preaching, baptizing, and starting new churches. Captain Chinjala, a layman, came by Publications and told us that his father had been saved. About 30 others in his village were baptized that year and another 20 were ready for baptism. The people were growing spiritually.

That same year, the missionaries were more intent than ever on "One on One" or "Small Group" discipleship training. It was real joy to see new Christians grow spiritually, and I was being challenged with memorizing scripture so I could keep up with the eagerness and enthusiasm of my discipleship group. I had completed "The Survival Kit" with Jean Ndjovu and three other young women. (I had even given Peggy, my daughter, a copy of "The Survival Kit" for her and Bruce to go through.)

Everything was really looking encouraging. We had gotten enough money to order four or five new cars to replace the worn-out Kombi vehicles. John Bisagno and First Baptist Church, Houston had given the mission enough money to purchase one vehicle.

Jerry went to the southern part of Malawi to preach where several village churches had come together. There were 27 decisions, and he returned praising the Lord. Some of the people, many barefoot, had walked 15-20 miles to hear the gospel.

Then Jerry preached 70 minutes. (When using an interpreter, that's how long it takes to deliver a 35-minute message.) The people killed a goat, and it was a big occasion. The people have such a sweet spirit it brings tears to my eyes when I think of their generosity and love for Christ.

I was honored with my first chicken. Mayi Kolako went home to her village to find her mother in the hospital. Mayi Kolako's mother insisted that Mayi Kolako go out to the village, catch a chicken, put it into a box, take it on the bus with her to Lilongwe, and "give it to Mayi Daud." (I had sent her some medicine for her arthritis, and she was so grateful.)

Another recent highlight was our annual Mission meeting. The missionaries had gotten together and planned our work and budget for the coming year. Dr. John Bisagno came and preached to us during that week. What a blessing he was. (Jerry and I were doubly blessed because he stayed with us in our home.)

We all just wanted to sit at Dr. Bisagno's feet and drink in every word he uttered. We had missed hearing great preachers, orchestras, choirs, and the surroundings of majestic church buildings.

Upon Dr. Bisagno's arrival, Capital City Baptist Church (CCBC) had invited him to speak to our church. We had built him up as a great and famous American preacher, emphasizing how fortunate we were to have him come to preach to our little congregation.

We had placed so much emphasis on the man that we failed to pray that the Holy Spirit would take control. I think this was the flattest church service we ever had at CCBC, reminding me once again that it is the power of the Holy Spirit working in man that causes things to happen.

I continued to work with the young people at CCBC. We had parties for them at our house and showed videos. I took a group to Lake Malawi and led a teaching on discovering your spiritual gifts. We had Bible Studies and lots of fun together.

Reflecting back on June 5, 1984, when the leadership of CCBC had their first meeting about constructing a church building, the church was going very well. We were attracting more than 100 on most Sundays. (We only had about 70 chairs, so that meant that a lot of people stood until the children left out for their Bible Study Class.)

We held our first Vacation Bible School at the National Public Library. Neil Weston took off work part of the time and was the primary director, and two Baptist Student Union girls also came to help. We felt it was a great success.

We had a celebration for our first anniversary and sent out invitations. We also visited people and gave them personal invitations. We were excited beyond measure that 156 people attended. (More people than could get into the little schoolroom we used for our church.)

I cut flowers from my own garden and made flower arrangements, and I was also in charge of the refreshments. Being the "church hostess" had somehow become my responsibility without the formal title.

———◆◆◆———

Ever since Jerry was elected to Mission Support, he seemed to spend a lot of time in meetings, and this required a lot of time. There were still the Mission/Convention personnel problems, and he was called in to meet with the Executive Committee several times.

The missionaries had voted to stand behind Bill, no matter what. They came to the consensus that making him go home for no reason was simply not right. Bill and the Mission decided together that maybe it would be better if he and Blanche cease to work with the churches in Zomba Association, so they agreed to give up their home on Zomba Mountain and move to Lake Malawi. This was a traumatic and difficult decision.

Jimmy and Charlotte Walker had stayed in Blantyre for months without working. The Mission supported them in trying a new approach to serve in a new area, but apparently there was so much conflict they decided to ask for a transfer — and they were transferred to another country.

Jerry and Joyce Spires wound up going back to the States. Joyce continued to have medical problems. (Once back in the States, her doctors discovered that when Joyce had been operated on, she had been sewn up incorrectly and this was the major cause of her problems.) Later they decided to just resign.

Mary Ann Chandler, Ernest and Auttie Sibley stayed in Blantyre.

All of these decisions had not set well with the Convention. At first the Convention Officer went to the Malawi Government and tried to get the missionaries kicked out of the country. However, since the missionaries were not in the country under the discretion of the Convention, the government would not become involved. (In fact, the Government was quite tough on the men who had reported the missionaries.)

The missionaries continued to work with the people and the churches who wanted to work with them. It looked as if there were just a hand-full of men who wanted the missionary houses and cars and budget for themselves. Once the officers worked through this problem, they began to realize that the missionaries felt that they were called to Malawi by God — and had no intention of being intimidated to leave. They realized the missionaries were willing to start a new convention or do whatever it took to be obedient to God's call.

During all this time, the church work had flourished. It was amazing how God had worked in the hearts and lives of the people. I was convinced that because the people were so receptive to the Gospel, the Devil's tactic of trying to stir up confusion was not successful.

Back home, Peggy, Bruce, and Ken continued in college. They each tried different kinds of jobs to try to subsidize what we gave them.

At the end of May, we made arrangements to meet them in England while they were out of school. We met them at Gatwick Airport one morning at 6:24 and went into London together. We stayed in a lovely little bed-and-breakfast, and we talked and visited and saw a lot of sights together. We jumped on little trollies. (Once we jumped on a trolley and all of us did not get on, so at the next stop we got off the trolley so we could regroup.) Then we rented a little car, and we were packed in like sardines. (Most of the European cars were quite small. Jerry and Ken each weighed in excess of 200 pounds. Bruce was pushing 300 pounds. If Ken sat in the back seat, he wanted to spread his legs apart and there was no room for anybody to spread any part of their body.)

Much of the time it was cold and rainy, but we just jumped and ran and laughed and did not let anything bother us too much. We looked at old castles, old ruins, old universities and took in all the usual tourist places. We stopped along the way and stayed in bed-and-breakfast homes with different people and enjoyed talking and having tea with them. We would eat a good breakfast, and then we'd be off to discover what we could see.

We drove all the way up the Eastern side of England to Edinburgh, Scotland to look at the Crown Jewels, and then we headed back down to Brighton. When we got back to London a week later, it had been a very full week. We enjoyed the trip in spite of our cramped surroundings. (Bruce said it was the best trip he had ever taken, and that pleased us.) The kids caught a plane back to the States and we caught a plane back to Malawi.

On July 4th, we hosted the missionaries and a few other Americans at our house. We had the house all decorated with red, white, and blue, and we had a little American and Texas flags on the wall. We barbecued a goat, roasted wieners from South Africa, and watched a video about the life of George Washington. It was a lot of fun.

The Parkers had decided that they would buy a pig at the Garners Agriculture Station. We had ordered one of the pigs, too. We waited until they got big enough to butcher, and the Parkers agreed to smoke our pig with their pigs.

These were big pigs. Jim Parker had never smoked a pig before, but he thought he knew how. He and his helpers gathered firewood and built a fire in a little shed and began to smoke the pigs. Jim would get up during the night to check on his fire. Jim called us to say he was not sure the pigs were going to be any good.

Upon our arrival at Lake Malawi where the Parkers were living, we knew something had gone terribly wrong with those pigs. From the moment we climbed out of our car, a powerful and foul odor enveloped us. We did not know if it was the kind of wood or what had gone wrong.

Nevertheless, we put our pig in plastic bags, thinking that maybe we could salvage some of it. We headed back to Lilongwe hoping that maybe after the pig aired out a little, it would taste just fine. (Pork is a rare delicacy, so we and the Parkers had really been looking forward to our pork!) Once in our kitchen, we opened up the plastic bag and laid a hunk of meat on my kitchen counter. While Jerry and I were trying to decide whether the meat should be thrown away or eaten, we were bombarded with big, green flies.

Then the flies really began to swarm on our kitchen window screen. After getting a whiff of that pungent aroma, they were attacking the house, swarming like bees. After this display, we decided the meat must be spoiled. Jerry and the gardener dug a hole in the back yard and buried our pig. That was the first and last pig we bought, but later we bought several goats. We learned that goats were really good when charcoaled outside, so that became our go-to party fare.

———◦•◦———

Charlie, Rebecca Phifer's son, was back home, so we decided to take Rebecca, her family, and Becky Scott to Nyika National Park, which was up north, west of Mzuzu. (I knew what kind of roads went up to Mzuzu and was not too sure I wanted to go to this game park, but since I had never been there before, I decided it could be fun.

Jerry borrowed the Parker's Nissan Patrol because it had four-wheel drive. We packed our food, water, and clothes and headed to the park. The Nissan was rough riding, and Rebecca complained that her leg kept hitting the handle used to roll the window down. She was certain she was getting bruises.

It was night when we arrived and located our little cabin. There were two bedrooms, and after we settled who would sleep where, we set into unloading the car. A cook came over to help prepare a fire in the wood-burning stove and to help us prepare supper.

We had seen a few animals on the way in. Since we were tired, we decided to wait until the next day to venture out onto the plateau to scout out the animals. We played games for a while and went to bed.

The next day we headed out early and saw innumerable antelope, zebra, and even a family of leopards. There were also mountain birds, elephants, and flat-topped acacia trees. Vivid proteas were dotted across the grassland as the wind made its swishing sound through the tall grass.

We drove into the rain forest, where we found ancient cedars of Lebanon and an array of tropical trees, flowers, and foliage. We marveled at the eerie mist that hovers around you as you walk. The road was muddy, but not too bad except in one spot. (Without the four-wheel drive we would not have made it through the rain forest.)

As we headed back to camp, a large antelope ran right out in front of us, and we were unable to stop. We hit the antelope, but fortunately he just shook his head and walked off. There did not appear to be any damage to the car, either.

At night, we drove around the park and shined spotlights into the trees looking for lions and nocturnal animals, but we only could see eyes reflecting in the light. We spent another night at the camp and then headed back to Lilongwe.

Our play time was over, and we needed to get back to work. Between our long days and nights of work, and our long days and nights at play, there was very little time for rest. We lived every minute in Africa to the fullest. We were so thankful that God blessed us with good health so that we could take in all the wonders of His handiwork.

Truly, this park was a breathtakingly beautiful place. The weather was perfect, at least to my liking. The jacaranda and tulip trees supplied a brilliant array of color along the streets of Lilongwe. The Acacia Candelabra trees sagged from the weight of their yellow blooms. Something always seemed to be in bloom.

Banana and Mango trees dotted the entire country. The tea plantations down South and the tobacco plants in the central region added beauty as well as economic gain. Corn and peanuts grew throughout the region. Cassava was a favorite plant in the North and rice was grown near Lake Malawi.

———•••———

During June and July, our winter season, we were able to build a fire in our fireplace. There was no heating system in the houses other than the fireplace. Sometimes at night, I would drag out a little electric space heater to get the chill out of the air. Sometimes I would wear a sweater during the day.

The work at Publications continued to progress pretty well. As the employees began to take a hold and learn a little, we began to tell them what to do and how to do it and leave the actual work to them with minimal supervision. I continued to do the books and Mr. Mkaka had the keys to the room which stored large amounts of paper. He was responsible for keeping up with the inventory. I had worked very hard to train him, and he had caught on.

36 Bridging Realities

I started playing bridge once a week with a group of ladies. (This gave me many opportunities to meet people and invite them to CCBC.) I was invited to play in a tournament where a hundred diplomatic women got together. Once, I won second place in a tournament and was presented with a bottle of liquor. (I had to graciously decline, so, they found me something else as a prize.) Bridge was so much fun I almost felt guilty. It was a good mental release for me, and I met people I never would have otherwise met. We had a lot of diplomatic people attend CCBC and hopefully some of them were due to my playing bridge.

Then, in February 1985, Mother fell and broke her hip. Doris called and said that she was in the hospital. Doris felt that it would be good if I could fly home; maybe I would be able to cheer Mother up. (She was quite depressed and felt that she would never be able to walk again.)

I made reservations on the first available flight and headed home. When I arrived at Dallas/Fort Worth Airport, there was an ice storm, and the streets were covered with snow and ice. I went to the hospital, and Mother was delighted that I had come. The hospital moved a little bed into the room, and they allowed me to stay with Mother at night.

Once before when Mother had gone into the hospital, Doris and I begged the hospital to allow us to stay overnight at the hospital with her. (We told them she was on medication that made her disoriented when she awoke during the night, and we were afraid she would need to go to the rest room.) The hospital flatly refused to allow us to stay at the hospital with her, and Doris and I had to go home. The next morning when I went to the hospital to see Mother, she was wearing a cast on her arm. She had gotten up during the night, wandered down the hall, fallen, and broken her arm. (I wrote the hospital administrator a letter stating my dissatisfaction with their policies and care.)

I don't know whether the hospital had made the connection between Mother's previous visit and this current one or if they just came to their senses, but when I arrived there was not one single word about whether I would be allowed to stay in her room. The hospital staff was extremely nice to me and to us all. I stayed with Mother for three days and three nights, without ever leaving the hospital.

On the fourth night in the hospital, Mr. Sellers, Ken's future father-in-law, came to the hospital and took me out to spend the night with him & Mrs. Sellers. I hardly knew them. Mother was released from the hospital and went back to the Masonic Home in Arlington, where she was living.

Ken and Suzanne were planning to be married as soon as Ken finished college. Suzanne had already graduated from Texas Christian University with a master's degree and was teaching school in Arlington. Ken was taking his final courses and planned to graduate that summer from T.C.U.

———————

Ken brought me a car from the Copy & Litho office, and I went to stay with Sandra and Ray Taylor while I was in the States. The Taylors turned a room of their house over to me because there was some business I needed to handle.

Our house on Bellaire Circle had finally sold, and the money was deposited into our bank account. Our accountant, who was taking care of paying some of our bills in the States, could write checks on our account pursuant to our requests. From time to time, he also wrote checks to Ken and Peggy and paid their tuition.

After the sale of our house, we had told our accountant to buy a certificate of deposit at Texas Commerce Bank once the money was in our account. We gave him these instructions verbally and in writing.

Because our bank statement went straight to the accountant, we never really knew what was going on with our account. We would write checks on the account and transfer money to Malawi each month to cover our living expenses there.

Then it came to our attention that our accountant had not purchased a CD with the proceeds from the sale of our house. Instead, he had helped himself to our money. He told us he had borrowed the money and fully planned to pay us back.

Since we had been so specific about what he was to do with the money, we realized he was an embezzler. Jerry and I were hurt over the loss of so much money, but we were hurt even more to think that a trusted friend would steal money from us.

I spent many nights being angry, mad, and hurt. I was so angry it was probably affecting my ministry. I tried not to allow it to bother me, but it really did. Jerry and I had worked hard for our money. We had lived conservatively, and now $100,000 had disappeared like a vapor. (That was a lot of money at that time.) The accountant said he would pay the money back, but we did not know whether to have him thrown in jail or make him sign a note and allow him to try to pay us back.

Jerry and I kept reading our Bible, trying to discern God's will. We prayed and tried to turn it over to the Lord as we came to the conclusion: "Vengeance is mine sayeth the Lord." (Romans 12:19-21, KJV)

Jerry seemed to handle this much better than me. Every once in a while, he would burst out with anger over the situation, but I was down-right hostile. We decided to turn it over to the Lord, and I believed that we made the right choice. We reasoned that filing legal charges would take time away from our work in Malawi, and we simply did not feel that was God's will for our lives at that time.

While I was home, I wanted to get all the bank statements and canceled checks and verify everything that had happened in that account since we went to Malawi. I had checks scattered all over the Taylor's office — and I made sure every check was accounted for. I made sure no withdrawals were made from the bank account I did not know about.

This was a mentally exhausting experience. When I had gone through all the checks, I called Jerry and told him exactly what had taken place.

There seemed to be little that we could do, but I made out notes and the accountant signed them, assuring me he would pay us back.

I did not think we would ever see that money again. The accountant was obviously in financial trouble, or he would not have taken the money in the first place.

Sandra and Ray were so gracious to put up with me during a very mentally demanding time in my life. Fortunately, they were very busy with their routine activities, and I was left alone most of the time to muddle through my muck and mire.

To finish what happened with the accountant, I will jump ahead. The next year Jerry and I went home and discovered that the accountant had taken money two more times without our knowledge or approval, so we took the checkbook away from him, which is what we should have done the first time he took money.

We went to see one lawyer and found out that his law firm was handling some of the accountant's business and had not bothered to inform us. We felt that this lawyer was involved in a conflict of interest, and I told him so to his face. He was appalled. I don't know exactly what had transpired with him — or between him and the accountant.

Both the accountant and the lawyer were prominent members of Travis Avenue Baptist Church. We went to another lawyer, and he told us we had legal grounds to file a lawsuit against the accountant. We again chose to try to recover the money instead of filing criminal charges.

We turned it over to the Lord, but for years, every time I thought about him stealing all that money from us made my blood pressure rise.

This is how God handled the situation. The accountant lost his business. He had a heart attack, and almost died. He and his wife had serious marital problems. He became a broken man. We have tried to remain civil toward him. He insisted that he was sorry.

I think he *was* sorry that he could not pay the money back, but I am not sure he is sorry that he *took* the money. I am also not sure he admits to God or himself that he *stole* the money. He tended to tell himself that because his intentions were good, it was fine for him to take that which did not belong to him.

That's how sin works. Mankind tries to justify sins and gloss over them. I believe God wants us to *admit* our sins and to *repent* — to be sorry for them — and to *refrain from repeating them*. Until we admit that we have committed a sin, then we can't repent.

After a month, I flew back to Africa. Mother was glad that I came home, and it was good to see some friends and the kids. I did the best I could with a difficult situation, but I felt I had just muddled through rather than professionally and efficiently handling a bad situation, because my emotions were too involved. Ray and Sandra Taylor were wonderful.

It was good to see Jerry and to be back in Malawi. A friend came by and brought a cake just before I got back. (She told me she found Jerry on his hands and knees cleaning floors and was greatly impressed.) Jerry had the house nice and clean when I returned. Because our cook had quit two days after I left, one of the first things I needed to do upon returning was to interview for a new cook.

While I was gone, Jerry had gotten a lot of printing jobs from the Ministry of Health. He was charging them enough to get Publications back on a sound financial footing. The health books had to be printed on a timely basis because they were being used in teaching.

As a result, the Mission got enough money to print five different tracts. Our employees did not know what it was to rush or hurry up, and Jerry wound up spending long hours working with the employees to meet deadlines. Throughout this process, Publications had a large inventory of paper and supplies, and yet, even after paying all their bills they still had several thousand dollars in the bank.

In June, J. D. Kelly and Jerry's sister Jann came to Malawi for a visit. Jerry was extremely busy with business, Publications and CCBC, but we made arrangements to take them sightseeing. When we decided to go into missions, Jerry gave up the Director of the Married Young Peoples department at Travis Avenue Church and started teaching a men's Sunday School Class; J. D. Kelly took over that class when we left Travis Church to go to Malawi. J. D. and this Sunday School Class had sent enough money to build Chidote Baptist Church in Malawi, and this church was going to have the dedication service while J. D. and Jann were in Malawi.

When we went to Chidote for this church dedication, the village people also served us lunch. Jann had a hard time eating, but J. D. just jumped in with his big hands and tried to eat like the nationals eat. (He got nsima all over his hand.) He made a valiant effort even if he was a mess when he finished.

During their visit we also visited Kasungu game park. J. D. was standing right by the window of the roundoval where we were staying when an elephant came up, stuck his head right up to the window (we could look right into one eye), and then stuck his truck and one tusk right through the window and into the room with us. In the process of trying to grab his camera to get that perfect picture, J.D. was making squeaking noises and fell across the bed trying to get away from the elephant while snapping some pictures. (He got away from the elephant but failed to get the photo. I don't know what the elephant thought.)

We ate in the Kasungu Restaurant, and after dinner we took some bread, sat on the steps, and a little deer came up and ate out of our hands. Hippopotamus snorted in the water, and at night as they grazed beside our roundoval where we were sleeping.

Jann had lost a lot of weight and she really looked good. She seemed to be feeling good, too, and took in all the sights. She brought me some goodies from home, and J. D. brought so many items the Prayer Group was sending us that he hardly had anything to wear in his suitcase. We had to keep washing his pants and underwear so that he would have clean clothes. When it got cool, he had to borrow a sweater from Jerry.

We had a good time just talking and recalling the memories we shared. We were at J. D. and Gypsy Kelly's house the night the first man walked on the moon. We did not know J. D. very well before that night. Then when Gypsy died not long afterward, J. D. was left with Gypsy's five daughters to care for. They had all graduated from high school by then, but they still needed a lot of attention. J. D. had adopted those girls when he and Gypsy were married, so he considered them his girls also.

Sometime later, J. D. married Joani Bodine Martin Kelly. Joani was small, lovely, and lively. She had two girls, Megan and Leslie, from a previous marriage. We spent many an evening playing bridge with J. D. and Joani. I always really liked Joani and knew her much better than I knew Gypsy.

Recently, J. D. and Joani had gotten a divorce. I knew there were problems before I left the States, so I was not surprised. One night in Malawi J. D. talked to us for a long time about their problems and divorce. It was still obviously painful for him to talk about, but he was determined to get on with his life. Our hearts were sorrowful as he shared his grief with us.

J.D. was very involved with the Men's Sunday School Class, and that helped to fill the void. He had brought enough money with him from his class and the Ruth Sunday school class to build a church at Makande Baptist Church, Ngabu, Malawi. Through the years, J. D. Kelly had become one of our dearest friends.

Jann and J. D. did a lot of shopping, and J. D. bought gifts for everyone. Both of their suitcases were bulging when they got ready to depart. It was always wonderful to have visitors from the States, but as soon as they were gone, we had to get busy again because we had not gotten much work done while they were with us.

37 Betrayal & Moral Struggles

We drove up to Publications one day and Jerry noticed that the paper he had brought from South Africa was missing from the storage room. We had stacked it to the ceiling in the front room at Publications, and through the small windows up high in the room, the paper could be seen from the outside.

We went in immediately, unlocked the storage room, and sure enough, a lot of paper was missing. After checking Bambo Mkaka's inventory and counting the paper left, we determined that more than $4,000 worth of paper was missing. That was a lot of paper. Because the 18" X 36" sheets of bond paper were packaged in 500-sheet reams it would have taken a truck to haul off that much paper.

I located all the recent job tickets to make sure we had not used all that paper. Sure enough, there was no error in Bambo Mkaka's inventory control. We questioned him about when he had counted the inventory and verified it to the inventory control. He assured us that he knew nothing about the missing paper.

Then we questioned all the employees, and nobody knew anything. We knew they would be afraid to tell us anything, even if they did know what happened to it. They would be afraid of retaliation from the medicine man. Then we told the Mission.

With all the problems we were going through with the Convention, now was not a good time to have another problem. Bambo Mkaka was the only one who had a key to the storage room besides us. And, Bambo Mkaka had been a trusted employee of the Mission for 18 years — and a convention officer.

Then there was Bambo Barnwell, the National Youth Director with whom we had been through so much. His daughters, Eslet and Annie — and his wife — had been sick so many times, and we had taken care of them. We had taken them to the hospital, given them money, and cared for them like they were our own family. (I even named his daughter, Annie.)

How could these people steal from Publications? The only admission they would make was, "It was spoiled." These were supposed to be Christians, trained for leadership.

We were still going through the deep disappointment with our accountant and now, on top of all that, this theft.

Didn't Christianity make a difference in people's lives? Our hearts were absolutely broken. It felt like this was the last straw.

The Mission was very supportive. Sam Upton said that almost every missionary had a traumatic experience during their first term of service. If that was so, this was our trauma.

We prayed diligently for God's leadership. Some of the missionaries thought that we should just let it go, just "sweep it under the rug." Others thought we should pursue justice and deal with the perpetrators regardless of who they were. But if we had not put a man from the States in jail who stole a large sum of money from us; why would we put a Malawian in jail for stealing $4,000 worth of paper?

After deep consideration, we felt we needed to call the police and get them involved. The police told Jerry they did not want to look for the thief, because every time a Christian filed charges they would get soft and not allow the police to do their work. Jerry assured the police that if they pursued the case, we would keep our hands off.

The police arrested five of our trusted employees, interrogated them, and put them in jail for two weeks. Their shoes and coats were taken away from them, they had no bed, no blanket, and they got one small meal per day.

When one or some of the men said that I had taken the paper, the police came to Publications and fingerprinted me. The young man who came to the office kept apologizing to me for having to fingerprint me. Then he apologized because he did not have any soap for me to wash my hands. So, with ten black fingers sticking up in the air, I went back to the restroom and washed my hands.

Bambo Sandalamu came by to plead with us to have the police release Bambo Barnwell. We told him we promised the police we would not intervene, so we could not go to the police. He was crying and heart broken, and I wanted to cry with him, but I did not.

After two weeks of interrogation, abuse, and neglect, the men began to break, and they began to tell the police what had happened. In the meantime, Jerry and I had played detective and learned a lot of things on our own. The employees had used the facilities to make paper and clear plastic picture frames for some of the National Officers. They had made scratch pads and taken them to the market and sold them. We found numerous infractions like these, but nothing significant.

Then the full truth came out. It seemed that another printer in town had bought the paper from our employees. He would come over to our publishing house when we went home for lunch and load up paper. They identified Bambo Mkaka as the ringleader.

Bambo Mkaka had seemed to be a sweet, gentle, man. I thought that he was a fine Christian leader. I could hardly believe that he was the ringleader. We kept thinking that one of the other National Officers had put him up to stealing the paper, and they had all shared in the gains. However, if anyone other than publication employees were involved, we never knew.

All five of our employees were charged with robbery, then released from jail. When they came by Publications to pick up their paychecks, they were so frail they were difficult to recognize. Those two weeks in jail had taken its toll on all of them. (Jerry had been by the jail to see them a couple of times, but I had not seen them.) I gave them their pay and they became "redundant" as the British would say — we fired them. All the missionaries, including us, really were sorry that this ever happened.

We realized we had given them too much responsibility and they did not know how to handle it. The temptation was just too great. They had never been responsible for anything of such a great value before. They were too immature.

A court date was set. Because Bambo Mkaka had suffered from tuberculosis, he was in a weakened condition. Recalling how he looked after just two weeks in jail, we knew that for him to go to prison for several years would be the same as a death sentence. We did not know what kind of sentence they might receive.

On the day that they appeared in court, Jerry was there. He went before the Judge and pleaded for mercy. Although we had promised the police we would not get involved — and we had not during the investigation — Jerry felt compelled to intervene on behalf of the employees.

When the Judge pronounced them guilty, he gave them all suspended sentences. They would not have to go to jail if they behaved themselves and reported regularly to the authorities.

I saw Bambo Barnwell only once or twice after that. I did not have any contact with the others except him. Once when I heard that his family and many people in his village were about to starve to death I took 1,100 pounds of corn to his house, and I encouraged him to take what he wanted and to share the rest with others.

Another time, I took one of the National pastors out to his church and Mayi Mkaka prepared lunch for us. They had a table, so we sat on chairs around the table, but Bambo Mkaka sat on the front step and would not eat with us. I did not know if he did not want to eat at the same table with me — or just why he did not come in to eat. The National pastor said Bambo Mkaka felt ashamed — and that *he* would not eat at the same table.

I could not keep from feeling sorry for Bambo Mkaka. He told me he was sorry for what he did — and I felt he had truly repented for his sin. Over the next several years, I continued to go out to his village and made an effort to help the people. I felt that my relationship with Bambo Mkaka was unusual. I forgave him, and in time, he forgave himself. Even though he did not go to prison, the penalty was great for him. He lost his job and was never able to get another one.

Bambo Mkaka became the pastor of the Baptist Church in his village, and he excitedly shared with me about the preaching points he had started. He said he made a mistake, but he did not blame God. He grew stronger and more dedicated. He learned from the error of his ways.

———•••———

We went to a Mission meeting during the publication problem, and the National officers and a few of the missionaries wanted to meet with us. The officers did not like the way that we were handling the problem. Bambo Kapalamula Banda, who was the natural whip for the group, accused us of taking the inventory. The other officers did not speak so bluntly but it was obvious that some of them were very hostile towards Jerry and me. (I felt they seemed especially hostile toward me.) I don't know what they really thought. I don't know what they thought after the police investigation. These were the same officers and other people we would have to work with if we continued in Malawi. After a grueling cross examination, the meeting was adjourned.

———◆◆◆———

The missionaries voted to invite Jerry and me to return to Malawi after our furlough. Since we had gone as associates, this was the standard procedure. Jerry said he wanted to return to Malawi, but that when we returned, we would not be running Publications. He had come to do other business work and that is what he wanted to do.

Van Thompson said that CCBC had extended a call for him to be their pastor. Jerry asked the Mission for permission for Van to accept that assignment. The mission was surprised, and after considerable discussion, approved his request.

Mary and Van Thompson, who were expecting their second son, wanted to move from Zomba to Lilongwe immediately. We said we would move into the guest house again and allow them to move into our house. The Mission approved their moving into our house with the stipulation that we would get the house back when we returned from furlough.

So, between the first of August and December, we would need to get Publications back on its feet. Gerald and Barbara Workman had agreed to take over Publications when we went on furlough. Jerry hired some new employees and got things moving again. This time he had enough money coming in to hire better qualified people for the work.

We thought the Workmans would do a good job at publications. They had worked with it some when the Kingsleys had been on furlough. Barbara was a fantastic typist and a capable bookkeeper. Gerald would be able to handle the printing side of the operation. Both of them were fluent in Chichewa, so that would be a real asset.

We still had a lot of tracts that needed to be printed, and Gerald needed more song books printed, so we scheduled the printing for those. Everything was running smoother than ever, but Jerry was having to work very long hours.

38 Delicacies & Reprieves

It just so happened that Janie House was coming to see us on Jerry's 51st birthday. First thing that morning, as I was trying to decide what to prepare for Jerry's birthday dinner, I had to take someone to the airport.

Each year after the crops are gathered, the fields are burned, and smoke fills the air and billows across the sky. When the fields are burned the fire runs the mice out in front of the fire, and small children run in front of the fire and grab the mice with their bare hands. Then they throw the mice into kettles of boiling water set up by the adults participating in this annual festival. These mice are boiled alive — hair, head, eyes, and all — and then the little boys skewer six or eight mice onto bamboo sticks and offer them for sale to people passing by.

As I drove back from the airport, the telltale smoke hung across the road, and some young boys were standing beside the road selling these "mouse-kabobs," as I called them. When one little boy held his skewer of mice out to me, I pulled over to the side of the road.

"How much do you want for the mice?" I asked.

The little boy said that he wanted ten tambala (about 10 cents) each.

"I'll give you fifty tambala for six," I offered.

He grinned and gladly accepted my offer.

I opened the trunk of my car, and he placed the kabobs on a piece of paper. I grinned as I drove back home. I now knew what I was going to serve for Jerry's birthday dinner.

I went into town to pick up a few things and just happened to run into Janie House and her niece.

"Janie, this is Jerry's birthday," I said, "and we are going to have the most wonderful appetizer. I have just purchased the perfect ingredients." I continued to talk about this appetizer until I was sure their mouths were watering — and I was sure I had their curiosity aroused.

When Janie and her niece arrived for dinner, I told Jerry I had gone to a lot of trouble for his birthday dinner, and I was sure he was going to be delighted. Then I told them all I was going to serve dinner Asian style, sitting on the floor around the coffee table in the living room.

For the main course, I had prepared chicken and dressing, and I opened my one and only can of cranberry sauce, a real specialty item. We would have strawberry short cake for dessert.

I excused myself and went into the kitchen to help my cook. I pulled out my finest China, and he placed one mouse-kebob on each of four China plates. He had their tails curled artistically, and each plate was garnished with parsley from my garden. We placed the plates on my best wooden tray, and I covered the tray with my finest linen cloth.

Now, unbeknownst to me, Janie had told her niece she had to eat whatever she was served because if she didn't it would offend her hosts. I walked into the living room and placed the covered tray on the coffee table as we sat on the floor with our noses directly over the little table. I mentioned that this was my nicest linen cloth, and that I hoped they enjoyed the appetizer because it was really special — a once a year local delicacy.

We all bowed our heads in prayer, and I could sense the anticipation of what we were going to have for dinner. Jerry began to pray. By this time, even he was beginning to wonder what I had prepared that I was *so* proud of.

When we raised our heads, I lifted the linen cloth that was covering the mice with a flourish. There they lay, their eyes wide open — and their hair still a bit wet.

At first everyone stared in wide-eyed shock. Then Janie's niece fell over backwards and wailed, "I can't eat that!"

Janie was speechless and pale around her mouth, and I was pretty sure I detected a green tint rising and then sweeping across her face.

Everybody seemed to be in such shock I wondered if I had overdone it this time. Then I began to laugh. I explained to Janie's niece that she did *not* have to eat the mice — it was just a joke. Then I explained that the Malawian people *do* eat these mice (and do consider them a once-a-year delicacy!), but I just thought that we could have some fun.

After they regained their composure, they agreed it was funny. But for a few minutes, there was nothing funny about those mouse-kabobs.

Janie then jumped up and said, "Let me run out to the car and get my camera!"

Then we all got our cameras and began to laugh and take pictures.

It turned out to be a fun evening. They all agreed that the rest of the food tasted good, and the next day I gave the mice to my gardener, who told me his family enjoyed eating mice.

Some years later, someone from Zambia came to our house and shared a story with us about one of the Zambia missionaries who visited Malawi and were served mice. He couldn't remember who the missionary was and wanted to know if we knew the story.

"I was that missionary!" I told him with more than a little glee that the story had achieved such status.

He looked surprised when I assured him the story was true and added the details. I don't know what he had intended to say. I later wished I had let him finish his version of the story just to see how it had grown.

We learned early on in our missionary life that if we were going to have fun, we would have to provide our own entertainment. We celebrated every occasion that came along from the birth of kittens to costume parties to the annual rodent harvest.

———•••———

We had a few vacation days coming so we told the Corleys we would meet them at Lake Kariba in Zimbabwe. We met them at Kariba and then caught a small plane and flew to Fathergil Island in the middle of Lake Kariba. Gayla and I flew in the plane with one pilot and Jerry and Charles flew in another one. (We split up families for safety reasons.)

We stayed in small buildings that were covered with thatched roofs that come down low on the sides and walls that came up about four feet high. The rest of the wall was wide open space. This was a resort island with trucks that took tourists out to view the animals. They provide nice meals and probably charge a fortune to tour groups, but they gave missionaries a special discount.

We climbed into a jeep and rode out to see a large heard of cape buffalo. We saw a lot of other animals, and during the day we went for a walk. We had walked across the small dirt airstrip and saw an elephant in the path where we intended to go, so we turned and took a different path.

As we got back to camp, someone yelled, "Come on, we have spotted some lions!" Several people quickly jumped onto the zebra-striped truck, and the truck drove right to where the elephant had been standing.

There they were — four lions eating a cape buffalo. If that elephant had not been in our intended path, we would have walked right up into a pride of lions. Our hearts skipped a beat as we realized how close we had come to danger. How many other times had we prayed for God's protection, and God had placed an obstacle in our path to protect us?

We played bridge and we played more bridge. We had a little candle at night that we used for light, and Charles also had a little flashlight on a hat he wore to shine on the card table so we could see well enough to play.

We laughed and laughed and said, "if people could see us, they must think we are crazy!" We did not care what people thought. We were enjoying getting away from the everyday stress and strain that comes from missionary life.

After a few days, we were back in Malawi, and a young man in our church was getting married. They asked me to provide the flowers for the wedding. This was a big job, but I enjoyed working with flower arrangements. (I guess I did fine, because this became my continuing job for weddings, in addition to my hostess responsibilities.

———•••———

Back in the states, Peggy and Bruce graduated from Texas A&M — and they both found jobs in Dallas — so they rented an apartment and moved from College Station to Richardson. They had Buster, the Cocker Spaniel, whom Peggy had adopted when we went to Malawi.

Peggy would say, "Buster, say your prayers!"

Buster would run to the couch, put his front paws on the front edge of the cushions, and place his head between his paws. (Sometimes he would also wag his tail-less behind.) He otherwise stayed very still; his eyes wide open.

When Peggy said, "Amen," Buster would jump up, so proud of himself.

Then she would say, "Buster would you rather be a Texas Longhorn or dead dog?"

Buster would then fall over "dead" with all four paws sticking straight up in the air.

She would commend him on his choice, and he would get up and wag his tail-ess behind even more.

Ken was scheduled to graduate from TCU at the end of the summer session, but his graduation ceremony would not be until January, so, we would be home on furlough for his graduation. It had taken him a long time, but he was determined to get that "sheep skin." Besides that, Suzanne said she would not marry him until he got his degree.

Ken and Suzanne planned to get married December 28, 1985. We would be home just in time for Christmas and the wedding. I was worried that I did not have a thing to wear, but Peggy assured me that we could run out the day after Christmas and pick up a pretty dress.

———◦•◦———

Van had arrived at CCBC and was well-accepted with about 156 people at the reception. We had moved into the duplex and were feeling a little cramped, but we managed to live there for another four months.

Our church had also started a mission at Chigwilizano. I took some of the Malawian young men from our church out there to preach, teach, and lead the music. Rebecca Phifer started going there, too, and she would take the young men sometimes. This was a difficult congregation to start because the area was predominantly Catholic.

Rebecca was going home on furlough about the same time we were going on furlough, and she said she would take our dog Princess with her to Houston. In Houston she would put Princess on a plane for Dallas/

317

Fort Worth Airport where Ken would pick her up and keep her until we would get home.

After being in Malawi for almost four years, we headed back to the States for a year. On the way home we stopped in Vienna, Austria, and saw the Stephansdom Cathedral. We went down into some of the old crypts, including the Imperial Crypt (or Capuchin Crypt) and the Franz Joseph vault. We viewed many statues, saw where the famous Vienna Boys Choir practiced, and viewed a performance of the famous Spanish Riding School. We secured a Eurail Pass and traveled over Europe for about three weeks before continuing home.

We stayed in Vienna with a missionary couple, enjoyed a weird little bed and breakfast in Venice that overlooked the Grand Canal, traveled by train across to Milan, Italy, and then boarded another train across Switzerland.

We came back to Italy and met the Corleys in Rome and saw the Coliseum and The Capitoline She-Wolf, the symbol of Rome. We saw the Vatican and the Sistine Chapel, and then we traveled to Pompeii to see the ruins. (Those were especially interesting.) After we parted company the Corleys, Jerry and I went on to Naples and Capri.

It was a whirlwind, three-week tour of Europe with one small suitcase each, filled with clothes and necessities. At the end of it we returned to Vienna and caught a plane to the States, returning home just in time for Christmas.

———•••———

We got together with the entire family on Christmas Day, and it was so wonderful to be back home. The best gift of that Christmas was just being together.

On the day after Christmas, Peggy and I hit the stores early in the morning, and I began to try on dresses. After four stores trying on numerous dresses, Peggy decided that maybe it would not be that easy to find a dress, after all. (Dresses that looked good on the hanger would not hang so great on me.) Finally, we went to Neiman Marcus, and I tried on a simple, straight, blue-brocade satin dress with just a touch of lace. I knew immediately that it was the one. We bought it, a pretty slip to wear under it, some hose, and a pair of white high-heeled sandals. I was finally ready for Ken's wedding.

By the day of the wedding, I was in such a whirlwind I could hardly remember anything. Suzanne looked beautiful. Ken looked great. Mr. and Mrs. Sellers were dressed in their finest. We all went to great lengths to look proper for this special occasion.

Ken and Suzanne were married in a Baptist Church in Arlington, by Pastor Lineberger. Both my family and Jerry's family made the effort to be at the wedding — none of us would have missed it.

After the wedding, Jerry and I headed to Fort Worth. Since we planned to be home for a year, we made arrangements to stay in one of the missionary apartments at Southwestern Baptist Theological Seminary. Jerry planned to attend the Seminary and wanted to get 20 hours credit that year.

We anticipated staying in the States all year during 1986, and we knew there were a lot of things that we needed to do. *What would this year bring?* we wondered.

39 First Furlough

After four years in the mission field, the Foreign Missions Board (FMB) allowed us to return to the States for a year's furlough. A furlough is quite different from a vacation. For one thing, there are certain requirements of missionaries in the States on furlough, including World Mission conferences, Girls' Camps, Boys' Camps, speak in churches about mission work, and sometimes attend other conferences.

When we came home, there were many other things which we wanted to do, so we signed up for the minimum speaking engagements. Jerry signed up for classes at Southwestern Baptist Theological Seminary (SWBTS).

I had made arrangements sight unseen for us to stay in the SWBTS housing for missionaries. (If I had looked at the housing before, I would have made other arrangements.) The first apartment they assigned us to was dark, and the rooms were oddly arranged, and our hallway was very uneven. (I think it must have been an abandoned government barracks, moved in and remodeled.)

I found the place very depressing. The building was sitting right beside the railroad tracks, and trains went up and down the tracks, blowing their whistles all hours of the day and night. It was not the kind of place that I would enjoy having friends over.

Jerry enrolled in his classes and was not at home much during the day. I enrolled in the health and fitness center and started working out with weights.

We got an old car from Copy & Litho, and Ray and Sandra Taylor had an old Oldsmobile they no longer drove, and they graciously offered it to us. Neither car looked very good, but both ran quite well and provided reliable transportation for us while we were home for the year.

When we first got home, we renewed old acquaintances with people from Travis Avenue Baptist Church. We were delighted to reconnect with Sandra and Ray Taylor, who hosted the monthly Dowdy Prayer Group Meeting at their home, and to see our friends who had been so faithfully praying for us, meeting monthly to pray for us.

Of course, one of the first things we wanted to do was spend time with our family. All were doing fairly well except Mother, who had moved to the Masonic Nursing Home in Arlington. Doris had faithfully looked after Mother and tried to meet her needs, but her health was failing.

Mother was always so special to me. As the year progressed, I had time to visit with Mother and bring her to our apartment for visits. As winter passed and summer approached, Mother's health continued to decline.

The Masonic Home administrator asked her to move from one floor to another floor. She would have a larger, brighter, and nicer room, and her favorite nurse was going to be moved to the new floor also. Mother agreed to the move, and everything would have been great, but at some point, during the move, the administrator took most of her clothes, put them in "storage," and would not let Mother have them back.

Mother became upset. Doris talked to the administrator and evidently had a real run in with her over the clothes. I don't know all the details, but in the process, Mother had a stroke and never recovered.

We did not insist that Mother be taken to the hospital — we left it up to the home to take care of her. We later found out that they did not even have a doctor to come and see her for several days. Neither Doris nor I was happy about the situation, but neither of us did anything. Maybe it would not have made any difference. Maybe it was for the best because Mother never had to linger in a mentally or physically handicapped situation.

Just before Jerry and I were supposed to do a Girls Camp in Dallas, my beloved mother, Ruby Ray Nicholson, passed away, and we held her funeral in Howe, Texas before burying her alongside Daddy at Cedar Lawn Cemetery in Sherman. Jerry wound up doing the camp by himself.

———•••———

Jerry and I continued dealing with our accountant who had stolen so much money from us. He was making some payments when we pressed him, but he was in deep financial trouble. We were also still grieving over our problems with the Publications employees prior to our leaving Malawi.

As I checked over the financial statements of Copy & Litho, it was obvious to me that there were also some problems there. I got copies of the depreciation schedule and started trying to track down the many machines on our depreciation schedule. There were hundreds of machines listed; maybe even thousands, and it was a long tedious task. It soon became clear that we were missing a lot of machines. I did not know whether people were stealing these machines, or if the accounting department had lost track of them.

After working for days, weeks, and months there were still hundreds of machines that could not be located. I enlisted Jerry to help me look at serial numbers and cross check every possible location, but the missing machines were nowhere to be found.

I talked with Linda and the manager at the office, and neither claimed to know anything about the problem. Linda assured me she had a record of every machine, but she had not been keeping records the way I asked her to.

Linda and I sat at the computer to cross check our machines' locations, and she finally had to admit that she did not have as good of records as she thought. She never admitted that she made a mistake, but she did not know where the missing machines were.

Even after Jerry and I worked on the depreciation schedule for several months, we still had not examined every serial number to see if each missing machines was sold (and just not taken off the inventory), out in a customer's office, rented, or still in our warehouse. After all this examination, I was pretty certain these machines were being stolen.

I was moderately depressed when we got home. Then we moved into that dark apartment, which added to my depressed feelings. All the additional problems with the missing copy machines became just too much.

My old problem of distrusting Jerry came back. Always lurking just below the surface, my distrust was causing me great difficulty. Our marriage was on the brinks of breaking up.

I got the name of a counselor from the Foreign Mission Board. His office was in Arlington, and Jerry and I began going to the counselor each week. Sometimes the counselor would meet with us together, and sometimes he would meet with us separately.

I began by telling the counselor, from the beginning, of my deep feelings of distrusting Jerry, going back to when Mamaw Maness passed away and Jerry did not stand up to his family and defend me. I told him about being sexually abused as a child. (I had never shared that with anybody.) I told him about all the times I felt that Jerry was running around on me. I had kept it *all* bottled up inside me — and now it was coming out.

I vacillated between believing that Jerry was guilty of gross misconduct and it all being in my imagination — and therefore, *my* problem. There were enough things that still distressed me, over the years, and if blame needed to be laid somewhere, I knew it was not *all* my fault.

My mind was a jumbled mess. I couldn't concentrate on Copy & Litho problems because my thoughts were consumed with thinking of "self" — and my marital problems.

We went to that counselor for several months. He gave me books to read. I wanted to get out of the mess I was in. I didn't want to get a divorce from Jerry, but I also did not want to live with him with the doubts I had.

Finally, Jerry admitted to the counselor, in my presence, that he did not love me. In counseling, things sometimes seem to get worse before they get better. With our situation at rock bottom, it was doubtful whether our marriage would survive. We still slept in the same bed, as if there was a wall between us — each careful not to touch the other. The pain was almost unbearable for me. I could not sleep, and I would lay awake and resent Jerry for his peaceful slumber.

Jerry offered to take a lie-detector test.

I said I did not think that would help.

Jerry talked to the counselor about taking a lie detector test.

The counselor convinced me that maybe it would help.

I agreed halfheartedly.

The counselor called someone and talked to them about giving Jerry a lie detector test, and then he gave me the name and phone number of the person. I called and made an appointment.

I was in no mental state to ask the questions I really wanted answered. We went in for the test, and I gave the woman a list of half-hearted questions. I felt terrible putting Jerry through this, and it was not my idea. And, while I hoped it would help, I did not trust those tests.

Jerry took the test, and the examiner met with me afterwards and told me that my husband was not guilty of adultery. I just sat there, not knowing whether to be happy or sad. (I think if he said Jerry was guilty, I could have dealt with that easier.) As it was, I felt I needed to go to Wichita Falls and commit myself to the insane asylum.

"Am I crazy?" I asked myself, then answered in the same breath, "I don't think I am crazy."

I was totally exhausted. Jerry was angry because he had gone through this examination, and he blamed me for making him take the lie-detector test. This all just seemed to add a new problem to our other problems.

Jerry and the counselor *insisted* I have Jerry take the test.

"How can this be *my* fault?" I thought.

We continued to go to the counselor, and little by little things seemed to get better between us. The counselor seemed to zero in on the fact that I had been abused by a relative. I did not have a good, respectful relationship with my father, and I did not have any other good male role model I trusted and respected. (Be sure to understand it was not my father who molested me.) That, the counselor surmised, was probably the reason I did not trust Jerry. I tried to believe and accept this explanation.

The counselor also explained that because Jerry had not had a good relationship with his own mother during his teenage years, he was transferring some of that hostility to me. The counselor also tried to convince Jerry to listen to what I *said* rather than to think he always knew what I wanted and needed. He tried to get Jerry to be more understanding and to realize that our problems were not all my fault.

The problems did not get completely corrected, but our relationship improved, and we were willing to work at the marriage.

—————•••—————

Peggy, who was expecting our first grandchild, had gained a lot of weight and I was concerned about her. She went into the hospital planning to have natural childbirth. (I tried to talk her out of that, but she was sure that natural childbirth was the way to go.) While Peggy was in the hospital, the doctor gave a woman in the next room a procedure that required him, by law, to stay with her. Peggy lay in the room next door, screaming in agony as her vagina tore. They had given her all the medication for pain that they could give her, and the doctor was finally able to come in and give her an episiotomy, but it was too late — the damage was done.

Bruce had sat by Peggy's bedside through the entire delivery. She had a baby boy whose head was quite large, causing childbirth difficult. They named him Zachery Chase Lawson, and he was a beautiful healthy child. She seemed fine after the delivery, but she must have been terribly sore. She and Bruce were all smiles and proud parents.

I wanted to tell that doctor that my daughter would have gotten better care if she had given birth on the ground under a shade tree in Africa with a midwife attending her. I felt that she had been given very poor care.

I stayed at the hospital with Peggy because they put the baby in the room with her. I stayed at the hospital at night with her but was unable to help her very much.

Then, after we took Zac home for a couple days, he became jaundiced and had to go back to the hospital. Peggy had to pump her breasts because she could not nurse him. Zac was a very good baby, and Peggy never complained. I just kept my mouth shut.

After staying in the hospital two or three days more, Zac's bilirubin came down and they released him from the hospital, but we still had to make sure he spent plenty of time in the sunshine for several more days.

Zac was such a good baby. After her baby was born, Peggy was still very large. I made her some skirts and tops and she looked very nice. As she nursed Zac and began to take better care of herself, she began to lose weight in a hurry — and was soon back down to a reasonable size. It was not until some years later that she looked at one of the skirts that I had made her that she realized just how big she had been.

During the year, one had died, and one had been born. We were so grateful for how God allowed us to be in the States for every major death, wedding, or birth. It seems that God saved up everything until we could be back in the States.

———•••———

Another thing which we had found stressful during the year was dealing with the sale of The Copy Center in Temple. Some years earlier, we had entered into a partnership with Ken Parma in which we put up some money and Ken Parma managed our business.

During 1985, the Internal Revenue Service decided they would do an audit on the business. Neither Ken Parma nor we saw this as any problem — just a little nuisance. What we did not know was that the person assigned to do the audit was totally unqualified — a young woman straight out of college who had probably never done a business audit before.

After going over our books, she decided that we could not depreciate the machines, nor could we consider the cost of the machine when the machine was sold. This meant that if we sold a machine for $1,000, we had to pay taxes on $1,000 rather than the difference between the cost and the sale price.

Our accountant tried to get through to the young agent, but she simply could not understand. After she turned in her report, we got a bill for over $300,000 — for a small business not worth $300,000.

Ken Parma called us while we were still in Africa, and we could not believe what had happened. Ken said he had a friend in Waco who was an accountant experienced in dealing with the IRS, and his friend was willing to fight the I.R.S. over this issue. Ken felt we should turn it over to him, so we agreed. The Waco accountant was confident he could not only win the case but also get enough money back to pay his fee. He said he would take the case if we would pay him everything that he got back as his fee. Certainly, this sounded more than fair to us.

He took our books, and starting from the time the business began he redid the depreciation schedule and got everything into a clear, understandable, acceptable accounting. He then began sending in appeals and continued until he got the case to the top court of appeals so he could talk to someone with a solid understanding of accounting who was authorized to make a decision.

Nearly two years later, the accountant got us back more than $30,000 instead of our having to pay $300,000. We were delighted with this accountant's work, and we also gave God some of the glory, because we had prayed long and hard about this problem as it lingered on and on.

While this lawsuit with the I.R.S. was going on, we had an offer for the business, and as Ken was tired of dealing with The Copy Center, we agreed to sell it.

The Copy Center sold copy machines, supplies, and services in Temple, Belton, and Killeen. We had about eight or ten employees who had basically run the business with very little supervision. Jerry and I went to Temple with Ken, and we told the employees that we were going to sell the business.

I did some work on the inventory and negotiated with the prospective buyer regarding a cut-off period for maintenance agreements that had to be pro-rated. We went through the accounts payable, accounts receivable, and inventory together, along with doing all the necessary things to do when a business changes owners.

We agreed upon a price, and all the necessary legal documents were drawn up so we could sign the papers to complete the sale of The Copy Center. Because the tax problem was still pending, we set aside most of the money until that problem could be settled.

We were delighted to liquidate this business, even though we had done almost nothing in regard to running it. We were grateful to Ken Parma for assuming all the responsibility of the day-to-day operations. All things considered, this business had been a real blessing.

———◦•◦———

It was hard to believe that the year was gone, and it was time to go back to Africa.

As we were making our preparations to return to Malawi, I left the Copy and Litho depreciation schedule with Linda and told her that was the only copy I had. This document held all the information about the machines I had collected. Because we never did find some of the machines, I asked Jim Moore, one of our accountants, to drop them off the schedule.

I had asked Linda several months before to finish the audit of the depreciation schedule, and she assured me that in two months she would have it completed. When I asked about it, I learned that she had accidently (or possibly intentionally) "lost" the schedule that contained all the information about the missing machines I had spent so many hours compiling. I was extremely suspicious and upset, but there was nothing I could do.

We were saying our good-byes to the people at the office, and I walked downstairs to do something. When I came back upstairs, I found Linda and Jerry in the middle of a passionate embrace. Even when I walked across the room and stopped at the desk of Eleanor Jackson, the kiss continued.

"I am not sure what the wife is supposed to do in this situation," I said to Eleanor.

Eleanor looked up and made no comment.

I just stood at Eleanor's desk and watched as Jerry and Linda walked out of Linda's office.

After all that counseling and all Jerry's vehement denials, witnessing this moment with Linda told me everything I needed to know about the validity of my suspicions. Jerry may have been able to fool a counselor and a lie detector test, but it was oddly empowering to know that I was neither crazy nor hysterical.

And now, I felt a strange new sense of assurance and clarity. In the fabric my life, my relationship with Jerry was but a single thread — a golden thread that connected it all — home, family, work, and most importantly, serving the Lord in whatever capacities we were called.

While Jerry's infidelity was personally insulting, and his denial of it and lack of remorse possibly worse, I realized in a flash of understanding that I had the power to choose whether to allow the obvious tarnish on that thread to unravel our future or to continue on. In refusing to allow Jerry's infidelity to define my worth or affect my joy in this life well-lived, I was liberated from this decades-long shadow in a way I never before could have imagined.

Ironically, it took this humiliating, but defining moment — seeing that my suspicions were both well-founded and completely irrelevant — to set me free. God's timing is perfect.

We said our goodbyes to friends and family and headed back to Africa.

40 Chongoni Retreat

After spending a demanding and draining 1986 in the States, we hit the Malawi ground running. Jerry started building an urban church at Lumbadzi. Gerald and Barbara Workman had been interacting with this little congregation, and Pastor Rubin Nkhata had been asked to become the pastor of this congregation.

Pastor Nkhata was married and had several children. He had graduated from the Baptist seminary in Zambia, worked there for several years, and received some valuable experience. He was doing a good job witnessing and ministering to the people at Lumbadzi, where most of the people were educated people and worked at the Lilongwe International Airport.

The membership of the church grew dramatically, and they anxiously awaited their new church building. The money for the building was provided by the Foreign Mission Board of the Southern Baptist Convention and the Lottie Moon Christmas Offering.

This new church in Lumbadzi would become one of the larger, nicer Baptist Church buildings. It was brick, with a high roof that could be seen for a mile in all directions. It was strategically located in the middle of the residential area.

Jerry spent the better part of several months building the church as well as a house for the pastor. (The money for the house was provided by special gift offerings.) Since we had given up Publications, Jerry's office was moved to the Bible School before we left.

While we were on furlough in the States, The Bible School had a roof problem; part of the roof fell in over Jerry's desk and all of his paperwork was drenched. They had started repairing it and the missionaries had dried things as time permitted, but things were still in a mess when we got back.

——————•••——————

I got involved at Capital City Baptist Church, and Jerry became an elder at the church, but Van Thompson was the head elder. With people from so many different denominations and nationalities, it was always a struggle to keep the church united in Christ. (This church must have been a lot like the church at Corinth.)

Van was good to confide in Jerry, and Jerry tried hard not to undermine Van's work. Because Jerry was the first CCBC pastor, he still carried a lot of influence in that church. Van showed a lot of maturity by not being jealous or intimidated with Jerry serving in the church's leadership. Van was an excellent preacher and interesting speaker.

I began working with the women in the church. I had a good women's group going before I went on furlough, and I was disappointed when I got back to find that there were some problems and the women's work had deteriorated.

I began organizing the women and planning a Chongoni retreat for two or three days. There were about 25 women who signed up to go, and I asked different women in the group to give Bible studies and talks on different subjects.

It was amazing to me how much talent there was amongst these women. I asked my good friend Marlene Logan to do a talk on prayer. When I first met Marlene, she would not even pray in public. I watched her grow and mature as a Christian — from one who was afraid to pray out loud to a leader who took on major leadership roles in the church. She helped me with everything.

As I recall, everything went pretty smoothly for the retreat, except for one small incident. Mary Thompson said she would not be attending the women's retreat because she had two small boys, and then, at the last minute, just as the women were gathering to depart, Mary decided to go.

I had asked Marlene to assign rooms rather than to allow everyone to stay with whomever they wanted. (We had some women who would not be asked to stay with anybody, so I was trying to avoid anybody feeling left out.) I also told the women that if there was someone they *really* wanted to bunk with, to let Marlene know and she would make the arrangements.

Since Mary was not in on any of the planning, she was not aware of any of the advance preparations. When she found out we were assigning roommates, she assured me it would never work. It was working fine, but she made a real scene, and I got upset. I was under a lot of stress because I had assumed the responsibility for everything. (I could have gotten along just fine without Mary coming in at the last minute and trying to tell me how to run the show.)

As a result of all this angst, I asked Marlene to just let Mary take care of the room assignments, and to help Mary if she required help. Marlene knew I was upset, and she graciously agreed to let Mary take charge and try to help Mary as needed.

Once we got to Chongoni and everyone got their room assignment, everything else seemed to run smoothly. Mary entered into and was an added benefit to the group. Each of the women who was part of the program did a great job.

Betty Day, who was married to Dick Day, who worked for USAID, was in charge of the singing. Betty got everything started with some lively music to help set the pace. (I did have to push on Betty to start on time. She seemed to always want to talk when I thought she should be ready to lead the music.)

I gave a brief talk on God's faithfulness and anxiety. Here's part of what I shared:

"It was a beautiful fall morning. Sunlight streamed through the kitchen window. Admiringly, I looked around the kitchen at my clean floor and stove, which I had set up the night before.

I had finished dressing Ken for school and was preparing Peggy's cereal which I sat on the table near her highchair. I gave Ken a quick once over, kissed him on the forehead, shoved his lunch pail into his hand and gently pushed him out the door. Joyfully, I was thanking

God for two such beautiful children who were healthy, happy, and well adjusted.

I turned from the door just in time to see Peggy grab the cereal bowl and pour it all over the floor — and then throw the bowl.

As I yelled Peggy, the phone behind her highchair began to ring.

I dashed toward the phone, slipping on some milk and landed directly on the puddle of cereal.

Momentarily, I thought I had broken my hip, my head began to throb. Peggy was pounding on her highchair with her spoon.

As I pulled myself up, I began to hear something boiling over on the stove. I thought to myself, "Answer the phone or grab the pot first?"

I trudged across the kitchen floor with cereal and milk oozing from my robe and house shoes.

Removing the pot, I headed back to the phone to catch it on the seventh ring.

"I was afraid I missed you," said the voice on the other end of the line. After I heard what she had to say I wished she had.

"My car won't start. Could you drive the carpool today?" the voice continued.

I took a quick glance at myself and the kitchen. "Sure." I said.

Ken came back into the house saying his ride hadn't shown up and started his usual 10 questions per minute.

I grabbed Peggy from the highchair, threw a blanket around her (tempted to stuff the blanket in her mouth to stop her infernal yelling).

I fumbled through my purse, looking for my keys.

I dropped it.

With a huff I kicked my purse halfway across the room, wailing, "Why me, Lord?"

It wasn't even 8:00 o'clock yet, and I was in a full-blown anxiety attack. I thought if I can ever get these kids to where they can bath themselves, feed, and dress themselves, how wonderful that will be.

Just a few short years later, they could do all of those things with the greatest of ease. Peggy has her hair smartly pulled back and tied impeccably with a bow, a cute T-shirt, and too tight blue jeans. I tell her how cute she looks and to have fun. She heads out the door for a party.

I remember the article I just read in the paper that said 75% of all girls in Fort Worth Schools experience sex and marijuana at least once before they finish high school. Abortions are at an all-time high. The *girls can go into an abortion clinic one afternoon and to school the next day. I felt I was sending her off to a den of pot smoking octopus.*

I pray, Dear Lord take care of my baby.

Ken comes in long enough to grab a bite to eat, shower and change clothes.

He's heading to a junior high party at the lake. I know the kids order beer trucks. I pray, Dear Lord protect Ken. Don't let him get to drinking, start driving home and have a wreck.

As the night wears on, I lie awake in the darkness, praying quietly until both of them have returned home safely and I say, Thank you, Lord, while knowing that these anxieties will go on for years.

I think, what we need is a little weekend, family trip.

We leave and all goes well.

We are on the last stretch home.

The kids have stopped asking "How much farther?"

We round the bend and the neighbor's house is in view and then we gasp.

Our house is not visible.

It looks like there has been a huge snowstorm. Sixteen-foot billboards and posters adorn the front lawn.

The entire football team, cheer leaders, and friends had had a weekend party at our house.

After purchasing all the toilet paper on the South side of Fort Worth, they had spent the weekend decorating our house and trees.

They had done a remarkable job.

It was almost dusk, but the neighbor dropped over to tell us that there had been a parade by our house all weekend and they had difficulty getting out of their driveway. They assured us that all 4,000 of the high school student body had been by to view the handy work.

I thought, "Well this is not too bad; at least it is not destructive."

I pushed my way through the toilet paper and found the door.

I grabbed the doorknob and felt slick, slimly substance ooze through my fingers. Gasping, I looked down at my hand to find it covered in Vaseline.

We all pitched in to clean up the mess. As we worked together, I tried to think of some redeeming factor in all this.

For the next 10 years, the Lord and I got very well acquainted. I was in an attitude of prayer almost from the minute they walked out the door until they returned.

I prayed for the Holy Spirit to help, for guardian angels to help, for God to send them good friends who could help them out of their depths of despair.

I kept reminding God of His promise, "Raise up a child in the way he should go and when he is old, he will not depart from it."

From the time Ken hit 16, he became his own person, developing his own set of moral standards, tasting and testing whatever the world had to offer, before he made up his mind which way he would go. I feared he would be in the wrong place at the wrong time and land up in jail, or even worse, in a morgue. Parents sometimes think the worst because we know that sometimes the worst happens.

I told you these things to say that God hears and answers our prayers. Even when we are in the pits of despair, God hears our moans, our cries, and He knows the longings of our hearts. God is faithful and he is in control if we have been faithful to raise our children in the way they should go, then He will step in when parent's authority means very little. I praise the Lord for he has brought me through troubled waters many times."

The women with small children seemed to relate to my story. Some of the women shared some of their feelings of doubt and discouragement. Each woman seemed to get something from the retreat, and we all had a good time.

———•••———

At the same time Jerry was working on the Lumbadzi Church building, we started making preparations and plans for Richardson Heights Baptist Church to come to Malawi on a mission trip. This turned out to be the highlight of the year.

In August, 36 evangelists and builders arrived from RHBC. Jerry had spent a lot of time preparing six villages for new church buildings, securing both permits and building sites for six new churches. The people from each of these new churches had to start molding their own bricks, drying them, and burning them. This process required clay, water, straw, firewood, and people coming together in a large-scale project to glorify the Lord in a marvelous way throughout all of Malawi.

We divided our RHBC volunteers into 12 groups of three. Six groups would build churches and the other six groups would hold preaching services where the Name of Jesus would be exalted throughout the land in 26 three-day revivals.

Jerry worked furiously to get all the foundations poured before the volunteers arrived. I worked on coordinating food, lodging, transportation, and assignments — who was supposed to do what and when and with whom.

A missionary was assigned to each of the 12 groups, and this meant that these missionaries had to give up their own projects for two weeks in order to work with and assist the volunteers.

The missionaries all supported one another wonderfully. There was so much excitement as we anticipated the arrival of these volunteers.

At last, everything came together just in time for their arrival. Because some of the churches had difficulty with their bricks, Jerry worked night and day to see that everything was ready.

When the day came for the RHBC group's arrival, we were ready! First, we held an orientation at Capital City Baptist Church as soon as they arrived. We explained many important things carefully. They were to: change money at the bank or with the missionaries only; listen to the missionaries and follow their instructions, and be careful not to take photos of any government buildings — or anyone without permission.

Do this. Don't do that. We went through the motions, but these volunteers had been traveling for about 36 hours and seemed too tired to hear or care. Part of the group got on a bus and had to go to Blantyre. By the time they got there, they were exhausted. They got settled into their sleeping quarters and then transported to where they were to work. Some of the group had nice, comfortable places to stay, while the others had what could only be called "a hardship assignment."

Three of the men had to stay in a village a few miles out from Blantyre and build their church with little assistance from any missionary. All the other groups had a missionary who stayed with them most of the time.

The village people were to be commended for all their hard work prior to the actual builders' arrivals. Each village had made by hand the 17,000 bricks needed for each church, with water and sand carried on the heads of their women. Jerry was responsible for getting the building materials such as cement, nails, lumber, and roofing materials on the sites when needed.

By the end of this amazing two weeks, through the cooperative efforts of RHBC, the Nationals, and the missionaries, six churches were complete. We were so excited and overflowing with praise of the Lord for this experience shared.

The revival teams, who did personal evangelism during the day, also held services each night. Sometimes the people were so eager to get a tract that the RHBC evangelists felt mobbed. (When this happened to one volunteer who was giving out tracts in the market, she screamed, threw the tracts, and ran.) It was clear to all of us that God had been at work preparing the hearts of the people — and they were fully receptive.

The hearts and lives of many Malawians were changed because of the love of these visitors. In addition to the physical construction of six new churches, we celebrated more than 1600 new decisions to trust Jesus as Lord and Savior. With tired minds and weary bones, we all rejoiced and praised the Lord together.

Even the three men who drew the "hardship assignment" survived the two weeks. Despite often being hungry they somehow managed to live in a village and get a church built in two weeks.

We did have one minor difficulty, however. One young man decided to take a photo of a *Gule Wamkulu* dance without permission. This was a big No-No.

Dance is a way of life in Malawi. They have a dance for war, a dance for love or hate. Their dance may express religion, politics, and a vast range of emotions. They dance at church and weddings. Dance can also be loaded with other cultural significance, as this young man discovered. And not all dance is something to take lightly.

Gule Wamkulu is a secret society of initiated men, the Nyau brotherhood. Their "Great Dance" is the most ritually significant dance in Malawi, filled with spiritualism and religious significance in which the dancer's identity is kept secret. The dancers wear feathers, animal skins, masks, grass, seed pods, strips of cloth, and hair.

Usually, the Gule Wamkulu dance late at night in and around the cemeteries. Sometimes, the older Gule Wamkulu will dance around and hit the ground with sticks to keep the evil spirits from coming out of the ground. Someone usually dresses in skins to depict times gone by when the people were hunters. A young man might dance depicting his initiation into manhood and pretend that he is masturbating. These dances are usually very private, not performed for the public.

The Malawian people are afraid of these people and won't have anything to do with them when they are all dressed up. Once the USAID director's wife organized an expedition and many of the missionaries attended because we had only seen the Gule Wamkulu walking beside the road, dressed in their elaborate attire.

Anyway, one of the young RHBC men, carried away with the mysticism of the costumes, decided to take a photo of one of the Gule Wamkulu. The people became very angry, abducted the young man, and held him hostage for several hours before the missionary could persuade them to release him. (This gave the young man quite a scare, I'm sure.)

It is difficult to emphasize the importance of following cultural rules and regulations when in a foreign land. Americans are often amazed at the result of breaking just one little rule in a foreign land and culture. I think this young man probably got the point.

On the last weekend before all the RHBC people went back to Texas, we took everyone to Lilongwe to visit Kasungu Game Park. About seven or eight of the missionaries took the volunteers inside Kasungu.

Steve and Charla Baker were new missionaries, and we asked Steve to drive his vehicle. Steve was about as green as the volunteers, and he was given the responsibility of a group of people. He was more than a little bit nervous, but he did not want anybody to know.

We figured if he could make it through the volunteers' two weeks and the game park, he and Charla would be able to handle Malawi. Sure enough, they were able to handle anything that was thrown at them after that. Although Steve was unsure of himself in the game park, he was not going to allow his group to get hurt, whether they saw any animals or not. Fortunately, they all saw quite a few animals and had a really good time.

The next day we took them back to Lilongwe for their flight back to the States. It had been a fruitful two weeks, and we were *all* ready for a long nap. Jerry was worn out, and I had been unable to take my group out to a preaching point one day. Nothing was wrong with me but exhaustion. But it was all worth it.

Since we were the ones who had asked that RHBC be invited, Jerry and I felt personally responsible that the trip was a success — for RHBC as well as the missionaries and the Nationals. Then, the project was over, and we were extremely pleased with the wonderful cooperation between the missionaries and Nationals.

———◆◆◆———

From the 64 who accepted Jesus at Capital City Baptist Church, we started a Bible Study at the home of Arthur and Elizabeth Kambwiri. We also began discipleship classes as follow-up.

We planned our vacation Bible School at CCBC, and I was the director. Julie Temple and Jolie Seligson, both summer workers from the USA, came over and helped with the Bible School, which we called "Good News Activity Time," which was the name CCBC coined for its vacation Bible school for children. We had an average of 77 children per day, and while it was a fun time, I was always relieved when it was over. (The summer workers did a really good job!)

That same year, we worked some with the Malawi Crusaders (National laymen), supporting them with money and transportation. Jerry and others took 30 Crusaders out to Kasiya village, left them for three days, and when he picked them up three days later, more than 500 people had turned their lives over to Jesus.

The people of Malawi were so friendly and open to the Gospel of Jesus. Mozambique, our neighboring country to the east, was still plagued by war and strife, and its people were struggling for survival. An estimated 416,000 people displaced from Mozambique flooded into already crowded Malawi.

———◆◆◆———

Dr. John Bisagno came to Malawi and was the guest speaker for the Malawi Mission Meeting to be held in Lilongwe that year. We were so blessed to have him stay with us again. He spoke on "How to get the Job Done," and it included the following major points:

I. The church must be strongly, pastorally led.

II. The pastor must preach to the congregation in God's words, as well as do expository teaching (verse by verse). (People want to know what God's word says rather than what you think it means.)

III. The church must have a warm, friendly, exciting atmosphere. (Generate excitement by doing exciting things that challenge the people.)

IV. In everything you do, do it with a since of urgency. (More money, more people, more buildings.)

He advised us to accomplish the above by getting a vision — and then he shared with us how to motivate others to follow that vision together.

41 Trouble at Copy & Litho

The Mission seems to settle down after our meeting in 1987, and we settled into routine daily activity. Jerry had seemingly become the builder for the Mission, building three houses in "Area 9" in Lilongwe and another out towards the Zambia border. Dan Robinson, who had started the last house, fell from the roof trusses onto the concrete floor below, broke his foot and had to return to the States. Jerry also continued to build church buildings as well as two or three pastor houses. Even with his business and construction work and taking care of the automobiles, Jerry still also served as an elder at Capital City Baptist Church.

I continued to support Jerry with his work. Whenever he needed help, I was there, driving a vehicle, picking him up, or going for needed items. I also played bridge once a week with women and sometimes we would have people over for dinner and then play bridge in the evenings. I was constantly entertaining with dinner parties, and I enjoyed my flower garden and often worked with my gardener.

I also checked the financial statements from Copy & Litho on a regular basis. It was obvious to me we had some serious problems with the company and our employees. God was so good in taking care of all our needs — and watching over our children and our company in our absence. Now was time for us to take a close look and make some changes.

Then, for the first time since we started Copy & Litho it began to lose money — about $5,000.00 every month — and if machines were also disappearing, our losses could be much greater. In addition, I noticed that our payroll had jumped up considerably in the sales department. After I brought this to Jerry's attention, he called the manager, and he admitted to changing the salary schedule of the Sales Manager, raising his salary by about $5,000 per month. (This was at a time when the sales were way down.)

If that Sales Manager was doing a fantastic job and experiencing tremendous sales growth, we would have been happy to give him a large raise. But that was not the case. Sales were totally stagnant, and the repeat paper, supply sales, and service department were the only things keeping the company afloat.

Then I noticed that the parts being used in the service department had elevated several percentage points. The manager had no explanation for this increase in the use of parts. This triggered in my mind the possibility that when they pulled parts to refurbish old copy machines, they were selling the older machines personally, and not running these sales through Copy & Litho. I never found any hard evidence this was really happening, but I am sure in my own mind.

It was clear we had a problem, and we needed to go home and take care of it. We had a furlough scheduled for 1989 anyway, so we just waited until we went home for our regularly scheduled furlough. In the meantime, Jerry told the manager in no uncertain terms to change the pay schedule of the Sales Manager back to the way it was.

The manager was indignant. This was the first time Jerry interfered with any decision the manager made. He did not want to do as Jerry instructed, but for once, Jerry stood his ground and would not relinquish his position.

———•◦•———

Once again, we packed our bags and headed back to the States. Since this furlough was for just a few months, we did not have to move out of our house. We just left it with the Mission that they could use our house, furniture, and everything, as needed.

When we arrived, we hit the road running. The employees at Copy & Litho knew right away that something was wrong. We assured them that their jobs were not at risk. We tried to not make too many changes or frighten the employees, but we let them know there were some problems — and that we would be making some changes to get Copy & Litho back on track. We told them that Copy & Litho had been losing money — and it was not so serious we could not turn it around with just a few minor changes.

Eleanor Jackson turned in her resignation. The employees liked her, and this made them jumpy. We assured them we had not fired Eleanor, she quit of her own free will, and she had tried to turn her resignation in twice before we ever got home. Before Eleanor left, however, she did share with me some helpful information about people in her area. As I did not know most of the employees, it was difficult for me to accurately evaluate the changes needed.

Then Jerry and I went to talk to the manager. We asked him what changes he thought could be made to get the company back on track. He offered no suggestions, so we negotiated a release for him. (The details are confidential, so that's all I can share.) The manager's departure did not bother the employees at all, and since he never received a call at the office after his release, there were no adverse effect with our customers.

I took over Eleanor's office and began going through every bit of data I could put my hands on. Linda was openly hostile toward me, and it was obvious she resented me being at the office after so many years of being away. She was of absolutely no help; in fact, she was a hindrance. When I asked her for information, she was reluctant to share anything with me, as if I was invading her private little world — and I had no right to information about our own company.

Then I called in the sales manager and asked him what he thought we could do to improve sales. I asked him to write down how he had been spending his time. He returned the information to me promptly and we evaluated what he was doing — and there was not one thing on the sheet that related to selling machines. Everything he listed was what the general manager should have been doing.

When I pointed this out to the sales manager, he said that someone had to do the things he had been doing. I told him he no longer needed to assume those responsibilities; he was to concentrate on selling machines, because that was his job. He was not to worry about the rest; we would take care of that.

The sales manager was not particularly happy after we talked. If he took control of the sales and start getting machines sold, his job would be saved; if he didn't do his job, I would be delighted for him to quit. (I did not tell him that specifically, but I am sure he got the message.) And, because the sales manager and general manager had been as thick as bees on honey, he was not happy about the manager's release. I learned that they were still seeing each other on a regular basis, so when the sales manager decided to quit, I counted it as a blessing.

After the sales manager left without any notice, he called Jerry and tried to sell him the information he had about our customers, such as where machines were on demo, and to whom they were trying to sell machines.

This really made Jerry angry. Jerry told the Sales Manager he had already paid him for that information once and he had no intention of paying him again. (This was downright blackmail.) I am sure he was angry; he never returned to the office.

Next, I shook things up in the paper-contract sales department, which was costing more than it was worth. We dismissed one of the girls, and then it got messy as we realized that the woman we planned to move into another position had gone to Las Vegas with the manager.

Then the Sales Secretary quit. Fortunately, I had already gone through some of the contracts and the residuals we received from our machine suppliers.

I learned that one of the salesmen was using only part of his time working on machine sales; most of his time was spent helping his wife with her flower business. This also turned out to be fortunate because he was being paid on a special commission plan that rewarded him more than the regular salespeople.

By the end of two months, everyone who was a drain on the company was gone. The next month our profits jumped back up where they were reasonable. The salespeople who remained seemed to do better on their own than with their previous "managers" around.

———•••———

One day before the manager left, I drove into the parking lot and four men were loading a refurbished copy machine onto our delivery truck. I would not have thought anything about that, except they all ran, except the young warehouse man. I did not recognize the other men. The warehouse man went back into the warehouse and left. (He never came back to the office, even to pick up his paycheck.)

I just let the machine sit there for several hours. When it began to look like rain, I went into the manager's office and told him about the situation — and he just laughed. I never accused anybody of stealing the machine, and he made no effort to investigate the situation.

While I was in the manager's office his phone rang and Linda's voice came over the intercom, "Hey. Pick up your phone."

He complied, and I felt certain she was talking to him about the machine sitting in the parking lot. (It was a weird situation.) After the manager got off the phone, I told him to have the machine moved back into the warehouse.

Jerry and Linda had been gone while the machine was being stolen. Jerry did not come into the office. He did not know what information I had — and he did not know what I was doing — but it was obvious the machine was being stolen and somebody in the service department had refurbished the machine, and I knew who it was.

———◆◆———

The days were long and stressful. Jerry and I were living in a house that belonged to Richardson Heights Baptist Church. So, every morning about 6:00 a.m. Jerry and I would drive from Richardson to Fort Worth, and we rarely got home before 7:00 p.m.

As soon as the dust settled around the Copy & Litho office, we began to gather the information we needed to sell the business. Jerry spent most of his time contacting and setting up appointments with people who were actively purchasing copy machine companies.

After learning the kind of information prospective buyers wanted to analyze, Jerry assumed responsibility for assimilating this data. We knew we had to make changes in using our accounting firm, so Jerry and Linda started talking about computers and which computer we should purchase. (Jerry got along very well with Linda.)

We had so many things going on and were making so many changes my head was swimming. I felt the stress of our situation acutely, and I think Jerry did also. We wanted to go back to Africa, but we could not leave until we got the business sold. We knew we could not turn the business over to an unknown.

344

We hired our son, Ken, to take the manager's place. He had been a salesman in the organization, so he was able to quickly assume some of the responsibility for day-to day-operations. He had a hard time with Linda — whenever he would ask her to do something or for information, she treated him much the same as she treated me. This did not make his job any easier. Ken looked for ways to cut expenses, and he began to make some changes, but we were concerned that this troubled business would be a lot to leave with Ken.

Also during our 1989 furlough, Pauline, Jerry's mom, got stomach cancer and within a matter of months she passed away. Jerry was really good about staying with his mother and helping her. When she got so weak she could not walk to the bathroom, Jerry took her in his arms and carried her to the bathroom. About a week after that, the hospice people ordered a bedside potty chair. Jerry resisted my many offers to help with Pauline's care, so I just took hands-off approach. After Pauline passed away and was buried at Restland Memorial Cemetery on Greenville Avenue in Dallas in one of the two cemetery plots Jerry and I had purchased.

With Pauline's illness, we had extended our furlough. We were supposed to go back to Africa in October. Ken seemed to be doing pretty well at Copy & Litho and we had not found a buyer for the business. We considered whether to leave the business in Ken's hands. (When people looked at the last year's profit graph from big losses to big profits, this looked suspicious to people who did not know us.)

Jerry contacted Danka Systems in Florida. Dan Doyle had started Danka after he left Royal Business Systems. (We had been on a lot of trips with Royal and Dan Doyle had planned the trips.) Dan had since sold Danka to a British-owned organization, and they were fast and furiously pursuing the purchase of other copy machine companies throughout the Southwest.

Dan showed some interest in Copy & Litho, and he was somewhat familiar with our organization. Jerry hopped a plane for Florida to meet with Dan, and Dan told Jerry he would buy Copy & Litho if we could come to a favorable agreement.

Then Dan sent a young man to Fort Worth to go over the financial statement and to question us on our accounting system and practices. We met him at Dallas/Fort Worth International Airport. (We really did not want the employees to know that we had the company up for sale, so it was difficult for us to get all the information without arousing suspicions.)

After Danka's people analyzed the information, they made an offer which was exactly what I told Jerry the company was worth. (Jerry and Ken both thought that the company was worth more) Jerry reluctantly agreed to accept their offer for the sale of Copy & Litho. We made no counteroffer, and I felt it was a fair deal.

This sale would give us a good retirement. We could go back to Africa and continue our missionary career as we wanted to do. It seemed like a perfect solution to me, and Ken was supportive of whatever decision we made.

Once we struck the deal, we took the information to Charlie Webb, our lawyer in Fort Worth, and he drew up the necessary legal documents. Dan Doyle and a couple of his employees came to Fort Worth to sign the sales agreement. Dan arranged for a wire transfer of the funds to Nations Bank in Fort Worth, and Jerry signed the stock over to Danka.

I arranged a little get together at Copy & Litho in Fort Worth and requested that all the employees meet at the office that afternoon. There were about 100 employees; we had called in our employees from the Dallas office and the Wichita Falls office, and the 60 or 70 Copy & Litho cars.

The parking lot was full, the streets were full of our cars, and the office was packed with people. (We did not have a meeting area this crowd could fit into at one time.) Some of the service men who were the last to arrive had to stand in the hallway. I tried to pack people into the lobby and demo area so everybody could get in and see Dan Doyle and Jerry.

First, Jerry announced that he had sold Copy & Litho to Danka. He said nobody would be dismissed; Danka had agreed to keep all the employees. This was a verbal contract, but we felt Dan would keep his word and only let someone go if they would not cooperate with the new management. Danka wanted the employees to stay even more than some of them wanted to stay. They were the company; they gave the company value.

Then Dan spoke to the employees and shared his plans with them. He said he would not demand that they make changes, but that he would expect results. If they could turn the numbers he wanted, they could do it their way. Then he showed them how his bigger corporation could offer greater advantages in buying power.

346

They could buy machines much cheaper than Copy & Litho. They could buy parts much, much cheaper than Copy & Litho. It was obvious to the employees that Danka had much to offer to help Copy & Litho remain competitive in a fast-changing industry. Then they were all invited to a steak house for dinner.

By that time, it was past their regular time to go home, so most of the employees went on home (Except the few we had advised they would be invited to dinner, and we suggested they accept.) Before everybody went their way, I cornered a few people and took them over to Dan and introduced them. I told Dan who they were and what part they played in the overall operation.

Two or three of the younger, newer employees came over and kissed and thanked me. I was moved almost to tears. (I was so surprised I had made a favorable impression with anybody.) Many of the long-time service technicians came by and shook hands with me.

Jim Moore knew I had put in a good word for him, and I told him he needed to go to dinner. He seemed a little shy about meeting Dan Doyle. (Linda never spoke to me, and I did not make any effort to introduce her to Dan, nor did I put in a good word for her.)

I felt I had worked with the employees and won all of them over but two. There were two employees that, when I asked them to do things, openly rebelled and would not comply with my requests. (Had I remained working at the office, those two people would have been dismissed.)

Ken negotiated an agreement to continue working for Copy & Litho/ Danka for two years, and they agreed to pay him a good salary. So, Ken stayed at the office and worked with the Danka people during the changes. Ken also became good friends with Danka's head man who had been sent in from Florida.

———◆◆◆———

The months in the States had been fast and furious. We only stayed a few blocks down the street from Peggy, Bruce, and Zac but we had spent precious little time with them. Peggy had gone on a mission trip with Richardson Heights Baptist Church to Montana, and I had kept Zac for the week she was gone. He was almost three and so precious.

While I was keeping Zac one morning, Jerry gave him a little coin purse with a few coins in it. He walked into the bathroom with me as I tended to my business there, and out of the clear blue sky, he said, "Nanna, do you have a penis?"

"No Zac," I said, "I do not have a penis."

He fumbled with his coin purse for a moment and then said, "I could buy you one."

"No, thank you, Zac," I said, "I really don't need one."

He calmly turned and walked out of the bathroom, still playing with his coin purse.

I couldn't keep from smiling to myself.

That same year Zac was playing with the phone at their house and accidently dialed 911. The police showed up and wanted to look through the house to make sure Zac was safe. It was that same winter when Peggy went out on the back porch to sweep. She had put a video tape into the player before she went outside, and Zac was sitting in his chair all relaxed.

While Peggy was sweeping, Zac got out of his chair, locked the sliding glass door, and then lay down in his chair and went sound asleep.

When Peggy got ready to come back into the house, she could not get in. All the doors and windows were locked. She banged on the door, no more than three feet from Zac, and yelled — all to no avail. Zac was sound asleep.

So, Peggy called Bruce to come home and open the door, but he was tied up in a meeting and could not get away. Peggy sat huddled on the back porch and watched Zac sleep until he woke up from his nap, about two hours later.

It was nice to be close enough to know all the cute things that he was getting into.

———•••———

It was almost October and time for us to go back to Africa. A lot had happened during this 1989 trip. We sold our business, Jerry's mom passed away, Bruce was selling valves for a company and doing well. Peggy was staying home, caring for Zac, and involved in church work. Suzanne was teaching school, and Ken was working for Danka.

We felt comfortable going back to Africa, and once again we climbed aboard a plane to travel halfway around the world from friends and family.

42 Kilimanjaro

Sometime after we moved into our Lilongwe, Malawi house, I decided to get out and walk around our block. (It was probably at least a half-mile.) I started walking and got a little more than halfway but was so tired I rested for a few minutes. That is when I realized my physical condition. If I had to run for my life, I might as well hold out my hands and say, "Here I am, come and get me." So, I began walking some at least three times a week. I walked a little farther each day until I could walk up and down the hills for a couple miles.

Jim Parrish was an avid walker. He had climbed Mt. Kilimanjaro several times, and several years later asked us to climb it with him. The thought intrigued us, but I was not sure I would be able to make it. Jim said if we could walk ten miles in two hours, we could climb the mountain.

So, Jerry and I started walking more seriously. At first, I could not keep up with Jerry. He would grab my hand as we started up a steep hill, and he pulled me along with him. As time went by, I grew stronger and faster.

Jerry measured five miles in the car, and we would walk as hard as we could. Jerry started walking ahead of me, and about every half-mile I would jog to catch up with him. I never could walk as fast as Jerry, who could walk a mile in 11.5 minutes. To finish the five miles with him, I had to jog.

Then I would be completely worn out and just want to fall over, but I knew I had to keep walking slowly until I cooled down. (Sometimes Jerry would drag me along until I got my pulse rate back down to normal.)

At last, we were ready. We told Jim we would like to climb Kilimanjaro with him, so he made the reservations for the month he thought would be best for climbing. His son and some of his English friends decided they would like to make the climb, too. In all, there would be about nine people climbing.

Then Jerry and I began to *really* train with diligence. We walked from our Area 43 home to old downtown Lilongwe (That was five miles), and then we would walk five miles back home. This was not easy for us because we were in our 50s at that time. Lilongwe was about 3000 feet altitude, but Kilimanjaro was about 19,000 feet.

The day came for us to depart. Jim and Liz were living in Tanzania at that time, and they asked us to bring them the little organ we had used when we started CCBC. Jerry said he would be glad to bring it on the plane from Lilongwe to Dar es Salaam, Tanzania.

We went to the church to pick up the organ. Jerry reached down to pick it up and grunted.

"My goodness that little thing is heavy!" he exclaimed. He had made a promise, though, and Jerry would take that organ to Jim, no matter what.

He got some rope and tied the organ up and made a good loop at the top so he could fit his hand into the loop. With a heave-ho he lifted the organ into the car. We packed our bags, and at the appointed time we were ready for our trip.

Just before we left, Jim called and said that Liz was sick, and he would be unable to climb with us. He said that one of the British Commonwealth drivers would meet us in the lobby of the Dar es Salaam Airport to get the organ from us. He also said that his son, David, would assist us with our climb and assume responsibility for the group.

When we got to the Kamuzu, Malawi airport, we boarded the plane without difficulty. Jerry kept insisting that one arm was longer than the other. When he was not carrying the organ, his body leaned the other direction, and he walked around with one arm "longer than the other," making monkey sounds. He was kidding around, but he really did think his arm had been stretched.

It was late afternoon when we got to Dar es Salaam Airport. We were the first to jump off the plane and head into the airport. In order to enter Tanzania, we had to get $25.00 U.S. converted to Tanzanian money. We were first in line to get our money exchanged.

We waited and waited. Finally, a man came out with a cigar box full of Tanzanian money. There were a lot of people in the line, but they only had enough money to let us in. I don't know what happened to the people behind us.

Unbeknownst to us, a pilot from the departure plane came around behind us and told all the people from our plane who were going to Moshi to follow him, and they could go through customs there.

We had to catch that plane, because we had arranged for a car to meet us at the Moshi Airport and take us to the Kilimanjaro Hotel, where we would spend the night. We would meet the others from England the next day, and then the day after that we would climb the mountain.

We were stuck trying to get through customs with our little organ, but the Tanzanian driver managed to expedite our entry. It still took quite a while to get through, and we were afraid we would miss our connection.

Gladly and gratefully, Jerry handed the organ over to the driver. By this time, he was hot and perspiring through his shirt, and you could wring water from his shorts. Once that organ was delivered, we breathed a huge sigh of relief.

We ran over to a ticket counter and asked where we needed to go to catch our plane. About that time, we looked out to the runway and there was a plane taxiing.

"Oh my gosh," I said, "I bet that is our plane!"

The ticket agent looked at us and confirmed that we had indeed missed our plane.

If we had not had that organ, we would have made it like everybody else. We felt a little irritated, but remembered the saying, "AWA" — "Africa Wins Again."

We asked the ticket agent if they had a place to put us up for the night. She assured us they did.

We had not had anything to eat, so we asked about food vouchers.

She told us that she would give us vouchers for dinner and breakfast. She told us to put our bags on the edge of the sidewalk and a pickup would come by to take us to the sleeping facility. The dining room was closed for the night, but she said we could get something to eat where we would be staying.

We stood on the sidewalk, in the dark, waiting for the pickup. Soon an OLD rickety pickup stopped, and the driver jumped out and started throwing our bags into the back end. (We did not know if he was stealing our bags or giving us a ride.) We could not speak whatever language he spoke (Swahili?), and he did not speak any English.

"Do we go with you?" we motioned to him,

In answer, he opened the truck door.

With great reluctance, we climbed into the front and only seat.

He drove to the end of the Airport and started down the fencerow. The farther we drove, the darker it got. We tried to find out some particulars about where we were going, and the man just seemed to confirm that everything was okay by nodding his head.

When we got to the end of the runway, the driver turned right and started down another side of the runways. By this time we were in total darkness. The pickup lights shined dimly. The road was dirt with numerous bumps. (I almost ended up on the lap of the driver, and Jerry's head almost hit the top of the cab.)

We were getting scared. We were in a foreign country with a driver going, we did not know where. How would we get back to the airport? All kinds of thoughts ran through my mind.

After we had been driving for what seemed to be an eternity, the pickup veered to the left, went a short distance, and stopped. There was a barbed wire gate with two military-looking men with machine guns standing guard. They came over to the pickup, peered in, and motioned us through. We bumped along for a while and then came to another gate and two more armed guards. They looked into the pickup and motioned us through.

We entered some kind of compound that was very dark, and we could make out two or three more armed, military-looking men. We strained our eyes, trying to see what lay ahead.

There were three small buildings, and the driver pulled up to the first one and motioned for us to get out.

We disembarked slowly. This did not look right — or like any hotel I had ever seen.

The driver motioned for us to follow him into the building as he carried our bags inside. We motioned that we were hungry and showed him our vouchers for dinner.

A man who spoke English came over and said there was no food. There was a drink machine, but the drinks were not cold.

I looked across the road, and beside another building was a bus.

I asked if that bus was going back to the airport.

He said it would leave about four in the morning and that he would take us back later. We go an orange Fanta and started to drink it. It was not only "not cold" — it was hot.

We walked to the room where he had set down our bags. It looked like there were four rooms connected to a small room. We looked at each other and at the room. There was no door to our bedroom. The floor was nasty. We placed our hands on the bed to find that there was no mattress. Old-fashioned metal springs lay on the bed covered with a sheet.

I needed to go to the bathroom, and with trepidation, I tip-toed into the bathroom area. It was just what I expected—intolerable. (But if you gotta go you gotta go.) It was either in the bathroom or out behind the building, so I carefully pulled up my skirt and squatted over the filthy commode to relieve myself.

"Don't take your shoes or clothes off," Jerry said.

As if I would!

We were so tired we laid down on the sheet-covered springs. There was no pillow, either, so we rolled up our jackets up and used them as pillows. We were hungry, tired, scared — and wondering if we would ever get back to civilization safely.

We set the alarm to make sure we wouldn't miss the bus. I am not sure either of us ever went to sleep; when we would try to turn over, a wire spring would jab us. We did not complain (much), because it would not do any good. Jerry had more of a phobia of lice, bedbugs, and filth than me. He was always sure he was going to catch the "mokus."

The next morning, I heard the bus start up.

"The bus has started." I said, and we bounded out of bed. We did not potty or wash our hands. We just grabbed our bags and hurried out to the bus. We asked the driver if he was going to the airport, and he nodded. We sat there a short while, and then we started off down the bumpy road past all the guards and gates.

We were relieved to see the airport lights. Our next hurdle was catching the plane to Moshi. We went into the airport and up to the dining room.

They brought us a menu.

"I will take some of that," I said, pointing.

Our waitress told us that our first choice was unavailable — they were out of that food.

After a few more tries, we said, "Just bring us whatever you have."

She brought us a scrambled egg, one slice of bread, a little jelly, and some good coffee.

We knew they were having a lot of shortages, so we were grateful to get anything. We sat there for a while, drinking coffee, then decided it was time to go down to the waiting room to catch the plane.

The room was full of people. People were everywhere, but we had not seen anybody out in the main terminal. Two seats were empty near the door where we would exit to get on the plane.

Jerry quickly walked to the departure door. "If all these people are supposed to get on that plane, not everybody will get on," he whispered, "So when that door opens, you run out the door and get on the plane."

Missionaries or not, we were *not* going to let anybody get in front of us. We knew that the plane was coming in from somewhere else, and it would probably already be full.

Sure enough, the plane landed and taxied up near the door near where we sat. When a stewardess came in and opened the door, Jerry shoved me out the door. We could hear her behind us on her loudspeaker, announcing for the people to board the plane. As the ladder was pushed up to the plane, Jerry and I were headed up the steps. As it turned out, there were only four seats available on that plane.

Did we feel guilty? NO!

Soon the plane took off and we flew a short distance to land at our destination. We departed the plane into a very small terminal. As we walked through the gate, we could see several old cars used as taxicabs.

One driver walked over to us and asked where we wanted to go.

We told him.

He said he would take us, and we agreed on a charge.

The driver had been rubbing the dust off the outside of his car, and you could tell he was very proud of his car. I don't know what it was, but it was far from new. It was clean, however.

We started driving. I think the trip was supposed to be about 45 minutes, and naturally, the road was bumpy.

All of a sudden, we heard a "Pow! Bump, Bump, Bump."

The driver stopped to see what had happened.

I felt so sorry for him.

One of the shock absorbers had broken. He got back in and started driving again. One side of the car went up while the other side was going down. Up, Down, Up, Down the car rumbled down the road. The shock was still attached, and it made a loud banging noise intermittent with the up-down rumble.

We could not keep from laughing at our situation. What else could go wrong? From here on it should be smooth sailing, right?

NO! NO! That was just wishful thinking.

43 Unexpected Adventures

Finally, we arrived at the hotel. It looked quite nice, freshly painted and all the windows looked pretty good. There were even flowers in the ground.

We checked in and they showed us to our room. We went to the bathroom and there was no water. There was also no light, but we knew there was a light bulb shortage.

"Do you have a room that has running water in the bath?" we asked.

They showed us to another room. It looked nice enough. There seemed to be a lot of people there.

This room had some light bulbs and water in the bath — but the commode would not flush. There was a bucket beside the commode. You filled the bucket with water and poured it into the commode, and it would automatically flush. That wasn't too bad. We had experience with this in Malawi.

We met our group in the dining room that evening and had our first good meal in 24 hours. David Parrish, a nice-looking man in his early 20s, acted very responsible. Most of the group was in their 20's. One girl was from Germany, and she was 16. She was the goddaughter of the Parishes, and her mother was a doctor in Germany.

We were told that past president Jimmy Carter had climbed Kilimanjaro the week before. He had his entourage of guards with him, and we were told that 13 people went up with him and nobody else could go up the mountain while he was up there.

As a result, people from all over the world who had been scheduled to climb the mountain that week, some using their life savings to climb that mountain, were stuck in the hotel — as well as all the people who planned to climb the same as us.

At first, they said that our group and all those who planned to climb with us that week would not be allowed to climb. We went to bed not knowing what was going to happen. We tried to look at it as a great adventure. Certainly, we had never experienced anything like it before.

The next morning, we got up, ate a good breakfast, and walked out to try to find out what was going to happen. David was our spokesman, and he had lived in Tanzania and knew the ropes.

A bus came and picked up the people who had been waiting a week. Then, a little later, they told us that we could go also, and we boarded the bus to the starting path. David decided to walk as fast as he could to the first base camp to try and get us a reservation for a bed.

The first day's walk was easy. We each picked up a stick and used it like a walking cane. This became my third leg. There were a couple of places where we had to climb a little, but it was just like walking up a hill. I had to urinate along the way, so I took my toilet paper out of my bag and stepped off the trail a few feet as instructed to take care of my business.

We got to the first cabin and David had booked us into a little A-frame house with three bunk beds. The building was just big enough to put one bunk bed down each sidewall and one across the end. There was about three feet between the beds. We were the last ones to go to bed.

Jerry and I had the end bunk bed, and the four other people were young men. The next morning, they bounded out of bed without any modesty. A Frenchman was on one of the upper bunks, and he jumped down in some little stretch bikini shorts. (I closed my eyes and turned over.) After they all left, and Jerry and I got up.

Each climber had a guide who carried the patron's clothes and food. We carried some snacks, raincoats, and water. We were rationed out our allotment for breakfast, but Jerry did not want to eat breakfast because he was afraid it would make him sick.

David and our group headed out together, but we soon scattered. Saying there would not be enough room for everybody, David walked ahead and to get us a place to sleep. The walk was a little harder the second day, but I seemed to be doing fine. I did not have any altitude sickness. I used my stick to keep my balance. (Because of my vertigo and motion sickness, it was harder for me to tell up from down than most people.)

While we were walking, two runners came down the mountain with a sled-like contraption. On it was a Japanese man who had wandered off the main trail and had been climbing when another climber above him kicked a rock loose and it hit him on the head. We were not sure if the man was alive or not, and Jerry and I stopped to pray for him.

When we reached the second night's cabin, there were a lot of people there — and we were told that we would have to sleep upstairs above the dining room. With my trusty stick I headed down the mountainside to the toilet. The mountain was fairly steep, and I had to be careful because my perception and balance was not very good.

I went into the toilet and looked down into the hole. I realized the toilet was built over the edge of the mountain, and when I looked down the hole there was a great distance between where I was and the ground, straight down below. Reluctantly, I sat down and took care of my business, trying not to think too much about it.

When I started back up to the cabin, my footing slipped, and I slid down. I felt a little uneasy when I arose. The cabin was a short distance away, and as I looked at it, I saw that sitting beside the cabin was one of those sleighs, with a body wrapped up in it. The head was covered, so I knew the person was dead. I later learned that he had gotten to the top of the mountain, got tired, and would not come down; he developed hypothermia and died.

We ate supper and went upstairs to bed. Wall to wall, there were people lying side by side, just as close as they could be. We walked to almost the end of the line and laid down between people. By the time everybody got up there, we were packed like sardines. If one person turned over, everybody had to turn over.

All through the night, people kept getting sick — altitude sickness, diarrhea, or something, and they would have to walk out, stepping between people's legs because there was no room for them to walk at the end of our feet.

I kept remembering the man who was lying outside dead.

There had been no difficulty with my breathing or getting tired. I was doing just fine. By the next morning, I told Jerry I was going to turn around and go back down.

During the night I had asked myself, "What on earth am I doing up here on this mountain? Two men were dead!" So, I turned around and walked back down with my guide.

Jerry walked on up to the next cabin, spent the night, and got up the next morning. This was to be the final day —they would reach the summit of Kilimanjaro and then walk all the way back down to the bottom the next day.

Jerry got up the final day and left with his guide before breakfast. He got up part of the way and wanted to stop to get something to eat out of his backpack, but his guide would not let him stop. They were near a cave, and the guide wanted Jerry to climb up to the cave. For some reason, Jerry could not climb any farther without something to eat, so he and his guide turned around and walked back down to the bottom of the mountain. All the rest of our group made it to the top. (I feel sure that if Jerry had eaten breakfast, he would have made it to the top, too.)

I had walked back down the mountain with a woman who, with her husband, owned a Mt. McKinley Climbing Guide Service. She had a cold and was afraid to go up any higher. While we were down that evening, we walked to the market together, and I spoke to some of the people in Chichewa. The people seemed very friendly towards me. The lady I was with thought the people treated me like a celebrity.

Much of our Kilimanjaro climbing difficulties related to too many people trying to climb the mountain at the same time because President Jimmy Carter climbed the mountain the week before. (We were told he made it to the top with some assistance from his guide.) Still, we experienced a wonderful and interesting adventure!

44 **Feet First**

As I look back on 1989, I can clearly see how God was in control of our lives and how he made our rough paths smooth.

This is the speech and announcement Jerry made to the Copy & Litho employees when we sold the business:

"On September 21, 1989, at 2:00 today, I sold my stock to Danka Industries of Tampa, Florida. Many of you are long time employees; others are so new I haven't even met you. To each of you, a very humble thanks for your faithful service to Copy & Litho and to Barbara and me.

This has been a difficult year with many changes. Those changes, with your dedication, work, and help has reversed a year which had reached a loss in February of nearly $150,000, to a profit during the month of September.

In all of the changes only one employee has been dismissed. I made every effort to assure you that I had no intention of disrupting our organization with personnel changes. I can assure you that the new owner of Copy & Litho has made the same commitment.

Meet Mr. Daniel Doyle, President of Danka."

This seemed like a very simple speech considering all the time, sweat, pain, and joy owning this business had brought. It had been a difficult year.

When we had started home March 21, 1989, we placed our hope and dependence on God, and He gave us the wisdom and strength that delivered us.

Before we went home, I prayed for God's wisdom, and I received a picture, an image of a man overseeing the office and Linda no longer there.

I prayed regarding Copy & Litho's accountant. The office they occupied was vacant — and then a dark black door closed my vision from the right. Then I could see the vacant office again — and a dark black door closed my vision of the office from the left.

I did not see who was to take care of our accounting. Then a bad thought came to my mind regarding our accountant.

The book of Isaiah says,*"And I will bring the blind by a way that they knew not; I will lead them in paths that they have not known: I will make darkness light before them, and crooked things straight. These things will I do unto them, and not forsake them."* (Isaiah 42:16, KJV) And then, a little later in Isaiah:*"Fear not: for I have redeemed thee, I have called thee by thy name; thou art mine. ²When thou passest through the waters, I will be with thee; and through the rivers, they shall not overflow thee: when thou walkest through the fire, thou shalt not be burned; neither shall the flame kindle upon thee. ³For I am the Lord thy God, the Holy One of Israel, thy Saviour . . . ."* (Isaiah 43:1-3, KJV)

Then on March 7, 1989, I taught a Ladies Bible study from Joshua, Chapter 3, in which. God told Joshua to tell the Levite priest to take the Ark of the Covenant and stand in the Jordan River. The waters were rushing because it was the rainy season. God worked a miracle holding back the rushing waters and allowed the people to go across on dry land.

But first the priest had to GO and put their feet in the water before God could work the miracle for the people of Israel. He brought the people across the river on dry land because they trusted and obeyed.

I felt this directly applied to us as we went home and put our feet in the troubled and rushing waters at Copy & Litho, but I knew if we trusted and obeyed, God would bring us through on dry land; but first we had to "GO" and get started working and rebuilding.

362

Our desire was that our lives might be single-mindedly committed to God and not have our minds and direction split between the things of this world and the things God wanted us to do as His ambassadors, His royal priests, and His servants.

Now as I ponder all that has happened, I can clearly see how God was at work in everything I did. God had given me a vision, a hope, and a dream. All I had to do was take the first step and trust in Him, and He would guide my path. It was amazing to see God at work in that time and also now as I reflect on God's bountiful grace and mercy. God has been so good to me that I feel like saying "Why me, God? Why have you been so good to me?"

I am truly thankful to God for the miracles He has worked in my life.

———————◆◆◆———————

Headed back to Lilongwe, Malawi, after eight months in the States, we flew by way of Amsterdam. With a 16-hour layover there we took the opportunity to go through the home of Anne Frank.

We left on Tuesday, November 16, and did not get home until Thursday afternoon about 2:00 p.m. It was nice to get home again. My dear friend Marlene Logan had been over with her Bambo for two days cleaning the house, and it really looked nice with a large arrangement of roses on the table. We had a burglary just before we left, and a window was broken out. The Mission had not repaired it until two days before our return, and an inch of dust must have accumulated.

The rains had already started, and our yard was green with flowers in bloom. Helen Friend had brought cookies over, Glenda Weston brought a cake, Rebecca Phifer gave us a jar of jam, and Mary Thompson had put bread, butter, and eggs in our refrigerator.

The next day after we got home, we had to go to Chongoni to a Mission prayer retreat that lasted until Sunday afternoon. We were tired from the year and the trip, but it was nice to see all the missionaries again.

As soon as we got back from the prayer retreat, I delved into the boxes and began to unpack and get the house back in shape once again. Packing and unpacking are all part of the missionary life.

The Mission had a welcome-home party for us, and that same night several missionaries drove in with four new cars from South Africa. So,

Jerry spent the next few days clearing the cars and all the goods they brought back with them. It did not take long for us to be back in the swing of things.

Now I had a new grandson's picture to put on the bookshelves in the living room, so everybody could ooh and ahh appropriately. Once again, it was difficult to leave the family, but there was no doubt that Malawi was where God wanted us to be serving Him.

We had a Thanksgiving pie supper at the Ambassador's residence, and we were reacquainted with our American friends. We enjoyed Thanksgiving dinner with the Lilongwe missionaries.

After a couple of weeks, our social and work life were back intact. We began to have people over. Capital City Baptist Church had completed their educational building and a house for the pastor. Jerry and I got back into our church life and began to look for a new pastor. Recently we had lost several of our finest Malawian families because they had moved to Blantyre and there was nobody to pick up the slack.

Jerry started working on purchasing land in Mchinji so a new missionary house could be built there. Then, since there were four new vehicles, he had four old cars to sell.

I started working with the health department regarding building some needed water wells near Lilongwe. I worked with Millie Munkondia from the church since she worked for the health department and the Ministry of Health.

The health problem was even worse than when we left, with an outbreak of cholera and meningitis. Several people died from these diseases, and we also still had the AIDS problem which is hard to measure. People got their immune system destroyed and then they died of malaria or something else before the AIDS got them. The government was trying to educate the people to change their lifestyles, but that is not an easy thing to get across.

Jerry was planning to fly to South Africa the first week of December to drive a truck back, but he did not go until January because the truck was not ready. Gerald and Barbara Workman also went to South Africa to drive an ambulance back for the Senga Bay Medical Clinic.

Jerry and I took the Jesus film out to Kiama Village. This is the village from which we heard drums beating late at night during the weekend. There are few Christians who live in that village, and my heart went out to these people.

We had a great time showing the film, and the people were very responsive. Over the weekend we walked to the river twice for baptism services, blessed the new babies, and had the Lord's Supper and preaching services.

Our family went to Albuquerque to spend Christmas with Jerry's brother and family, Norman, Peggy, Mark, and Kathleen. We had not spent much time with Norman, who had gone to Texas A & M right after we got married and then into the service, but we always enjoyed the time we spent with them. We were all together when Jerry's Mom passed away, and we hated to be away from the family during Christmas, but being with our missionary family was the next best thing.

Before we left, we bought Zac a bicycle for Christmas. Then we learned that his other grandfather bought him a bicycle, too. When I talked to Zac on the phone, and he told me he got two bicycles for Christmas.

Jerry and I took Marlene and Ian Logan to dinner at the Capital Hotel to thank Marlene for being so nice to clean our house for our return. The food was very good, and we had a nice visit. Jerry thought he was coming down with malaria and did not feel well, so he took a malaria cure. We were never sure he had malaria, but he felt bad and just dragged around for the next few days.

That first month back in Malawi was back to our usual busy schedule. Bennie Banda, a young man who had been one of the backbones of Capital City Baptist Church, was getting married. They had a lovely wedding at the church. Ten little girls danced down the aisle and bowed to one side and then to the other. They were all dressed alike with two colors of dresses. They were so cute. All the little girls were Malawi Nationals except Lisa Weston.

Lisa and her family were from New Zealand. Lisa had always taken a liking to Bennie. She would run to him, and he would pick her up and carry her around. It was special for him to ask Lisa to be in his wedding, but she stood out, being the only little white face.

After the wedding Neil Weston and Frances Sutcliff came over to talk to Jerry about some problems in the church. Mary and Dan

Robinson came by before the meeting was over. Then we went to the Korean restaurant for dinner with them.

Ted and Dot Lewis came to Malawi to supervise the Medical Clinic at Senga Bay, and they knew how to play bridge. These were the first missionaries who knew how to play bridge, so we invited them to dinner and to play bridge. Dot was a nurse and was well-accepted by the people. They were very good at the clinic, and she also worked with the people and taught the women how to sew and cook. I am sure she taught them many other things.

Hank and Francene Van Veleen, a very devout Christian couple, were from Amsterdam. They were in Malawi working at the Reserve Bank. They had us over to their house for dinner. I always enjoyed talking to Hank because he was always in the know about a lot of things related to the Malawi government.

———•••———

I got back into the interdenominational Ladies Bible Study Group. It had gone very well while I was gone, and there were about 25 to 30 women who attended each week. Of all the Bible Studies I have been a part of, this group was the most blessed. My spirit was always lifted at our meetings.

We would start with a fellowship time, then singing, then prayer, and then the Bible study. Everybody volunteered their home, or snacks or would lead in the singing or prayer time, and a few of the ladies would teach the lesson. It was always just wonderful.

They asked me if I would have a Christmas get-together at my house. (I had not intended to put up Christmas decorations, but I said yes.) So, on December 12 I had that group over for a little party.

One of the women, Maureen Green, wrote this little poem.

Why are you feeling so guilty?
This problem is not coming from me,
I died on the cross for your freedom.
I carried your guilt on the tree.

I'll show you when sin is your problem.
I deal with them one at a time,
I never will tell you you're worthless,
I love you, you're precious, and you're mine.

Stop trying so hard to be worthy.
Relax in my love and be free.
You don't have to work any harder
You are just what I chose you to be.

So please relax and be happy
Enjoy my blessings each day.
It's easier for you to know me.
When you're peaceful and happy each day.

45 Matters of Life
& Death in Malawi

December, January, and February are the most difficult months for the people of Malawi. Their crops have all been eaten and the new crops are not yet fully grown, so the people without paying jobs have difficulty just surviving. One day I received this letter :

Dear Rev. and Mrs. J. Dowdy,

I write this letter to you all because I have been a long time without seen you or writing you a letter. I will be very grateful if you are all well and doing fine. Here at home, we are doing fine.

First, I want to give thanks about your help last year during the time of troubles. I have received what you have sent to me Mayi Dowdy, thank you very, very much.

I have finished the Bible School last year, but I want to continue about my studies going to Seminary just pray for me although I am a pastor of Mphindo Baptist Church, but I want if my Lord allows me to go to Seminary. This year I will apply to go to Seminary.

Secondly pray for us about our trouble more especially during the months of January and February at the Village that are hungry months even the clothes are very shortage. You can see necked children. Pray for us please. We are in great trouble because it's almost five years without working all the maize have completed in August last year.

I will be very grateful if I can just find a piece work even cutting grass and can do in order just to be helped about the hungry and poverty in the village. Sometimes you can just come and see what people are eating bananas without ripe just to cook in the pot.

> *Your son in Christ,*
> *R. N. Mkaka*

So, I went out to Mphindo Village. And sure enough, there was much poverty. I saw one child about 18 months old try to take something from the mouth of another child who was about three years old. Another child about three years had picked a few kernels of corn from the ground and handed one kernel of corn to the 18-month-old. He put it into his mouth and began to chew happily on the raw corn. At least the rains had come early that year and the crops would come in early.

Before I left the States, someone had given me an anonymous gift of $100.00 to be used to help the people. I took the money and bought corn and gave them the money that was left over to buy beans and oil. Probably many lives were saved by this one gift of $100.

It is hard for Americans to realize just how important $100 can be in Africa. It can be the difference between life and death.

This is the thank-you letter that was given to me to send to whoever had given the money, so I forwarded the letter to Richardson Heights Baptist Church.

Dear Brother and Sister in Christ,

I write this letter to you in order to give many thanks because of your gift which you sent to our church through Rev. and Mrs. J. Dowdy. We have received the gift of maize and also money to buy salt and beans.

We appreciate your gift reached us in time of trouble, even though our church is not in the town or city of Lilongwe, it is in the village, but Mrs. Dowdy tried her best wishes to help us.

Many fellow friends in Christ are suffering from the hunger and poverty. We appreciate what you have done for us, please don't forget us. Pray for us and help for us, the same you did for us already just to continue.

May the Lord Jesus Christ bless you and lead you in everything that you have done in the name of our Lord Jesus Christ.

Warm Greetings are due to you all.
Your Brother in Christ
On behalf of all members.
Pastor: R. N. Mkaka Banda

The country of Malawi is rich in so many ways. The people are wonderful. There is also so much pain everywhere. The government operates some aspects in opulent style. Big black government Mercedes speeds here and there. Large sums of money are withdrawn from the banks so that government officials can have spending money above and beyond lavish expense accounts. It is as if the government goes looking for a hand-out, and at the same time, they want to look top-notch. They want to travel first-class.

During June I took Malawian Young Adults to Lake Malawi for a retreat. We had a good study on the Holy Spirit. We had a good fellowship and good time together. I had been apprehensive about food, water, and getting everything down there that we would need. I took my cook with me so he could handle the cooking. As the Lord was good to answer my prayers, everything went well. Nobody went hungry or thirsty, even though the food was very simple.

While at Salima one night, I was walking back from the big house over to the guest house, and I stepped across a cobra. Ed Barnes and the Bambo killed the snake, and this gave all of us quite a scare. It was not unusual for the Barnes to find snakes on the compound.

Chigwirizano Baptist Preaching Point is making plans to start the construction of a new church building. Rev. George Mwasi is doing a great job preaching and ministering to the people in that area. All our work seemed to be going well.

By mid-May the nights were beginning to feel cool. Our cook, Leonard Chipalaza's wife, gave birth to a baby boy. We had been awaiting this baby for months. Leonard said she had gotten pregnant in

June of 1989 and now it was eleven months later. (I felt sure that Leonard did not know.) He is pretty well-educated and more open about such matters than most Malawian men are, or he would not have talked to me about such matters. I talked to several of the missionaries; they all told me that it was not unusual for a woman to carry a baby for eleven months. They attribute this to poor diet and health. Both mother and baby were fine.

I took the Single Young Adults to the park for a picnic. We played some fun little games. We had relays. I blindfolded two people and let one feed a banana to the other. (They had never played such games!) They were good sports and seemed to have a good time. Some young people passing by thought we looked like we were having fun and wanted to join in. They said they would attend CCBC.

Kawali Baptist Church asked Jerry to preach on Sunday. They had been having some personal struggles since their pastor, Bro. Chisi left. They were looking for a new pastor. Bro Chisi was in the service, and they asked him to interpret for Jerry.

Jerry preached a message on the people getting right with one another. Just at the peak of the invitation, when Jerry was trying to get people to be reconciled one to another, there was a huge whirlwind that circled the church, dust came up so that you could not see out the windows, dirt began to come into the church, the shutters began to bang, and everybody experienced an eerie feeling. People began to go down the aisle, and it still gives me chill bumps to think about it.

During the following week, I talked with Bambo Chisi, and he was still excited. He said the whirlwind was the Lord's confirmation.

Then one of my single adults shared with me about an evil spirit which was troubling her. She was sent home from school twice because she had been thrown down on the ground by this spirit. She looked wild, her eyes bugged out, and she talked in a strange language, her brother told me. (This sounds far-fetched to most Americans but is fairly common in Malawi.)

I had just finished reading *This Present Darkness*, so, with fear and trembling, I prayed about what to do. I asked a few of our Malawian leaders over to our house to pray for Mary. I felt as if I was called upon to have a confrontation with the Devil. I had prayed and studied the scriptures all day.

Anyway, the Malawian friends arrived, and we began to read scripture and pray. We talked to Mary and asked her about what had been going on in her life. She said a couple of times that she felt like evil spirits were going to attack her. Then she began to pray, and as she said the name, "Jesus," she began to shake and then shrieking sounds began to come out of her — and she seemed to almost pass out.

Everyone in the room jumped up automatically from our chairs and ran to Mary. We began to pray for the evil spirit to come out of her, in the name of Jesus. Frances Mkondawiri asked her to say the name, "Jesus," over and over.

At first, she had a hard time saying "Jesus." After a little while she was able to say Jesus without trembling. Finally, a spirit left, and she thought that there was still a spirit in her. So, we prayed until it was gone. Now, she is telling everyone that she is cured. We all thanked the Lord for what He had done. Neither Jerry nor I had ever experienced anything like this. After it was all over, we all just sat speechless. We were completely drained of energy. We were exhausted.

After Jesus prayed at Gethsemane, he must have been completely exhausted. I had never realized how tiring intense praying can be.

I started to wash my hair and there was no water. Then I went to make a phone call and the phone was out. The electricity still goes on and off. But, probably, all in all, our utilities are better than the other countries around us.

———•••———

In October 1990, a couple of unusual things happened. First, an Englishman who owned a chicken farm in Lilongwe died. We had met the man and he had kindly delivered some chicken manure for my flower garden. We did not know them very well, but he and his wife seemed friendly; we had never been able to get them to visit our church.

Jerry was asked to preach at his funeral. We felt pretty certain that the man was not a Christian. (I always wonder why non-Christians want Christian funerals.) Jerry agreed to speak, but he was not sure what he would say.

When he arrived, the man had been cremated and his ashes were in a wooden box. All the guests were standing around on the lawn at the chicken farm and drinking, laughing, and having a good old time. When the man's wife announced that it was time for the funeral, everyone set their drinks down.

Jerry began to share the word of God with the people. He even shared the plan of salvation with them. When he finished, they picked up their drinks and began to party again.

Then just a week or two later, our only other chicken farmer, a South African man, was killed in a car wreck. (Both men were quite young.) We had met this man, too, and he and his family had visited our church a couple of times.

Jerry was asked to perform this funeral, as well.

Jerry and I went over to talk with the wife and help her with whatever arrangements she needed to make. She said she wanted her husband cremated so if she went back to South Africa, she could take the ashes with her. She did not, however, know anything about how to get the body cremated, since there is no actual funeral home or mortuary in Malawi.

Jerry checked around and learned that the Hindus are the ones who do the cremating. So, he made arrangements for a Hindu man to come out to the home of the bereaved wife to talk about the procedure. We sat and listened. When the Hindu man asked if she wanted all the ashes, she said yes.

She was told that this process would take about 72 hours. Jerry preached the funeral at CCBC. The wife stood beside the casket as people walked by and viewed the body for the last time. After the funeral, the body was taken to the Hindu place for cremation. The people from the church watched as the casket was taken into the ampa-theater looking place.

People sat on bleachers around this open area. A large pile of timbers was cut and placed in a rectangular pile in the center. Hindu men carried the casket around the wood pile in a ritualistic manor. They chanted, and at certain corners, they would turn the casket around and walk around in the other direction. Finally, the casket was placed on top of the woodpile.

Then sticks with large cloths wrapped around the ends were dipped into buckets of butter. The butter was wiped and strewn all over the woodpile. While the bereaved wife and friends looked on, the fire was set. Flames flashed into the sky all around the casket. Soon the casket caught on fire.

46 Home from Africa

Our years in Africa were wonderful years. As we began to plan our return to the States for our required two-year leave, we did not know where to live. Because our farmhouse, near Southmayd and Sherman, Texas, was vacant, we decided to move into that house until we could decide where we wanted to live permanently. (We wound up living there for 9 years.)

After we arrived home, unpacked and settle in for a bit, we began remodeling the house and working on the land. In 1991 we installed central heat and air. Then Loren Bradshaw came up with a couple of men and built an oversized two-car garage with an electric garage door. Then we had storm windows installed. (Jerry tried to install the windows, but after working on one almost all day, he decided to hire someone.)

In 1992 we completely remodeled the old farmhouse. Jerry turned the back porch into a bathroom and a large closet to hold all our clothes. (Jerry did some of this work and hired help as needed.). We tore out the old kitchen cabinets and installed new cabinets, ceiling, floor, and walls. Then we papered the walls in the kitchen and eating area. We then hired Perry Fleeman from Richardson Heights Baptist Church to install another bathroom where the old main bathroom had been.

Perry and Jerry tore out the walls, ceiling, and floor. (The old shower had rotted the floor out, so that it is a wonder the bathtub had not fallen through the floor.) We had white marble installed on the walls and in the new shower. The bathroom was small, but everything was new, and it really looked nice. Perry did a wonderful job.

Then we turned our attention to the yard around the house. Herb and Faye Crocker came up, and they brought Herb's little tractor and terraced the North lawn just outside the driveway. Jerry and I installed railroad ties to hold the terracing in place. We had the crossties stacked at the fence line west of the house, so we loaded them into the pickup and then unloaded them to maneuver them into place. They were really heavy for me to handle, but I was not one to back away from picking up heavy furniture, copy machines, *or* cross ties. Little by little, we terraced the grounds around the house.

Jo and I were in the same Bible Study in Denison, and one day she was late. When she came in, I noticed she was wearing a red slip. (I am not sure what the story was about red slips, but Jerry evidently used it over and over with various women.

I also suspected that Jerry was having an affair with Myra. Then one Sunday she came into church wearing a red dress, red slip, red hose, and red shoes. (As far as I was concerned, she looked ridiculous.)

We went to marriage counselors, but Jerry would never admit that he had done anything wrong, and they could not help him unless he was willing to be honest. I spilled my guts to them about myself, vented a lot of repressed anger, and learned a lot about communication. I listened to tapes, read books, and did everything I could — except tell them what Jerry had been doing. (I wanted him to reveal that part about himself, and I wanted him to get help.

I knew he definitely needed help. You don't live with someone for 40+ years without knowing them pretty well. (I also learned in one of the tests that I was "very perceptive.")

It was strange how I could live with Jerry, even with all his wandering ways. Surprisingly, we were very compatible as long as I did not mention his extra-curricular activity. I did become very quiet, and we began to talk only about whatever business we needed to communicate about.

Jerry was usually quiet with me, but with other people he was the life of the party. I admired Jerry for all his accomplishments and abilities, but I hated his lifestyle. One day he said that maybe he was a schizophrenic, and I told him I would not buy that. He never mentioned it again.

Life on the farm was a mixture of joy and distress.

———◆●◆———

Sometimes early in the morning Jerry would bring me a cup of coffee in bed while I did my Bible study. Then he would take his cup of coffee into the back yard and sit.

There was a skunk that would often come up to Jerry as he sat there, close enough that he could pet it. Other times, when Jerry would get up and walk toward the barn, that skunk follow him and walk between his legs.

One day as Jerry was sitting in his chair drinking his coffee, along came the skunk — with three little skunks following. It was as if the mother skunk was showing her babies to Jerry.

This went on for quite a while, and then one day there was a foul odor coming from the culvert (the large pipe beneath the driveway to barn). Apparently, the mother skunk and her babies were living in that culvert.

Jerry waited until he was sure the skunks were gone, and then he got the water hose and washed out the culvert and then installed wire over both ends so the skunks could not get into their home.

———◆●◆———

One day when Jim and Liz Parrish were visiting from Yorkshire, England, Jerry saw the armadillo on the driveway that had been rutting up our grass looking for food. He got his gun and shot the armadillo right in front of the Parishes. Liz was aghast that he would shoot the creature. (I think he probably shot it just for the Wild West effect.)

There was also a cat living under the house when we first returned from Malawi. She was scared of us and would run away as fast as she could every time she saw us. Sometimes we would put food out for her.

One day we realized we had not seen her in about a week. Then during breakfast one morning Jerry saw her laying in the yard. She looked nearly dead. Jerry got some milk and put it in front of her, and she was barely able to lift her head to drink. Then he took some food out to her, and while we were gone, she ate the food and moved back under the house. After that she was much friendlier, and she even got to where she would let us pet her when we sat down outside.

One day we walked out into the garage and the garage door was up. The cat got in front of us and tried to keep us from walking into the garage — she hissed and meowed and hissed, trying her best to stop us.

"What is wrong with that crazy cat?" I asked.

As she grew downright hostile, we looked past her into the corner of the garage — and there was an opossum. Because that opossum, a nocturnal creature, was out in broad daylight, it was probably sick or maybe even rabid. The cat was trying to protect us.

"Stay here while I get my gun," Jerry said,

So, the cat and I just stood there and watched each other and waited. Jerry came back with the gun and shot the opossum dead.

———— •• ————

We had not been back from Africa very long when one night we heard a scream coming from out in the pasture, down toward the trees behind our house. It sounded like some woman was being beaten to death. Several times we heard that sound and then one morning while I was sitting in bed, I saw a black panther. I could not believe what I was seeing, but I couldn't think of anything else it could be.

We asked our neighbors about it, and they said there was a flood a while back at the Gainesville Zoo, and the animals were released — and some were never found. (After that I was very careful about walking down into the pasture.)

Sometimes early in the morning or late in the afternoon we would see deer walking across our place. They would get to the fence and just sail over. They were so beautiful. Jerry bought a deer feeder and put it down among the trees so we could feed the deer during the winter. Watching the deer and other wildlife was the most pleasant thing about living on the farm.

Birds chirped as we drank coffee on the front swing Ken and Suzanne gave us one Christmas. On crisp, cool mornings I would bundle up with a coat over my nightgown; Jerry and I would sip coffee and listen to the birds and look at the late blooming roses. Sometimes we walked around the yard and checked the grass, trees, and flowers.

During the winter, Jerry would build me a fire in the fireplace. I loved to sit on the hearth and feel its warmth. There always seemed to be something that needed to get done, so we stayed busy. We checked the stock market regularly to try to decide where and when we needed to sell or invest our money.

We attended First Baptist Church of Sherman regularly. In just one year's time, there were four close friends from our Sunday School Classes who passed away: Buddy Pitzer, Jane Grimes' husband who directed the Zambia Boys Choir, Jean Martin, and Carolyn Noble. Since that left Barbara Pitzer and Jack Noble single, they fell in love and got married to each other.

———•••———

We joined an FBC Sherman mission trip from Sherman, Texas to just north of Calgary, Canada to work on the Seminary there. The trip was comfortable even though our truck was an old Ford, and we were pulling our fifth wheel camper.

As we drove into the grounds, we saw this seminary building was very tall and being built into a mountainside, making the back of the building a long way from the ground. Jerry was 61 years old by then, and I told him he should not be climbing on top to work on the roof.

We found the campground and got our camper hooked up. We were traveling up there with Myra and Bob Cravins and a Mr. and Mrs. Juntinen (whom we did not know). Myra had been bugging me all the way up, talking back and forth with Jerry on the two-way radio. (Finally, I just turned our radio off. It had been a long trip.)

The first morning I looked out and what did I see? Jerry on top of the seminary building. As it turned out, he was one of the youngest volunteers there — and he was helping to set the trusses. But even when they got the trusses up, he continued to work on the roof. (We were there for about a month, and he was on top of the building for much of that time.)

There were a lot of volunteers, and I helped out with the cooking. (The women did all the cooking.) While we were there, many more people came in with their trailers. Eventually, there were no more electricity hook-ups available to plug into, so, the volunteers had to run additional electric lines. It was quite a sight to see all those campers parked side by side.

After we left the Seminary, we stopped in Banff where Jerry played a round of golf on their beautiful course. The elk roamed around the town. (We heard that sometimes tourists acted like these were tame animals and they got mauled.) Then we drove west toward the Pacific Ocean.

We stopped at a campground where you could see a train going into a mountainside and then it would go around, and you could see the tail of the train — you could see the engine coming out as the caboose was going in. The mountains and scenery were lush with foliage.

Once we got to British Columbia we drove on into Vancouver. We looked around their beautiful gardens and had dinner with Nazim and his wife, whom we had met in Kenya. Nazim was originally a Muslim, but he said that now he was a Christian. He went to see his parents, who were Muslim, every Friday night — and his wife was not welcome to visit.

We took a boat over to Victoria to see the Butchart Gardens. This garden, which had once been a rock quarry for rock used to make cement, was transformed when Mr. Butchart allowed his wife to make a flower garden out of the rock pit. These gardens are really one of the showplaces of the world. (The house they lived in was quite simple in comparison.) After that, we drove all the way back to the farm.

Later that same year, FBC Sherman sponsored a week where people volunteered and repaired houses, painted playground equipment, or did whatever else the city needed to make things look better. Jerry was responsible for the First Baptist Church project, a house on which they completely renovated the exterior.

Volunteers scraped and painted, and the Bill Steele family worked on the yard. They loaded truckloads of debris from the back yard and took it to the dump. (While going through the debris they found a pearl-handled pistol.)

Once the yard was cleaned up, the team planted some shrubs. The people at FBC were so good to help with all the projects. Mr. Andrews, the man who lived in that house, had never accepted Jesus as his Savior, so I witnessed to him — and he confessed Jesus as his Savior. Jerry and I gave him a little tape player, and we would take him tapes on the Bible from time to time so he could listen to them.

———————•••———————

In July, we planned a Malawi missionary retreat in Sherman, and the Kingsleys and their daughter Karen, the Westers, the Spires and their daughter and Rebecca, the Workman's daughter Debra and her son, the Herifords, the Swaffords, Jeanette, Charles Middleton, and many other volunteers came. In all, there were nearly 30 people there. We ate, slept, looked at pictures, shared all kinds of stories, and reminisced about the past.

———————•••———————

Ken and Suzanne's daughter, Alayna, turned five that year, and she had a birthday party as always. It was a big affair. Alayna's maternal grandparents, Sam and Peggy Sellers, were also there. The theme was farm animals, and her cake had pigs, sheep, dogs etc. on it. All of our grandchildren — as well as several of Alayna's friends — were at Ken and Suzanne's house for the party.

Corbin, Peggy's youngest son, who was about the same age as Alayna, was so excited for Alayna and looked over her shoulder every time she opened a present and would hug her just as if he had gotten a gift. The children swam in the swimming pool in the back yard. Then truck loaded with farm animals arrived and was unloaded in the back yard for the children to pet.

Zac, who was older than the other children, did not know if he fit in better with the adults or the little children.

Andrew, Ken and Suzanne's son, was walking well, and he loved to pet the animals.

Peggy and Jerry's sister Jann were there, watching and helping.

I sat down on the grass and helped Andrew with his cake and punch. He wore blue and white overalls with a birthday hat on his head. The rest of the children wore swimsuits.

I paused to reflect on how sweet it was to be able to participate in little family moments such as this. We had missed so much when we were in Malawi.

———••••———

Peggy came up to the farm one weekend with her boys, Zac and Corbin (Lawson). I got the neighbor boy to bring over his horse so the boys could ride. Zac rode by himself, but Peggy rode with Corbin.

Hay had just been cut, baled, and picked up in the pasture, but the grass was still green, and it looked really good. The boys rode their go-cart round and round the drive and up the road as fast as it would go. Jerry had installed a lawn mower motor on the go-cart, so it went faster than it was designed to go. I was terrified they would go off the road and decapitate themselves on the fence or otherwise badly hurt themselves. Fortunately, they were good drivers, nothing bad happened with the go-cart, and the boys had a great time.

———••••———

We had Christmas at the farm that year. It was one of the few Christmases that Ken, Suzanne, Alayna, Andrew, Peggy, Bruce, Corbin, Zac, Jann, Jerry, and I had Christmas together. I had the house all decorated. I had my Heritage dining room table and chairs along with my beautiful buffet and credenza. I used my Grand Baroque sterling silver along with my Royal Dalton, Rose Garden China. I placed my crystal on the table, and everything looked perfect. I cooked a lovely dinner and all the food taste good.

Besides our family there for dinner, we hosted a crowd of friends from our church and local community including Doris, Lindy, Roger, Delaine, Kenneth, Marsha, Bob, Duane, and a few others. I read the Christmas Story and got together costumes for people to dress up for a live Nativity. Duane, Bobby, and Kenneth were wise men. The children played Joseph, and Mary; Andrew, Ken's son (who was called Drew by then) was an active Baby Jesus. I was surprised how cooperative everyone was. It was a lot of fun for me, and I think everybody enjoyed it.

Most of our years were filled much the same way. It seems like we were always busy.

47 Called Again to Serve

During the summer of 1993, when Jerry and I had been back in the States on a two-year leave from serving in Malawi, I received a phone call from Mary Faulkner, the wife of John Faulkner who was director over Eastern & Southern Africa for the International Mission Board of the Southern Baptist Convention. (It had changed its name from The Foreign Mission Board.)

Our furlough time as missionaries was about to run out, and we had thought we would just resign and stay in the States. We were busy on the farm and had made a lot of improvements to the old house, added a barn, repaved the road, bought several pieces of farm equipment, and landscaped the garden. Everything was beginning to look pretty good.

Then Mary Faulkner asked if Jerry would like to go to Somalia as the director of our relief operations there — and if I would be willing to help with the treasurer job. We thought about it a little. (I could sound holy and say that we prayed about it — and I suppose we did.)

We decided to accept the position. It seemed to be the right thing to do; they needed someone to fill in those positions while George and Sally (not their real names) took a much-needed vacation.

A war was going on in Somalia. There were three tribes fighting to be the leader of the country. The United Nations was directing the assistance, and the United States had a large envoy stationed there.

We packed our bags and flew to Kenya. Tim Smith, who owned the farm north of our property, on Southmayd Road, would manage the land and keep an eye on the house. Bob and Myra Cravens would spend the night in the house once a month to keep our insurance in force. We stored some of our furniture in the barn.

———•••———

We arrived in Nairobi, Kenya, where we would make our home, and Jerry would fly in and out of Mogadishu, Somalia from there. We learned that we had people in three or four countries and about 15 employees in Mogadishu.

Dr. Gene and Laura Moore were doing medical work.

Gary Tapp was a pharmacist and Judy Tapp was a nurse and they worked in Djibouti.

Mami Wright was a nurse from Florida, and she was there working in Mogadishu.

Al and Neva Crows were coming to Kenya to work in Mandera, Kenya, the upper corner where Somalia, Ethiopia, and Kenya come together, where a refugee camp is located. They were coming to replace Todd and Karen Helms.

At times Dr. Gene Moore or others in our organization would go to Mandera or Mogadishu, Somalia, or other places to perform surgery or do various types of relief work.

We were not allowed to do much sharing of the Gospel. If someone asked us a question, we could answer him or her.

———•••———

We had no more than landed when I learned that I was not expected to *help* with the treasurer work, but that I was already approved as *the treasurer*. There was nobody else there to help — it was just me. My concern was not about the accounting part, but I had a lot of reservations about the computer. I had done word processing and Quicken and that is about the extent of my computer experience. I felt I had been brought there under false pretenses but decided I would keep my mouth shut and accept the challenge.

Sally was to teach me my job, but her husband George felt that a half-day training was all I needed, so he always threw up roadblocks to keep me from working with Sally. I think Sally didn't feel confident in her job and therefore didn't feel that she was qualified to teach me. She said that she had gone on furlough and left the treasurer job in the hands of another woman who had just put the receipts in a shoebox and had not done anything. (I could certainly understand why, because Sally would not teach me, either. I am sure she had not trained the other woman.

George trained Jerry on what to do, and we learned it was a big responsibility. I had been told that I would not have to go into Somalia. (The idea of going into a combat zone held no appeal for me.) George also advised me that I was not to give out any information to anybody. Jerry was to be the only one to share any information about our work.

John Faulkner was our director. He and Ann were sweet, lovely people and took us under their wings and were most gracious. We did not work with the missionaries of Kenya since we were there to do relief work with a different branch.

———•••———

George and Sally were packed to leave. It was the end of the month, so Sally had to close out the books. I worked with her one full day, and we balanced the books. About half the work was done by hand and the other half was done on the computer. I learned that she was using a computer accounting system that nobody else in Africa was using. If I had a problem, there was nobody to help me. I felt the system of bookkeeping was antiquated, and it made it very difficult to file end-of-the-month reports. But I understood what she was doing.

Then Sally told me I would need to go into Mogadishu. I mentioned to George that I was told I would not have to go into Mogadishu. He said I did not *have* to go, but I would understand the relief work better and the Baptist work better if I went.

Operating the short-wave radio when Jerry was out of Nairobi would be my responsibility. I was also told that I would not understand how to communicate with our people if I didn't go into Somalia.

So, with trepidation I agreed to go.

Because there were no commercial planes going into Somalia at that time, George made arrangements for us to fly in on a U.N. flight. About the time George made our reservations, "Black Hawk Down," otherwise known as The Battle of Mogadishu, happened. The Somali Civil War was really heating up. An American Soldier was stripped of his clothes, tied to the back of a Jeep, and dragged around K4, a roundabout. CNN captured this dragging on film, and across America, people saw this on television. The Americans became irate and said it is time to bring our boys home. This "Black Hawk Down" incident was made into a movie that very accurately depicts what was going on in Somalia at that time.

About three days after all this was going on, we had our reservations to go in. Sally gave each of us a $100 bill for expenses. Jerry gave me his new $100 bill for safekeeping. When I got to the airport , I pulled the $100 bill out of my billfold to pay our $20-per-person Airport Fee, and the cashier gave me $60 change. A few moments later I realized I gave the teller $200 instead of $100. (Evidently, the new bills had stuck together) I went back to the cashier, and he denied that I had given him $200. Not a good way to start the trip.

We went into the area to catch the U.N. flight. (We did not go through immigration or anything.) When we got into the waiting area, there were soldiers from several different countries sitting around. Several had about 30 dozen eggs tied together in crates. Others were carrying live chickens. Still others had food items they were taking back into Mogadishu.

As I looked at these men and thought about how young they seemed, they were probably eyeing me and thinking, *why in the world is that old woman going to Somalia?*

I was wearing a long dress that was tie died and it covered some of my arms. I had a little scarf tied around my head to cover my hair. I did not have to dress like this, but out of respect for the Islamic culture and for protection of my life, I selected this attire purposely.

With chickens cackling and goats bleating, we all climbed aboard the United Nations plane. I don't know if Jerry felt any apprehension — we never discussed our feelings or what we might be getting ourselves into.

George was with us, and he knew the procedures. The flight was quiet with few people saying a word.

As we approached the Mogadishu Airport, I could see a sight like I had only seen in movies. Around the edge of the landing strip were soldiers behind piled up sandbags. They were armed with machine guns and AK 47's. Tanks were scattered around, and helicopters buzzed overhead all around us, so many it called to mind the image of a dragonfly convention.

I could see the so-called terminal, one lone building with three sides made of sheet iron. Bombed-out buildings lay just outside the airstrip.

With trepidation and silence, we all climbed off the plane and walked across the pavement to the terminal. There were only a few people in there. We did not go through any customs or security. It seemed that everybody there saw someone they recognized, and they all departed.

Two young Somali men and Frank Ritz met us. We only had a little bag, and we climbed into two pick-up trucks with Somali men on each side of us. Each pick-up had a machine gun mounted in the back and a man with an AK 47.

Wide-eyed, we departed the airport area, taking in the bombed-out roads and abandoned vehicles beside the roads. Some were burned while others were splattered with bullet holes. The buildings that were still intact stood riddled with bullet holes; the others were piles of rubble.

Once Mogadishu had been a beautiful city with large flat-top homes, businesses, and wide paved streets. Bullet holes revealed the gray cement beneath the buildings' whitewashed facade, now fractured and peppered with holes.

We stopped at a checkpoint, and an armed soldier questioned our driver. We had a flag on the right fender of our vehicles that identified us, and he motioned us through the barricade. Four of our Somalia guards picked up their AK 47s, and they sat on the outer parts to protect us.

We approached a large, white house surrounded by thick, white, cement walls, and our driver honked twice. Two Somali men opened the two sheet-iron gates. As I looked up to the roof of this house, I saw two armed soldiers with AK 47s. They were with the U.N. from Nepal.

We learned that the Nepal command post was adjacent to ours, and they guarded our property in order to protect theirs. They also kept a U. N. white tank in our compound.

We climbed out of the truck and went inside for our instructions.

Jerry would be responsible for the two to five fellow workers from the States we usually kept in Mogadishu and the 15 or so Somalian employees. I was responsible for the accounting, and although going into this country was not part of the deal, I was determined to learn everything I could since I would be responsible for these people in Jerry's absence.

The work in Mogadishu, Somalia consisted mostly of medical work, feeding people, and getting assignments from UNISOM (United Nations in Somalia) of needs we were qualified to handle.

George showed us around our Compound. Our electricity came from a generator, and water was brought in by a truck and emptied into an underground tank.

We walked out on top of our house and looked around. Flat-topped houses sprawled across the city. We could see the Nepal military personnel behind their bunkers. I waved at them, and they waved back.

George explained how two Nepal solders had been killed guarding our gate. (That did nothing to make me feel safe.) The bottom floor of the house consisted of an area where corn was stored. Medicine was stored in one room, and each day before the staff went out to do medical work, medicines were dispensed into little plastic bags.

The upper floor is where our U. S. staff lived. We had a Somali lady who was our cook, and she purchased our food and prepared our meals. Food was limited, and meat was limited to camel. The vegetables were whatever she could buy. The U.S. Military had also given us C rations to eat sometimes. (Each packet contained a small bottle of Tabasco sauce. The food was actually edible, but I would not want to make it a steady diet.)

The first night Jerry and I slept in a side room with sheet iron roofing, and all night long we heard rats jumping from the adjacent roof down onto our roof. All night we heard gunshots and helicopters keeping vigil. They were U.S. flyboys, but somehow that did not make me feel particularly secure. (After a while we become accustomed to these new sounds, and they virtually disappeared from our awareness.) Soon it all seemed somewhat normal and routine, and we began to feel "this is normal life."

48 World of War: Somalia

The next day we went to the Pakistani Headquarters to offer our condolence. Twelve of their soldiers were killed while guarding our people in a village where our staff was running a medical clinic. The Post Commander greeted us and served us tea in a little tent.

I sat in the back of the tent and struck up a friendly conversation with a Pakistani soldier. He said he was a sharpshooter. and I thanked him for protecting our people.

I guess we were talking too loudly because the commander gave me a hard look.

I apologized for being disruptive. I explained that I meant no disrespect and offered my deep appreciation for their soldiers' brave and gallant protection of our people. I was so deeply sorry for the loss of his men.

When we went back to our compound, I realized I had mud on my face, so to speak. In an Islamic country, women are supposed to keep their mouths shut. Just by talking to that soldier I had really overstepped my bounds, but nobody in our group reprimanded me or mentioned it.

Rent on the house was $3,000 per month. We also rented two pickup trucks with a driver, two men armed with AK 47s, and a machine gun mounted into the bed of each of the trucks. Each of those cost $1500. We rented the trucks, and the truck owner supplied the armed men to protect his investment.

Everywhere we went, we always took both trucks. That way, if one broke down or had a problem, everyone could jump into the other truck.

UNICEF reimbursed every project we accepted and completed. The salary of our people from the States was basically the extent of our expenses. Jerry wrote up the projects as we completed them. Once he submitted them, UNICEF reimbursed us.

George had requested that UNICEF pay us for one specific project in Somali Dollars. Of course, that money was of little or no value. It took about S5,000 in Somali dollars to equal $1 U.S. A truck brought the money to the house, and they weighed it instead of counting it. (This is what happens when someone does not understand currency and what makes it valuable.) So as a result, we had a room filled with money that could be used in Somalia but nowhere else in the world. The house and vehicles had to be paid for with new U.S. $100 bills.

The second day we did not leave the compound because the U.N. said it was not safe. I watched some television that came from a U.S. satellite, and the picture and sound was perfect. Then I began watching the medical team package medicine.

I noticed that one of the girls was packing some of the packages and placing them in one place and some in another place, and I felt that something was wrong. Come to find out, the girl's father owned a pharmacy, and she was supplying his pharmacy with our medicine for a tidy little profit for her family at our expense.

That same night, one of our employees came to us, and by candlelight he shared that years earlier an American soldier had shared Christ with him, and he accepted Jesus as his Lord and Savior. He said he wanted to be baptized. George promised him his confession and desire for baptism would be kept confidential.

Later, when George went back to Mogadishu, the U.S. military base made arrangements for this employee to be baptized in a canvas tub. The only problem was that George took a photographer from the IMB in with him, and when the young man was baptized, photographs were taken. George had told us that the Muslims read every religious magazine. I knew about the baptism, but I did not know about the photographer.

Jerry, George, and Frank Ritz went to the U.N. meeting early the next morning and they were advised that we could go to Afgoye village, where the Pakistani soldiers were killed, and hold a medical clinic. So, our staff climbed into the two pickups and headed out. The driver dodged the holes in the bombed-out road and the wrecked vehicles alongside every street.

We came to K4 circle and could see where the American Black Hawk helicopter had gone down. I didn't want to think about our soldier boys and what had happened to them. I did not want to think about the half-naked American soldier that was tied to the back of a jeep and dragged around K4 with onlookers jeering. Only a few days before, fighting was taking place right where I sat. What was I doing here? Was I crazy? No. It just seemed to be the thing God wanted me to do.

I did not stop to ask why. Even now, I don't know why I was there. I learned a lot about war, the Islamic Religion, and the Muslim tribes. God must have had a reason for me to go through this experience.

As we made our way down the street, every few minutes there would be a roadblock and soldiers with weapons. We would stop, the drivers would have to give our information, and then we would be allowed through.

As we rode along, George pointed out a concrete foundation for a large building. Long steps had gone up to this large building, now leveled. He said the building had been a Christian Church. Once there had been a large contingency of Christians in Somalia, but by 1993 there were only 22 known Christians (and of course they could not admit they were Christians, or they would be killed). Christianity and Islam go together like oil and water. The Muslims do not allow Christianity.

We drove down to a checkpoint and Mami Wright, our staff nurse, had forgotten something. As we waited beside the road for her to go back and retrieve the forgotten article, I looked around to see if there were any weapons pointing at us. I was wearing a long African dress with a scarf tied around my head. Mami always wore her cross, but I had left mine back in Nairobi.

When Mami returned, we bumped along with our security guards until we reached a little village. There was a hole dug with the dirt piled around the side to protect the medical clinic area. The Pakistani soldiers who had guarded us along this trip set up their tanks and posted men with rifles.

Our group unloaded, got out the medicines, a little table, and about three stools. Sick villagers had already gathered to be treated. Dr. Gene Moore, Nurse Mami Wright, Jerry and I, and all our Somali paid staff set up for the clinic. As people came up to the little table, we registered, questioned, and examined them before dispensing medicine.

Patients came and went. After a while, George suggested that Jerry and I go with him to a water well being dug. Abdul, our Somalian leader, went along with us. As I got out of the truck, a woman came up to me and tried to give me her daughter, who looked to be about 13 years of age. In broken English, she said the girl's father was an American, and she wanted me to take the girl to America with me.

The village people laughed at her, but she was very sincere. She was probably the village prostitute. I felt so sorry for her and the girl. I can't imagine what their lives must have been like. As I talked to her, many people gathered around.

The others in our group had gone on toward the well. Abdul came back for me and told me to come on, speaking in a tone of voice that made me realize I was alone and in possible danger. Hastily I moved to catch up with the others.

Because the water well was being paid for by Americans, the villagers said the well was cursed. They assume that all Americans are Christians because the Islamic government and religion are combined, and there is no separation of government and religion.

After a while, the most emaciated old man I have ever seen was pulled from the well. He came to me, put out his hand, and begged for money. I did not have a cent of any kind of money. I asked George for money, then I asked Jerry, and finally I went over to Abdul and asked him for money. (I am sure he had money, but he would not lend me any.)

Back at the house, we had a room full of money, but I had nothing to give this poor man. Maybe it was for the best. If I had given him money, the villagers would probably have beaten him up and taken it away from him. My heart really went out to him, but I had no way of helping him.

He was placed back down in the deep dark hole. We could not let the well fail because it was a battle between God and Allah. We prayed to our God for water to show His power. (After months of prayer and digging, water was eventually struck.)

We headed back over to the medical camp. The woman approached me again and begged me to take her daughter. This time I stayed with the group. She was in a desperate situation, and I could do nothing. I cannot keep from wondering, *what if I had been born in that woman's situation? Why did God choose me to be born in a freedom filled country with plenty? And why was this woman born in Somalia in her situation?*

I can only be thankful to My God.

When we got back over to the medical clinic, I climbed to the top of the mound of dirt surrounding the clinic. The Pakistani soldier I had met at the Pakistani headquarters came over and began talking to me. Then he began to trace the stitching on the chest of my dress with his finger.

He was coming on to me! I was shocked. Here I was about 60 years old — and he was not more than 21. I gasped, stepped back, and pointed to Jerry, telling him that Jerry was my husband.

In response, the soldier walked down to Dr. Moore and asked him if Jerry was my husband. He also questioned the color of my hair, since there was a little hair sticking out from under the scarf. Gene Moore told him I used Henna, and he accepted that.

There was an old woman who started forward to the table, and she could not see how to sit on the stool. I walked over, took her hand, and tried to pull her arm down so she could feel the stool to sit on. With great difficulty she sat. The team then interviewed her and dispensed the medicine she needed.

After everybody was treated, we headed back to Mogadishu and arrived without incident.

My few days there seem like a dream.

———•••———

Jerry, George, and I headed back to Nairobi. We loaded into a large cargo plane that was big enough to drive tanks, trucks, and jeeps into. Along the sides of the plane are mesh seats to sit in. The noise on these planes is so loud you must plug your ears. In the center of the plane there was a huge pile of chains and tires.

As nature would have her way, Somalia's (known in Mexico as Montezuma's) revenge struck. I asked for direction to the rest room, and George pointed to a curtain near the front.

A soldier was seated right next to the toilet behind the flimsy curtain. I climbed through the chains and tires and finally reached the curtain.

I felt all eyes on me.

It was dark behind the curtain, and there was virtually no space. After quite a struggle, I finally sat down on the tiny toilet, and my knees pushed through the curtain by about six inches.

The C rations and camel had not been bad going down, but the odor coming out was spectacularly foul. Somehow in the darkness I located some paper, completed the task, and readjusted my clothes. Then, as I started trying to find where to flush the pot, my butt shifted from one side of the curtain to the other, fanning the terrible aroma throughout the plane. Just when I thought I would have to ask the man sitting there, "How do you flush this thing?" I found the button.

When I finally got back to my seat, mortified, I could tell Jerry was embarrassed. "Why did you keep fanning that curtain back and forth?" he asked through tight lips.

I whispered back my best possible explanation.

He said nothing.

The rest of the ride back to Nairobi was long, loud, bumpy, and smelly. It gave me more empathy for our military for enduring such simple things.

49 Mogadishu Mission Work

Once we had learned our way around Nairobi, we had a taste of what life in Mogadishu was like. With very little actual training George and Sally handed the reins to Jerry and me.

In Somalia I felt anger and frustration I had never felt in Malawi. We met a lot of nice people and felt that, with God's help, we would be able to accomplish what He called us to do there.

Sally and I went over the books and bank accounts, and I verified that what she showed on the books was correct. With this last meeting the treasurer' responsibility was turned over to me and I could write a check up to $100,000 without any question or authorization needed.

We had work in Mandera, Kenya, where at least one couple was always present at its large refugee camp. We had a nice little house that was modestly furnished. The office was at one end of the house with an air-conditioner in one window.

Jerry got involved in his job, and I began to sort through the accounting. It was fairly simple accounting, since little or no taxing was involved. I did work with five different currencies and had to convert all accounts to U.S. dollars. Although the computer automatically made these calculations, I had to know what number to plug in and which buttons to push — and whoopee! Accounting functions accomplished!

Then the computer numbers had to be manually converted to a spreadsheet. Sandy, a missionary from Ethiopia, came by and helped me figure out which columns to add and which ones to subtract. (I placed little plus and minus signs over each column so that the next month it would be easy for me to balance the books.) Sandy was a real "God send".

I had to turn in an accounting report on a certain date each month. The area treasurer then collected and combined these reports from all the Southern Africa regions and sent the compilation to the International Missions Board by a certain date. (If you did not get your report in on time, the treasurer would report to the IMB that his report was incomplete because you had not turned in your report.)

———•••———

It was obvious to me that my accounting program needed some radical changes. So, after a few months a computer tech named Orvil Boyd Jenkins came by and installed the BMAS computer program so that I would be on the same program as our other Southern Baptists treasurers. This meant there would also be someone to communicate with in case of a problem or something I did not understand.

The weather was hot, and I worked day and night trying to input all the information to bring this new program online. I had the air conditioner going full blast. Whenever my little laptop computer got hot and began smoking, I would push back from the desk, take a deep sigh, and wait until it cooled off. After I dealt with this for a while, Jerry put a fan next to my computer to help keep it cooler. (This helped the computer but blew my papers; you just can't have everything.)

After I had input most of the data, within a little over a week, the bottom fell out. Nothing worked. Had I burned up the little computer? Or had something else happened? We called in the IT support tech, and he said he had failed to put in one of the stops — and that I had a hard drive crash. I had lost about 80 percent of the data I had input.

Fortunately, I did not mind typing on the computer, so I took this with a grain of salt. (I think he expected me to throw a fit.) He knew it was his fault, but I knew there was no need to cry over spilled milk. He corrected the problem, and I got to work redoing things.

I went over to the area office to talk to the area treasurer. I did not intend to mention the hard drive crash, but he smiled as he brought it up. He evidently had received a full report of the incident.

So that is how my work in Somalia started. At last, I got the program up and running and really enjoyed my work. The area treasurer and I had a good rapport. On the final day my report was due, I took the report over to him.

"I have already sent my report in and said that I had your report," he said, "I knew you would have it in before the day is over."

Jerry was also doing a fantastic job. Networking with people was his forte. He could talk to people, and they loved him and wanted to please him. They would go to extra lengths to accomplish great things.

One day I had a phone call from the area photographer, and he wanted some information about Somalia. Since George told me that I was not to give out any information, I would not talk to him about Somalia. He prodded me, but I would not answer his questions. I could tell he got really mad at me. Evidently, he went to the area office and reported me to the area director, John Faulkner.

About two months after the baptism, I received a fax from friends in New Zealand. There was a photo of the young man being baptized. The news had traveled to New Zealand and the information had gotten back to me. Remarkable!

I have never been so angry in my life. (And I am slow to anger.) This was righteous indignation of the highest degree. I took the faxed copy over to the area office and confronted John Faulkner in the office in front of everyone. When the people in the other offices heard me, they came out to see what was going on.

I was not professional or tactful. It never occurred to me to suggest that John and I adjourn to his office. I broke loose right there on the spot.

"Did you authorize this photo release?" I demanded.

Much to my astonishment, John said, "Yes."

"I was there when the young man was promised that his baptism would be kept confidential," I said. "Now I received a fax from a friend halfway around the world with a *picture of it!*"

John said that if the area photographer called and wanted information about Somalia, then I was to give it to him.

I was beside myself. "If anything happens to this man, his blood is on your hands," I said with a huff. I had lost my cool in front of my boss and all his peers. I had lost my tact and professionalism.

I told him that if the photographer called, I would give him any information I had.

I am not one to cry, but if I were, this would have been an occasion to cry. In a huff I turned around and walked out the door with the words of Pilot when the people wanted Jesus to be crucified echoing in my head.

Sometime later we learned that the young man (I will refer to him simply as "A".) was going home from work one day and a friend stopped him and told him not to go home. A was then told that his pregnant wife was forced to abort their baby and she was taken from their home to be married to a businessman she did not know. Their house, with all their belongings, was burned. The Muslim leaders were looking for "A" and were going to kill him before sundown.

"A" went into hiding. Our organization hid him for a while, and for about three months he was hidden by different organizations. Several months later, he was outside at a coffee bar on the opposite side of town. While relaxing and drinking his coffee, a man came by on a motorcycle and shot him dead.

We as Americans sometimes make bad choices because we do not understand other religions or culture. This had turned into a deadly mistake, and I am sure it still weighs heavily on the hearts of those who made the wrong choices.

Sometimes people say it doesn't matter what you believe, as long as you are sincere. I want to tell you being sincere is not enough. You'd better be correct in your choice. The choice you make may ruin your life or end someone else's. It may make the difference of whether you spend eternity in heaven or hell. Jerry and I never really discussed this situation, and I did not mention it to anybody in Kenya.

———— •••• ————

One of my responsibilities as treasurer was to go to the bank. To carry on our work in Somalia, we needed new, one-hundred-dollar bills. To secure the money we needed there, I would usually go into the bank in Nairobi and ask for $20,000 in one-hundred-dollar bills. They would show me into a little half-walled booth off to the side of the bank. This was not a private room — people going up to the tellers could see me in there, and they knew I was dealing with a lot of cash.

This task was dangerous because thievery was prominent in Kenya. If you wore jewelry in public, people would run up to you and yank it off. One of our missionary boys lost a gold chain he wore around his neck, and he chased the thief and got his chain back. (This action was not recommended.) Another missionary was resting his forearm on the open car window while stopped at a red light and someone came along and yanked his watch right off of his arm. There were much worse stories than these, and this was a common occurrence.

The IMB director advised me to be aware of my surroundings all the time — and of the safety procedures to observe. Before I got out of the car, I was to look around. As I walked down the street, I was to be aware of everything going on around me. When I left the bank, I was to walk straight to the car, get in fast, lock the doors, and go straight home.

We had a little safe at home that I would put the money in until we could take it into Mogadishu. One of the other relief organizations got robbed when they returned home from the bank, and they were roughed up a little and had their money stolen. I realized the danger associated with my job, but I tried not to dwell on it.

Jerry usually went with me when I went to the bank, but he could not always go. Often, I did this errand alone. One day when Jerry and I got back to the car I noticed a very skinny woman and a baby sitting on the sidewalk. Because I had $20,000 in my purse I headed straight to the car. As I closed the car door, the baby toddled toward us and placed one hand on the car. She was begging; she could not have been more than two years old. I told Jerry to start the car and go.

After we went about half a block, my conscience got the best of me. I asked Jerry to drive around the block so I could give the woman something to eat. When we got back around, she was gone. To this day I believe they were angels God sent to test me, and I had failed the test.

This was about the third time in my life that a small, needy child came to me for help, and I failed to help them. For these occurrences, I am ashamed of myself. God gave me so much, and sometimes, for stupid reasons, I failed to help others.

———◆◆◆———

Christmas was a sad time for us when we could not celebrate with our children and family. All of Ken and Peggy's grandparents were gone except Arvil, their paternal grandfather. Ken, Suzanne, and Alayna lived in Arlington and would have Christmas with Suzanne's parents and family. Peggy, Bruce, Zac, and Corbin lived in Houston and would have Christmas morning at home. (They always wanted Santa to come to their home and opened gifts on Christmas morning.) Andrew, my other grandchild, was not yet born.

John and Anne Faulkner were very nice to invite us to their home for a lovely Christmas lunch with several other friends. The food was good. Their house was small, but we all managed to find a place to sit and eat. Somehow missionaries make the best of all situations. Their lawn was beautiful. The weather was nice and sunny but not too hot.

During the week after Christmas, I closed out the 1993 books, balanced everything, and submitted my year-end reports. The year was coming to a close, and we had gotten into the swing of things in Somalia. Something was always changing, people were coming and going, and we took everything as it came, trying to stay focused on God and the jobs we were there to do.

50 Fun in Kenya

While we were living in Kenya, we took a lot of short, tourist-type trips. There was a game park right at the edge of Nairobi. The game park did not have a fence around it, but because the animals usually prefer to be where people are not living, they stay in this "park" area. (Once in a while a giraffe would decide to wander down the streets of Nairobi to look around, and the rangers would come and escort the giraffe back home.)

The first time we drove into this park, a huge giraffe was standing right at the entrance. I thought maybe it was not real, but then I saw its head move and mouth open, and it began to eat leaves from the top of a nearby tree. We drove within eight feet of this giraffe, and it never paid us any attention. It was the largest giraffe I had ever seen.

As we drove further into the park, we saw all kinds of African animals: elephants, baboons, lions, gazelles, impalas, warthogs, numerous species of birds, and hyenas. We came upon trees filled with monkeys, and we stopped and watched them jump from limb to limb. Some would swing by their tails, holding their babies onto their chest. It was delightful to watch them chase one another and play happily in their "treehouse."

These animals were so accustomed to cars driving around they usually did not pay much attention to us as long as we kept a sensible distance. We enjoyed a few hours there and then drove back home to Nairobi.

We took another trip for a couple of nights. We first stopped at the Blue Hotel, not far out of town for lunch, and we watched the little waterfall there. Along the side of the hotel there were little booths set up, and people were selling all sorts of curios — purses, belts, hats, baskets, and wooden animals. Carved giraffes seemed to be the most popular item — they had chiseled giraffes from tree trunks, necks intertwined, and bodies curved around each other. They were exquisite. (Whenever you see carved wooden giraffes in the States, they are often from Kenya.)

Then we drove to an area where we could walk out where giraffes were just roaming around. (We tried to stay a little bit hidden so as not to disturb or scare them.) We found that we could walk up pretty close to them, and they would just wander away.

A few other animals were there, as well. We had to keep reminding ourselves that these were not domesticated animals — they were wild animals that could turn on us without a moment's notice.

The scenery was beautiful — some places were lush and green, and other areas featured stretches of tall brown grass that had fallen over, depending on the season and location. Most of the trees are fairly small and looked much like the Mimosa tree. Some had little thorns and others had pink, orange, or yellow flowers.

Next, we went out to "Noah's ark," a hotel shaped like Noah's ark might have appeared from its exterior. There was a sand pan (watering hole) outside a viewing window where visitors could get a cool drink, sit, and watch the animals come, drink, and leave, and then other animals would come. There seemed to be a pecking order of who came first and then who got to come next, but not many animals came while we were there.

In this hotel, if you wanted to be awakened during the night when exotic animals came up, you were to leave your shoes outside your door. We left our shoes outside the door, but nobody woke us up. After all our years in Africa, we were no longer tourists who got very excited at the sight of wild animals, but I never tired of seeing elephants.

One weekend while we were living in Kenya, we went up to Lake Nakuru to see the pink flamingos. There had been some kind of disease that hit flamingos and caused them to die by the thousands. While we were at Lake Nakuru, however, we saw hundreds of large pink and white flamingos in the lake. It was a breathtaking sight to see so many birds swimming in the water, bobbing their heads up and down, twisting their necks around to pick at the feathers on their backs, flapping their wings, and ruffling their feathers.

We drove on to the town of Nakuru (Nakuru was north of Nairobi about a day's round trip.) and spent time just wandering around and trying some of their local cuisine. We ate from street venders and wherever the local people ate. (I don't know if we had strong stomachs or if it was God's protection, but we just went, ate, and enjoyed everything.) All of it was new to us, and we were interested in everything from the way people dressed, to how they lived, shopped, set up shops, and marketed their wares.

Another place we took visitors was out to Karen Blixom's home. The movie, "Out of Africa" was about Karen. She loved the people, and the people loved her. She begged the city leaders to care for "her people." (There is actually a town there that is named Karen.)

We went up the little mountain where her lover was buried. They say that the lions still come and lay on his grave at night. The road up there was very bumpy; we drove part of the way and walked the remainder. It is so interesting to see places you have seen in the movies — and now, somehow, I felt I was part of that life.

Near Karen is a place where exotic African dances are held for the tourists, and on certain days the different tribes come in and dance. It was so much fun just to watch them and consider the symbolism and meanings behind the movements and pageantry. All of the "tourist places" have stores and wares for sale. I always enjoyed looking and buying, but by then I had lost most of my fervor for shopping.

In this same area there was an ostrich farm where we once took two missionary kids, Alicia Sibley, and Brian Collier, for sight-seeing. Although the ostrich farm birds were fenced in, you could feed them through the fence. (If you are brave enough, you can stick your fingers through the fence and rub their feathers, too!) Ostrich can run up to 80 miles per hour and kick like a mule. (They can also peck a chunk out of your arm.) In South Africa they are tamed a little bit and people try to ride them, but I did not see any place in Kenya like that.

———•••———

One of the most popular souvenir items to buy is a necklace made with wild animals carved out of wood. (I must have bought two dozen of them.) Some are quite lovely with balls of blue or green wood. Many also have earrings to match.

There was a woman living in Kenya who had a heart for the street women. (In this culture, when a woman had been married and was kicked out, she was considered soiled and did not have a way to make a living for herself except prostitution.) So, this kind lady started molding, painting, and firing beautiful necklaces and earrings, and she brought in these "street women" to help her make this jewelry. She turned this mercy mission into a good business, and I bought these items because I liked them — and I also wanted to help the women involved in making them.

———•••———

While living in Kenya, we found time to do all kinds of tourist things. It was wonderful to have our own car and enough time to make short trips. It was fun to drive to Mombasa and see the Maasai (a Kenyan tribe renowned for its natural abilities as long-distance running) running along. The tall, graceful Maasai runners are known for their physical beauty—not just their strong, lithe physiques but also for their unique body ornamentation — including colorful wide necklaces that bounce up and down as they run. They ran in perfect rhythm and harmony, never turning their heads to the right or the left; their eyes stay focused straight ahead.

The Masai had a long gourd shaped something like a funnel that they would place under a camel to milk the camel. Then they would make a small cut in the neck of a camel (or sometimes a cow) and mix the blood with the

404

milk and drink it. (This did not harm the animals.) We never became friends with any of the Maasai, so we were never offered this delicacy.

While in Kenya this time we also had the opportunity to see a wildebeest migration. (We had witnessed this spectacle once before when we had visited Kenya when Don and Barbara Messer hosted us on a train trip from Nairobi to Mombasa.) This time, however, we were in a car and could drive slowly and really take in the majesty of these beasts. (I think they are called "beast" because they are one of God's ugliest animals.)

I spent most of my time in Nairobi. Jerry split his time between working in Nairobi, Somalia, Mandera, and other locations. One day when Jerry was gone, I learned that Scott Ritz needed $20,000. So, I went to the bank and got the $100 bills.

None of our people were going into Mogadishu, but I understood that the U.S. Embassy people would take money into Somalia for us. I was not sure what the procedure was, but I went to the embassy and contacted the lady identified as someone who could help with this task.

I wanted a receipt for the cash I was handing over, but I did not know whether I should ask her for one or not. It was difficult for me to turn $20,000 over to a complete stranger without a receipt. I had to account for this money, but I did not know if she would want to assume this responsibility.

I was so relieved when she said, "Would you like a receipt?"

"Yes," I said, breathing out my relief. "I sure would appreciate it."

There were several occasions when I went to the Embassy on business. While we were living in Kenya, someone threw a bomb onto the steps of the American Building across the street from the American Embassy, killing more than 1500 Kenyans. I never learned who was responsible, but it was probably related to the war in Somalia.

During our year in Kenya and Somalia, we had made quite a few friends. We really enjoyed spending time and playing bridge with Clyde and Anne Berkley. Clyde had retired from the military; Anne taught school at Rift Valley Academy. The Berkleys continued to be great friends even after we left Kenya.

I loved all the missionaries I worked with. God was so good to provide just who and what I needed, just when I needed it. John Faulkner was a great boss, and I appreciated how he and Anne took Jerry and me in and helped us with whatever we needed. (Even after we were back to the States, Anne went back to Kenya and bought me a pair of earrings because I had lost one of mine.)

When George and Sally returned to Kenya, ready to resume their jobs, we could have stayed another year, but we opted to return to the States. I told Sally I had changed the program on the computer and offered to show her how to operate it, but George said that would not be necessary, and Sally did not seem interested in my helping her.

We changed over the bank account and audited the books together to make sure what I showed was accurate and correct. (This was the reverse of what we did when I arrived to become the treasurer.)

A lot happened during that year in Kenya and Somalia. I learned a lot of new things. I experienced things I never could have imagined. Some of these things were fun, and others tragic. I felt as if I had been taken up in a whirlwind and then, one year later dropped back down into my "real" life. As I look back on that year, it almost seems like a dream. And, while I am delighted to have had that experience, I would never want to do it again.

I learned a lot about Arab Tribalism, Islamic Religion, and Muslim people. Once Christians lived in Somalia; now they do not. Once the women there wore Western dress, but now they must dress in the traditional Arab attire. Once they thought for themselves; now they are totally subject and subservient to their husbands, according to the law.

Jesus died for both men and women, and he set us free to make our own choices. The choices we make may cost us or someone else their life. Experiencing life in Somalia made me more thankful to my forefathers, our military, and for America: "The land of the brave and the free." GOD HELP US TO PROTECT OUR FREEDOM!

51 Back to Farm & Fort Worth

We went back to the states and settled at the farm for a few years. Jerry seemed to be having some minor memory problems, and as these worsened, we decided it best to just leave the farm with a real estate agent to rent the house. Our neighbor, Tim Smith, agreed to take care of the land.

About the time we were getting ready to move back to Fort Worth, my brother Duane became ill, and we drove out to see him as often as we could. On several occasions as we were driving back and forth to his place, I noticed a really nice area of homes in the southwest part of Fort Worth. One day we went over there and looked at the houses in that area to see if any were available. We purchased a house in Hulen Bend Estates soon afterwards.

———◆●———

Once settled back in Fort Worth, we re-joined Travis Ave. Baptist Church. We had been gone for 21 years, and the people had changed so much. I noticed right away that they had gotten older — and then I realized that we had gotten older, too. As we walked down the halls at

Church, Jerry would ask me their names. He could hardly remember anybody. I often had to think about it, but most people's names came back to me.

It was not long until we were back in the swing of things. Jerry started teaching a men's Sunday School Class. I participated in a women's class. I started playing bridge again with Sandra Taylor, Bobbie Roberts, Billie Keeton, Maxine Irwin, Gladeene Lee, and Barbara Quillen; and Pat Pearson and Bettie Johnson were learning to play. Someone was always out, and Sandra spent half her time in Frazer, Colorado, where she and Ray had bought a beautiful home.

Several times, Sandra and Ray Taylor invited us to stay a week with them in Colorado, and we were always glad to go. These were always wonderful times — they are great cooks and hosts. Jerry would ski with them in the winter, we played a lot of bridge, and I did some reading. They always had one or more couples up there at the same time.

———◆◆◆———

The grandchildren were all growing up fast. Zac, Corbin, and Andrew were playing football and baseball, and Alayna played volleyball. (All of them seemed to excel in sports.)

From time to time, they would come over to the house. Alayna and Andrew would draw pictures and write each other notes. One would go upstairs and sail a note down to the other. They enjoyed playing together. Alayna and Corbin took the dominoes and spread them on the floor, and then they would build towers. Sometimes they would use the cards to make multi-story buildings. It was amazing how high they could stack the cards and the dominoes before they would fall.

Zac and Corbin loved to throw a football or baseball to each other in the backyard. (Sometimes they would miss the ball and it would crack the fence.) Peggy and Bruce had a big Labrador Retriever, and he broke boards in the gate while we were gone. (I did not mind just as long as they would come to visit.) I loved to see the grandchildren play together.

Shortly after "911" Andrew's teacher gave his second-grade class an assignment: finish the sentence, "I hold in my hand the key." (I happened to be staying with him at the time). That evening Andrew sat down at their kitchen table and began to write. Within 20 minutes, he read me what he had written, and my mouth dropped open in amazement.

I was thinking *a key that would open a door or a trunk or a treasure chest*, but this is what Andrew wrote.

I hold in my hand the key to truth, wisdom, and lots MORE.
It's like a normal key, but it's FAITH.
Faith means trust, like you should trust in GOD.
Keys can unlock doors, but that's not the key we're talking about.
We're talking about the key that unlocks the goodness of OUR
    COUNTRY.

By: Andrew Dowdy, Age 7

In John F. Kennedy's inaugural address, he wrote. *"For man holds in his mortal hands the power to abolish all forms of human poverty and all forms of human life. And yet the same revolutionary beliefs for which our forebears fought are still at issue around the globe—the belief that the rights of man come not from the generosity of the state, but from the hand of God."*

If other kids are thinking like Andrew, our future generations should be in pretty good hands.

———•••———

One day out of the blue, Jerry said, "I am not going to teach Sunday school anymore!" When people in his class would comment on how well he taught, I would tell them I thought he should resign. I alone knew that he was working for hours on end to prepare his lessons. He struggled so hard to get the lessons written down so he could more or less read what he wanted to say. Each week after he had taught his lesson, he would be sick. His stomach stayed in knots.

Jerry was scared. He thought he was losing his mind. Finally, he stopped his Bible Study Fellowship class and resigned teaching Sunday school. He was always worried that things would break and that he could not repair them.

409

I knew Jerry was having problems, and shortly after we moved to Fort Worth, Dr. Simpkin diagnosed Jerry with Alzheimer's disease and Lewy bodies Parkinson's. His hands and body did not shake at first, but as time progressed his hands and legs would jerk slightly. I asked the doctor if there was any trial or research project Jerry could join, but there was no such placement for him. Little by little, Jerry's life deteriorated.

Peggy sent me an email with these scriptures:

"Be strong and courageous. Do not be terrified; do not be discouraged, for the Lord your God will be with you wherever you go." (Joshua 1:9)

"And we know that in all things God works for the good of those who love him who have been called according to his purpose." (Romans 8:28)

"One night shortly after we had your (Daddy's) final diagnosis," Peggy wrote, "I sat down as usual with Corbin to have our nightly bedtime prayer. As I prayed for you, I began to cry. Corbin reached over to comfort me, and he hugged me tightly. He said with all confidence, 'Mommy, don't cry. It will be all right. God doesn't make any mistakes. He knows what He is doing, and He will make everything all right'.

"Who knows," Peggy continued, "what we face now may strengthen your grandchildren's faith and lead them to a lifelong commitment of service to God. I love you both and pray for you daily."

I started out having part-time help with Jerry's care and then progressed to 24-hour-a day, seven-days-a-week support. By March 7, 2004, Jerry had difficulty finding our bathroom. He could not dress himself. If I buttoned the first two buttons on his shirt, he was able to button the remainder. He required assistance to remove his clothing. He needed assistance getting into and rising up from the bed. When the nurse and I put him to bed, I had to move his legs and straighten them out or bend them into a comfortable position.

410

Marcia Jones, Jerry's main nurse from the time we needed skilled nursing, was a real blessing. She could handle him better than anybody, but she could not work all the time. The other help I employed was good, but they just did not have the knack that Marcia had acquired through her years of experience. Marcia really liked Jerry, and everybody also liked her.

As I looked at the man I was married to for 50 years, I realized he was slipping away — and there was nothing I could do. I could not even cry; it hurt too much. *Where has my husband gone?* I wondered every day. *This is not the man that I married. His brilliant mind has slipped into some dark pit. His strong arms and legs have become weak and frail.*

I loved Jerry and I still love him. My heart still bleeds with his struggles and his moans. At times, I felt so lonely and depressed. When he sat in his chair, I tried to sit in his lap, but that hurt his legs, so I would sit on the arm of the chair and lean over to hug and kiss him. On some level, I think he knew I was there and that I loved him. He never got so bad that he could not call "Barbara?"

When he called my name, I would ask him what he wanted. Sometimes he wanted something, and other times he just wanted to know I was there. We had not slept together for over a year, but one night before he got so bad, he wanted to crawl into my bed. I helped him get into my bed. We were alone. He was so weak and frail, but in his own way he showed me that HE DID LOVE ME at the end of his life. As I look back on our life together, that gives me peace and a lot of joy. This single moment of connection was his special gift to me.

If I have any advice for newly married couples, it would be to share your feelings and thoughts as they come to mind. Not in a blaming way, but "this is the way I felt when so and so happened." Or "I feel this way" about something. If you hold your feelings back, after a few years you will not have anything to say to each another.

When Jerry prayed, he always said, "God forgive me for my shortcomings."

I began asking Jerry to ask God to forgive him for his sins.

He did.

That was the first time in all our years I ever heard Jerry pray for forgiveness of sin.

52 **End Notes**

Sometimes Ken would come over and supervise his dad for the day. If Jerry wanted to go out to eat, Ken was able to get him out to the car and we ate out. Once when Jerry tried to eat cashew chicken and rice, he had difficulty, but he was able to eat some chicken tenders before he got too bad. Suzanne, Alayna, and Drew came to visit from time to time. Peggy and her family were also very supportive.

Around March 28, 2005, Jerry became completely incontinent. He had also developed a bedsore between his buttocks that we could not get healed. Although the nurses worked diligently to help it heal, it was to no avail. His pain continued to get worse.

On a Tuesday morning Jerry had eaten breakfast as usual, and then he was helped to his chair where he went to sleep. When Marcia tried to awake him, he could not open his eyes or speak, and he seemed to be in a coma.

I called Ken and Peggy. I called friends and asked them to pray. Ken and Suzanne came right over. Peggy got ready and headed for Fort Worth from Houston.

After a little while, Jerry awoke. We made him a chocolate malt, and he drank that and went back to sleep. Later, Sandra and Ray Taylor came over and he woke up, talked, and laughed with them really well. (Ray had always been able to make Jerry laugh.) Then, he went back to sleep and slept most of the afternoon.

Jann arrived about 4:30 p.m. and Peggy arrived at about 5:45 p.m. Marcia said she thought Jerry had a transient ischemic attack (TIA), which is a temporary period of symptoms similar to those of a stroke. He slept well that night.

Going back a bit, to the end of 2004, I had begun to have issues of my own — I began to fall occasionally. Once I was taking our dog Pumpkin to the groomer, and I fell in front of the pet shop while trying to step up on the curb. I really hurt myself, and Pumpkin got out of her leash, and I was afraid she would run out into the busy street. Finally, she came back to me, and I got her leash back on.

I looked down the sidewalk and there was a man standing there. He was wearing ragged and tattered clothes, and the thought came to me that he was an angel. Slowly, I got up as he walked toward me. I crossed the sidewalk and leaned against the building, noticing as I did that my billfold lay where I had fallen. I waited until the man (or angel) got to where I was standing.

He looked at my billfold and pointed to it.

I gestured for him to bring it to me.

He hesitated, then picked it up and handed it to me.

I looked into his eyes, and he looked into mine.

He never said a word.

I think I mumbled out a "thank you." I knew God had placed him there to help me.

He turned and walked away, and I turned my attention back to Pumpkin. Then I thought, *what if he is just a poor street man and I should have offered him some money?*

I turned and looked back, and he was gone. There were buildings lining the sidewalk and he had no place to disappear.

My balance and the growing pain in my back soon got so bad I had to use a walker. I went to the doctor, and after many tests and several more doctors, I was diagnosed with a tumor between my spine and spinal cord that was about four inches long and one-half inch wide. The doctor told me they could do surgery and relieve my pain, and that I might have 100% recovery, or I might be totally paralyzed from my bustline down.

While I was busy going to one doctor after another for all of these tests, Jerry suffered another TIA, and he seemed to be even more out of it. His speech was slurred, his left eye was drooped and red, his left lip hung down slightly, and he was beginning to hallucinate some.

Meanwhile, I developed numbness in my legs and feet. I fell, and my big toe became black, blue, red, and purple, but it did not hurt. That night I read John Chapter 3 with Jerry and said a prayer. He went to sleep and slept well.

Clyde and Ann Berkley from Abilene came to visit Jerry, and he was feeling good enough to enjoy them. They had a nice visit.

———•••———

We made the decisions that I would have back surgery July 1, 2005. I was in such pain by that time I really don't remember the details. I know I went into surgery without thinking about the results. My faith told me that whatever happened was God's will and that He would take care of me and meet all my needs.

Without God, I don't know what I would have done. I can't imagine going through all that was happening in our lives without FAITH.

Ken, Peggy, and others visited me when I came out of surgery. The operation went well, and while the surgeon said he felt he had not damaged any of the nerves, he still did not know the prognosis of my walking again.

I was kept sedated for a week, and I knew very little about what was going on. Friends took turns staying with me all day. I could usually rouse enough to know when someone was there. Staff members from Travis Avenue Baptist Church came by and looked in on me. I spoke to them when I could, but I could not talk much.

After about a week, I moved into Health South Rehabilitation center. Peggy was beside my bed, and I asked her why they had rolled up a towel and placed it under my side. It was very uncomfortable. She told me that there was nothing under my side. When the nurses would get me up to go to the bathroom, my legs moved every which way. Transferring to the wheelchair was difficult and took two nurses.

I could not tell where my legs were unless I looked at them. I could only move them slightly. I did have some feeling in them, but virtually no control. It is a strange sensation to not know where your feet and legs are. They would get tangled up in bed, and I would have to push the covers back so I could see my legs to untangle them.

I worked as hard as I could. I desperately wanted to be able to walk. I strained and wet all over my clothes, my chair, and myself. One of the physical therapists took me back to my room and gave me pads to wear, because I was incontinent. So, what else could happen?

———◆•◆———

Charles and Gayla Corley and Clyde and Ann Berkley came to visit me and brought Marcia and Jerry to see me. They picked up Kentucky Fried Chicken and we ate lunch together. Ann Brosius purchased socks and pajamas for me. Many other friends came to visit. I spent most of my days working out and eating, and in late afternoon I would take a nap before dinner.

Marcia brought Jerry to visit me several times. Jerry could not understand why I wasn't at home. He began to think I was running around on him, and he would talk to Marcia about these thoughts. She would assure him I was sick in the hospital and could not come home yet. He simply could not comprehend why I was not at home.

At last, I started walking, two or three feet on a walker with one of the nurses holding on to me at first. Then I could walk five feet. I would be completely exhausted by the time I got back to my chair.

Little by little, I walked ten feet very, very slowly. After a month, I went home and had a therapist come over every day for a while, and then three times a week.

Then I went back to Health South for about three months, and then to Carter Rehabilitation Center for a while to continue my outpatient rehabilitation. Various friends would take me to Carter, stay for an hour, and then take me back home. I can't remember everyone who took me, but Don and Peggy Barnard, Maxine and Holland Irwin, and Wilma and Andy Litzler were some of the ones who were so faithful to help me. My Travis church friends were the ones I depended on most.

Ken was the one who usually took me to the Doctor. Sandra & Ray Taylor drove me to the doctor when I got my final diagnosis and prognosis. Because I could not remember all the things the doctor said, I asked Ray to take notes. He wrote down all the important points the doctor expressed, and I carried that paper in my wallet for years afterward. Basically, it said that I might be able to walk, or I might never be able to walk without a walker. Although my walking improved over time, I was never able to walk without a walker.

———◆◆◆———

We had a hospital bed for Jerry and another one for me set up in our bedroom at home. The caregiver would sleep in our queen-size canopy bed. I did not think we could fit three beds in our bedroom, but Peggy measured and showed me how the bed would fit. Sure enough, they fit in nicely with plenty of space to walk around.

Jerry's health continued to decline. He seemed more content just to have me in the house with him. He never got to the point where he could not recognize the children or me, but he was in a great deal of pain. His food had to be pureed, and it did not taste good to him. He ate some, but then got to where he could not eat.

We knew it was time to call in hospice. They put him on morphine, and the family came in and spent more time with us. The hospice nurses stayed around the clock. Marcia remained during the day to help bathe me and cook for me.

Jerry was put into a coma. He had a living will and did not want any tubes or needles. He could not eat or drink anything, but his heart was strong, and his kidneys were in good shape.

He lived for about three weeks without any fluid or food. The Hospice nurses were amazed. (I did not believe that people could live more than a week without food or water.) One day the nurse looked into our backyard and told everybody to look at the water fountain.

Perched on the fountain bowl were eight or ten doves just sitting there, all facing the bedroom window. We knew that they were angels waiting to escort Jerry home to the Father. Marcia said she had seen a figure in his bedroom, and she knew that angels were there attending him.

Then Jerry breathed his last breath. His body was there, but I knew my husband of 50+ years was gone. As Jerry passed from this life, the doves flew.

The tarnished gold thread of my life now gleamed as new; the blood of Jesus Christ cleansed and restored it, shiny and bright.

www.ingramcontent.com/pod-product-compliance
Lightning Source LLC
Chambersburg PA
CBHW060418100426

42812CB00030B/3231/J